CW01669352

Richard Wagner's Zurich

Studies in German Literature, Linguistics, and Culture

Richard Wagner's Zurich

The Muse of Place

Chris Walton

CHRISTOPHER.H.PLOMER M.B.E
96 EAST MUIRLANDS ROAD
ARBROATH, ANGUS
DD11 3HF
TEL: 01241 873970

CAMDEN HOUSE
Rochester, New York

First published 2007
by Camden House

Camden House is an imprint of Boydell & Brewer Inc.
668 Mt. Hope Avenue, Rochester, NY 14620, USA
www.camden-house.com
and of Boydell & Brewer Limited
PO Box 9, Woodbridge, Suffolk IP12 3DF, UK
www.boydellandbrewer.com

ISBN-13: 978–1–57113–331–1
ISBN-10: 1–57113–331–3

Library of Congress Cataloging-in-Publication Data

Walton, Chris, 1963–
Richard Wagner's Zurich: the muse of place / Chris Walton.
p. cm. — (Studies in German literature, linguistics, and culture)
Includes bibliographical references (p.) and index.
ISBN-13: 978–1–57113–331–1 (hardcover: alk. paper)
ISBN-10: 1–57113–331–3 (hardcover: alk. paper)
1. Wagner, Richard, 1813–1883. 2. Music — Switzerland — Zurich — 19th century — History and criticism. I. Title. II. Series.

ML410.W12S93 2007
780.9494′572—dc22

2007011073

A catalogue record for this title is available from the British Library.

This publication is printed on acid-free paper.
Printed in the United States of America.

For Margaret Eglington and Jean White, with much gratitude

Contents

Illustrations

Figures

Music Examples

Tables

Acknowledgments

NUMEROUS INDIVIDUALS AND INSTITUTIONS have been of assistance to me during my work on this book. While I conducted most of my research when the Head of Music Division of the Zentralbibliothek Zürich, my subsequent relocation to the land of nurture of my wife left me often reliant on the support of several colleagues when sources had to be consulted at the other end of the planet. Without their help, this book would never have been completed, and I owe particular thanks to Harry Joelson of the Stadtbibliothek Winterthur; Martin Germann of the Burgerbibliothek Bern; Armin Trösch of the Swiss Wagner Society; Pfarrer Christian Radecke and family; Bernhard Päuler of Amadeus Verlag; and Heiri Aerni, Christian Aliverti, Stefan Dell'Olivo, Rainer Diederichs, Christoph Eggenberger, Urs Fischer, Dani Gloor, Heidi Kaufmann, Hermann Köstler, Michael Kotrba, Alice Robinson, and Angelika Salge of the Zentralbibliothek Zürich. The staff of the Music Library of the University of Pretoria (Isobel Oosthuizen in particular) have been as patient with my incessant requests as they have been generous with their time. Without their active assistance I would simply not be able to find the sources I need for my research. And were it not for Jim Walker's initial expression of interest, and his subsequent patience and enthusiasm in equal measure, this book would not have been written at all.

I am further indebted for help, assistance, and encouragement, to Zdravko Blažeković of the Répertoire international de littérature musicale; Peter Jost, Christa Jost, and Egon Voss of the Wagner-Gesamtausgabe in Munich; Jürg Obrecht of the Library of the Zurich Tonhalle Orchestra; Evelyn Liepsch of the Goethe- und Schiller-Archiv, Weimar; Ilona H. Macht; and the students of my fourth-year history classes at the University of Pretoria, namely Marica Hattingh, Karien Labuschagne, Jenny Rabie, Janette Richter, Annemie Stimie, Suzy du Toit, Carina Venter, Etienne Viviers, and Sophia Welz. Karien and Annemie kindly typeset my music examples for me. The following individuals have also helped me in ways too numerous to mention, and I hope to be forgiven for listing them here merely in alphabetical order: Judith Cabaud, Chats Devroop, Uwe Eckardt, Reiner Habering, Beat Hanselmann of the Peter Mieg Archives in Lenzburg, Volker Harms-Ziegler, Armin† and Lore Hartwig, Alexander Johnson, the Kammerorchester der Kirchgemeinde Witikon, Axel Langer of the Museum Rietberg, Barry Millington, Robert Münster, Stephanus Muller, Marlene van Niekerk, Guillermo Peretti, Dieter Rebentisch, Alexa

Renggli, Ralph Schmidt, Elisabeth Schniderlin and the Eidgenössische Stipendienkommission, Stewart Spencer, Dan Thokoane, Rigbie Turner, Derek Watson, Franz Wesendonk, and Jürg Wille. As always, especial thanks go to to my wife and children: Riëtte, Isa, Elza, and Alvaro, for their patience during my months of writing.

The sections in this book on Otto Wesendonck, Theodor Kirchner, and Wagner's conducting activities are based on material first published in *The Musical Times*, in *Wagner*, the journal of the British Wagner Society, and in *Fontes artis musicae*, and I am indebted to their respective editors, Antony Bye, Roger Allen, and Maureen Buja, for permission to revise it for use here.

Chris Walton
University of Pretoria
Michaelmas 2006

Abbreviations

The following abbreviations are used in this book.

ML Richard Wagner. *Mein Leben*. Edited by Martin Gregor-Dellin. Munich: List Verlag, 1977.

SB Richard Wagner. *Sämtliche Briefe*. 14 vols. Leipzig: Deutscher Verlag für Musik, later Wiesbaden: Breitkopf & Härtel, 1967–.

Vol. 1. Edited by Gertrud Strobel and Werner Wolf. Leipzig: Deutscher Verlag für Musik, 1967.
Vol. 2. Edited by Gertrud Strobel and Werner Wolf. Leipzig: Deutscher Verlag für Musik, 1980.
Vol. 3. Edited by Gertrud Strobel and Werner Wolf. Leipzig: Deutscher Verlag für Musik, 1983.
Vol. 4. Edited by Gertrud Strobel and Werner Wolf. Leipzig: Deutscher Verlag für Musik, 1979.
Vol. 5. Edited by Hans-Joachim Bauer and Eva Gerlach. Leipzig: Deutscher Verlag für Musik, 1993.
Vol. 6. Edited by Hans-Joachim Bauer and Johannes Forner. Leipzig, Deutscher Verlag für Musik, 1986.
Vol. 7. Edited by Hans-Joachim Bauer and Johannes Forner. Leipzig: Deutscher Verlag für Musik, 1988.
Vol. 8. Edited by Hans-Joachim Bauer and Johannes Forner. Leipzig: Deutscher Verlag für Musik, 1991.
Vol. 9. Edited by Klaus Burmeister and Johannes Forner. Leipzig: Deutscher Verlag für Musik, 2000.
Vol. 10. Edited by Andreas Mielke. Wiesbaden: Breitkopf & Härtel, 2000.
Vol. 11. Edited by Martin Dürrer. Wiesbaden: Breitkopf & Härtel, 1999.
Vol. 12. Edited by Martin Dürrer and Isabel Kraft. Wiesbaden: Breitkopf & Härtel, 2001.
Vol. 13. Edited by Martin Dürrer and Isabel Kraft. Wiesbaden: Breitkopf & Härtel, 2003.
Vol. 14. Edited by Andreas Mielke and Isabel Kraft. Wiesbaden, Leipzig and Paris: Breitkopf & Härtel, 2002.

TB Cosima Wagner. *Die Tagebücher*. 2 vols. Munich and Zurich: Piper, 1976–77.

Introduction

> And so I grasped eagerly the aid recently offered to me from Weimar in order . . . to seek out a place of refuge that had nothing to attract me, except precisely the complete and utter hopelessness of achieving anything there along what had thus far been the path of my life. This, then, was Zurich: completely devoid of any public art form, where, for the first time, I had come upon some simple people who knew nothing of my work as an artist, but who seemed to have found friendly sympathy for my person alone.
>
> Richard Wagner, *Mein Leben*, 435

HE LIES, OF COURSE. Zurich in 1849 was neither devoid of art nor populated by the simple; nor was he unknown in it. But Wagner's autobiography *My Life* as a whole is a virtuosic interweaving of fact and fiction, truth and invention, and this is just one of countless such passages that flirt coquettishly with the *vérité*. When he dictated the above passage to his lover, Cosima von Bülow, in late 1868, Wagner was keen to depict himself as a very large fish in a very small pond. This was in itself nothing new, for he had long been concerned to appear the focal point of every event, place, and conversation. But he was now, perhaps, compensating for a specific matter of frustration. He had recently taken up residence in Switzerland once again, less than a decade after leaving it, in ignominy, in 1858, after his failed affair with the wife of his then benefactor. He had in the intervening period been called to Munich as the guest of King Ludwig II of Bavaria. But within less than two years, his meddling in both affairs of state and in Hans von Bülow's marriage had made it impossible for his host to retain him. The result was yet another departure, and in equal ignominy — a matter in which Wagner was now becoming a serial perpetrator. His newest place of exile was again in Switzerland, but this time Tribschen, a brisk twenty minutes' walk from Lucerne, and far more isolated than had been Zurich upon his arrival there in 1849. Thanks to the benign cultural influence of the Catholic Church, Lucerne had in fact for most of the previous three hundred years enjoyed a far more active artistic life than had the northern, Zwinglian, city of Zurich. But the industrial revolution had long since reached the north, and the resultant surge of capitalist endeavor, coupled with advanced political, social, and educational ideals, had ensured that Zurich in the mid-nineteenth century was healthy, wealthy, and wise, while Lucerne remained a small, provincial town with beautiful but oversized, over-elaborate, overstaffed churches. To be sure, the magnanimity of its northern compatriots had allowed Lucerne, too, to enjoy the fruits of economic expansion. So when Wagner arrived in 1866, he came not by post coach as he had in 1849, but by means of the railway system that was spreading rapidly across the land. But not even the existence of a railway station could obscure the fact that Lucerne was still a very minor place indeed.

Richard Wagner's renewed flight had surely prompted unhappy memories of previous experiences, and this most probably resulted in his projecting the isolation of his current place of exile onto its predecessor; hence his harsh criticism of Zurich. The above passage from Wagner's memoirs is, in fact, contradicted immediately by its author. For he then admits to having lodged in Zurich with the composer and pianist Alexander Müller, who was a close colleague from his early days in the Würzburg theater, and for whose musical skills he expresses unreserved admiration. He also tells us that one of Müller's pupils, Wilhelm Baumgartner, had once visited him in Dresden and had taken away with him a full score of *Tannhäuser* as a gift for his teacher. So the "simple people who knew nothing of my work as an artist" in fact boasted gifted men among them who were well acquainted with his music. And Wagner would himself soon become deeply involved in the city's existing "public forms of art," sowing the seeds of major reforms that would help to shape the course of Zurich's musical life for many decades to come.

Despite such self-contradictory moments, *Mein Leben* as a whole does indeed portray Zurich as a backworldly place of little intellectual interest before its author's arrival. And the musicians whom he found there are, on the whole, accorded but condescending praise, tinged with heavy sarcasm. But in fact, Zurich at the time was a hive of intellectual activity. Switzerland had in late 1847 emerged from a brief, largely bloodless civil war that had been victorious for the forces of liberalism, federalism, and secular democracy. In the rest of Europe, however, the continent-wide revolutions that broke out shortly thereafter ended largely to the satisfaction of the old order. Switzerland now became a secure little island in the midst of a sea of belligerence either real or latent, and many radicals and intellectuals fled their homelands to find a new life there — Germans, French, Italians, Austrians, and others, of whom Wagner was merely one, and by no means the most prominent. Famous artists of all kinds also visited Zurich in these years (first among them Clara Schumann and Franz Liszt), either with the aim of visiting Wagner or of giving concerts (though they often ended up doing both). The city's history during the First World War has been told many times — how artists, writers, and painters, from James Joyce to Ferruccio Busoni and the Dadaists, flocked there to escape the turmoil of the world around them — but its situation was in the early 1850s almost identical.

It is all too easy, however, to portray Zurich as a convenient "empty" vessel into which the surrounding nations poured their genius. The city in fact produced its own fair share of remarkable men and women, many of whom belonged to Wagner's circle of friends and acquaintances. This has in some cases merely served to push them into obscurity, for music historians have in large part taken as their prime source for those years the accounts of Wagner himself, or the accounts of other historians based on his. And Wagner was ever adept at placing himself as the bright sun at the center of a vast, largely empty universe, populated otherwise only by distantly orbiting satellites of subsidiary significance. But history has hardly been any kinder than was Wagner to those other composers who were active at the time in Canton Zurich. The fact that the majority of them espoused an aesthetic much closer to Mendelssohn and Schumann than to Wagner was probably a hindrance to their posthumous reputation. But, as is discussed in chapter 6 below, several of them are worthy of serious critical attention, and — to judge simply from the availability of their music on CD — the past decade has even seen a revival of interest in them (most notably Wilhelm Baumgartner, Johann Carl Eschmann, and Theodor Kirchner). But Wagner's associates were naturally not confined to musical circles. Among the earliest admirers of the libretto to the *Ring des Nibelungen* was the celebrated novelist and Zurich Cantonal Secretary Gottfried Keller. Johanna Spyri, the author of *Heidi*, was the wife of Wagner's greatest supporter in the Zurich media, the newspaper editor Bernhard Spyri. And Wagner's landlady was the portraitist Clementine Stockar-Escher, whose brother Alfred Escher was not just the leading politician in the canton but one of the most remarkable venture capitalists in mid-nineteenth-century Europe. No distant, insignificant satellites these.

One of the few men to acknowledge the importance of place in Wagner's works of his Swiss exile was Ernest Newman, who in the second volume of his mammoth biography of the composer remarked

> The sublimity of the Swiss scene had given wings to his cramped and harassed soul: it is fairly safe to say that the *Ring* would have been something less titanic than it is had Wagner not lived in Switzerland during the years when he conceived and realised the main portion of it.[1]

And yet, despite the oft-repeated commonplace that the bibliography on Richard Wagner is longer than that on any composer, the current portrait of the artist in his Zurich years (1849–58) remains in many respects the one that Wagner later drew himself in his autobiography. There is no daily or weekly record of his life, as is the case for his final years, after his second wife Cosima began her diary; and almost all the letters from his most important Zurich correspondent — his "muse," Mathilde Wesendonck — are lost, after being wilfully destroyed. The first studies of Wagner's Zurich years date from the very early twentieth century. Hans Bélart published two small volumes entitled *Richard Wagner in Zürich* (*1849–1858*), which rely heavily on other sources that are readily available today (such as Wagner's letters), but which also contain useful firsthand information.[2] From 1901 to

1903, the Zurich historian and music critic Adolf Steiner published three even slimmer volumes, also entitled *Richard Wagner in Zürich*, which despite their slimness are particularly useful because of Steiner's long acquaintance with several of Wagner's Zurich friends.[3] The only detailed study of that period in Wagner's life is one by the Swiss historian Max Fehr (*Richard Wagners Schweizer Zeit* [Richard Wagner's Time in Switzerland]), published before the Second World War, and covering the years from 1849 to 1855. It is full of carefully researched detail — as is its companion volume, published twenty years later, dealing with Wagner's last years in Zurich and his time in Tribschen. But Fehr's work is tainted by his hagiographical stance, while his open anti-Semitism and his German supremacist leanings simply make his writing difficult to stomach today at all.[4] Of contemporary commentators, the most significant is Werner G. Zimmermann, former City Archivist of Zurich, whose two volumes of documentation are essential reading on the Zurich years, though their format did not allow the author to engage in extensive critical comment (*Richard Wagner in Zürich: Materialien zu Aufenthalt und Wirken* [Richard Wagner in Zurich: Materials Pertaining to His Stay and Activities There][5]).

It was in Zurich that Wagner wrote his most important theoretical works. There, cut off from the mainstream of German musical life, he found the financial and intellectual freedom to be able to put his theories into compositional practice; there he was engaged for the last time in intensive rehearsal and performance of the staple orchestral and operatic repertoire with a regular ensemble;[6] there he held the first ever "Wagner Festival," three concerts of his works at the time of his fortieth birthday; there he began work on the music of his *Ring des Nibelungen* and embarked upon *Tristan und Isolde* and *Parsifal*; there he conceived the idea of a theater devoted to his own works; there during his years of exile he met the two women who were to play a determining role in the remaining three decades of his life: Mathilde Wesendonck and Cosima Liszt-von Bülow; and there his anti-Semitism, which has since dominated the reception of his music, first found expression in print. Nor is it impossible — though it remains unproven — that the pageantry of the Zurich guild processions at their annual rite of spring named *Sechseläuten* might even have left a mark on the third act of *Die Meistersinger*. Particular attention will be paid in these pages to the role of Mathilde Wesendonck, who is presented in the literature as a largely passive muse, when in fact her role in Wagner's life and work — as I will posit below — was almost certainly far more active than hitherto imagined. Since most sources pertaining to Mathilde in the 1850s are lost, her literary works (hitherto all but dismissed by Wagner scholars) and her later correspondence with other composers — Theodor Kirchner and Johannes Brahms in particular — will be read "backwards" in order to try and establish the real nature of her relationship with Richard Wagner.

My aim here is to place both Wagner and Zurich in (each other's) context during his years of residence there. First, I sketch out the musical and historical situation of his place of exile; there then follows an overview of Wagner's years in the city. The issues I touch upon in this latter chapter — Wagner's friends and patrons, his loves, his hates, his musical activities, and his state of health — I then consider in greater detail in the ensuing chapters. The reader looking for an analytical discussion of individual works, or forays into the influence of (say) Feuerbach and Schopenhauer on Wagner, will find such matters mentioned here only within their historical and biographical context. All translations (mostly from the German, occasionally from the French or Italian) are my own; the original is also given in those cases where the wording or vocabulary is of specific importance. Except where custom or common sense dictates otherwise, the titles of works both musical and literary are given in German, accompanied by an English translation; the latter is given alone on subsequent mentions where the English form is the more user-friendly.

Even a brief consideration of the available evidence can leave one in little doubt that Wagner's Zurich years must be seen as crucial in his development as a man and an artist, and a source from which he drew inspiration for many years thereafter. But my purpose is not simply to chronicle the life and work of Wagner during his years of exile in Zurich, nor just to examine the effect that Wagner's presence had on Zurich and its musical and intellectual life. Most important, I shall endeavor to uncover the "Muse of place" referred to in my title, namely to ascertain the impact that Zurich itself — the city, its institutions and its people — had upon the man and his oeuvre; how his geographical location, his physical space, impinged upon his life and work. I thus wish here to uncover not merely "Wagner's Zurich" and "Zurich's Wagner" but also, above all, "Zurich in Wagner."[7]

Notes

[1] Ernest Newman, *The Life of Richard Wagner*, vol. 2 (Cambridge: Cambridge UP, 1976), 143–44.

[2] Hans Bélart, *Richard Wagner in Zürich (1849–1858)*. Two vols. (Leipzig: Hermann Seemann, 1900 and 1901).

[3] Adolf Steiner, *Richard Wagner in Zürich*. Three vols. (Zurich: Orell Füssli, 1901–3).

[4] *Richard Wagners Schweizer Zeit* (vol. 1: Aarau/Leipzig: Sauerländer, 1934; vol. 2: Aarau/Frankfurt am Main: Sauerländer, 1953). The second, postwar volume — not surprisingly — is less vociferous in proclaiming its author's racist views than is the first. For examples of Fehr's anti-Semitism, see, e.g., 1:38–40, with its discussion of the "high degree of topicality" of Wagner's anti-Semitic tract *Jewishness in Music* and Fehr's criticism of the "cultural Bolshevism" of contemporary Wagner productions.

[5] Werner G. Zimmermann, *Richard Wagner in Zürich: Materialien zu Aufenthalt und Wirken*. Two volumes (Zurich: Hug, 1986 and 1988).

[6] Wagner's engagement with the Philharmonic Society in London in spring 1855 — discussed in chapter 8 below — actually postdated his regular conducting activities in Zurich, but constituted a concert season of just three months, with only one rehearsal per concert, whereas his work with the Zurich orchestra lasted from 1850 to 1855, and would usually entail at least three rehearsals for a single symphony.

[7] In an example of synchronicity that would undoubtedly have delighted Wagner himself, it has transpired that Eva Martina Hanke of the University of Zurich has just completed a doctoral dissertation on the composer's Zurich years: *Richard Wagner und Zürich: Ein Individual und seine Lebenswelt*. This dissertation became accessible online just before the present book went to press, at: www.dissertationen.unizh.ch/2006/hanke/diss.pdf.

Figure 1. Map of Richard Wagner's Zurich, with the City Theater and Casino on the Hintere Zäune to the left, and the Escherhäuser, where Wagner lived for several years, on the Zeltweg at the top. Used by permission of the Zentralbibliothek Zürich.

1: Wagner's Zurich

> "Away with the mumbling of your songs, nor do I want the sound of your lyres."
>
> Huldrych Zwingli

IT IS AN ODD FACT, but the greatest reformer of Zurich's musical life before Richard Wagner was the man who did away with it: Huldrych Zwingli (1484–1531), who here quotes the prophet Amos as his justification.[1] The charismatic leader of the Zurich Reformation was a gifted musician who played numerous instruments and composed music to his own poems, with one of them ("Herr, nun heb den Wagen selbst") even surviving in the German hymnbooks of today. But he was also insistent that music did not belong in the church, and so had all of Zurich's organs removed and destroyed, along with every other ecclesiastical ornament and adornment. A few extant travelers' reports suggest that Zurich in the late Middle Ages had boasted some of the most elaborate musico-liturgical ceremonies of the Alpine region; it was also, it seems, the place of origin of the famed "Manesse" manuscript of *Minnesänger* songs. But almost all the documents that would have allowed us to reconstruct a clearer picture of Zurich's musical life, pre-Huldrych, also fell foul to Zwingli's iconoclastic orgy of destruction.

The ban on singing in church was eventually lifted when Zurich's first hymnbook was published in 1598.[2] The psalms and hymns therein were set merely to unaccompanied melodies, though at least they were taken seriously enough for the local schoolchildren to receive regular instruction in singing them. However, while music was squeezing its way back into the Zurich liturgy, it was at the same time being squeezed out elsewhere. For the city fathers now banned all theatrical performances, whether with or without music. Only the private sphere remained for real music-making, and there it blossomed. In about 1600, a "Music Society of the Canons" was founded (namely the "Chorherren" of the "Grossmünster" or "Great Cathedral"). It is still in existence today, albeit under a different name, and is thus quite possibly the world's oldest surviving music society.[3] A similar society, the "Music Society of the Music Room at the Corn House," was founded in 1613. The plague had visited the Canton of Zurich in 1611–12, killing over a third of the population, so perhaps the sudden flourishing of private music-making was also a means of distraction from the horrors of everyday life and death. By 1641, matters had relaxed enough for the expanded third edition of the Zurich hymnbook to abandon monody in favor of *a capella* harmony, in four parts, albeit very foursquare. And in 1679, the city's music scene was further enlivened by the founding of a third music society, the "Music Society at the Fraumünster," later known as the "Music Society at the German School" since it used the premises of the local primary school that taught in the vernacular (as opposed to the high school, where Latin was employed). The three societies differed in their membership (at least at first), but all had the same purpose: private music-making on a regular basis. An early emphasis on vocal music gave way to an increasing use of instruments. Over the decades, a certain rivalry developed between the societies, not least because the number of potential members was naturally small in a city whose population was just a few thousand in number. In 1685, the "Music Room Society" began to publish annual *Neujahrsblätter* (New Year's Brochures) every 2 January, the local festival of *Bächtelistag*. The Society of the German School followed suit in 1713. These each comprised a slim booklet with a frontispiece depicting a biblical episode or local scene, followed by a religious poem set to music in three or four parts. This format was retained until the early nineteenth century, with various local poets and composers providing the necessary content. The libraries of the three societies also grew considerably during the seventeenth and eighteenth centuries, as did the music collection of the City Library (founded in 1629). They are today a veritable treasure trove of music, both printed and in manuscript, from all over Western Europe, and even include a number of works that have survived nowhere else. The reasons are both geographical and economic: Zurich's position at the crossroads of Europe made it an obvious meeting point for merchants and goods traveling between France, Germany, Italy, and Austria. Its music-loving citizens thus had the opportunity, and the means, to acquire music from abroad, either from travelers passing through, or from the city's merchants who purchased it while on their own travels abroad.

By the end of the seventeenth century, the Music Room Society had established itself as the most successful of the three institutions, with its members being called upon to provide official city functions with music. In 1684, the city financed the building of a proper "music room" for it, and when a second, bigger room was built for the society in 1717, it was accorded a grand opening that featured a brief cantata by the City Trumpeter Johann Ludwig Steiner (1688–1761) and was attended by the Mayor, the members of the Small and Great Councils — the two bodies that formed the political power in the city and canton — and also by the Venetian ambassador. It was in this same Music Room that Wagner held many of his orchestral rehearsals in the 1850s. And when the building was demolished in the late 1800s, its elaborate ceiling was preserved; today it adorns the Municipal Music Room in the Zurich Town Hall.

The two leading composers in Zurich in the first half of the eighteenth century were Steiner and Johann Caspar Bachofen (1695–1755). The former wrote many of the *Neujahrsstücke* for the Music Room Society, while the latter was for many years responsible for those of the German School Society. In 1723 and 1735 Steiner also published his *Neues Gesangbuch*, a hymnbook in two volumes[4] that was some 1624 pages long and became one of the most important Pietistic song collections of the eighteenth century. In 1727 — spurred on, no doubt, by rivalry with Steiner — Bachofen, too, published a volume of hymns: the *Musicalisches Hallelujah*, which enjoyed a total of eleven editions over the next eighty years. Bachofen's hymns are quite pretty, with some of them even finding their way into today's hymnbooks. But when compared to what was being composed in the rest of Europe, this and all the other music written in Zurich in the early eighteenth century remained basic in both form and harmony, even amateurish. The reasons are not difficult to ascertain: the city was very small, and its music-making was supported neither by the Church nor by a prince or duke, but was indeed the domain of amateurs. To cap it all, those amateurs channeled their limited energies into three different societies that were by this time all running their own ensembles and putting on concerts of symphonies, cantatas, and the like. The Chorherren and the German School societies fused in 1772, but this new society retained its rivalry with the Music Room Society for another forty years. By contrast, just fifty miles to the south, the composers of Lucerne, such as Joseph Franz Xaver Dominik Stalder (1725–65) and the German-born Constantin Reindl (1738–99) — who were supported by the Catholic Church — were writing symphonies and instrumental concertos on a par with most of their European contemporaries. Lucerne even boasted the first German Swiss opera: *Hans Hüttenstock* (1769) by Franz Joseph Leonti Meyer von Schauensee (1720–89). Protestant Zurich, however, was still opposed to the theater in all its forms. In 1730, the city's ecclesiastical authorities declared that "There are sad examples that prove that people keen on theater merely experience a stronger urge toward Papal worship rather than true religion."[5] A few traveling troupes were in the mid-eighteenth century occasionally allowed to put on plays during daylight hours, but these were rare events indeed.

Although its musical and theatrical achievements ranged from the meager to the non-existent, Zurich in the mid-eighteenth century nevertheless began to excel in other artistic fields. Indeed, the city became a veritable power-house for the Enlightenment, even dubbing itself an "Athens on the Limmat." This was thanks, in part, to a high degree of seriousness in matters of education, but also to the very factors that also made it so weak in music: a liberal, democratic tradition, the absence of an overbearing aristocracy, and neither princes nor bishops to determine the cultural agenda. The leading Enlightenment figure in Zurich in the 1700s was Johann Jakob Bodmer (1698–1783), who became a keen Anglophile, published a German translation of Milton's *Paradise Lost* in Zurich in

1732, and in imitation of Addison's *Spectator* founded the *Discourse der Mahlern* in 1721, one of the very first literary journals in the German-speaking world. Great minds from all over came to pay homage to Bodmer. It was even he who suggested to Christoph Martin Wieland that he should translate Shakespeare — which is not without irony, since Shakespeare, along with every other playwright, could not be performed in Bodmer's own city. It was also Bodmer who announced to the world the "rediscovery" of the medieval *Nibelungenlied* that would later form the basis of Wagner's *Ring* tetralogy.[6]

Small publishing houses sprang up in Zurich, new journals were founded, and so were assorted learned societies with diverse scientific, scholarly, and humanistic ends. One of Bodmer's many disciples was Johann Caspar Lavater (1741–1801), a theologian and poet, whose fame at the last exceeded that of his mentor. Another was Heinrich Füssli, who later emigrated to the England that his teacher admired so much, and there (as "Henry Fuseli") achieved fame as a painter of wonderfully dramatic scenes from Shakespeare and the *Nibelungenlied* (to which Bodmer had drawn his attention). But Fuseli and Bodmer were not the only Anglophiles in Zurich. The city soon saw the publication of several different translations of James Thomson's *The Seasons*, and it even enjoyed its first musical setting there, half a century before Joseph Haydn's oratorio. In 1747, the Zurich publisher Heidegger brought out a cantata based upon it by the local composer and agronomist Hans Jakob Ott (1715–69). It was set for three solo voices, three-part chorus, bass continuo, and solo cello, and was obviously modeled on Benedetto Marcello's psalm settings of 1724–26.[7] At fifty-six pages of full score, it was the most ambitious musical work hitherto composed in the city. While such elaborate examples of music printing were rare in Zurich, it should not surprise us that the technical means were available to achieve them, for Zurich in the eighteenth century was home to some three dozen publishing companies[8] (while comparisons are always a little absurd, one can gain an inkling of just how active was the intellectual life of Zurich when one considers that eighteenth-century London would have had to have boasted some seven thousand publishing houses in order to achieve a similar concentration).

It is surprising that, when music did begin to enjoy an upsurge of importance in Zurich in the second half of the eighteenth century, the impetus came not from the city itself, but from an even smaller town some twenty kilometers to the east called Wetzikon. The local vicar was one Johannes Schmidlin (1722–72), who was born in the city of Zurich itself and had also studied there, and besides his pastoral activities devoted himself to the composition of a large oeuvre comprising religious songs and small cantatas.[9] Schmidlin founded a choir and a "Musicum Collegium" in Wetzikon, and exercised such an influence on music-making there that this little place saw the emergence of the three most important Swiss-born composers who were active in the city of Zurich in the last decades of the century: Johann Jakob Walder (1750–1817), Johann Heinrich Egli (1742–1810), and Hans Georg Nägeli (1773–1836).[10]

The second half of the eighteenth century also brought yet more foreign literati to Zurich — Goethe, for example, visited Lavater on his trips to Switzerland in 1775 and 1779. But there were also increasing numbers of foreign musicians passing through. The most famous of these was the young Mozart, who stopped off there with his family in 1766, on the final stage of their Grand Tour, to play for the members of the Music Room Society.[11] In 1786, Zurich briefly hosted an itinerant composer and violinist from Bohemia named Franz Christoph Neubauer (ca. 1760–95), who a few years later was appointed the successor to Johann Christoph Friedrich Bach (the second-youngest son of JS) as Kapellmeister to the court of Bückeburg (though Neubauer died, in an alcoholic haze, shortly afterwards). Neubauer is noteworthy in our context, for at a time when the publication of opera scores was a rarity in the German-speaking countries, he published in Zurich the full score of a singspiel entitled *Fernando und Yariko* — a typical Enlightenment tale of wicked, greedy Europeans and noble North American "savages," not too far removed from the recent Disneyfied version of the Pocahontas story.[12]

Several foreign musicians also came for longer, as the local music societies realized that it was in their interest to entice professionals from elsewhere to come and lead their respective ensembles. Friedrich Leopold Graf from Rudolstadt settled in Zurich in 1758, where he played in the orchestra of the Music Room Society (he was a brother to the better-known composers Friedrich Hartmann and Christian Ernst). In 1788, one Ernst Häussler (1761–1837) arrived, a touring cellist-cum-countertenor from Stuttgart, who remained in Zurich for the next nine years. We know little about him, except that he was responsible for what must have been the first-ever operatic performance in Zurich. His opera *Partenope*, to a text by Metastasio, was given a concert performance in April 1797. I note with some regret that this apparently seminal event provoked no Zwinglian riot, no *Rite of Spring*-style scandal incited by black-clad clerics. Indeed, while there must surely have been *someone* offended by it, their opinions have dissolved into the mists of history, and no one seems to have remembered it at all until, rummaging in archives, I stumbled upon the briefest of mentions of it.[13] Häussler does seem to have left the city shortly afterwards, but there is no proof that his departure was under any kind of cloud.

Another visitor from abroad who stayed from the mid-1780s until the late 1790s was one Johann David Brünings, of whom we again know almost nothing, except that he thereafter departed for St. Petersburg and was never heard of again. Three opus numbers of his survive, each in only a single copy, but his music is testament to a considerable talent; two of his piano sonatas have in the meantime appeared on CD.[14] The most interesting character in Zurich's musical life in the last two decades of the eighteenth century, however, was undoubtedly Philipp Christoph Kayser (1755–1823) from Frankfurt am Main. While still at school, he became friends with Friedrich Maximilian Klinger, whose play *Sturm und Drang* would just a few years later give a whole literary movement its name. Their circle was soon joined by Johann Wolfgang von Goethe and Jakob Michael Lenz. In 1774, they met Lavater, then 33 years of age, who was taking the waters in nearby Bad Ems (just as would Richard Wagner, as it happens, a hundred years later). Kayser was throughout his life possessed of a melancholic disposition, and was at this time — as was his wont — unhappily in love. He seems to have decided that a fresh start in life was necessary, that Lavater's Zurich might fit the bill, and so he moved there in 1775. He was soon giving enough music lessons to make a decent living; he published a volume of songs later that year, and then another two years later. The latter collection includes five Goethe settings — quite possibly the earliest ever published. In 1777, Kayser accompanied Lenz on a walking tour through Switzerland, and it was after the latter continued alone through the Veltlin that he suffered the nervous breakdown described many years later by Georg Büchner in his short story *Lenz*. Kayser and Goethe collaborated on an opera, *Scherz, List und Rache*,[15] they visited Italy together in late 1786, and Goethe even wanted his friend to take up a position as Kapellmeister in Weimar. But they quarreled, and Kayser returned to Zurich, where he remained, unmarried and subject to increasingly dark bouts of depression, until his death in 1823. Kayser was the first of many leading musicians in Zurich to become a Freemason (a tradition that is still alive today), joining the local lodge "Modestia cum Libertate" in 1775. The Lodge disbanded in 1786, but was refounded in 1811, at which time it transpired that Kayser had in the intervening 25 years kept its old insignia safe and sound.

Some of Kayser's extant music is beautiful, especially his songs, so it is a matter of regret that he seems to have stopped composing in the late 1780s. As a teacher and an orchestral player (the viola was his main instrument), he remained a significant figure on the local music scene. But he and all other musicians of Zurich were soon to be overshadowed by a man who would dominate Zurich's musical life for many years to come: Hans Georg Nägeli, publisher, music dealer, entrepreneur, organizer, choral conductor, aesthetician, philosopher, pedagogue, politician, and probably the worst composer ever to have his name grace monuments and streets in a European city. Nägeli was born in Wetzikon in 1773, moved to Zurich, studied with Brünings, and at the age of 18 opened his own music shop. It ran so well that he began to publish music, too — and herein lies his real importance. Brünings introduced Nägeli to the works of J. S. Bach, whereupon Nägeli realized just how difficult it was to procure his music. Ever practical by nature, he decided to do something about it. Thus, some three decades before Mendelssohn's "rediscovery" of Bach, Nägeli brought about a revival of interest in the composer by publishing his music in new editions. These included the *Well-Tempered Clavier* in 1801 and the *Art of Fugue* in 1802. In the latter year, Nägeli also bought the autograph of the B-minor Mass from the widow of C. P. E. Bach and succeeded in publishing the Kyrie and Gloria from it, thirty years later, in 1832. Had the Zurich city fathers been a little more prescient and a little less miserly, they could have acquired the autograph after Nägeli's death. But they weren't, so they didn't, and thus it lies today not in the Zurich Central Library but in Berlin. It was not just the music of the old masters that intrigued Hans Georg, though. He also brought out a series of modern piano works, including five sonatas by Beethoven (op. 31, nos. 1–3, op. 13, and op. 53, the "Waldstein") and works by Clementi, Tomaschek, Steibelt, and himself.[16]

Like many other enlightened citizens of Zurich, Nägeli was attracted by the liberal ideas emerging from France in the wake of the revolution of 1789, though he recoiled from the bloodshed that had resulted from it. Despite increasing economic wealth and the burgeoning of liberal ideas, the political system of Zurich had changed little in the course of the eighteenth century. Although ostensibly possessed of a democratic constitution, it was *de facto* still ruled by the guilds and a few old families. The city ran most of the rest of the canton of Zurich by means of decrees that were enforced by its appointed bailiffs and *Landvogte* (governors). Not only were the roughly two hundred thousand citizens in the greater canton beholden to decisions made by a city of just ten thousand, but the latter group enjoyed greater freedoms and more rights than the former. The fact that the cantonal areas had already embraced the industrial revolution, with spinning and weaving factories springing up in Knonau, the Zurich Oberland, and elsewhere, merely made it all the more inevitable that opposition to urban rights and privileges would grow swiftly. In 1794, the citizens of Stäfa, a small community on the eastern shore of Lake Zurich, drew up a petition to the city fathers, requesting legal, social, and political parity with the citizens of the city itself. In a knee-jerk reaction, the city's troops occupied Stäfa and imprisoned its leaders. Several of them only just escaped the death penalty, thanks in part to the advocacy on their behalf of Lavater, who protested vigorously in his sermons. His views were shared by many other local intellectuals, including Hans Georg Nägeli.

In January 1798, under threat of a French invasion, the Great Council declared an amnesty for the rebels of Stäfa, but their safe return merely sparked off renewed calls for greater freedom. Within days, Zurich was forced to declare at last the equality of all citizens of city and canton; but these concessions were made too late, for the advancing French armies were already sweeping all conservative opposition aside. In March, "trees of liberty" were erected across the canton, though the farmers that danced around them were able only to sing psalms in celebration, as their Zwinglian upbringing had expunged all other song from their communal memory. On 12 April 1798, a new, Helvetic Constitution was accepted in Aarau, which annulled all cantonal boundaries and created for the first time a single, unified, Swiss state in which the citizens were now declared sovereign. The President of the Helvetic Senate was Paul Usteri, a Zurich man from one of the city's old ruling families.

The French occupied Zurich in late April 1798. For much of the next two years, eastern Switzerland was the site of several battles in the War of the Second Coalition, in which French, Russian, and Austrian troops harried each other, back and forth, across hills, plains, and valleys. The most prominent casualty was Johann Caspar Lavater himself, who was shot by a French solider during the second battle of Zurich in September 1799, never recovered properly, and finally died of his wounds on 2 January 1801 (he was accordingly featured on the frontispiece of the 1802 *Neujahrsblatt* of the Music Room Society). Lavater had protested against both the inequalities of the old order and the excesses of the new, but he had remained a figure of international repute. His funeral in the Grossmünster was one of the grandest events that Zurich had ever seen (or ever would), with a total of 137 performers and some three thousand in the congregation.

The Helvetic Republic was far from popular with everyone. The Music Room Society, as it happens, was open in its support of the new régime. It featured a "tree of liberty" with the legend "Freedom and Equality" on the frontispiece of its *Neujahrsblatt* for 1799. But on the whole, for a country that had hitherto barely been a "country" at all, comprising instead over a dozen largely independent statelets with their own monetary, legal, political, and educational systems, to be run now by a five-man directory was too much to ask. Not until 1803 did Napoleon recognize that the Swiss were by nature incapable of functioning under a single, centralized government. His Mediation Act of that year restored the sovereignty of the cantons, though in an overall system far more federal in form than had been the case before 1798. The cost of the French occupation and the Helvetic experiment was vast, not just with regard to the energies invested in fighting for and against change (depending upon where one stood), but also in sheer economic terms — one historian suggests a total loss of some fourteen million francs to the Canton, with the biggest burden falling on the city itself.[17]

One of those badly hit by the economic consequences of war was Hans Georg Nägeli, who by 1807 was no longer able to continue with his business. He sold it to one of his financial partners, a certain Jakob Christoph Hug, in whose family the firm remains to this day as "Musik Hug," Switzerland's biggest chain of music, music instrument, and CD shops. But Nägeli retained the right to publish his own works, even traveling to

Paris that same year in order to establish new business contacts (by 1818 he would be in a position to open yet another music company).[18] Even before his business problems, however, Nägeli had begun to diversify. In 1805, he had founded his "Zurich Singing Institute," with rehearsals on Monday evenings for children, on Wednesdays for women and girls, and on Fridays for a mixed choir. He soon also founded a "Harfenchor," or harp ensemble, and wrote several works for one or more harps. His daughter Ottilie played the harp — indeed, she was still playing it half a century later, in 1853, when Wagner was preparing the local orchestra for the first-ever festival devoted solely to his music. Unfortunately, she insisted on knitting during the rehearsals, kept missing her cues, and had to be replaced.[19]

In 1810, Nägeli founded a male voice choir. This was perhaps the single most important event in the history of Swiss music of the nineteenth century, for it became the model for similar ensembles all over German Switzerland and Germany itself. Nägeli composed more than a thousand straightforward four-part songs for male choir, simple enough for amateurs to sing, and his example was copied everywhere. Nägeli was sure that he could with choral singing unite his patriotism, his passion for democracy and liberalism, and his love of music: "Nationalheiligtum soll die Tonkunst unter uns werden," he cried — "music should become a holy relic of the nation." And indeed, the genre of the male voice chorus soon became inseparable from patriotic ideals. Choral singing was still the main musical activity in the city when Wagner arrived forty years later (and would still be when he left nine years after that). But Nägeli's intentions were in fact primarily educational. He was a supporter of the ideas of the reforming pedagogue Johann Heinrich Pestalozzi — who like Lavater had belonged to Bodmer's circle — and believed that education should be both available to all and adapted to man's natural development. In the same year that he founded his male-voice choir, he published, together with one Michael Pfeiffer, his *Gesangsbildungslehre nach Pestalozzischen Grundsätzen* (A Singing Method According to Pestalozzian Principles). In it, Nägeli praises music as an ideal means to develop a child's emotional and intellectual abilities, and it is full of pedagogical advice for teaching children that is as valid today as it was then. The subscription list of the *Lehre* included addresses as far away as Königsberg, Lübeck, and Paris, and his methods were soon even being taught in Russia.

Nägeli's reputation as a composer, however, was not that much better in his day than in our own. Carl Maria von Weber found his works "odd" and "far too uninspired,"[20] while Louis Spohr — whose fifth violin concerto Nägeli published in 1807 — wrote in his autobiography that "Mr. Nägeli . . . may as a theoretician and as a writer on music have done great things, but on the practical side of music and in the formation of taste he does not seem to have got very far."[21] Spohr was far more impressed with Nägeli's main competitor in Zurich, Anton Liste. Liste was born in Hildesheim in 1772, the son of the cathedral organist, and had studied with Georg Albrechtsberger in Vienna in 1789. There are also unconfirmed reports that he may even have studied there with Mozart. It was thanks to Nägeli that Liste applied successfully for the job of music director of the Music Room Society in Zurich in 1804. He soon established himself as a teacher of piano and singing, and he published three piano sonatas and a bassoon sonata with Nägeli in the ensuing years. They are undoubtedly the best music to be composed in Zurich to that date. While this in itself was hardly an achievement, Liste's music is in fact very fine indeed. His Piano Sonata in A Major, published in 1811, displays the obvious influence of its dedicatee, Beethoven. But Liste was no mere imitator, and he indulged in frequent experimentation. His Piano Sonata in G major is cast in a single movement, the middle section of the slow movement of his bassoon sonata is written without bar lines, and his excellent Sonata in B Flat major for Piano Duet (published by Breitkopf & Härtel) even ends with a fugue.[22] His "Sehnsucht nach dem Rigi" ("Yearning for the Rigi") became highly popular, even eliciting the admiration of Franz Liszt.[23] Liste was also one of Zurich's many musician Freemasons. And, just a year after Nägeli, in 1806, Liste founded his own mixed choir, at first named the "Kleine Musikgesellschaft" ("Little Music Society"), and then, after 1818, the "Listesches Singinstitut" ("Liste's Singing Institute").

Nägeli and Liste were not the only men to bring new vigor to the musical life of Zurich in the years after the restitution of cantonal sovereignty. In 1806, a "Casino" was built there that was not, despite the oddness of its name to Anglo-Saxon ears, a place of betting and gambling but the venue that for the next sixty years would serve as the city's principal concert hall. With its neoclassical façade, it was in appearance not dissimilar from the concert halls and theaters being built across Europe in the late eighteenth and early nineteenth centuries. It had seating for only about four hundred people, which meant that bigger events had to be organized elsewhere; but it was still a major improvement on the facilities hitherto available to the city's concert organizers (and it still stands, today serving as the cantonal courthouse). It was the Casino that was the venue for most of Wagner's concerts in the 1850s.

In 1807, a major step was taken to establish firm structures for the country's musical activities, with the creation of a "Swiss Music Society." Although the notion of a centrally organized government had been abandoned four years earlier, the experiment of the Helvetic Republic had obviously convinced many outside the purely political field that a closer working relationship between Swiss citizens of different cities and cantons might be a good thing. It was therefore decided to hold an annual music festival in a different city each time, at which every member would be allowed to play. The founding festival of 1808 was held in Lucerne, the first event of its kind in Europe (not until 1810 did a similar festival take place in Germany). At the first festival, the orchestra numbered eighty, the choir only thirty-four; at the second festival, in Zurich in 1809, Hans Georg Nägeli conducted an orchestra of 114 in a Haydn symphony and a choir of a hundred in choral pieces by Handel and Friedrich Ludwig Aemilius Kunzen. The audience in the Grossmünster totaled two thousand people. The festivals acquired such prestige that personalities from abroad even deigned to attend, such as Carl Maria von Weber and Giacomo Meyerbeer, who both came to the 1811 festival in Schaffhausen. This festival also saw the debut as a composer of Xaver Schnyder von Wartensee (1786–1868), another musical member of Zurich's Masonic Lodge. Although his compositional gifts were limited, Schnyder later proved a witty autobiographer, whose memoirs are enlivened by cameos of many of the most prominent musicians of his day — it was he who, shortly afterwards, delivered to Beethoven a copy of the piano sonata that Liste had dedicated to him, and forty years later, Schnyder would even pay a friendly visit to Wagner in Zurich, testified to by Wagner's letter of thanks (*SB* 7:423–24).[24]

The democratic ideals of the Swiss Music Society, however, were not always compatible with the exigencies of coherent musical performance. At the 1812 festival, for example, held once more in Zurich, the orchestra numbered 194 players, including eighteen flutists and ten bassoonists. Nor did standards improve vastly over the years. Four decades later, Wagner would be made an honorary member; but his only engagement as its conductor would be cut short when he fled in horror after the first rehearsal. Nevertheless, the Society performed a vital function in propagating music on a scale far more ambitious than had hitherto been attempted. And its example seems also to have prompted the two remaining music societies in Zurich to combine at last. After all, if the musicians of the whole country could work together, why not those of a single city? Both of the Zurich music societies were using the Casino as their concert hall, and they were already coordinating their concert and rehearsal activities to avoid clashes. So a union must have now seemed the most natural course of action. The "Allgemeine Musikgesellschaft Zürich" (Zurich General Music Society, henceforth AMG) was accordingly founded in July 1812; it boasted 114 members in total. It took on not just the concert activities of its two predecessors but also the task of bringing out a *Neujahrsblatt* every year. From 1813 to 1822, these comprised settings by Nägeli of poems by Martin Usteri; from 1823 to 1829 they consisted of texts on the annual festivals of the Swiss Music Society; but in 1830, they took on the form of brief monographs on music and musicians, and this remains their format to this day. The earliest were short biographies of musical "greats" such as Beethoven, Mozart, and Weber, but soon local personalities began to be featured, such as Nägeli in 1838. The *Neujahrsblätter* today provide our biggest and best source of information on the music history of Zurich and its environs.

Nägeli's reputation as an aesthetician of European import was cemented by a series of lectures that he gave across Germany in 1823 and 1824, speaking on Johann Sebastian and Carl Philipp Emanuel Bach, Haydn, Mozart, and Beethoven. He published his lectures in book form in 1826, dedicating them to Archduke Rudolph of Austria, Beethoven's patron. Nägeli praises both Bachs, declares Beethoven "the great hero of art," but expresses grave reservations about Mozart because of his supposed "lack of style" and disregard for the true proportions of a work of art. That Nägeli here goes against the grain of what we today hold to be true should by no means encourage us to belittle him. These lectures are in fact of considerable historical significance, not least because their aesthetic is not far from that espoused by Eduard Hanslick thirty years later in his *On the Beautiful in Music*. But they are also fascinating in our context, because here — a quarter of a century before the "Musician of the Future" Richard Wagner descended upon Zurich — the city's most prominent musical son declares the following to be the true goal of art:

> Newness. We do not need a new world all at once, but one that is constantly being renewed, if we wish to lead a truly ideal life in this field of artistic endeavor where the mind must maintain its creative strength in a boundless play of forms.[25]

Nägeli was still to have his own share in "newness," though not in the field of music. After Napoleon's fall from power, the conservatives in Switzerland had hoped that his political reforms would be abandoned altogether. But any notion that the status quo of 1797 might be restored was quashed by the Council of Vienna. The great powers allowed the cantons to regain much of their former independence, but were keen that the country — now expanded by the addition of the cantons of Valais, Neuchâtel,[26] and Geneva — should remain enough of a single entity to play a role in keeping the balance of power in their new Europe. So, above the cantons, they placed a federal diet. The period of 1815–30 has often been referred to as that of the "restoration" in Zurich history,[27] but the position of the conservatives in fact became increasingly precarious. This was due in part to various scandals, financial and otherwise, but also to a sheer lack of ideas, initiative, and energy just at a time when these were needed.[28] The liberals were supported by the local press, in particular the *Neue Zürcher Zeitung*, which received the "New" in its name in 1821, when Paul Usteri — the former President of the Helvetic Senate — became its editor. It was Usteri who was primarily responsible for successfully defending free speech when new censorship restrictions were proposed by the Swiss federal diet in the 1820s. The *Neue Zürcher* remained long at the forefront of liberal thinking in Switzerland (though, as we shall see, it would at first prove undeniably impervious to the charms of Richard Wagner's *Zukunftsmusik*).

Change for the city of Zurich now came, just as it had over thirty years earlier, via France. The July Revolution in Paris in 1830 set off a chain of protests and gatherings across Switzerland, and within just a few months eleven of the cantons had drafted and accepted new liberal constitutions. As in the 1790s, it was the little towns to the east of the metropolis that sparked off the political upheavals in Zurich, with the citizens of Uster this time playing a key role in demanding — yet again — greater political parity between the city and the canton. The conservatives capitulated, and in 1831, Zurich accepted a new constitution that declared the people of the canton to be sovereign. Paul Usteri became the new mayor, but he died within days of taking office and was succeeded by Konrad von Muralt. The liberals, who now held all the important offices of the state and judiciary, went about constructing a modern society with astonishing zeal. The penal code was reformed; new, streamlined tax laws were introduced; the administrative structures of the canton were modernized; the city walls were dismantled, walls that had long been a visual signifier for those outside them of the autocratic power exercised by the city of old; new streets, quays, and bridges were built to improve transport within the city itself; and new municipal buildings were erected, such as the Post Office and the Corn House. But arguably the biggest changes of all came in education. An *Erziehungsrat* or "Education Board" was created to reform all levels of schooling, and on the panel for the reform of elementary schools sat none other than Hans Georg Nägeli. He was one of several who now ensured that the pedagogical ideas of Pestalozzi (who had died in 1827) began to achieve general acceptance. The schools in the canton were completely overhauled, and an emphasis such as would not be seen in England, for example, for many decades yet was placed on general education of the youth. School attendance became compulsory for "children from all classes of the people," as the very first paragraph of the new Education Act made clear.[29] School was to last from the sixth to the fifteenth year, and was to be free for those from the poorest families. A new system of secondary education was introduced, with academic and technical high schools. The "simple people" whom Wagner would encounter in Zurich just a few years later were thus, in fact, the most literate and best-schooled in Western Europe.

A teacher's training college (*Lehrerseminar*) was now created in Küsnacht, just down the lake, to provide the teachers for all these new schools in the canton (the *Lehrerseminar*, as it happens, would later establish a fine musical reputation, and some of the country's best composers of the twentieth century would study or teach there, ranging from the Boulanger pupil Hermann Haller to the avant-gardist Klaus Huber). The Education Act of 1832 was 119 pages long and gave detailed information on every aspect of the Canton's new policy, including the syllabus to be taught. Music figured large here, with particular emphasis given to singing. In light of this fact, and given his knowledge of Nägeli's pedagogical work, Wagner's suggestions to the Zurich authorities in the 1850s for establishing more concrete structures for music training in the city (see chapter 2 below) appear less impractical than one might otherwise suppose. Although he was to be disappointed, he would at least be arguing within a system that had already acknowledged the importance of the arts in education.

Most significant of all, the Act provided for the establishment of a university in Zurich, which then indeed came about in 1833. Its early years were turbulent, not least because the liberals who had founded it made a point of inviting top-notch scholars from Germany to take up important teaching posts, and many of these — such as the first Rector, Lorenz Oken — were radical in their politics. The arrival of Wagner and his fellow revolutionaries from Dresden, some sixteen years later, was thus no unnatural occurrence for Zurich but merely formed part of an established tradition of welcoming political radicals from the north. Among the young refugees who arrived at Zurich University in its early years was Georg Büchner. He submitted his doctoral dissertation in 1837 and was then appointed to the lecturing staff, but he died soon afterwards without having completed his most recent play, *Woyzeck*. The house in which he lived, and died, still stands today, on the Spiegelgasse — the "street of revolution" celebrated in Tom Stoppard's play *Travesties*. Eighty years after Büchner, the house next door was home to Lenin before he departed for the Finland Station; a few seconds' walk down the street takes one to the site of the Cabaret Voltaire, where Dada was founded, and a few doors away in the other direction stands the house occupied by the opera singer Lucia Popp in her final years, when she sang regularly at the Zurich Opera House. Although Büchner's death by no means went unnoticed, the educational world in Zurich was in fact still very much in mourning for Hans Georg Nägeli, who had died in December 1836. In his final years, he had turned increasingly to politics, even becoming a member of the Great Council in 1835. He spoke out vigorously against the death penalty, in favor of trials with jury, against harshness in the penal code, and for maintaining the right of asylum (for which Wagner should no doubt have been grateful).

The political and social upheavals of the 1830s brought little change to the city's concert life. The new, united music society had maintained the tradition of its forerunners by bringing in Germans to direct its orchestra. Its first music director was one C. Ochernal from Erfurt, who had succeeded Liste as director of the Music Room Society's ensemble. He was followed in 1814 by Franz Beutler, a "Bayrischer Kammermusikus" (Bavarian Chamber Musician), then in 1817 by the German violinist and composer Heinrich Joseph Wassermann (1791–1838), a former pupil of

Louis Spohr's. When he left in 1820 to become the leader of the orchestra in Donaueschingen, he was succeeded, briefly, by a local violinist — the first Swiss to have the job — named in the records as "Gall der Ältere" (Gall Senior). But soon afterward, in 1821, another foreigner was chosen for the post. He was Casimir von Blumenthal: violinist, composer, and conductor, who was born in 1787 in Brussels as the son of a baron, but whose family had lost the greater part of its fortune in the wake of the French Revolution. Casimir had studied in Vienna with Abbé Georg Vogler and afterwards enjoyed a somewhat peripatetic existence, playing — as far as we can tell from the scanty records — in Vienna, Prague, Brno, and Bratislava before taking up his new position in Zurich.

The AMG Orchestra was still very much an amateur affair, with its numbers bolstered by just enough professionals to ensure a moderate standard of performance. Blumenthal was by all accounts a perfectly competent musician. But he "showed understanding for the amateur orchestra, and was accommodating toward it. Its members felt this, and rewarded him with great loyalty and friendliness."[30] An accommodating conductor to whom his players feel great friendliness is hardly a taskmaster such as is needed to bring real results — and we can now begin to understand the lackadaisical circumstances with which Wagner found himself confronted, a quarter of a century later. Blumenthal was at least responsible for introducing the symphonies of Beethoven to Zurich, albeit "rarely, and with reservations."[31] He liked Zurich, married a local girl, acquired citizenship, joined the local Masonic lodge, founded a choral society of his own, and obviously made himself comfortable and popular. He directed the festivals of the Swiss Music Society in Geneva in 1824 and in Zurich in 1828 and 1838, and only retired from his post in 1846 (he died three years later in Lausanne, of an "inflammation of the brain"). Blumenthal also deigned to perform the music of other local composers on occasion; the AMG library today still holds the manuscript of a Symphony in D, dedicated to the Society, and written in the early 1820s by one Jacob Zeugheer (1805–65; also known as "Jaques"). Jacob played the bassoon in the AMG Orchestra but emigrated to England in about 1837 and later became the founding conductor of the Liverpool Philharmonic Orchestra. It was his brother, the architect Leonhard, who would later build Otto Wesendonck's villa in Zurich and renovate the house next door that became Wagner's home, his *Asyl* or "refuge."

Blumenthal's most important contribution to Zurich's musical life, however, lay in his bringing opera to the city. Since the French invasion of 1798 had swept away the old régime, theatrical troupes from France and Germany had been allowed to visit the city with greater regularity than the hitherto all-powerful Zwinglian authorities had deemed permissible. Some of them even performed operas, though the facilities available to them were apparently as poor as were their offerings. The notion of building a theater in the city was still anathema to many. The AMG regularly performed overtures and individual arias, but in the 1820s, under Blumenthal, it began to give concert performances of whole operas, ranging from Mozart's *Don Giovanni* and *Die Zauberflöte* to Rossini's *Moses in Egypt* and Carl Maria von Weber's *Freischütz* and *Preciosa*. This explains why the AMG's library today possesses early or first printings of the orchestral parts of many operas, obviously bought at a time when theater was still forbidden in the city.

In 1830, an Italian operatic troupe run by one Giordani visited the city, and this seems to have been the catalyst that prompted several prominent citizens to ponder whether it might now be time to erect a theater of their own. They founded a provisional "theater committee," and in October 1832 asked the city for a suitable building in which their theater might find a home. The head of the Zurich church, Johann Georg Gessner, was so horrified by the idea that he published a pamphlet to warn of the immense moral threat that such an institution would pose to society, and of the concomitant dangers to impressionable youth. Perhaps it was, then, a certain sense of ironic justice that now prompted the city fathers to allow the theater committee to buy and convert a former monastery church for their wicked endeavors: the *Barfüsserkirche*, which had most recently been used as a corn warehouse, and was situated just behind the Casino. In order to cover the costs of the building, a joint-stock company was founded in late 1833 — an "Aktiengesellschaft," hence the official name, "Aktientheater," of the theater itself. Two hundred and fifty shares were offered at two hundred gulden each, and within weeks they were all sold. The members of the "Theater Committee" bought twenty-five each, the canton ten, and the AMG and the city council five each. The Zurich theater was one of the first independent city theaters in German-speaking Europe. The board of the shareholders decided upon one Ferdinand Deny from Berlin as its first director. Like all the directors who followed him during the first decades of the theater's existence, he had to hire the theater at his own expense and run it strictly as a business in order to make it worth his while. He had to pay thirty gulden for each performance; the AMG provided the orchestra for musical productions but charged 10% of the takings for plays with incidental music, and 15% for operas and singspiele. Furthermore, the AMG's music director Blumenthal now functioned as Music Director for the theater.

In the second half of 1833, Richard Wagner was reputedly offered the post of "music director" at the theater in Zurich, though this prospect was apparently dashed when the Leipzig authorities denied him a passport (*SB* 1:137). However, since the theater did not actually open its doors until late 1834, this is improbable. Furthermore, he had only just begun his career in the profession, having taken up his first job, as chorus director at the theater in Würzburg, in early 1833. It is naturally one of music history's intriguing "what-ifs" to ponder what Wagner's career might have been had he taken up a post in Zurich at such an early date. As it happens, however, one of his friends in Würzburg, Alexander Müller (1808–63) from Erfurt, a former pupil of Beethoven's friend Johann Nepomuk Hummel, did soon to move to Zurich. In *Mein Leben* Wagner later wrote of Müller, "[He] impressed me [with] his truly great dexterity in improvising; he was able to hold me spellbound for hours on end, improvising on themes he was given (*ML*, 83)." Such examples of unequivocal, unqualified praise are not common with Wagner, so Müller must have been gifted. In any case, he soon established himself in Zurich as a piano teacher and choral conductor, and — like Blumenthal and others before him — joined the local Masonic lodge. Soon after arriving in Zurich, Müller took over the directorship of the former "Listesches Singinstitut" (whose founder had died in 1832); was this, perhaps, really the "conducting job" that Wagner had been offered, and had Müller taken it in his stead? This is, however, sheer speculation, and while it would be a convenient means of tying up a couple of biographical loose ends, we shall never know for sure. But Müller and Wagner did not forget each other, and — as I mentioned in the introduction above — it was to Müller that Wagner would turn, sixteen years later, when he arrived as a refugee in Zurich.

The Zurich Theater's opening night was on 10 November 1834. The first item was an overture by Blumenthal based on popular Swiss melodies. This was followed by a "festspiel" or celebratory play by one Professor Hottinger, and then a prologue spoken by Madame Deny. The main item on the evening's program was Mozart's *Die Zauberflöte*, and it was a huge success. Although the theater was intended from the start to cater for all tastes, both musical and non-musical, the fact that the bulk of the opening night was devoted to an opera, not a play, was a significant statement regarding the importance that the authorities assigned to the art form. The theater had seating for only eight hundred people, and many had to be turned away. In fact, the performance had only taken place at all because Deny had managed more or less to "steal away" from the Basel Theater a soprano named "Demoiselle Podlesky" who was starring there as the Queen of the Night, and was apparently also the only singer far and wide who was up to the role.

Not every subsequent production was as successful as this, of course, and the theater's program over the next years had to be as popular as possible in order to fill the auditorium and stave off the constant threat of bankruptcy under which all its directors had to live and work. It is therefore not a little surprising that the first season saw no less than fourteen operas performed — one would imagine that the most expensive art form would have been kept for special occasions. But the Zurich public was obviously so keen for musical theater that they were prepared to turn up in large numbers and pay the increased ticket fees. The operas performed in that first season included several of the staples from the European repertoire of the time, such as Adrien Boieldieu's *La dame blanche*, Joseph Weigl's *Die Schweizerfamilie*, Ferdinand Hérold's *Zampa*, Auber's *Fra Diavolo*, Weber's *Freischütz*, Cherubini's *Les deux journées*, Rossini's *Otello*, and Mozart's *Don Giovanni* and *Figaro*.[32] Among the regular members of the audience in these early years was no less a figure than Prince Louis Napoleon, Bonaparte's nephew and later Emperor Napoleon III, who spent his youth in Arenenberg, to the north of Zurich near the border between Germany and Switzerland.[33]

Deny's reign was not long, however, and he was soon complaining in public that the members of the Theater Committee were trying to make all his decisions for him and were even distributing dozens of whistles among the audience in order for certain actors to be heckled. So he left to run the theater of Bern instead. He was followed by a Carl Friedrich Breuer from Cannstatt, who was also more or less chased away, though he apparently managed to go bankrupt first.[34] Not until 1837 did the theater find a director who could satisfy all its needs — economic, artistic, and political — and it was a woman: Charlotte Birch-Pfeiffer. She was not just one of the best-known German actresses of her time but was also a skilful authoress whose plays remained in the repertoire until well into the twentieth century. When she gave a guest performance in Zurich in April 1837, she was so successful that the Theater Committee offered her the directorship. She accepted, and conveniently she had a husband in tow who was able and willing to take on the technical aspects of running the institution. Her political astuteness was soon proven when she shortly thereafter produced a heroic play of her own entitled *Zwinglis Tod* (The Death of Zwingli), starring herself as Zwingli's wife. How better to ingratiate oneself in a city where it was the arch-Zwinglians who had hitherto been the most vociferous against the very existence of the theater? Birch-Pfeiffer's tenure lasted until September 1843, when she left for the Court Theater in Berlin. She had campaigned, unsuccessfully, for financial support from the city, and finally had to realize that winning her way into the hearts of the Zurich populace was far easier than winning her way into their pockets. In April 1841 she had even published a tract outlining her views and her ultimate goal of creating a theater with a fixed ensemble — exactly ten years, almost to the day, before Richard Wagner would do the same (and with a similar lack of success).

In artistic terms, however, Birch-Pfeiffer's tenure was of immense significance to the city. The operas that she produced during her six years included not just the staples by Adam, Auber, Boieldieu, Mozart, and Weber, but also Meyerbeer's *Les Huguenots* (Meyerbeer soon became one of the most popular composers with the Zurich public; by 1859, his *Huguenots* had clocked up forty performances and his *Robert le diable* forty-two[35]). Birch-Pfeiffer also put on the occasional local work. Thus

Alexander Müller's opera *Die Flucht nach der Schweiz* (The Escape to Switzerland) was first performed at the Zurich theater in 1841 — an appropriate title, given that his home would be Wagner's first port of call, eight years later. Sadly, neither the music nor the libretto of Müller's opera has survived. The possibility cannot be excluded that the work in question might be the opera of the same name by Friedrich Wilhelm Kücken, first performed in Berlin in 1839; or perhaps the names of Müller's and Kücken's operas have simply been confused, for in 1853, the AMG would perform in one of its concerts an "overture from the opera *Der Flüchtling* [*The Fugitive*] by Alexander Müller," which is probably the same work as was performed twelve years earlier in the theater.[36]

Birch-Pfeiffer was not just an actress, an organizer, and a playwright but was also active on occasion as a librettist. Among the composers who are recorded as having set her libretti to music are Adolf Schmid (1801–86) with his *Die Walpurgisnacht*, first performed at the Theater an der Wien in 1830, Conradin Kreutzer (1780–1849) with *Der Edelknecht* (Wiesbaden, 1842) and Michael Hebenstreit (ca. 1812–50) with *Das Posthaus zu Sèvres* (1843 at the Theater an der Wien). After her move to Berlin, she translated — together with Ludwig Rellstab — Scribe's libretto for Meyerbeer's singspiel *Ein Feldlager in Schlesien* for its première there in 1844; and when Meyerbeer decided to set Scribe's libretto for *L'Africaine* in the early 1860s, after the poet's death, Birch-Pfeiffer was one of the authors whom he engaged to help prepare the text for him. It was as a librettist, in fact, that she would later make a brief appearance in Wagner's autobiography, for in 1851 he turned down a commission to orchestrate an opera composed by Duke Ernst of Coburg to a libretto by her, *Santa Chiara* (*ML*, 477). It is an odd fact, however, that she was not the only librettist living in Zurich in these years. One Leonhard Widmer (1808–68) from Feldmeilen, just outside Zurich, is known today almost solely because he wrote the words of what is now the Swiss national anthem. But in his youth he had moved to Lausanne and there met the composer Andreas Späth, for whom he wrote four opera libretti, which were all performed in Coburg between 1833 and 1842. Although Widmer returned to Zurich in 1833, there is no record of his operas ever being performed there. His musical interests were extensive — besides being a keen amateur singer, he even set up a lithographic workshop, where he printed many choir songbooks, and seems to have dabbled in composition himself.[37]

During her time in Zurich, Birch-Pfeiffer was also responsible for drawing men of talent to her theater. Thus in the autumn of 1837 she engaged as harpist one Karl Oberthür from Munich, who stayed until 1839 and in the late 1840s emigrated to London, where he established himself as one of the leading harpists of the day (his *Universal Method for the Harp* is apparently still in use today). In 1840, the violinist and composer Gustav-Adolf Kölla (1822–1905) joined the theater orchestra, the same Kölla who from 1829 onwards had toured the courts of Europe with three of his brothers as a "Wunderkind" string quartet (he would later settle in Lausanne, but returned to Zurich to participate in the Wagner festival of 1853; he subsequently founded the Lausanne Conservatory). In 1841, Birch-Pfeiffer brought the young Franz Abt to Zurich as conductor of the theater's chorus. And in 1843, in her final month at the theater, she was able to engage as a guest artist the famed soprano Wilhelmine Schröder-Devrient. Just a year before, Schröder had sung the role of Adriano in the world première of Wagner's *Rienzi*, and she had followed this with a brilliant portrayal of Senta in the première of *Der fliegende Holländer* under the composer's baton, also in Dresden, on 2 January 1843. It was in the wake of that première that Wagner was appointed Kapellmeister in Dresden. The appearance of Schröder-Devrient in Zurich was such an event that one of the orchestral musicians even made a note of it in his part for Weber's *Freischütz*.

Birch-Pfeiffer needed all her political acumen from late 1839 onwards, for September 1839 saw a reversal of fortunes for the city's liberals, one that gave both the German and, thereafter, the English language a new word: "putsch." The victory of the liberals in 1830–31 and the ensuing reforms had by no means won over all the citizens of the city and canton, and local politics had instead become highly polarized. In a desire to bring their ideas of reform also to the ecclesiastical structures of Zurich, the liberal government decided in 1839 to appoint the controversial theologian David Friedrich Strauss to a professorship at the University. But this was the straw that broke the camel's back. The city authorities had not realized the degree of popular disapproval of Strauss and his ideas, and were forced to pension off Strauss even before he had arrived to take up his post. It was too late, however, and the "September Putsch" that followed saw the tables turned on the government. A general purge ensued that saw off the members of the *Erziehungsrat* and even threatened the continued existence of the university. The sudden increase in influence of conservative clerics naturally had an impact on the theater, too. Although it was not closed — both it and Birch-Pfeiffer were probably too popular for that — censorship restrictions meant that certain plays (such as Karl Spindler's *Waldmann*) could no longer be performed, while others — including Goethe's *Egmont* — had to have any and all passages removed that might have offended either the church or the new political dispensation.

The victory of the reaction was relatively short-lived, however, for in the elections to the Great Council of 1842, just as many liberals were returned as conservatives, and in the elections of 1844, the liberals won the upper hand. The new mayor was one Hans Ulrich Zehnder — the first time that a man from outside the city had been elected to the position. He was succeeded in early 1845 by the new leader of the liberal party, Jonas Furrer, a brilliant young lawyer from Winterthur, a small town to the north-east of Zurich. The liberals in Zurich, as elsewhere, had always tended toward a unitarian, federalist view of their country, while the conservatives — who were strongest in the Catholic cantons — were traditionally in favor of greater cantonal independence. These two diverging views of what Switzerland could be, or should be, now came into real conflict. The liberal government of Aargau had in 1841 confiscated the monasteries in its territory, which had provoked outrage among the Catholic cantons such as neighboring Lucerne. In part to spite its liberal, Protestant brethren, Lucerne soon decided to place the running of its higher education system in the hands of the Jesuits, who accordingly arrived in the capital of the canton in October 1844. The Jesuits in the early twenty-first century arouse little of the suspicion that was their lot in the mid-nineteenth. Indeed, in more recent history, it has been members of that order who have been at the forefront of left-wing theological movements in Latin America and elsewhere. But a hundred and fifty years ago, the Jesuits were a bete-noire for both Protestants and liberals alike. To draw a more contemporary analogy: Zurich, Aargau, and the other Protestant cantons regarded Lucerne's move with a horror that would be matched in the USA today if, say, Canada were to place the running of its schools *en masse* in the hands of an alliance of Osama bin Laden, Fidel Castro, and Kim-il Sung.

A number of outsiders, together with allies inside the canton, now attempted insurrection in Lucerne — twice — but were defeated, and many of them imprisoned (even the young poet Gottfried Keller took part in the second insurrection, though in the event he did not get any further than the boundaries of his own canton). The leader of the Lucerne liberals, Robert Stieger, was sentenced to death but managed to escape. Such harsh reprisals on the part of Lucerne's government merely increased the political polarization at a national level. At the end of 1845, Lucerne formalized an alliance with the (Catholic) cantons of Uri, Schwyz, Unterwalden, Zug, Fribourg, and Valais, which became known as the "Sonderbund" or "extraordinary union." Over the coming months, there was increasing concern in the rest of the country that the intention of the Sonderbund was to secede from Switzerland altogether; apart from anything else, such a move would have severed in geographical terms the southwestern, Protestant, French-speaking cantons from their German-speaking allies in the northeast. In July 1847, the Swiss federal diet voted by a narrow majority to demand the dissolution of the Sonderbund. The latter responded by mobilizing its armed forces, bolstered by arms shipments from a sympathetic Austria. The other cantons mobilized too, but enjoyed only a slight advantage in numbers. The conservatives among the great powers that had guaranteed Swiss neutrality in 1815 — most notably Austria and Russia — were nervous about the prospect of a victory of the liberals. So Furrer and his allies knew all too well that a prolonged conflict would almost certainly prompt foreign intervention. This was clear, too, to the commanding officer of the federal troops, Henri Dufour, who in a series of impressive tactical moves managed to cut off and defeat Fribourg in mid-November 1847 before turning his army on Lucerne itself. He defeated the remainder of the Sonderbund's forces in the Battle of Gislikon just a few days later. The total number of dead was less than a hundred. Thanks to the delaying tactics of Lord Palmerston, the note of protest that the signatories of 1815 sent to Switzerland did not arrive until several weeks after the civil war was over. Switzerland was in any case saved from the danger of last-minute intervention from abroad when revolution broke out across Europe in 1848 — in France, Austro-Hungary, and the various smaller states that would later unite to form Germany and Italy.

In the meantime, the Protestant victors were forging ahead with their reforms of the Swiss state. Zurich had indulged with relish in the symbolic act of regaining the weapons of Huldrych Zwingli — taken from his corpse after the Battle of Kappel in 1531, and kept as a trophy in Lucerne for the next three hundred and sixteen years. But otherwise, the defeated cantons were treated with remarkable tact, in order not to prejudice them completely against the new order. By the end of 1848, the Swiss cantons had voted for a new constitution that created a bicameral parliament after the American model, and the new federation swiftly assumed control of all aspects essential to running a modern state, centralizing the post office and the customs and monetary systems. All the old forms of currency were abolished, and a decimal "franc" was introduced with parity to the French franc. Bern became the new permanent capital, and the first President of the Swiss Confederation was Jonas Furrer. His position in Zurich was thereupon taken by his colleague Alfred Escher, just thirty years old, the son of a millionaire businessman, and the man who would dominate politics in his home canton for the next two decades: leader of the city's liberals, founder of the Credit Suisse bank, founder *de facto* of the Swiss Federal Technical University, the "railway king" of eastern Switzerland, and the organizational genius behind the building of the Gotthard Railway. His sister, the painter Clementine Stockar-Escher, was to be Wagner's landlady and would also paint what is the most famous portrait of the composer from his years in Zurich. Escher's former position of Cantonal Secretary — "Staatsschreiber" — was taken by his friend and ally Johann Jakob Sulzer, two years his junior. Sulzer would in later years become the president of his native city of Winterthur; as we shall see, he became one of Wagner's first patrons, and closest friends, after the composer's arrival in Zurich.

The political events of the 1840s seem not to have had any major influence on the musical life of Zurich, except in that the more liberal members of the *Stadtsängerverein* — one of Nägeli's former choirs — formed a splinter group in 1841, called themselves the "Harmonie," and had such success that they became responsible for organizing in 1843 the first *Eidgenössisches Sängerfest*, a massed choral festival-cum-competition that was run under the auspices of the recently formed *Eidgenössischer Sängerverein* (Swiss Singer's Association), and which from 1846 onwards was held every two years. Franz Abt had lost his job at the Theater when his protector Birch-Pfeiffer had resigned, but he had remained in the city and was becoming increasingly important on the local choral scene. In November 1844, the Harmonie elected him as its new conductor. One measure of his success is the fact that he and the Harmonie twice — in 1848 and 1852 — won first prize at the *Eidgenössisches Sängerfest*; another is the fact that various other choral societies also appointed him as their conductor: the Stadtsängerverein, the Studentengesangverein, the Cäcilienverein, and the Limmatthal-Gesangverein.[38] And when Casimir von Blumenthal retired from his position as music director of the AMG Orchestra in 1846, it was Abt who, after the orchestra's brief interregnum under one Wilhelm Bärwolf, was asked to be his successor. When Wagner arrived in Zurich, then, it was Franz Abt who was essentially the city's "music baron" — and that fact was probably enough for Wagner to want to oust him, as indeed he would. Besides Abt, the most prominent musician in the city at the time of Wagner's arrival was undoubtedly Alexander Müller. He was not just active as a choral conductor but was also responsible for teaching much of the best talent that Zurich could offer. His pupils included Wilhelm Baumgartner, whose songs Wagner would later go so far as to praise in print; the pianist, singer, and composer Fanny Hünerwadel (1826–54); and the pianist Henriette Eschmann (1829–96), of whom Müller would later claim that she was his finest ever pupil (she was the sister of the violinist Jean Eschmann and cousin of the composer Johann Carl Eschmann; see their family tree in chapter 6).

After Birch-Pfeiffer's departure, the Zurich Theater suffered uncertain times. By 1846, the AMG had even seen itself forced to annul its contractual obligation to provide an orchestra, for the theater had ceased to pay its percentage. The names of her successors, Gerlach, Henckel, and Hehl, feature nowhere in the literature today except in lists of Zurich's post-Birch directors. Their fate might well have been shared, too, by one Philipp Walburg Kramer, who came to run the theater in 1850, were it not for the fact that he would employ Richard Wagner as a freelance on his staff and would be the first man to give Hans von Bülow a conducting job; as it happens, the Theater Board under whose auspices both Wagner and von Bülow were appointed included among its members none other than Alfred Escher. It would be wrong, however, to suppose that Zurich's cultural life was barren of all but the activities of the dilettantes, for it was, and would remain for many years, on the touring circuit of various musicians and actors. Even Liszt came there to play two concerts in July 1845; during his visit he found the time to be given an honorary membership in Zurich's Masonic Lodge.

A consideration of the musical life of Zurich at the time of Wagner's arrival would be incomplete, however, without also casting a glance at the city of Winterthur. Today, it takes one barely twenty minutes to travel by *S-Bahn* from one city to the other. But while the post coach in Wagner's day would commonly take two-and-a-half hours to cover the distance, it had nevertheless long been normal for musicians from Winterthur to commute to Zurich to play in the orchestra there. Once the railway link was established between the two places in June 1856, contact naturally increased vastly.[39] Winterthur had a population roughly one-eighth the size of Zurich, and it existed then, as it does now, in the shadow of its bigger brother to the southwest. But its musical life was in many ways more vibrant. The arts prospered there in the nineteenth century, not least because it became a center of industry, the captains of which were both interested in the arts and of a philanthropic disposition. The fruits of this can still be seen today, most noticeably in its magnificent art collections, acquired by its prominent citizens and now displayed for all to admire. Winterthur had reintroduced the organ to its Protestant churches many years before Zurich made the same great liturgico-theological leap forward, and in 1843 Winterthur took the admirable step of appointing to the post of City Organist a brilliant young musician from Saxony by the name of Theodor Kirchner (1823–1903), a protégé of both Schumann and Mendelssohn. He was joined in 1845 by an assistant organist named Oswald Lorenz (1806–89), a fellow Saxon, and the dedicatee of Schumann's song cycle *Frauenliebe und Leben* (The Love and Life of Woman). Lorenz had been writing for Schumann's *Neue Zeitschrift für Musik* since 1837 and in fact had edited it himself in 1839 and in the winter of 1844–45. He continued to write for it from Winterthur (Wagner even mentions him in that capacity in a letter of 4 February 1852 to Franz Brendel, a later editor of the journal [*SB* 4:481]). But Winterthur also had its own native artistic talent, most notably the composer Johann Carl Eschmann (1826–82), another pupil of Mendelssohn's, whose life and oeuvre will be discussed at greater length in chapter 6 below, and the painter-cum-writer August Corrodi (1826–85), yet another ardent Schumannian, who had studied painting in Munich before returning to join the circle around Kirchner and Lorenz. Corrodi's literary works attracted praise from Jacob Grimm and others, and even included poems and plays in his local dialect. It was into that same dialect that he translated poems by Robert Burns and plays by Plautus and Oliver Goldsmith.[40] Corrodi was also familiar with Wagner's works. In his *Reisebriefe aus der Schweiz und Mailand* (A Traveler's Letters from Switzerland and Milan), published in 1857, he even quoted (twice) from the song of the Young Sailor in the *Fliegender Holländer* ("Ach, lieber Südwind, blas' noch mehr").[41]

The revolutions that swept most of continental Europe in 1848–49 have one thing in common: they failed. The forces of reaction triumphed everywhere

— except, however, in Switzerland. When Wagner fled there in May 1849, he thus arrived in the only country on the continent where the liberals had been able to consolidate their position, despite the upheavals of the previous two years. The attempt to create a unified Germany under democratic principles had proven a failure, and many members of the German Parliament in Frankfurt — so newly created, and so soon dispersed — had fled in fear of their lives. Their number included one Hugo Wesendonck, the brother of a north-German silk magnate of whom we shall learn more later. As the radical movements that had sprung up in Europe's conservative states failed one by one, many of those who escaped capture made their way to Switzerland, whose long-held policy of granting political asylum was well known. This caused no small problems for the new confederation, especially when the failure of an uprising in Baden, just over the border to the north, prompted over three thousand soldiers to seek refuge across the Rhine in July 1849 — including the poet Georg Herwegh and his formidable wife Emma, who had arrived for battle with a haphazard German Legion, drummed up in France, and supported by the revolutionary government in power at the time in Paris. By this time Switzerland was already sheltering several thousand refugees from neighboring countries, and Johann Jakob Sulzer had become president of a "Committee for the Support of German Refugees" in Zurich. It was their self-appointed task to aid the needy and to help those who stayed to find jobs — some six hundred refugees had now settled more or less permanently in the city. These refugees were joined by others over the next few years. Some fled from France after the coup d'état of Louis Napoleon in late 1851, while others arrived in Zurich after having tried their luck elsewhere, such as the architect Gottfried Semper, the historian Theodor Mommsen and the literary historian Francesco De Sanctis. Other prominent men and women of arts and letters who found their way to Zurich in the 1840s and 1850s — some as a result of politics, others simply to take up employment there — included the Classical scholar Hermann Köchly (who had fled from Dresden, like Wagner), the noted aesthetician Friedrich Theodor Vischer, the lawyer Robert Ottensoser (who worked there ca. 1850 as a theater critic), the buffo bass Franz Orth (who would on one occasion sing under Wagner), the composer, violinist, and conductor Christian Gottlieb Rabe (who settled in nearby Lenzburg, but now and then played as an extra in the Zurich orchestra), the military historian Wilhelm Rüstow (who would later fight alongside Garibaldi in Italy), the politician-cum-journalist François Wille and his novelist wife Eliza, and the literary historian Ludwig Ettmüller; among the Swiss nationals who also settled in Zurich at this time were the painter Rudolf Koller and the scholar Jacob Burckhardt. In 1855, the Zurich-born novelist Gottfried Keller also returned to his native city, after a lengthy stay in Berlin (no revolutionary he).

When Wagner described Zurich several years later as "completely devoid of any public art form" he was lying, though he was also skillfully picking upon the weakest point in the city's cultural life. For it was in the public manifestations of art — concerts and theater — that Zurich was still heavily provincial. Wagner's purpose was rather, we must assume, to hide what would in retrospect have been embarrassing for someone in the meantime so accustomed to seeing himself as the brightest star in the firmament. Let us not forget that, although his position as Kapellmeister in Dresden was enough to make of him a celebrity in the provinces, his reputation as a composer at the time of his arrival in Zurich was founded on only three operas — *Rienzi*, *Der fliegende Holländer*, and *Tannhäuser* — none of which had achieved the wide currency enjoyed by the operatic works of his contemporaries Verdi, Meyerbeer, or Rossini, and none of which could have led any of his contemporaries to suspect that he would, within less than a decade, compose with the mastery displayed in *Die Walküre* and *Tristan*. In Zurich in the 1850s, he was in fact merely one prominent name among many others. When, however, Wagner the autobiographer of the late 1860s came to portray his younger self as the creator of a new world in art, then for that he needed as his geographical and metaphysical location a *terra nulla*, even if it could be constructed only in retrospect, and only in his imagination. Ironically, it is not hyperbole to claim that nowhere else in the mid-nineteenth century was there such a limited geographical area that could boast such a concentration of leading liberal and radical intellectuals from so many different fields and cultures. It was, arguably, this highly charged environment in Zurich that in fact propelled Wagner on his path of rapid artistic evolution in the years from 1849 to 1858. If, upon fleeing Dresden, he had been free to choose a city where he might seek heightened intellectual stimulation among the like-minded and the similarly gifted, then he could hardly have come to a more perfect place.

Notes

[1] "Thuo mir das gmürmel diner gsungen hinweg, und das gsang diner lyren wil ich nit." See Markus Jenny, *Zwinglis Stellung zur Musik im Gottesdienst* (Zurich: Zwingli Verlag, 1966), 9. See Amos 5:23; the King James translation runs thus: "Take thou away from me the noise of thy songs: for I will not hear the melody of thy viols."

[2] See Chris Walton, "Die 'synopsis isagoges musicae' von Johannes Fries 1552," in *Zentralbibliothek Zürich: Alte und Neue Schätze*, ed. Alfred Cattani, Michael Kotrba, and Agnes Rutz (Zurich: Verlag Neue Zürcher Zeitung, 1993), 66–69.

[3] There are, of course, performing ensembles that claim to be considerably older, such as the Royal Danish Orchestra, the Sächsische Staatskapelle, or several of the English cathedral choirs.

[4] The title runs: *Neues Gesangbuch auserlesener, geistreicher Lieder zum Lob und Preis Gottes . . . [mit] zu drey und vier Stimmen gesetzten Melodeyn, und einem richtig-gezeichneten General-Bass versehen* (Zurich: Heidegger and Rahn, 1723 and 1735).

[5] Reinhold Rüegg, *Die ersten 50 Jahre des Zürcher Stadttheater, 1834–1884* (Zurich: Verlag der Züricher Post, 1925), 10.

[6] The so-called "Codex C" of the *Nibelungenlied* was discovered by Jacob Hermann Obereit in Hohenems (just across the border from Switzerland) in 1755.

[7] For extensive information on Ott and his contemporaries, see Walton, "Three Men for All Seasons: Musico-Horticultural Flights in Enlightenment Zurich," in *Bunte Blätter: Klaus Mecklenburg zum 23. Februar 2000*, ed. Rudolf Elvers and Alain Moirandat (Basel: Moirandat AG, 2000), 315–39.

[8] Paul Leemann-van Elck, *Druck, Verlag, Buchhandel im Kanton Zürich von den Anfängen bis um 1850* (Zurich: Leemann, 1950), especially 37–92.

[9] See Walton, "Three Men for All Seasons," 330–34.

[10] A number of works by Bachofen, Schmidlin, Walder, and Egli can be heard, performed by the Choir of Gonville and Caius College Cambridge, on the CD *Zurich, Arise!* Guild Music GMCD 7175.

[11] The Zurich Central Library today holds the manuscript of a little keyboard piece — now known as K33b — that the young Wölferl scrawled in a childish hand on the back of a program sheet while in Zurich.

[12] Franz Christoph Neubauer, *Fernando und Yariko* (Zurich: Orell, Gessner & Füssli, 1786). For more information on Neubauer and Zurich, see Walton, "Pocahontas in the Alps: Masonic Traces in the Stage Works of Franz Christoph Neubauer," in *The Musical Times* 146, no. 1892 (Autumn 2005): 43–56.

[13] The manuscript score and parts of the opera are today held by the Zentralbibliothek Zürich, shelfmark AMG XIV 737 and AMG XIII 764/a-o.

[14] On *Goethe-Lieder and Chamber Music*, Guild Music GMCD 7163.

[15] Goethe/Kayser, *Scherz, List und Rache*, ed. and arranged in vocal score by Hermann Dechant (Vienna: Apollon, 1999).

[16] A selection of works published by Nägeli is recorded on *Hans Georg Nägeli: Verleger und Komponist*, MGB CD 6193.

[17] Gordon A. Craig, *The Triumph of Liberalism: Zurich in the Golden Age* (New York: Collier, 1990), 36.

[18] See Leemann-van Elck, *Druck, Verlag, Buchhandel*, 68.

[19] Werner G. Zimmermann, *Richard Wagner in Zürich: Materialien zu Aufenthalt und Wirken* (Zurich: Hug, 1987), 1:8.

[20] Rudolf Hunziker, ed., *Der junge Hans Georg Nägeli: Achtzehn Briefe aus den Jahren 1790–1808* (Zurich: Hug, 1937).

[21] Louis Spohr, *Selbstbiographie* (Basel: Bärenreiter, 1954), 252.

[22] Liste's bassoon sonata and his piano sonatas in G major and E-flat major are available on Guild Music GMCD 7154; his A-major piano sonata, his piano duet sonata, his Cantata for the Opening of the New Masonic Hall in Zurich and various songs have been released on Guild Music GMCD 7184.

[23] See La Mara, ed., *Franz Liszts Briefe an eine Freundin* (Leipzig: Breitkopf & Härtel, 1894), 92.

[24] See also Xaver Schnyder von Wartensee, *Lebenserinnerungen* (Zurich: Hug, 1887).

[25] See Nägeli, *Von Bach zu Beethoven*, ed. Willi Reich (Basel: Schwabe, 1946), 67.

[26] Neuchâtel was still nominally Prussian territory, an odd state of affairs that would only be rectified several decades later; but to all intents and purposes, it was a "Swiss" canton, and is thus treated here as such.

[27] See, for example, Anton Largiadèr, *Geschichte von Stadt und Landschaft Zürich*, vol. 2 (Erlenbach: Eugen Rentsch, 1945), 90.

[28] See, for example, Craig, *The Triumph of Liberalism*, 41–42.

[29] Anon., *Gesetz über die Organisation des gesammten Unterrichtswesens im Canton Zürich* (Zurich: n.p., 1832), 3.

[30] Heinrich Weber, *Zürichs Musikleben von 1812–1850*, vol. 1 (Zurich: Allgemeine Musikgesellschaft, 1874), 14–15.

[31] Weber, *Zürichs Musikleben von 1812–1850*, 1:15.

[32] Rüegg, *Die ersten 50 Jahre des Zürcher Stadttheater*, 76.

[33] Hans Erismann, *Das fing ja gut an: Geschichten und Geschichte des Opernhauses Zürich* (Zurich: Verlag Neue Zürcher Zeitung, 1984), 26.

[34] Erismann, *Das fing ja gut an*, 29.

[35] Rüegg, *Die ersten 50 Jahre des Zürcher Stadttheater*, 79.

[36] The poster for that concert is reproduced in Max Fehr, *Richard Wagners Schweizer Zeit*, vol. 1 (Aarau and Leipzig: Sauerländer, 1934), 211.

[37] See Walton, *Richard Wagners Zürcher Jahre, 1849–1858: Ein biographischer Index* (Zurich: Hug, 2000).

[38] See Weber, *Vierundsiebzigstes Neujahrsblatt der Allgemeinen Musikgesellschaft in Zürich* (Zurich: Orell Füssli, 1886), 6–7.

[39] See Rudolf Hunziker, "Theodor Kirchner in Winterthur," in *Schweizerische Musikzeitung* 74, no. 7 (1 April 1935): 229–42; here, 235.

[40] Rudolf Hunziker and Paul Schaffner, *August Corrodi als Dichter und Maler* (Winterthur: Literarische Vereinigung, 1930), 27 and 34.

[41] August Corrodi, *Reisebriefe aus der Schweiz und Mailand* (Lucerne: Kaiser, 1857), 83 and 95.

Figure 2. Richard Wagner. Lithograph by Caspar Scheuchzer (1852), after a portrait by Ernst Benedikt Kietz. Used by permission of the Zentralbibliothek Zürich.

2: Zurich's Wagner

When Richard Wagner was appointed Kapellmeister at the Dresden Court Opera on 2 February 1843, the contrast to his previous miserable existence in Paris — his "hunger years" — could hardly have been more acute. His new base at one of Germany's most prestigious opera houses afforded him a first-rate ensemble to perform his own operas, untold possibilities to hone his art of conducting, and also — for the first time in his life — financial stability and considerable social status for both him and his wife Minna. For five years, he remained a dutiful servant of the King's theater. He had the time and energy to sketch out numerous dramatic projects, of which two were completed, namely *Tannhäuser* (premièred in Dresden on 19 October 1845) and *Lohengrin* (finished in mid-1848). Wagner mingled as an equal in Dresden with fellow composers, musicians, artists, and intellectuals, ranging from Robert Schumann to Gottfried Semper, and he had the means to visit spas in his summer vacation in an effort to alleviate the numerous ailments, mostly intestinal, that were to plague him over the years. One matter that did not change, however, was his virtuosity in living beyond his means, regardless of whether those means were minimal or generous. But his position also allowed for a certain financial cushion — thus he was granted a loan from the Dresden pension fund in 1846 in order to cover his most recent debts. Wagner's desire for more than he had, however, extended beyond the merely financial. He grew weary of the Kapellmeister's daily round and drew up a detailed plan of how the Dresden theater might be reorganized and expanded. It was rejected, of course; and while it would be overly convenient to suggest that this rejection by the court authorities turned Wagner from a royalist into a republican determined now to overturn the old order altogether, it would not be completely without foundation. Be that as it may, the revolutionary fervor that swept Europe in 1848 did not leave him untouched, and in the course of that year — aided, abetted, and encouraged by his friend and colleague August Röckel (a nephew of the composer Johann Nepomuk Hummel, as it happens) — Wagner wrote and published a series of articles that his superiors could not have interpreted as anything other than of a politically subversive nature. At the same time, he was sketching new, grandiose dramas, including *Siegfrieds Tod* (Siegfried's Death), *Jesus von Nazareth*, *Achilleus*, and *Friedrich Barbarossa*.

After the German parliament in Frankfurt failed in early 1849 to unify the country under a democratic dispensation, Prussia moved to disperse its members by force. Keen to reaffirm his own power, the Saxon King Friedrich August II dissolved his parliament, too, at the end of April, even though this was in violation of the constitution. Open revolt broke out in protest in the Saxon capital, Dresden. The king and many other residents fled the city — Robert Schumann was among them — but many others stayed to fight. Barricades were erected, Prussian troops were sent in to save the Saxon monarchy, and within less than two weeks the uprising was quelled. Accounts of Wagner's participation in the revolt vary drastically, depending on the agenda of the author in question — did he or did he not order hand grenades? Did he or did he not ring the storm bells at the outbreak of the uprising? Did he or did he not try to burn down the *Prinzenpalais*? His own version of the tale in *Mein Leben*, written some twenty years after for the eyes of King Ludwig II, is a veritable tour de force. He manages somehow to place himself always in the thick of things (for where else could Wagner ever be, but at the center of events?) while not actually having done anything that might appear even vaguely anti-monarchist in the eyes of his new royal patron. One of the more recent Wagner biographers, Joachim Köhler, argues not unconvincingly that Wagner's role in the uprising was in fact an active one, and there are several other commentators who are of a similar opinion.[1] But there are also contemporary reports that his part therein was far less heroic. In his memoirs, Gustav Adolph Kietz wrote that Wagner had never stood on the barricades and had never carried a weapon but had always been dressed impeccably, unsullied by even a single spot of gunpowder. A similar claim was made, independently, by Wagner's wife Minna, while the memoirs of his friend Röckel mention Wagner only in passing, without any reference to revolutionary activity on his part.[2] These skeptics, on the whole, seem the more reliable sources.

What we know for certain is that Wagner did ally himself with the revolutionary forces and was in close contact with several of their leading lights. We also know that it was a series of chance events that allowed him to escape capture while others, such as Röckel and the Russian anarchist Mikhail Bakunin, were caught and imprisoned. Wagner fled first to Franz Liszt in Weimar. With his help, and with an expired passport once belonging to a Professor Widmann, Wagner managed to travel through southern Germany, from where he crossed the border into neutral Switzerland. He headed straight for Zurich to his old friend Alexander Müller. He arrived on 28 May 1849, but Müller was not at home, and so Wagner was compelled to spend his first night in the Hotel Schwert. He descended on his friend the next day, and they were soon joined by Müller's pupil Wilhelm Baumgartner — the same who had visited Wagner once in Dresden in 1845. Together, they went to see the two Cantonal Secretaries, Jakob Sulzer and Franz Hagenbuch. According to *Mein Leben* — though the veracity of this point is in some doubt — Wagner now gave them all a recitation of his libretto to *Siegfrieds Tod*. Undeterred by this — indeed, veritably impressed, it would seem — they

Figure 3. Minna Wagner, mid-1840s. Used by permission of the Richard-Wagner-Stiftung, Bayreuth.

provided Wagner with the necessary passport to enable him to travel on to Paris. It was there that he intended to begin a new career, just as he had tried, and failed, ten years before. Back in Dresden, Minna was hoping and expecting that Wagner would do his best to establish himself there. He accordingly left for Paris on 30 May, but there did little and achieved nothing, so returned instead to Zurich in early July. He found both the city and its people sympathetic. With Wilhelm Baumgartner (whom he called "Boom"), Jakob Sulzer, and Bernhard Spyri (the editor of the *Eidgenössische Zeitung*) he soon struck up a firm friendship, referring to them as his "Dreieinigkeit" or "Trinity." Sulzer's wine cellars in particular were to be a frequent consolation to the composer in exile.

Minna joined her husband in early September 1849, together with their dog, their parrot, and Minna's illegitimate daughter Natalie — the product of a teenage liaison who had been brought up believing that she was Minna's sister, in order to avoid the stigma that her real status would have brought upon both of them. Upon his return from Paris, Wagner had moved in with Alexander Müller, but in September he and his family rented their own apartment in the "Escherhäuser," a long apartment block situated on the Zeltweg in the suburb of Hottingen. It is today a part of the city proper, just a six-minute tram ride from the center of town and the main station. Their landlady was Clementine Stockar-Escher, the sister of Alfred Escher. Wagner had not composed anything since completing *Lohengrin* in 1848, nor did he start again now. Instead, he devoted himself over the next two years to writing a series of tracts that offer a heady mixture of aesthetics, politics, and history (both real and postulated). Wagner was not the first musician to write about music, of course. Over the centuries, many of the composers who regarded themselves as reformers in musical aesthetics had put pen to paper to justify their actions, from Peri and Caccini in ca. 1600 to the Gluck of *Alceste*. Two of Wagner's idols, E. T. A. Hoffmann and Carl Maria von Weber, had even written important articles that served to define the early Romantic music aesthetic of their day. But no musician before him had embarked upon a "reform" project of such scope as the one that he now attempted, and none had yet coupled aesthetics with politics in so open a fashion. That he should have begun this project in Zurich was particularly apposite, as the previous decade had seen a surge of political publications in the city (as will be elaborated further in chapter 5). Switzerland was now, of course, more or less the only remaining German-speaking area where free speech was guaranteed.

Wagner's first two tracts, *Die Kunst und die Revolution* and *Das Kunstwerk der Zukunft* (Art and Revolution and The Artwork of the Future), were written in the second half of 1849, and published shortly afterwards by Wigand in Leipzig. It had long been a commonplace for any artist keen to "renew" his art to call upon the Ancient Greeks for aid. The members of the Florentine Camerata who had founded the genre of opera in the late 1500s had drawn on what they believed to have been the true form of Greek tragedy; Gluck had justified his operatic reforms of the 1760s in similar fashion; and Wagner now did the same. In *Art and Revolution*, he bemoaned the dissolution of the unified art form that (so he believed) had been the tragedy of the Ancient Greeks and maintained that it would only be attained once more through "the great revolution of mankind." It was "revolution, not the restoration, [that] can give us that highest form of artwork once again."[3] Here, and in his subsequent writings, he couples the rise and fall of the drama directly with the history of the city-state of Athens, and in so doing, of course, opened up the possibility — most fully exploited, as we know, fifty years after his death — of coupling the fate of his dramas with that of his own nation.

The Artwork of the Future was written in part under the influence of the philosopher Ludwig Feuerbach and accordingly dedicated to him (he acknowledged its receipt with gracious praise[4]). Wagner had naturally heard of Feuerbach back in Dresden but by his own admission had read nothing of him until Wilhelm Baumgartner brought him a copy of Feuerbach's *Gedanken über Tod und Unsterblichkeit* (Reflections on Death and Immortality), after his return from Paris in the summer of 1849. Baumgartner's own interest in the philosopher was almost certainly thanks to the influence of Gottfried Keller. He and Baumgartner were old friends, and Keller had just months before written to Baumgartner from Heidelberg, overflowing with praise for Feuerbach,

> . . . with whom I spend almost every evening, drinking beer and listening to his words. . . . Although he is not really a born lecturer . . . it is nevertheless highly interesting to listen to a man lecturing on his own philosophy of religion who is currently by far the most important historical person in philosophy . . . this much is clear: I shall make *tabula rasa* with all my hitherto religious ideas . . . until I am on Feuerbach's level.[5]

Wagner declared of Feuerbach in *Mein Leben* that "it seemed to me laudable and rewarding to know that the sole true immortality was assigned to a noble deed or a wise work of art" (*ML*, 443). It was, of course, the immortality of that "work of art" that concerned him most. His *Artwork of the Future* elaborates on the arguments presented in his previous tract. He now considers each of the arts in turn — dance, music, poetry, architecture, sculpture, and painting — and declares:

> The highest unified work of art is the drama, which can only exist in its greatest possible fullness if every type of art in its own greatest fullness is present in it. True drama can be contemplated only as the common urge of all the arts toward an immediacy of expression to a common public.[6]

This would all be elaborated yet further in *Opera and Drama* a year later, but for the moment these two tracts were followed by the article "Art and Climate" and a prose sketch for an opera intended for Paris, *Wieland der*

Schmied (Wieland the Smith), both written in early 1850. Wagner was at this time earning some money from his published writings — five *louis d'or* (i.e. SF 100) each for *Art and Revolution* and *The Artwork of the Future*, for example — but he obviously needed more in order to support himself and his family (we can see from a letter he wrote to Minna that he himself reckoned the basic weekly costs of accommodation and food for two people as being about SF 17 [*SB* 3:102]). He turned to Liszt, as he had before and would so often again, but Liszt was, for once, unable to help. Instead, he recommended that Wagner earn a little money by returning to the conductor's podium. So this he did. His fame as composer and conductor had long before reached the city, of course, and his having (supposedly) manned the barricades in the Dresden uprising had no doubt enhanced his status in a city proud of its liberal politics. So the local music society (the AMG) now willingly engaged him to conduct its semi-professional orchestra on an *ad hoc* basis. To what extent its nominal conductor Franz Abt was consulted in this, we do not know. Wagner began his career as guest conductor of the AMG orchestra on 15 January 1850, with a performance of Beethoven's Seventh Symphony. Many more such appearances would follow in the next five years (as is explained in detail in chapter 8 below), but for now, he decided — egged on by Minna and others — to try his luck again in Paris.

Wagner arrived in Paris at the beginning of February 1850, but once more he had no success. In March he accepted an invitation to go to Bordeaux and visit a Scottish widow he knew there, Ann Taylor. She had formerly lived in Dresden, hence their acquaintance. Together with another Dresden friend, Julie Ritter, she now offered to give Wagner an allowance of three thousand francs a year. This would have been enough for him to devote himself in future to composition alone, without the need ever to take on another full-time Kapellmeister post. Ann Taylor's daughter, Jessie, as it happened, had shared the same Dresden piano teacher as Hans von Bülow in the early 1840s (one Cäcilie Schmiedel), and was by all accounts a fine pianist (Wagner later wrote in *Mein Leben* of her giving a convincing performance of Beethoven's *Hammerklavier* Sonata, op. 106, which remains today one of the most fiendish works in the repertoire [*ML*, 450]). Jessie had in the meantime married a wine dealer from Bordeaux named Laussot, hence her, and her mother's, current address. Julie Ritter was the mother of Karl and Alexander Ritter, both of them musicians. Alexander would later marry Wagner's niece Franziska and four decades afterwards would exert a powerful influence on the young Richard Strauss; Karl — a former pupil of Robert Schumann — would for the next few years move in and out of Wagner's life in the guise of occasional surrogate son-cum-assistant-cum-loving disciple. Wagner's reminiscences of him paint a somewhat depressing picture of a young man uncertain as to what he wanted from life, and generally too untalented to achieve it anyway; but he does seem to have had a genuine affection for the lad at the time, despite assuring others that Karl's sensitive, somewhat feminine nature was a result of excessive masturbation (*SB* 4:383; Wagner would reach similar conclusions about Friedrich Nietzsche, two decades later).

In early March 1850, Wagner received word that his friends and erstwhile fellow revolutionaries August Röckel and Mikhail Bakunin were about to be executed for their part in the Dresden uprising (though their sentences were later commuted). The current lack of security and certainty in Wagner's life was undoubtedly weighing heavily upon him, and it seems that this news was the catalyst in his decision to make some important changes. He found himself falling rapidly in love with Jessie Laussot, whom he also discovered to be unhappily married — and although we have only Wagner's word on this, rather than that of any objective observer, it does seem that domestic bliss was not her lot. He now hatched a madcap plan to elope with her to the Middle East, leaving by boat from Marseilles and traveling to Asia Minor via Malta and Greece. For the moment, however, he returned to Paris, where he finalized his plans and wrote to Minna and to various friends (including Julie Ritter, Wilhelm Baumgartner, and Liszt) in order to say goodbye. He wrote to his wife from Paris on 16 April that he could no longer bear the pressure that she exerted upon him to live the life of a run-of-the-mill musician, and that they must now live apart (*SB* 3:275–88). In early May, he wrote to Gustav Kietz in Paris: "I *had* to undertake something unusual now, in order to cure myself in every sense. I hope to see you healthy and well again, at a time when our homeland is also in a better state" (*SB* 3:293–95). He then returned to Bordeaux to whisk away his love, only to find that she had already been whisked away by her husband instead. The same husband was furthermore contemplating Wagner's whisking away, though to a place yet more distant than the Middle East, and by means of not a boat but a bullet. Wagner escaped unshot and unscathed, though emotionally bruised, and did not see Jessie again for over two decades. With her, of course, disappeared the half of his annual allowance that her family had planned for him. He now returned instead, not a little sheepishly, to Zurich and to Minna, who herself put on a brave face and endeavored, with him, to bring some order and dignity back to their marriage. Minna was no saint herself — she had run off with another man not long after marrying Wagner, who had then begged her back. But she never forgot, nor quite forgave, the Laussot affair, and it undoubtedly colored her reaction to her husband's later infatuation with Mathilde Wesendonck. The closest that Wagner would ever get to the Middle East was when the neck of the dragon for the first production of the *Ring* in 1876 would by mistake be sent, not to Bayreuth, but reputedly to Beirut instead (*TB* 1:1243 and 2:715).

There is an odd postscript to the tale of Jessie Laussot, however. For Wagner never forgot her, and even in the midst of his passion for Mathilde

Wesendonck in late 1857 was trying to find out where she was and what had happened to her (*SB* 9:84). In fact, Jessie — newly single again — had moved to Florence, where she set up a music society named the "Società Cherubini," and from where she corresponded regularly, and on an apparently equal footing, with some of the leading musicians of the age, including Franz Liszt.[7] Hans von Bülow did not lose touch with her, it seems — in 1857 he even dedicated his first and only song cycle to her, oddly entitled *Die Entsagende* (The Woman who Renounces). Whether or not this signified an untold passion on Hans's part, it was to Jessie Laussot that Hans fled, after Cosima abandoned him in late 1868 in order to go and live with Wagner in Tribschen. For two years after his break with Cosima, Hans shared Jessie's house in Italy. It was maintained that their relationship was platonic — he himself wrote to his mother, pointedly, of Jessie's "sisterly" care for him[8] — but whatever the precise nature of their relationship, Hans could hardly have done anything better calculated to incite Wagner's jealousy (and calculated it surely was). In the mid-1870s, after Hans's return to Germany, Jessie began a liaison with the German writer Karl Hillebrand (yet another former revolutionary from 1848–49, as it happens), and Wagner and Cosima even paid them a visit when they holidayed in Italy after the first *Ring* production of 1876 (*TB* 1:1018). Jessie and Hillebrand married soon after, though he died just a few years later, in 1884; Jessie lived on in widowhood until 1905.

While Wagner was cavorting in France in the first half of 1850 and planning his abortive forays yet further afield, Minna was concerning herself with domestic practicalities back in Zurich. In her husband's absence she now moved their abode to the suburb of Enge, on the other side of the Zurich Lake, into a house named "Zum Abendstern." A month after his return Wagner began sketching the music for his opera *Siegfrieds Tod.* Franz Liszt was urging him to write the work, dangling before him the possibility of both a commission from Weimar and an imminent performance. But Wagner reached only the scene where Siegfried leaves Brünnhilde before breaking off his work — a total of some twelve minutes of music (which in recent years have even been recorded[9]). However, the opening of the sketch does seem to have left its mark on the beginning of *Rheingold* three years later, both in its key (E flat minor here, E flat major in the latter) and in its bubbling semiquaver accompaniment.[10] Later in August, Wagner returned instead to his journalistic activities and completed his article *Das Judentum in der Musik* (Jewishness in Music) — the text that, more than any other, has overshadowed Wagner's work and reputation. Several scholars believe that it was in fact not new but had been drafted two years earlier. The only "proof" of this, however, lies in a letter that Minna wrote on 8 May 1850, at the height of the Laussot affair, when she mentioned in disgust an article that Wagner had written "two years before," "worin Du ganze Geschlechter schmähtest, die Dir doch im Grunde

Liebes getan" ("in which you maligned whole races who had, nevertheless, basically done kind things for you"[11]). Others interpret the letter differently. Stewart Spencer is surely right to point out the good sense of the "traditional chronology, whereby the growing anti-Semitism of *Art and Revolution* (July 1849) and *The Artwork of the Future* (October/November 1849) . . . culminated in *Judaism in Music* in August 1850."[12] He suggests that Minna is in fact referring to the anti-French sentiments of Wagner's article of 1848 entitled "How do Republican Aspirations Stand in Relation to the Monarchy?" But she could just as well mean the aristocrats whom he had served as Court Kapellmeister, and whose downfall Wagner there demands; he in fact uses the word "Geschlecht" in that article specifically in its alternative meaning of (aristocratic) "house" or "lineage."

Jewishness in Music is particularly remarkable for its high degree of irrationality, and what one commentator has termed its "sexual-sadistic" nature.[13] It was clear even to several of Wagner's contemporaries[14] that the article was born in large part out of envy of Meyerbeer and Mendelssohn — the former immensely successful, both in Wagner's field of artistic endeavor and in Paris, the one geographical place he would always desire, and fail, to conquer; the latter born into wealth and breeding and possessed of a natural talent that neither Wagner nor any of his contemporaries could match. The issue might have been further complicated if Wagner, as Nietzsche was the first to suggest, had indeed believed that his biological father was Ludwig Geyer (his parents' lodger, then his mother's second husband), and that Geyer might have been of Jewish descent (let us not forget that Wagner had grown up in Brühl, a suburb of Leipzig where a large proportion of the city's Jewish population lived). But there is simply no firm proof that Wagner harbored any such doubts about his lineage at this time. In any case, Meyerbeer — Wagner's elder by just over twenty years, and a man to whom he owed so much, both personally and professionally — seems to have already acquired, in part, the role of "father figure" to him, at least in artistic terms. *Jewishness in Music* could thus constitute to some extent a "cutting of the apron strings," albeit a violent one in which they are not just cut but metaphorically shredded, burned, and flushed away too. It would be tempting to suggest that Wagner's metaphorical "execution" of Meyerbeer might in some way have been a surrogate act intended to expunge any fears of his own possible Jewish heritage, but this would be perhaps too neat and tidy to be really true.

All the same, the highly personal tone of Wagner's tract is undoubtedly that of a man who "doth protest too much." Wagner's principal argument here against the art of Meyerbeer and others was in itself nothing new, and it would persist — thanks in part to him — well into the twentieth century. He maintained that "the Jews" are somehow an alien race incapable of true artistic expression, their art remaining always one of surface effect. That this was merely an insidious means of denying profundity to the music of composers whom Wagner envied hardly needs to be elaborated here. And while Wagner cannot, of course, be held directly responsible for the fact that these absurdities were believed and propagated eagerly by many others after him, most notably by the adherents of National Socialism, it is not possible to absolve him of all culpability for the crimes of those who used his arguments to help justify their activities.[15] Ulrich Drüner has in recent years argued persuasively that Wagner's article was intimately related to the conception of *Siegfrieds Tod*, and that it is merely one example, albeit the most crass, of a deep-seated psychological need on Wagner's part to create turbulence in his life in order to "kick-start" his muse. Drüner argues pertinently that Wagner's decision to reprint *Jewishness in Music* in brochure form in 1869 was closely connected to his resuming work on the *Ring*. And he also offers convincing proof that those who maintain to this day that Wagner's anti-Semitism did not enter into the fabric of his works are guilty at best of naivety.[16]

August 1850 brought not just *Jewishness in Music*, but also the world première of Wagner's *Lohengrin* in Weimar, two years after its completion. Wagner had sent Liszt the score of it, in the hope that he would perform it, and so he did — the date chosen being the 28th, Goethe's birthday (Wagner would over the coming years show an increasing interest in doing things he considered important on "significant" dates of the calendar). His status as a political exile meant that he could not attend in person, of course. Instead, he and Minna undertook a short walking tour over the Rigi mountain in central Switzerland. Karl Ritter did attend the première, however, as did Franz Abt, Wagner having begged Liszt for a free ticket for each of them. Commentators have usually stressed the antagonism that existed between Wagner and Abt, though the latter's willingness to travel all the way to Weimar was an open gesture of support for his colleague that makes Wagner's later contempt for him seem not a little churlish.

In October 1850 Wagner returned to the orchestra pit for the first time since leaving Dresden. The director of the Zurich Theater, Philipp Walburg Kramer, had tried to convince him to take on the musical directorship of his ensemble at a fee of SF 200 per month (*SB* 3:455). Wagner had refused, determined to stay away from what he regarded as the drudgery of Kapellmeistership, and suggested Karl Ritter instead. Wagner offered a guarantee that he would step into the breach if Ritter should encounter any problems, and Kramer agreed. As Wagner must have anticipated, Ritter proved quite inadequate, and so the guarantor had to step in to save the day, subsequently conducting several operas over the next few weeks (see chapter 8). It is not impossible that Wagner had calculated in advance that this would be the best way for him to begin conducting at the theater: he could appear at the last minute as a knight in shining armor (shades of *Lohengrin*, perhaps), and he would in that capacity have more freedom to pick and choose which operas he was willing to conduct. He would also have been well aware that he would have to keep his promise, for the Theater Committee not only included the mighty Alfred Escher but also was presided over by Franz Hagenbuch, the Cantonal Secretary who, together with Sulzer, had put Wagner's papers in order in Zurich (he was also the son-in-law of the president of the AMG). This season also saw Wagner return to the podium for the Allgemeine Musikgesellschaft, picking and choosing which works he desired to conduct, and leaving the rest to Franz Abt.

As luck would have it, in late 1850 Hans von Bülow, whom Wagner also knew from Dresden, was staying at his father's villa in Canton Thurgau, several miles to the northeast of Zurich. He was engaged in a battle of wills with his family, who did not want to acquiesce in his desire to devote himself to music. Wagner now intervened and called Hans to Zurich. Bülow was an old schoolfriend of Karl Ritter's, and it was Karl who went to fetch him. Perhaps Hans's decision to take the plunge into music was made with the example of Wagner before him, who had, of course, recently set himself "free" and thereby risked far more than parental displeasure. Be that as it may, Wagner now propelled von Bülow on his musical career, by engaging him to conduct in Ritter's place at the Zurich Theater. Hans also made his Zurich debut as a pianist that winter, in one of the concerts of the AMG. But an intrigue at the theater by the ensemble's principal soprano, one Rosine Gindle-Rauch, soon prompted von Bülow to resign. He thereupon left Zurich for St. Gall, taking Karl with him, where they both took up posts at the local theater. Within a few weeks, however, von Bülow left again, this time for Weimar, where he now began his studies proper with Liszt. At Wagner's suggestion, Franz Abt took over the conducting at the Zurich theater, though it was not long before Wagner began to express dislike toward him. Perhaps Abt had at long last — and understandably — tired of having to pick up the scraps from under Wagner's table; or perhaps Wagner had expected the theater's ensemble to crumble without him and was offended when Abt managed to hold it together. In any case, we know that Abt was thoroughly popular in Zurich, which will not have pleased Wagner at all. The city, it seems, was in the long run just not big enough yet for two crowd-pleasers.

The winter of 1850–51 saw Wagner back at work on assorted theoretical writings. The biggest of these — indeed, his longest single piece of prose before *Mein Leben* — was *Oper und Drama*, which he completed in early 1851 and published with Weber of Leipzig toward the end of the year. In it, Wagner expands upon ideas that he had begun to formulate in his previous theoretical works. *Opera and Drama* has had its admirers — Richard Strauss in particular judged it one of the most important tracts on the subject[17] — but most find it prolix and heavy going, devoid of the lightness of touch that had characterized Wagner's shorter prose pieces of the early 1840s. But it does provide us with much accurate information on how Wagner intended to proceed with his art, and it lets us see just how closely he did in fact keep to his theories (at least at first). In this three-volume tract, Wagner sketches out the history of opera in order to demonstrate how, as he writes, music has come to dominate everything. The fundamental premise of opera, he assures us — that it should convey a drama — has been lost amidst a wash of notes: "In opera, a *means* of expression — the music — has become an end, while the *end* of expression — namely the drama — has been made the means."[18] The aria must be jettisoned, he tells us, as must end-rhyme, with the latter replaced by alliterative *Stabreim*, for which the German language alone, he assures us, is suitable. The melody must grow out of the words themselves. He goes so far as to employ a sexual metaphor, namely that "music is a woman," who must be impregnated by the poet's seed in order to give birth to melody. His metaphors are somewhat reminiscent of the ideas of the Young German movement of the 1830s, where "free love" was postulated, and whose predilection for the virtues of sensuality had been celebrated by Wagner himself in his early opera *Das Liebesverbot* (The Ban on Love). As for the topics of opera, Wagner states that historical themes must now be abandoned and the Germanic myths embraced as a suitable contemporary equivalent of what the Greek myths meant to the Ancients. Also in *Opera and Drama* is a remarkably accurate description of what would become his leitmotif technique (though he did not call it thus), with characteristic "melodic moments" woven together that themselves create the "form" of the music. This web of motives also allows the orchestra to fulfill the role of the Greek chorus in Ancient tragedy, by offering a commentary on the action as it happens.

There are two possible outside influences that might have prompted Wagner's increasing interest in Germanic medieval epics during his early Zurich exile. The first might simply have been the everyday language that he heard around him. For the German dialects spoken in Switzerland have to this day retained many characteristics of Middle High German (the language of the *Nibelungenlied*) that are no longer present in High German (even the very first line of the *Nibelungenlied* contains a past participle of the verb "to say" that is almost identical to its Swiss-German form — *geseit*, as opposed to the High German *gesagt*). Strictly speaking, the Swiss-German dialects are in fact a far cry from Middle High German itself, though to a High German speaker with a smattering of *Mittelhochdeutsch* such as Wagner, the superficial similarities can appear striking, and it might well have appeared to him upon arriving in Zurich that he had entered a linguistic time capsule.

The second, more obvious, influence upon him was Ludwig Ettmüller — scholar, translator, and professor at Zurich University — with whom Wagner became closely acquainted shortly after settling in the city. Wagner had possessed a copy of Ettmüller's *Vaulu-Spá* of 1830 in his Dresden library,[19] and he receives a single mention in *Mein Leben* on account of his apparent enthusiasm for Wagner's recitation of *Siegfrieds Tod* (*ML*, 437). As it happens, he first surfaces in Wagner's correspondence in mid-1850, just before Wagner embarked upon his first sketches for the music of that opera (*SB* 3:360). Wagner and Ettmüller undoubtedly had much to discuss. It was almost certainly Ettmüller's own modern German translations of the Edda texts that provided Wagner with the model for the meter and *Stabreim* of his libretti for the *Ring des Nibelungen*.[20] Stanley R. Hauer maintains that "virtually everything that Wagner understood (or at times misunderstood) about Old Norse metrics comes from Ettmüller."[21] In 1830, Ettmüller had also published an edition of a medieval text that oddly brings together several figures (even including "Klinsor") that feature later in Wagner's operas *Tannhäuser*, *Lohengrin*, and *Parsifal*, namely: *Der Singerkriec uf Wartburc: Gedicht aus dem XIII. Jahrhunderte; zum ersten Male genau nach der Jenaer Urkunde nebst den Abweichungen der Manesse und des Lohengrins herausgegeben* (The Singers' Battle on the Wartburg: Poem from the 13th Century, Published for the First Time Exactly as in the Jena Charter and alongside the Variants of Manesse and Lohengrin).[22] In later years, however, the position of the two men was somewhat reversed, with Ettmüller following in Wagner's footsteps by publishing in 1870 a drama on the Siegfried myth: *Sigufrid*,[23] with roles for "Wôdan," "Mime the smith," "Sigufrid, Sigmund's son, a Welsung," "Grîmhild," "Krunhild" (a "Walaküre"), the elf "Albgast" and his son "Hagano," plus the latter's half-brother "Gundahari," the king of the Rhine. In chapter 10, below, Mathilde Wesendonck's play on the same topic — written after Wagner, but before Ettmüller — will also be discussed.

Wagner resumed his intermittent conducting for the AMG in early 1851, but he did not stop writing. In April 1851, he published *Ein Theater in Zürich* (A Theater in Zurich), a brochure outlining how the local theater could and should be reorganized. It shares with several of his other theoretical writings an admixture of utopianism and down-to-earth common sense, both couched in occasionally tortuous prose, and put together in such a manner that it was all but bound to be either ignored or at best read and then promptly forgotten. That is a pity, for besides his idealistic plea for all good men to come to the aid of the theater, Wagner does make perfectly reasonable, concrete suggestions, such as organizing the ensemble in a manner that would allow for adequate and intensive rehearsals before the start of the season, and reducing the number of theatrical performances per week (and at the same time increasing the number of concerts). Wagner manages in passing to praise the work of Hans Georg Nägeli in the choral field but cannot resist taking a sideswipe at Birch-Pfeiffer, who was still in the memory of many as having initiated a golden age in the brief history of the theater in Zurich. He did not stop to await

Figure 4. The 1858 Festival of the "Eidgenössischer Sängerverein" in Zurich. Used by permission of the Zentralbibliothek Zürich.

the reaction to his text, however, before continuing with his authorial activities. In late May, he wrote the prose draft of a new opera: *Jung Siegfried* (Young Siegfried), to precede his opera *Siegfrieds Tod.*

On 1 May 1851, Wagner interrupted his work, briefly, in order to take part in the celebrations for the five-hundredth anniversary of Zurich's admission to the "Eidgenossenschaft" (in other words, the loose union of cantons that would later become Switzerland). This was only one example, however, of the local pageants and processions that Wagner would have observed in these years. It has even been postulated that the vibrant life of the Zurich guilds, with their annual spring celebrations known as "Sechseläuten," might well have exercised an influence on Wagner's portrayal of the Nuremberg guilds when he composed his *Meistersinger* in the mid-1860s.[24] It is perfectly possible, of course; but if the scene of the guilds on the *Festwiese* (the "festive meadow") in the opera were indeed the result of an outside influence, a more likely candidate would be the massed singing festivals that were a regular occurrence in both Switzerland and Germany in the mid-nineteenth century. Wagner had himself conducted the première of his *Liebesmahl der Apostel* — the *Love Feast of the Apostles* — at just such a giant festival in Dresden in 1843, and the *Eidgenössisches Sängerfest* of 1858, with over four thousand singing participants, in fact took place in Zurich from 17 to 19 July, just a few weeks before his departure from the city. Wilhelm Baumgartner was the chairman of the jury, and had written a special song for the occasion, to words by Gottfried Keller. Even though Wagner was occupied at the time by his personal woes, he would not have remained unaware of the event, for he would have been unable to venture into town without coming across hordes of singers. Certain extant pictorial records of the Swiss *Sängerfeste* from these years bear an undeniable resemblance to the scene that Wagner depicts in the third act of his *Meistersinger*, with thronging crowds and many flags and flowers on festive meadows. And, of course, what the *Sängerfeste* have in common with Wagner's Nuremberg festival, and that "Sächseläuten" does not, is the simple fact that they were singing competitions.

In July 1851, Wagner began work on a new autobiography, entitled *Eine Mitteilung an meine Freunde* (A Communication to My Friends), which Breitkopf and Härtel published at the end of the year, in a volume that also included the libretti of his operas *Der fliegende Holländer*, *Tannhäuser*, and *Lohengrin*. It was also in July that Wagner first made the acquaintance of the poet Georg Herwegh, a fellow exile with whom he would retain friendly relations throughout his Zurich years. They would even make an abortive attempt together, in late 1851, to bring the philosopher Feuerbach to Zurich (*SB* 4:205–6). The most important event of this month to Wagner, however, was a visit from Theodor Uhlig, his former colleague from the Dresden orchestra and his most important correspondent at this time. It was with Uhlig that Wagner was most open about his artistic plans and hopes, and their surviving correspondence is one of the most significant sources of information available to scholars on Wagner's life and work. It came to an abrupt end when Uhlig succumbed to consumption in early 1853. Wagner later recalled that Uhlig was already visibly weakened when he arrived in Switzerland to visit him, but that he had insisted on carrying out the extensive walking tour that they had planned, which included ascending the Säntis, the highest mountain in eastern Switzerland. They were joined on the first part of their tour by Karl Ritter, who had remained in nearby St. Gall after Bülow's departure some three months before. It was Uhlig who now urged Wagner to undergo the latest pseudo-medical fad, namely a water cure. After Uhlig's return to Dresden, Wagner followed his advice, submitting himself from mid-September to mid-November to the rigors of hydrotherapy at an institute especially founded for the purpose over a decade earlier in Albisbrunn, to the south of Zurich. There he drafted the libretti for *Das Rheingold* and *Die Walküre*, though it was not until over a year later that he would finish the final, versified libretto of the whole of the *Ring des Nibelungen*. He returned from Albisbrunn in late November 1851 to a new flat; Minna had in his absence organized a move back to the Escherhäuser on the Zeltweg, this time to a ground floor apartment. Their financial position was improved by the news from Julie Ritter that she was now in a position to provide the Wagners with the full three thousand francs per annum that she and the Taylor/Laussot family had planned to give him, until Wagner had imprudently suggested to Jessie that she might form part of the deal. Three thousand francs was no small sum at the time; Franz Abt's annual salary from the AMG, for example, was just over one hundred francs — though he was obviously expected to supplement this paltry sum with part-time income from elsewhere, as he could expect his basic accommodation and food costs alone to be some eight times that amount. As it happens, Abt resigned as conductor of the AMG in a letter of October 1851, citing too much other work — teaching, commissions from publishers, and the like.[25] His place was taken by Alexander Müller.

Wagner's conducting activities with the AMG resumed in early 1852, inspired in part, perhaps, by his elevation to honorary membership in the Society in mid-1851. The orchestra's committee now displayed its keenness to please him by engaging a number of musicians from outside. It had long been common practice, as mentioned above, for the orchestral musicians of Winterthur and Zurich to help each other out in their respective ensembles when necessary. But this time, players of excellence were even brought in from Germany — and not just for a single concert, but for the whole winter season. Two of the new additions warrant closer attention here. One was the then famous Viennese cellist Carl Leopold Böhm, who had been based at the Court Orchestra of Donaueschingen under the direction of Johann Wenzel Kalliwoda, and who had on occasion in the 1830s and 1840s already appeared as a soloist in concerts of the AMG in Zurich. The revolutions of 1848 had seriously disrupted artistic activities at the Court, after which Böhm had moved first to Strasbourg, then to Vichy, before returning to Donaueschingen. He was now engaged in Zurich not just as a soloist but as a member of the AMG Orchestra proper — though he did also give two solo performances and was accorded a benefit concert on 10 February 1852.

Another first-class musician to be hired this winter was the violinist Max Seifriz (1827–85), who brought along his brother Emil, also a violinist. Not unlike Böhm, Seifriz too was a "victim" of the revolution. Since his early teens he had been based at the Court Orchestra of Prince Constantin of Hohenzollern-Hechingen, who in 1848, when chaos broke out, simply handed over his territory wholesale to the Prussian King, receiving in its stead the residence of Hohlstein Castle in Löwenberg, in distant Silesia. The Court Orchestra was dissolved, as had been the case in Donaueschingen, and the musicians had to find work elsewhere. Seifriz not only played in the AMG Orchestra in the 1851–52 season, but on one occasion (17 February 1852) played a solo piece of his own, and even acted as an occasional copyist for the AMG. A few months later, Seifriz returned to the service of his prince, who had reassembled his orchestra at the other end of the country and for the next one-and-a-half decades would invest his energies and money into promoting the works of the "New German School" in a manner unparalleled for any prince before the advent of King Ludwig II of Bavaria. Constantin even went so far as to give financial support to the *Neue Zeitschrift für Musik*, which under Franz Brendel was the most vocal source of support for the composers of the "School." Seifriz, who succeeded Thomas Täglichsbeck as director of the Löwenberg orchestra in 1857, became the prince's right-hand-man in his devotion to Wagner, Liszt, Berlioz, and von Bülow, and was highly regarded by them all, even eliciting a positive review from von Bülow for his own compositions too.[26] In April 1860, Seifriz conducted one of the very first performances of the *Tristan* prelude. Wagner was himself invited to conduct a concert at Löwenberg in December 1863, and he received a much-needed gift of money from the prince. As for Seifriz, in the late 1860s he was even considered a serious candidate to replace Balakirev as conductor in St. Petersburg but instead ended his career as Hofkapellmeister in Stuttgart, where he also co-wrote a violin tutor with Edmund Singer and taught the American composers Victor Herbert and Edgar Stillman Kelley.[27]

Any notion that the Zurich orchestra was of purely provincial quality in Wagner's time must thus be revised, at least from the end of 1851. Wagner's first concert in the new season took place on 20 January 1852. It began with Beethoven's music for Goethe's *Egmont* and ended with the same composer's Seventh Symphony. Sandwiched in the middle — not conducted by Wagner — were a work each by Böhm and Seifriz and a song by one Valentin Becker. The audience included a Beethoven-lover by the name of Otto Wesendonck and his wife Mathilde. They had arrived in the city the previous year, after the end of the concert season, and were living semi-permanently in the Hotel Baur au Lac. They made the personal acquaintance of the conductor in February 1852, after another Beethoven concert. More Beethoven followed in March, when Wagner conducted the *Pastoral* Symphony and his own overture to *Tannhäuser* — the latter at Georg Herwegh's request — which concert was generally considered to be a highpoint in Zurich's musical life during those years.

From 25 April to 2 May 1852, Wagner conducted four performances of his *Fliegender Holländer* at the Zurich theater. He had been urged to stage it by the music director of the Zurich Theater at the time, Rudolf Schöneck, with whom he felt a particular empathy. But what really seems to have swayed him was the prospect of having a direct influence on the sets. Wagner wrote to Uhlig on 22 January 1852 that "the director [Wilhelm Löwe] promises to achieve the unthinkable with regard to the décor" (*SB* 4:255). The director's first choice was a stage designer from Munich, but he pulled out, supposedly on account of lack of time (or had Löwe perhaps used him to entice Wagner's participation and then simply not come up with the necessary money?). Löwe's choice then fell upon one Ludwig

Caësmann, originally from Hamburg, who happened to be in the Zurich area (though we do not know why), and of whom Wagner admitted that his sketches "demonstrated great skill" (4:313). On the day of the fourth and final performance, Wagner wrote to Liszt — who was planning a production of the opera in Weimar — that the scenery arrangements in Zurich had been made according to his precise instructions, and that Weimar would be wise to buy Caësmann's designs from him (4:484). After the performances were over, Wagner wrote to Wilhelm Fischer that they had been of a higher standard than in Dresden back in 1843, whose décor in particular he now criticized (4:360). But just a few weeks later, he seems to have changed his mind about "Caëssmann," as he calls him, when the designer demanded five *louis d'or* (SF 100) from Weimar as payment for his sketches. Wagner now wrote to Liszt that he was "really incredibly mediocre," and that his only good quality had been his ability to follow his, Wagner's, instructions precisely (4:367). Caësmann's designs have not survived; even if Liszt did buy them, they are not in his archives in Weimar today.[28]

The theater's orchestra was increased in size by about a third for the production, with extra musicians being brought in from as far away as Canton Bern. Not only — so Wagner claimed — did he pay for some of the extra players out of his own pocket, but he declined to accept any fee himself. The high opinion of the production among public and press alike seems to have served to increase Wagner's standing in Zurich society. He had been away from the orchestra pit for more than a year; whether or not it was this success that now prompted him to return to his newest musico-dramatic projects, we cannot know. But we do know that the next two months saw him complete both the prose version of the *Walküre* story and its final versified libretto. We also know that it was in May 1852 that he first visited François and Eliza Wille in Mariafeld, just down the lake from Zurich, for Eliza herself wrote of it in her memoirs; it was Georg Herwegh who introduced them. François (1811–96) was a north German of Swiss descent who had been a fellow student of Otto von Bismarck and had acquired enough notoriety for his fierce dueling skills to warrant a mention in Heinrich Heine's *Wintermärchen*. But in the chaos of 1848–49 he had sided squarely with the liberals, he had participated in the failed German parliament in Frankfurt, and in 1851 he had moved to Switzerland, where the democracy he preached was, he felt, being put into practice (though, ironically, members of his family were among Adolf Hitler's earliest financial supporters several decades later).[29] Eliza (1804–93) was of English descent and had in the mid-1830s begun a part-time career as a writer. She later became one of Wagner's most trusted confidantes, though neither she nor her husband tolerated any greater degree of intimacy. In fact, Minna would often accompany Wagner on his visits to their house.[30]

Wagner and Minna spent the rest of May and June 1852 on holiday, out of the city, in Fluntern on the Zürichberg. Today, Fluntern is simply a suburb of Zurich that one can reach swiftly by tram — it is a journey of a quarter of an hour from the Central Station — but in Wagner's day it was still a semi-rural, agricultural community (Brahms would later also succumb to its delights, for he would work on his German Requiem there some fifteen years after). Hardly had Wagner returned from the one holiday than he embarked on another, this time a walking tour that took him first to the Bernese Oberland, then to Italian Switzerland, then back to Zurich via Geneva (this time by rail) almost a month later (this holiday is discussed in greater detail in chapter 3 below). Wagner wrote the final libretto for *Rheingold* after his return, between 15 September and 3 November, and soon after made his final revisions to *Siegfrieds Tod.* The new concert season was about to begin, and it brought with it a major change in personnel, for Franz Abt had now decided to leave Zurich. He had presumably had his fill of playing second fiddle to a man whom he must have known had begun to despise him. But in any case, he now had an offer from Brunswick to work at its Court Opera, which was a far more prestigious theater than any in Switzerland. Wagner's disparagement of Abt's abilities, which is repeated in all the literature, can easily mislead us. Abt's further career was, in fact, highly successful. He turned down an offer to move to the Vienna Court Opera in 1855, preferring to remain in Brunswick, where he had in the meantime been put in charge of both the opera and the symphony concerts. His reputation grew immensely, such that a tour he made to the USA in 1872 ended with a farewell performance in Boston of his song "Wenn die Schwalben heimwärts ziehn" sung by twenty thousand voices. Nor does he seem to have borne any grudge against Wagner, for he later ensured that Brunswick was one of the first German theaters to present both the *Meistersinger* and the *Ring des Nibelungen.*

Abt had already given up his job with the Stadtsängerverein, which was now under the baton of Wilhelm Baumgartner. Ignaz Heim succeeded him as conductor of the Harmonie chorus. Since Alexander Müller was already conducting the AMG Orchestra, this meant that all three of Abt's successors were keen members of Wagner's circle. This now made Wagner, at a stroke, the kingpin of Zurich's musical life — no mean feat, when one considers that he himself did not hold any official posts at all. The support of Heim, Baumgartner, and others would soon prove of vital importance for his newest organizational plans.

Wagner gave the first reading of the complete four libretti of his *Ring des Nibelungen* on 18 and 19 December 1852, at the house of François and Eliza Wille at Mariafeld. He had the whole set published in fifty copies in early 1853, to be sent as a gift to friends, both real and potential. Despite his productivity, however, Wagner was far from well that winter. His digestive system failed him, and he was having difficulty sleeping. His exile from Germany was gnawing at him, as was his inability to see his own works performed by professional ensembles. The success of his *Holländer* in Zurich, as a result of his own considerable investment of time and energy, probably brought home to him just how much easier matters had really been when he had been at the head of a full-time, permanent, first-class operatic ensemble in Dresden. In a letter to Liszt of 9 November 1852, he cried out: "Do you know — *Zurich??* — I *have* to go mad here, nothing else is possible!" (*SB* 5:95). This should hardly surprise us; even in a city full of foreign intellectuals such as Zurich (with a new influx having arrived recently, in the months after Louis Napoleon's coup d'état), one cannot expect to find adequate compensation for having been expelled from one's native environment. As many of the German exiles of the 1930s and 1940s found in Hollywood, New York, and Oxford, no degree of intellectual stimulation can replace "home" in full, if one has been exiled not by free will but by necessity.

In early January 1853, Wagner received word that Uhlig had died. This must have multiplied vastly his feelings of isolation, for he was now deprived of the one man with whom he had, since his flight from Dresden, been able to discuss openly all the aesthetic and musical matters that concerned him. He was now more desperate than ever to hear his *Lohengrin* — no doubt so that he could prepare himself all the better to embark on his *Nibelung* project. To this purpose, "in order just to hear *something* from *Lohengrin*," as he wrote to Julie Ritter — though in fact, more specifically (as he later admitted in a letter to Louis Schindelmeisser) in order to hear that opera's prelude (*SB* 5:299), with its unusual orchestral effects employing divided strings — he had decided to organize "a kind of music festival" with musicians from far and wide. Furthermore, he told her, the coming summer would bring him visits from Liszt, Franz Brendel, Louis Schindelmeisser from Wiesbaden, Gustav Schmidt from Frankfurt, and Alwine Frommann from Berlin, though they did not all turn up in the end (*SB* 5:192–93). If he could not go to Germany, then Germany, it seemed, would have to come to him.

In the meantime, Wagner embarked on a heavy work schedule. He sent out his privately printed copies of the *Ring* libretti on 11 February 1853, conducted Beethoven's Seventh Symphony on 15 February, and on the evenings of 16, 17, 18, and 19 he read the four dramas of his tetralogy to an invited audience in the Hotel Baur au Lac. He later wrote in *Mein Leben* that the audience had grown with each day, and that "it was the most serious men of the university and the government from whom I won the greatest assurances of recognition, even positive expressions regarding their understanding of my poem and its concomitant artistic intentions" (*ML*, 505). Three days after the last reading, Wagner wrote to the Committee of the AMG to propose what he had mentioned in his earlier letter to Julie Ritter, namely a series of three concerts in the coming May, featuring bleeding chunks from his operas, to be held in the theater, and using extra players brought in from outside. He was already popular with the AMG, not least because ticket sales went up whenever he conducted. As an example: the number of tickets sold outside the normal subscription had been 186 for his concert on 15 February; the previous concert in the series, conducted by Alexander Müller alone, had sold just 53 extra tickets. Not only did the AMG Committee present Wagner with a coffee set at the end of March (worth SF 273), but they agreed to assist him with his planned concerts in May. Wagner's recent ill health abated in the course of February. He ascribed this to his new doctor, who thereby acquired his full confidence: one Konrad Rahn-Escher (1802–81), a graduate of Göttingen University, who was the father-in-law of the AMG's actuary, Moritz von Wyss. As Wagner later admitted in *Mein Leben*, Rahn was sensible enough to not pump him with medicines but simply prescribed basic measures to calm his nerves, such as plenty of rest and drinking tea. This, coupled with the outward success of his readings and concert (followed by an *Eroica* on 8 March that Wagner himself regarded as particularly successful [*SB* 5:229]), seems to have alleviated his worst symptoms.

Wagner already had experience of gathering together extra musicians from outside Zurich to perform under his baton. His plans for the coming May, however, necessitated bringing together a much bigger, better orchestra of some seventy players, plus a chorus of over a hundred. He needed money for this; but he also needed to find the players themselves, ensure that they had somewhere to stay and somewhere to rehearse, and cope with all the mishaps and petty jealousies that one encounters when trying to organize nearly two hundred musicians and singers, professionals and amateurs alike, and mold them into a passable ensemble. He also needed to advertise in order to get an audience big enough to make the venture economically viable. It would perhaps be an exaggeration to claim that Zurich's Wagner festival of May 1853 was a kind of pre-run *en miniature* of the first Bayreuth Festival of twenty-three years later. But there were undoubted similarities, and there is no denying that the former was the first real test of Wagner's organizational talents and capacity for "multitasking" such as he would also require in Bayreuth. The financial requirements for the Zurich festival were in fact solved in a manner that would be repeated in order to finance the first *Ring* festival. The initial plan in Zurich for a subscription had proven inadequate to the tune of almost three thousand francs, and so a system of "patronage certificates" was introduced that were then bought by various interested parties (including the AMG itself) — a system that proved equally successful in Bayreuth two decades later. Wagner also had financial guarantors, however, including Konrad Ott-Imhof (the clarinetist in the AMG Orchestra) and — more important — Otto Wesendonck. Both Otto and Mathilde were taking an increasing interest in Wagner and his music, and from the little that survives of their letters to both the Wagners it is clear that a mutual friendship did for a while exist between all four parties, even between Mathilde and Minna.

As for the musicians necessary for the enterprise, Wagner's extant correspondence shows that he made enquiries both in Switzerland and abroad, in Bern, Munich, Wiesbaden, Bienne, Basel, Schaffhausen, Murten, Hechingen, Lausanne, St. Gall, and elsewhere in order to find the best players, and to convince them to come for the smallest possible fee. It is a sign of Wagner's growing reputation that some, such as a certain F. Wenzel from Bienne, offered to come for no more than their expenses (*SB* 5:268), while even experienced violinists such as the leading local instrumentalist Jean Eschmann were asked (and apparently agreed) to play the viola in order to boost the numbers of that section. Yet others who had not been asked to play had to be written to in order to smooth their ruffled feathers and urge them to come as members of the audience instead (*SB* 5:294). Ignaz Heim and Wilhelm Baumgartner rehearsed the choral parts with their respective choirs, the Harmonie and the Stadtsängerverein (Franz Abt's former ensembles). The soprano soloist for Senta's Ballad was Ignaz's pretty young wife Emilie (1830–1911), to whom Wagner was particularly attracted.

The three concerts were fixed for 18, 20, and 22 May, the last being on Wagner's fortieth birthday. They included excerpts from four of his operas: *Rienzi*, *Holländer*, *Tannhäuser* and *Lohengrin*, and were held in the Theater, not the Casino. As Wagner had requested in his original proposal, a "Schallgehäuse" was constructed according to his own design (literally a "sound casing" or "sound shell") and placed on the stage in order to reflect the sound into the audience (he had done something similar for his performance of Beethoven's Ninth Symphony on the stage of the Dresden Opera House in 1846; his interest in architectural-acoustical matters would later aid him in the design of the Festspielhaus in Bayreuth). Wagner complicated his tight rehearsal schedule, not only by moving apartments in mid-April (albeit only from one side of the Escherhäuser to another, at Zeltweg 13), but by further organizing readings of the libretti of *Holländer*, *Tannhäuser*, and *Lohengrin* on 10, 12, and 14 May. Wagner negotiated with Alfred Escher (successfully) for the use of the Casino for his readings — this being the first written proof of any direct contact between the two men (*SB* 5:288). As mentioned above, Escher's sister was already Wagner's landlady; it was during the preparations for the May concerts that Clementine Stockar-Escher painted the now famous portrait of Wagner that he, and others, found particularly accurate — so accurate in fact, that he had it lithographed afterwards and sent copies of it to those whose role in his concerts he deemed particularly worthy of recognition. She also painted Minna's portrait at about the same time. Wagner's extant correspondence for April and May 1853 totals over sixty letters, but he refers there to many other written communications that have not survived.

Given the number of musicians and singers that he had to organize, we can assume that this is a mere fraction of the total number of letters that he wrote in order to get his enterprise off the ground; it also shows how remarkably efficient was the postal service of the day, as he was still writing around, looking for musicians, just six days before the first rehearsal took place (*SB* 5:294).

As has often been reported in the literature, this — the first-ever "Wagner festival" — was by all accounts a complete success. Not only performers came from afar for the concerts, for the town also swelled with visitors who came just to be in the audience. Max Fehr — in such matters a reliable source — investigated the hotel lists of the day and found that the days of the festival saw a third more tourists staying in Zurich than was the case in the weeks before and after.[31] Reviews were published as far away as Berlin. Not only the concerts but even Wagner's readings in the Casino were apparently attended by full houses; and even the *Neue Zürcher Zeitung* and the *Eidgenössische Zeitung* almost managed to agree in their enthusiasm (though the former could not help but express its reservations regarding the degree of enthusiasm shown by the latter). A banquet was held in Wagner's honor on 21 May, and the final, birthday, concert on 22 May ended, as Bernhard Spyri reported in the *Eidgenössische*, with bouquets flying, the presentation "by the prettiest of the ladies" of a laurel wreath to the composer/conductor, and the reciting by one Wilhelm Niedermann-Studer of an anonymous poem of praise that we now know to have been written by Spyri's wife Johanna — they had married just over six months before, and this was, it seems, the very first time that she would present one of her works before the general public (not until 1871 did she publish her first novella, anonymously, with *Heidi* appearing — also anonymously — nine years later).[32] This Wagner festival did not just end with flowers and a poem, however, but with a deficit of over a thousand francs (this despite the fact that the takings had reached SF 7000, far more than Wagner had originally envisaged would be the total cost of the enterprise). The AMG, however, recommended that Wagner not be left with the bill, and so it was paid instead by eight of its prominent benefactors.

Wagner himself was delighted with everything — well, almost everything, for a few musicians did not turn up, with unfortunate consequences for several wind passages (*SB* 5:299) — and he wrote to his Dresden friend Ferdinand Heine on 10 June that: "My music festival was wonderful, and has given me great hopes of realizing unheard-of things here in the future" (*SB* 5:320) He wrote to Liszt in similar vein, expressing not merely astonishment that the men of Zurich had been able to drum up the necessary finances but also, implicitly, his confidence that they would do the same in the future (*SB* 5:305). He added in his letter to Liszt that "the women have all been good to me, and for *one* beautiful woman — I laid the whole festival at her feet!" The woman in question, of course, was Mathilde

Wesendonck, and it was for her, too, that he now broke his creative silence of five years (if one discounts the abortive fragment of *Siegfrieds Tod* of 1850 and a couple of other, tiny, sketches in the meantime). Oddly — given his assurances in his theoretical writings that the days of absolute music were over — the first pieces that he completed since *Lohengrin* were now a Polka for Mathilde, dated 29 May, and a sonata for her, completed by mid-June, both for piano solo. The sonata is anything but substantial in either content or length (it lasts for ten minutes), but a careful interpretation can also succeed in overcoming the common assumption that it is a slight, occasional work. It is cast in one movement, as was Liszt's almost exactly contemporaneous B minor sonata — though the latter is, of course, on a far more ambitious scale.

Wagner's high spirits were dampened by the news in mid-June that the "wanted poster" that had been issued after his escape from Dresden had now been reissued. The King of Saxony was thus still in no mind to grant a pardon, and Wagner would have to continue to make do with what Zurich could offer him. However, the arrival of Franz Liszt for a week's visit in early July buoyed him up once more. They made a one-night trip to Brunnen with Georg Herwegh in order to walk in the footsteps of William Tell but otherwise remained in Zurich, playing and discussing their music, and wining and dining with assorted friends and colleagues, including — at Liszt's specific request — Johann Carl Eschmann and Theodor Kirchner. The Wesendoncks missed his visit, as they were taking the waters at Bad Ems. Three days after Liszt's departure Wagner was honored with a torchlight procession to his flat on the Zeltweg by the members of the Stadtsängerverein and the Harmonie, as well as the members of the theater orchestra and (it seems) of the band that Philipp Fries ran, the "Dilettanten-Harmonieverein."[33] A laudatory speech written by Karl Keller was read out, diplomas from both choirs were handed over that declared Wagner their honorary member, and the assembled singers gave of their best in one of Baumgartner's songs and the sailors' chorus from *Der fliegende Holländer.* In reply, Wagner promised that he would repay the citizens of Zurich with "something extraordinary," as the papers reported. The next day, he left for a cure in St. Moritz, which was followed, after just two weeks back in Zurich, by an extended holiday that took him to Italy — in particular, to Genoa and La Spezia — where he saw the Mediterranean Sea for the first time. He arrived in La Spezia after a stormy, seasick-ridden nocturnal boat journey, his ill health compounded by dysentery after his arrival. It was there — according to *Mein Leben* — that he fell into a half-sleep, felt himself sinking into water, and conceived in this dreamlike state the music in E-flat major, portraying rushing water, that became the opening of his *Rheingold.* But since he seems to have sketched the so-called "nature theme" that opens the prelude some time before, and since he did not tell his tale of this inspirational moment until over a year later, it is now generally assumed that it was yet another example of the composer twisting his biography to fit his art.[34] It has also often been pointed out that Wagner's description is startlingly similar to Schopenhauer's discussion of the state of "half sleep" in his *Parerga und Paralipomena*, which the composer read in late 1854.[35] But perhaps his reminiscences were in some way also prompted by the knowledge that the poet Shelley had drowned, in a night-time storm similar to his own, in the same bay of La Spezia, thirty-one years before him — for Shelley was by all accounts one of his favored poets in these years; perhaps even the name of Shelley's boat — the "Don Juan," with its Mozartian resonances — had played a contributory role in Wagner's subconscious (*SB* 4:256). Seeing it in this light, we can interpret the tale as Shelley being "trumped" by Wagner: the former sinks into water and drowns, while the latter's (metaphorical) immersion at La Spezia ends with his "rebirth," now at a stroke the composer of the *Ring*. A further possible interpretation of the La Spezia "vision" will be investigated in chapter 4 below.

Wagner's concerns were at this time squarely with his *Nibelungen*. He was already thinking of yet another "Wagner festival," this time to produce the whole of his (as yet un-composed) tetralogy in Zurich. He had also recently sent an official proposal to the AMG Committee for an overhaul of the city's music scene.[36] These suggestions, not unlike those in his earlier brochure on the Zurich theater, were grounded in common sense. They envisaged a close cooperation between the theater and the concert hall, doubling the number of concerts per season from six to twelve, and postulated the creation of a conservatory of sorts. Not for the last time, Wagner had assumed that the generosity of his friends and colleagues in financing his activities would inevitably be but the start of a yet more generous relationship to his benefit. Wagner's optimism was to prove unfounded, however, for the deficit that his festival had incurred seems to have depressed the AMG Committee at least as much as its artistic success had impressed them. When it met again, in September, the Committee declared curtly that "sufficient ways of bringing together the necessary means could not be found," and that was the end of Wagner's grand plans. His proposals would eventually come to fruition — for they were indeed sensible — but not for many years to come. It would be more than a decade before the citizens of Zurich would go about putting even their orchestra in order (with the founding of the Tonhalle Society), and the rest would take yet longer still.

The beginning of October 1853 saw Liszt involved in a music festival in Karlsruhe, just a few hours away to the north, where music of his own and excerpts from Wagner's *Lohengrin* were on the program. Since Wagner could not set foot on German soil, Liszt and a group of friends and colleagues — Hans von Bülow, Joseph Joachim, Peter Cornelius, Richard Pohl, Dionys Pruckner, and Eduard Reményi — set off for Basel just after the festival, where Wagner joined them. Wagner then left for Paris, together with Liszt (who paid the hotel bills). It was there, on 10 October, that he met Liszt's three children for the first time, including Cosima, then fifteen (though she was for now overshadowed in Wagner's eyes by her "stepsister" Marie, the daughter of Liszt's current partner Carolyne von Sayn-Wittgenstein, whom he also met in Paris. Although equal in age, Marie was striking in appearance where Cosima was plain) (*SB* 5:476). The Wesendoncks were also in Paris this month, and they met up with Wagner for a morning visit to the Louvre on the nineteenth. Minna joined him the next day, though they stayed for only a week before returning to Zurich, traveling through rainstorms via Strasbourg, where the tips of the cathedral spires were obscured by mist.

On 1 November, Wagner at last began work on the music of *Das Rheingold*. He had written the libretti for the *Ring des Nibelungen* more or less in reverse order, but would now adhere to the chronology of the plot when composing the music. Astonishingly, he finished the complete draft of *Das Rheingold* in just eleven weeks (in performance, it lasts some two and a half hours); by the end of May 1854, the instrumentation draft would be finished. The rest of his work on the tetralogy, by contrast, would take him over twenty years more. Throughout this winter he was also conducting again, with Beethoven center-stage: between November 1853 and the end of March 1854, he conducted the symphonies nos. 4–8, the Fifth Piano Concerto (with his friend Alexander Müller as soloist), the *Leonore* Overture no. 3, and excerpts from *Egmont*; also among the works on his programs were Mozart's *Jupiter* and Haydn's 104th symphonies, and Gluck's Overture to *Iphigenie in Aulis* in an arrangement of Wagner's own, with a new concert ending that he published separately in the *Neue Zeitschrift für Musik* three months later.[37] Alexander Müller was still officially the conductor of the AMG, and as a rule was now responsible for the first half of the concert, with Wagner being assigned the "cherries on the cake," as it were, in the second half.

Wagner's reasons for conducting so much in this season were largely financial. He had hoped for extra income from performances of his operas in Germany — *Tannhäuser* in particular was proving increasingly popular in his home country — and it seems that he had begun to live more lavishly in that expectation. But his hopes, as so often before and after, were in vain. He had been borrowing money from Sulzer, whose patience was extensive but not boundless, and he simply needed to earn some money. However, it also seems that Wagner was making an effort to repay debts of a nature other than financial, for on 14 February 1854, Müller conducted the Concerto for Four Clarinets by Louis Schindelmeisser, Wagner's friend (now in Darmstadt), who had provided several musicians for the May Festival of the previous year, and was now planning a production of *Lohengrin*. It was not the first time that a work by Schindelmeisser had been heard in Zurich — his Overture to *Uriel Acosta* had been performed on 23 December 1851 — and it seems highly likely that the inclusion of his music in the AMG's programs was thanks to his longtime friendship with Wagner.

The 1853–54 season also brought a new face to Zurich, whose future devotion to Wagner's cause would have unusual consequences, namely Carl Ludwig Eberle (1826–71). He was appointed music director at the Zurich Theater, where his wife, Barbara, was also engaged as a singer. They had both come straight from a previous engagement at the theater of Magdeburg (one of Wagner's own earliest places of employment). Although Eberle conducted nothing of Wagner's while in Zurich, he caught Wagner's attention, and when their paths crossed again, over a decade later in Munich, Eberle was a répétiteur for the world première of *Die Meistersinger von Nürnberg*. Wagner thought so highly of him as to recommend him as conductor for the Munich world première of his *Rheingold* a year later. But by this time, Eberle had been struck down by psychiatric illness, and within two years he would die in a mental institution in Munich — upon which the *Neue freie Presse* in Vienna would gleefully ascribe his condition to the ill effects of a surfeit of Wagner's music.[38]

Wagner had not yet given up trying to get the AMG to think on a grander scale than that to which they were accustomed. In early 1854, he proposed a performance of Beethoven's Ninth Symphony, to be held in the Theater, though only upon the construction of a "Schallgehäuse" like the one built the year before. The AMG was not opposed to the idea *per se*; but its members had obviously had their fill of issuing financial guarantees to a man who, it must have seemed, was bound to go over budget.[39] For the second time in just a few months, therefore, Wagner was forced to abandon his ambitious plans for the Zurich orchestra on account of a lack of money. But he was not easily put off, and it was also at this time that he seems seriously to have considered taking over the running of the Zurich Theater. The previous director, Wilhelm Löwe, had died six months earlier after an accident during a performance of *Uncle Tom's Cabin* in nearby Baden. His widow Karoline had assumed his position in Zurich but within a few months had fallen into massive debt, with the result that the whole personnel was sacked without notice on 31 January 1854. We do not know to what extent Wagner truly considered taking on the job, nor to what extent the local authorities took him seriously (probably not very, given his financial record), but the notion, in retrospect, is naturally a fascinating one. Wagner did, however, conduct a benefit concert for the suffering theater staff on 30 March, the generosity of his gesture being underlined by the fact that he was this time — unusually — responsible for the whole program. He had also, in the meantime, submitted a third and final proposal to the AMG for the reorganization of its orchestra. It entailed a close collaboration with the theater director, and also came with a detailed plan of the necessary costs. He was obviously still considering how to bring about a state of affairs that might make a production of his *Nibelung* tetralogy a possibility. But in June 1854, this plan, too, was turned down, and Wagner must have at last begun to realize that republican Zurich was just not going to open its pockets wide enough to give him all he craved.

On 28 June 1854, nevertheless, Wagner embarked upon the draft for the music of his *Walküre*. This would take him until the end of the year, but when one considers the length and complexity of the work, and the fact that during these months he was also writing out the fair copy of the *Rheingold* score, the speed of its composition cannot but astonish us once again. Within the space of just a year, the first two dramas of his tetralogy would be finished in draft, with the first of them ready in full score. His work was interrupted in early July by the necessity of traveling to Sion to conduct the festival orchestra of the "Swiss Music Society" — that same organization mentioned in chapter 1 above, whose mammoth concerts had featured large on the national music scene since the second decade of the century. Wagner had been made an honorary member three years before but had hitherto shown no inclination to repay the honor by taking part in its activities. Now, however, he needed any money he could lay his hands on and so had agreed to conduct its festival orchestra in Beethoven's Seventh Symphony. But the orchestral musicians arrived late and proved inadequate to their task, and so Wagner, in a huff, handed over the direction of the symphony to Adolf Methfessel, and slunk off angrily, now even more out of pocket than before. The young German composer Robert von Hornstein, who had attended the May festival concerts in Zurich a year before, met up with Wagner and Karl Ritter in Martigny on the way to Sion. He later recalled how Wagner had talked incessantly of his work on the *Ring* and of the theater he was going to have built for it, at Otto Wesendonck's expense, in Zurich. "If someone uninitiated had listened in," he wrote, "he would have taken the man for a Barnum . . . that the man's persuasive talent, if possible, was even greater than his other talents became clear to everyone on this journey."[40] Wagner spent the latter half of July 1854 on the opposite bank of Lake Lucerne from Brunnen, at Seelisberg, where Minna was taking a cure. To all intents and purposes, his money had already run out. He had begged Liszt for five hundred francs in late June, and received it within days (*SB* 6:165, 175); by late July, he was begging him to drum up larger sums of money, with promises that his income from opera performances would in any case soon be flowing in. As Liszt will surely have expected, given Wagner's financial record, the latter had to write on 16 September that his opera income was now, in fact, at zero. He then asked instead if Liszt thought he might be able to earn ten thousand francs from organizing a music festival in Holland and Belgium similar to that of May 1853 (*SB* 6:186–87, 224). Grand ambition and near-stupidity were obviously close companions now. Lasting help, at last, came in the autumn from Otto Wesendonck and Jakob Sulzer. Wesendonck cleared Wagner's debts of some seven thousand francs and promised him an annual income of SF 2000, to be paid in quarterly installments, while Sulzer was to take charge of all of Wagner's financial affairs in the hope that together he and Wesendonck would be able to rein in their friend's spending (Wagner now began to address his letters to Sulzer — with whom he was on first-name terms — as "Lieber Vormund," "Dear Guardian").

The autumn of 1854 did, however, bring two events of consequence for Wagner's future career. The first was his success in arranging for Gottfried Semper to take up a professorship in architecture at the recently created "Eidgenössische Technische Hochschule" (ETH) in Zurich, the federal technical university. Wagner had been lobbying for Semper to come to Zurich for some three years by this time, and his close acquaintance with him from their Dresden days made him the obvious choice as a go-between when the Zurich powers-that-be finally decided to offer Semper a job. Semper accordingly visited Zurich briefly in September 1854 to conduct negotiations for the post and then returned the following June to assume his professorship. Wagner, of course, was not without personal reasons for having his friend nearby. As early as February 1855, he was writing to Eduard Devrient of his plans to stage his *Nibelung* tetralogy in 1858, adding that "Semper will build me my theater" (*SB* 6:343). The second event of importance in the latter half of 1854 was Wagner's acquaintance with the philosophy of Arthur Schopenhauer, thanks to the mediation of Georg Herwegh. Schopenhauer's *Die Welt als Wille und Vorstellung* (The World as Will and Representation) had been published over thirty years before but had long remained little known. Wagner was soon announcing him boldly to his friends as "the greatest philosopher of our time" (*SB* 6:308). He was more precise in his correspondence with Liszt, to whom he now explained both Schopenhauer's philosophy as he understood it, and the effect it had had upon him:

> What charlatans are all these Hegels etc. when compared to him! His principal thought, namely the final renunciation of the will to life, is of a terrible seriousness, but uniquely redemptive. It did not really come to me as new, and no one can think it at all without already living in it. But not until this philosopher had anyone awakened it to clarity within me. When I think back on the storms of my heart, the terrible spasms with which it hung on to life's hope, against my will — yes, when it still now often swells up to a hurricane — now have I found a palliative against it, that at last alone helps me to sleep in my waking nights: it is the heartfelt, inner yearning for death; complete loss of consciousness, utter non-being, the disappearing of all dreams — the only, final redemption! (*SB* 6:298)

Wagner's wildly enthusiastic reaction to Schopenhauer is reminiscent to us — as it no doubt was, too, to Liszt — of his equally wild enthusiasm for social revolution back in 1848–49 or his water cures two years after that.

As usual, Wagner took from his philosophers what suited him for his aesthetic purposes and ignored the rest. The logical consequence of "renouncing the will to life" as Wagner describes it, would of course be suicide, though this naturally did not match either Schopenhauer's beliefs or his intent. The parallels with certain of his operatic characters were probably what appealed to Wagner with the most immediacy. In that same letter, he himself mentions his *Holländer*, in which, of course, Senta sacrifices herself for her love; and, closer to home, there was Wotan, who engages in self-destruction in the *Ring*. In light of this it is instructive to consider how Wagner's heroes changed during these years: Jesus Christ was abandoned; so were Achilles and Friedrich Barbarossa. But Wotan remained: the only god who willed his own annihilation.

There is, however, a theatricality to Wagner's espousal of Schopenhauer that speaks volumes. Here a lover of the grand gesture has at last found a philosopher who will allow him the grandest gesture of all: the public "embracing" of death itself. Liszt will hardly have feared that his friend was about to take a boat out on the Zurich Lake and drill a hole in the bottom, or throw himself on the railway lines of the recently completed *Spanischbrötlibahn* between Zurich and Baden. After all, Wagner could only enjoy his grand gestures for as long as he stayed alive, and he had no intention of giving up that enjoyment for the moment. A further point that will have made Schopenhauer attractive to Wagner was the importance that the philosopher gave to music in the greater scheme of things, for he regarded it as the highest of the arts and, on account of its non-representational nature, a direct expression of "the Will" itself. This paramount importance of music naturally ran counter to the arguments that Wagner had put forward in his aesthetic tracts of his first years in Zurich, when music was supposed to be subservient to drama. Wagner himself and various subsequent commentators were to expend many words and much energy in endeavoring to square this particular circle, and somehow prove that he really did not change his basic aesthetic beliefs at all. This debate will probably never cease completely. But if one takes the straightforward view that Wagner was a pragmatic thinker who would always take and espouse whatever philosophical notions he needed for his art at any time, then the many undeniable self-contradictions in his writings, large and small, in fact appear of little real consequence for his artworks themselves.

Wagner's discovery of Schopenhauer had a more immediate use, however, for it also coincided with his deepening passion for Mathilde Wesendonck, the unapproachable wife of his financial savior. He was probably already groping, as it were, for some means of accepting and explaining to himself the fact that he would probably never be able to consummate his love for her. This means he now found in Schopenhauer, who not only took a dim view of the sexual urge in general, but whose philosophy — in Wagner's superficial explanation — offered redemption through renunciation. He did not hesitate, of course, to explain Schopenhauer to Mathilde herself; though if he had hoped (as is likely) that she might be willing to apply the philosophy of renunciation to her marriage, but not to him, then she was to disappoint him. All this, however — Mathilde, Schopenhauer, chastity, renunciation — came together in his idea for a new opera, based on the medieval legend of Tristan and Isolde. In the letter to Liszt quoted above, Wagner continued as follows:

> Out of love for the most beautiful of my dreams of life, namely young Siegfried, I will probably have to finish the Nibelung pieces . . . but since I have never in my life enjoyed the real happiness of love, I wish to create a monument to this, the most beautiful of all dreams, in which this love shall have its proper fill, from beginning to end. In my head, I have sketched a Tristan and Isolte [*sic*]: the simplest, but most full-blooded musical conception. With the "black flag" that flutters at the end, I will then cover myself in order — to die. (*SB* 6:299)

In late 1854 Wagner was also dealing with far more prosaic matters. Relations between the theater and the AMG were at an all-time low, with the one boycotting the other and the orchestral musicians of the city caught in the crossfire. The AMG wanted Wagner to conduct again — after all, he was best able to bring in the crowds — but he replied on 23 November by insisting that the AMG be prepared to compromise with the theater, in which case he would indeed be prepared to accept their offer. He had already allowed the new theater director, Ernst Walther, to announce on 15 November that *Tannhäuser* would be featured in the coming season, and we can probably assume that Wagner was playing both sides off against each other in order to exert enough pressure to make them come together. If that was indeed his intention, then it worked, for by December, the warring parties had finally agreed to compromise. The musicians were once more allowed to play for both organizations, and Wagner subsequently kept his side of the bargain with the AMG. For all his financial recklessness, he was now proving himself no mean politician; and for all his selfishness, he was also quite capable of using his political tact for the greater public good. Wagner conducted on 9 January 1855 for the first time in this season, and ticket sales (aside from existing season tickets) immediately shot up by over a hundred compared with the previous concert of 26 December. This huge increase then almost doubled again by the time of Wagner's last concert, on 20 February 1855. The final concert of the season, at which he did not conduct, saw a drop in sales of over 180.[41]

Wagner's second concert, on 23 January, included the world première of a revised version of his *Faust Overture* of 1839–40. He had begun the scoring of the first act of his *Walküre* at the turn of the year but had interrupted it for some ten days in order to carry out his revisions to the earlier piece. He had probably been prompted in part by Franz Liszt's announcement in a letter of 1 January that he had finished his own *Faust Symphony*, though in *Mein Leben* Wagner claimed to have been motivated by a desire on the part of his "friends" to hear the work at last. He might even have heard, perhaps via Theodor Kirchner, that Robert Schumann, too, had recently finished his own large-scale choral and orchestral work based on *Faust* — and we do know that Wagner was taking a closer look once more at Schumann's scores in the first quarter of 1855 (*SB* 7:39).

The score of Wagner's newly revised *Faust* bore the letters "S. l. F.," which Minna presumably interpreted as "Seiner lieben Frau" ("To his dear wife"), though most commentators agree that the "F." meant "Freundin" (the feminine form of "friend," "girlfriend"), that is, Mathilde; she was, it seems, the "friends" who prompted the work. To the program of the first performance, Wagner added a motto from Goethe's play on which the overture was based that reflected his new, "Schopenhauerian" view of things. The last two of its six lines run: "And thus my existence is a burden to me; I wish for death and hate life." At Liszt's urging, the overture was published that same year by Breitkopf & Härtel, while Hans von Bülow shortly afterwards published arrangements of it for piano solo and piano duet. Wagner repeated his overture in the second half of the concert of 20 February, which he this time conducted in its entirety. It also included the prelude and Elsa's Bridal Procession from *Lohengrin* and the overture to *Tannhäuser*. This was the last concert that he would ever conduct in public in Zurich. His last public performance in the city, however, came three days later, in the theater. As promised, Ernst Walther was bringing *Tannhäuser* to the Zurich public for the first time, and Wagner had already been deeply engaged in all aspects of its production. The conductor was one Louis Müller, originally from Frankfurt, and Wagner was perfectly happy with him. In a letter to Julie Ritter of 17 February, the day after the première, Wagner wrote of his satisfaction, and of how his own input had brought forth remarkable results from the "very mediocre singers" at his disposal (*SB* 6:356–57). Such statements were not unusual for him, of course, but while they can justifiably be interpreted as a result of Wagner's need to prove that he was ever the secret ingredient that could turn base metal into gold, his surprise at the results seems genuine, nor can we really doubt, either, that his vast experience could indeed have proven vital to the success of the enterprise. For the third performance — at the special request of Mathilde Wesendonck, so he wrote to Hans von Bülow (*SB* 7:39) — Wagner deigned to conduct himself, with the result that the theater was full to overflowing.

Two days after his appearance in the pit for *Tannhäuser*, Wagner left for London. The conductor of the Philharmonic Society, Michael Costa, had resigned in November 1854, and Wagner had a few weeks later been approached with a view to taking on their coming concert season from

March to June. The Society's treasurer, and Master of the Queen's Musick, George Anderson, even came to Zurich in early January in order to sort out the details. Wagner at first hoped to make money from the venture, but as he related in a letter to Julie Ritter (*SB* 7:357), he realized, even before leaving, that of his fee of two hundred pounds (about SF 5000) little would be left after three months of living in London, where his weekly costs for food and accommodation alone would prove to be almost four pounds (ca. SF 100). The fact that he could speak almost no English was also a hurdle. But he would have the opportunity to hear at least a few of his own works played by a fully professional orchestra; and his patrons Wesendonck and Sulzer would probably have taken offense had he turned down a perfectly good offer of paid work from a reputable source. Indeed, Wagner used the London offer to rub Sulzer's nose in it. A brief letter exists in which he announces to his friend the imminent arrival of the treasurer of the Philharmonic Society, and he adds "Now smell that!" (*SB* 6:337). What Wagner presumably did not know was that the Society had actually first tried, but failed, to procure Louis Spohr. They had then kept their options open by writing to both Berlioz and Wagner on the same day. The former, however, had already agreed to conduct the rival concert series of the New Philharmonic Society and so could not oblige. And if Wagner had said "no," then Anderson's instructions were to go to Weimar to procure Liszt, and then, as a last resort, to try for Franz Lachner in Munich.

Wagner's quite specific hope was that success on the London concert scene might procure him the chance to return the year after to put on his operas. This, of course, was just about as utopian an idea as any of the others that he had recently entertained (as he would indeed soon find out). Nevertheless, he left Zurich in late February, returning only at the very end of June, a mere thousand francs better off than before, and depressed after the drudgery of English concert life with its minimum of rehearsals. There were at least three bright spots, however: he got to know Liszt's former student Karl Klindworth (1830–1916), who would later make the vocal score of the whole *Ring des Nibelungen* (they could not know, of course, that Klindworth's later adopted daughter, Winifred, would marry Wagner's son Siegfried over half a century later); Wagner also established a closer acquaintance with Berlioz (who arrived in June to conduct the concerts of the New Philharmonic); and he was received by the Queen and Prince Albert, whose public display of sympathy was a gesture generous to a man wanted for revolutionary activities in his native Germany (which was Prince Albert's homeland too, of course).

The latter half of July 1855 saw Wagner back at the Seelisberg with Minna, where she was to take another cure, and where he continued work on the score of his *Walküre*. He was still planning on finishing his *Nibelung* operas in the near future, and still pondering where to perform them. He now even considered the possibility of setting up a wooden theater for them in Brunnen. In early August Wagner and Minna returned to Zurich, where he worked throughout the autumn and winter on the *Walküre*. He soon received his by now customary annual invitation to conduct the orchestra of the AMG, but this time declined, citing "poor health." Since we know that he had a bout of erysipelas that autumn, we should not assume that Wagner's excuse was merely arbitrary — indeed, he even wrote to Liszt in December, advising him not to visit him as they had originally planned, on account of his state of health (*SB* 7:315). But it also seems that, for the moment, Wagner had had his fill of conducting. An offer now arrived from America for him to spend six months conducting in New York. But not even what seem to have been promises of huge sums could sway him: "I had enough with London," he wrote to Ferdinand Praeger (*SB* 7:277). Nor was the hundredth anniversary of Mozart's birth the following January able to entice him back to the podium, though both the AMG and the new theater director (Karl Scholl) asked him to conduct commemorative performances.

The winter of 1855–56 brought a new figure to Wagner's circle, when the writer Gottfried Keller returned to his native city after several years in Germany. It was Sulzer who provided the funds that Keller needed to be able to return at all, and it was apparently Sulzer, too, who introduced him to Wagner. The two were no strangers to each other; Wagner had already praised Keller's poetry in a review of Wilhelm Baumgartner's songs four years before, while Baumgartner had also kept Keller informed by letter as to Wagner's activities. In fact, Keller had written to Sulzer from Berlin on 16 November 1855, specifically expressing regret that his imminent return would mean missing the forthcoming production of *Tannhäuser* in Berlin.[42] As early as 13 January 1856, Keller was writing to Lina Duncker about dinners *chez* Sulzer, where he came together with Wagner, Semper, and others; he also told her that the Wesendoncks had made him welcome. Wagner gave Keller a copy of his *Ring* libretti, and Keller was so impressed that he wrote as follows to Hermann Hettner on 16 April 1856:

> If you find the opportunity to read his Nibelungen trilogy [*sic*], which he has had printed for friends, do it. You will find that it exudes mighty poetry, truly German, but purged by the tragic spirit of the Ancients. On me, at least, it made this impression.[43]

Keller's prose in turn made a lasting impression on Wagner, for Cosima remarked repeatedly in her diary, twenty years later, of the pleasure that reading his works gave both her and her husband.[44]

Wagner's erysipelas might have made him unwilling to appear in public, but it obviously did not prevent him from socializing privately. Nor did it stop him from composing. In March 1856, he finished the orchestration of *Die Walküre*, and on 26 April, he presented its first act to his friends for the first time. To a small, invited audience that included the Wesendoncks, Wagner sang the roles of both Hunding and Siegmund, with Emilie Heim singing Sieglinde; Theodor Kirchner accompanied. As is discussed in greater detail in chapter 9 below, it was the impact of this performance that prompted Otto Wesendonck to increase his financial support for Wagner, to enable him — so he thought — to finish the composition of the whole *Ring* without money worries. Wagner's mind was already moving on to other projects, however. *Tristan* was still occupying his thoughts, while in May 1856, he also made a sketch for a drama based on the life of the Buddha, entitled *Die Sieger* (The Victors), which topic would remain at the back of his mind for many years to come. May also brought a visit from the tenor Joseph Tichatschek, who had sung the part of Rienzi in Dresden fourteen years before. But Wagner was being plagued once again by his erysipelas. In early June, he left for another water cure, this time in Mornex near Geneva. This one, however — though by what precise means we do not know — actually managed to cure him. He was not affected by erysipelas for another twenty years. Even his bowels stopped troubling him to the dreadful degree to which he had become accustomed. He stayed in Mornex until mid-August, stopping off at Bern on the way back to meet the Wesendoncks, who happened to be visiting the city.

Wagner's mood this summer was thus at first decidedly positive. His health was improving, he was absurdly confident that Breitkopf would buy his (as yet unfinished) *Ring des Nibelungen* for forty thousand francs (!), he was just as confident that he would now be granted an amnesty from Germany, and he began dreaming of acquiring a little house by Lake Zurich where he and Minna could live out their days in domestic bliss. But the owner of the piece of land that he deemed necessary for this blissful state, Heinrich Bodmer-Stockar, decided not to sell, as his son-in-law was considering moving there. And within just a few weeks, Breitkopf had turned down his *Nibelungen* and the Saxon King his amnesty request.[45] But while his ebullient spirits were dampened, this seems not to have altered his determination to continue with the *Ring*. It was in this summer of 1856 that Wagner changed the titles of the last two operas of his tetralogy, from *Jung Siegfried* and *Siegfrieds Tod* to *Siegfried* and *Götterdämmerung* (Twilight of the Gods). On 22 September, he began work on the music of the former. He was determined to conduct no more in Zurich, and he made this clear in a letter to the AMG of 12 October 1856 ("I in no wise find it possible for me to participate any more in the concerts of the Music Society," it said [*SB* 8:183]). His work on *Siegfried* was interrupted in mid-October by another visit from Liszt, this time together with his partner, Princess Carolyne von Sayn-Wittgenstein, and her daughter, Marie. They lodged in the Hotel Baur au Lac (where the Wesendoncks were still living). The Princess, who herself not only possessed a considerable intellect but was perfectly aware of it, proved a remarkable attraction to the intellectual elite of Zurich and Winterthur, with the local professors more or less lining up to meet her when she held court at her hotel — Hermann Köchly, Theodor Vischer, and Jacob Moleschott in particular found the atmosphere enchanting around her and Liszt. These were leading intellectuals who had hitherto shown no desire to court Wagner in any way; nor would they in the future.[46] In *Mein Leben*, Wagner remarked that "It was as if Zurich had at one stroke become a kind of world-class city." This can hardly be anything but sarcastic, for it would otherwise naturally presuppose that Wagner regarded his own presence in the city as of lesser consequence. Indeed, his reminiscences suggest that, even at more than a decade's distance, he was still envious that someone else should so suddenly have become the center of attention (*ML*, 552–55). He, Liszt, and the latter's entourage nevertheless all attended the opera together — Halévy's *La Juive* (The Jewish Girl) on 20 October — and went to an organ concert given in Winterthur by Kirchner and the young Alexander Winterberger, one of Liszt's protégés. On 22 October, Liszt's forty-fifth birthday was celebrated in their hotel in Zurich by another performance of the first act of the *Walküre*, plus a scene from the second act. Once more, Wagner and Emilie Heim sang, but this time with Liszt himself accompanying. Liszt stayed until mid-November, when Wagner accompanied him to the border at Rorschach. They traveled via St. Gall, making use of the recently finished railway line from Zurich to that city, and there they halted for several days. The St. Gall music director of the time, Heinrich Sczadrowsky (1828–78), was a refugee from the Baden uprising of 1848. He had already made a point of including excerpts of Wagner's works in his programs and had now managed to convince both Wagner and Liszt to conduct at one of his subscription concerts. This took place on 23 November 1856, with Sczadrowsky himself conducting Liszt's *Orpheus* and two arias by Gluck. Liszt then conducted his *Les Préludes*, while the second half of the concert comprised Beethoven's *Eroica* Symphony, conducted by Wagner. In the days thereafter, there was a visit to the famous St. Gall Monastery Library, and there were various society invitations and dinners. Liszt and the Princess left for good on the twenty-seventh. The concert in St. Gall is especially significant, for — as László Eösze has remarked — this was the first time that Wagner had the opportunity to hear any of Liszt's symphonic poems performed by an orchestra (as opposed to hearing Liszt demonstrate them at the piano). The closing bars of *Orpheus* would appear to have left their mark on the music of *Parsifal*, while Liszt's technique of thematic transformation, as demonstrated in *Les Préludes* and elsewhere, is remarkably similar to Wagner's symphonic treatment of his leitmotifs.[47]

Wagner now returned to his work on *Siegfried*. Although his original notion that the whole cycle would be complete by 1856 had proven too optimistic by far, his pace of work was still, by any standards, remarkable. The orchestral score of the first act of *Siegfried* was finished on 31 March 1857. Less than a month later, the Wagners left their apartment on the Zeltweg and moved to a small house on the edge of the city, in the western suburb of Enge, a few streets from the lake, which Wagner henceforth dubbed his *Asyl*, his "refuge" or "asylum." It stood next to the huge plot on which the Wesendoncks were having a villa built. To his consternation, Otto had discovered that a psychiatric doctor was planning on having an "asylum" of another kind installed in the house next door. So he promptly bought it up, and now offered it to Wagner for a rent of one thousand francs per annum (*SB* 9:256).[48] Wagner accepted; it underwent some minor renovation work under the auspices of Leonhard Zeugheer, the Wesendonck's architect, and in late April, the Wagners moved in. However, they did not pay any rent until the following October, and even then, to judge from the letter that Wagner sent with the money, it was not the full amount (*SB* 9:49). It seems that Wagner was already reneging on his assurances, mentioned to Liszt earlier in the year, that he would maintain his independence by paying fair and square for the house (*SB* 8:256).

Not long after arriving in the *Asyl* Wagner made his first sketch for the libretto of *Parsifal*, but then set it aside — where it would remain for the next two decades. He was still busy with the second act of *Siegfried* but in June 1857 decided to halt work on it. He would now compose *Tristan und Isolde* instead. He wrote to Liszt: "I have led my young Siegfried into a beautiful woodland solitude, have there left him under the linden tree, and with heartfelt tears have taken my leave of him"; though in fact he resumed work on the opera just a few days later, completing the second complete draft of the second act on 9 August 1857. He now indeed abandoned his work on the *Ring* and would not return to it for several years. Wagner began the libretto for *Tristan* just before the Wesendoncks moved into their new villa, on 22 August. The late summer brought more socializing. Hans von Bülow had married Cosima Liszt on 18 August, and they spent the latter part of their honeymoon — almost a month in all — in Zurich with the Wagners. Wagner finished the text for *Tristan* on 18 September, and soon thereafter there took place what must be one of the oddest events in Wagner's biography, when he gave a private reading of the libretto to an audience that included his wife, his muse Mathilde Wesendonck, his patron Otto, and Hans and Cosima von Bülow. Wagner began the music of *Tristan* on 1 October, though he interrupted his work on it several times over the coming months in order to set to music five poems by Mathilde, the first of these in late November 1857, the last of them in early May the next year. Whatever Otto Wesendonck's reasons for letting Wagner live next to them, relations between the two families were becoming — inevitably — more and more complicated. The precise dynamic involved will be investigated in detail in chapters 9 and 10, but — as is today well known — Wagner's infatuation with Mathilde Wesendonck became increasingly pronounced, their geographical proximity merely serving to enflame him all the more.

Otto had to travel to the USA in late November 1857 because of a serious business crisis. It was while he was still away that Wagner organized an early-morning serenade for Mathilde's birthday on 23 December, at which he conducted a version for solo violin and small orchestra of the song "Träume" (Dreams) that he had recently composed to one of her poems. The concert took place at seven in the morning and also included the March of the Messengers of Peace from *Rienzi* and the Entrance of the Guests in the Wartburg from *Tannhäuser*. Minna was by no means excluded, for she was in charge of providing coffee and sandwiches for the musicians, who, she wrote to her friend Mathilde Schiffner, numbered nineteen of "the best" available. We do not know for certain who played in the ensemble, but Minna states that they took part "as a favor." She does mention, however, that she and Wagner gave the "organizer of this little band of musicians ['Musickergesellschaft' (*sic*)] a gift of money of several times twenty francs" for his trouble. She also implies that the band in question comprised mostly wind instruments.[49] The two main bands of this kind in Zurich were run by members of the AMG orchestra: the oboist Philipp Fries (whose career I shall discuss in greater detail in chapter 8) and the brothers Rudolf and Hans Jakob Bär. We know that Fries had made arrangements of the marches from *Rienzi*[50] and *Tannhäuser*, and also that Wagner had at some point attended a performance of the latter. But just about every band that played in Zurich in these years, whether from the city itself or from outside, took the trouble to play the marches from Wagner's operas; and Fries would in any case not have been needed for the performance of "Träume," since it is scored only for solo violin, strings, and two each of clarinets, horns, and bassoons. It was thus most probably the Bär brothers' ensemble that played on that December morning.

Otto returned just before Christmas, to find that Wagner's whims had become a determining factor in how his household was being run, even down to when the heating was to be turned on. Otto apparently thought of expelling Wagner from his *Asyl*, but then gave in to his wife's insistence that he remain. Wagner traveled to Paris in January 1858 in order to let matters calm down, and upon his return a degree of normality was restored. He even conducted a concert of movements from assorted Beethoven symphonies at the Wesendonck villa on 30 March, in belated celebration of Otto's birthday, and obviously in compensation for the private concert to which Mathilde had been treated on her own birthday three months earlier. The center of attention remained not Otto, of course, but Wagner, who was that evening publicly presented with an elaborate conductor's baton that Mathilde had occasioned to be made, to designs especially commissioned from Semper. A report on the concert in the *Tagblatt der Stadt Zürich* of 8 April 1858 remarked that Wagner had employed members of a "Harmoniemusikgesellschaft" (a wind band) alongside instrumentalists from the Theater Orchestra. Since Philipp Fries received a personal invitation to play at Otto's concert, with no mention of his wind band, we must assume that the ensemble involved was that of the Bärs (which would also make it more likely that it was indeed the Bärs who had helped to organize Mathilde's concert, too).[51]

If Wagner was now trying to patch things up with the neighbors, matters nevertheless took a turn for the worse within little more than a week of Otto's concert. On the morning of 7 April 1858, Wagner sent his servant to Mathilde, bearing a draft for the prelude to *Tristan* and an accompanying letter now generally referred to as the "Morgenbeichte" or "Morning Confession." It never reached its addressee but was instead intercepted by his wife Minna, and (partly mis-) interpreted by her as a declaration of love to their neighbor. She complained to Mathilde, Mathilde was forced to tell her husband, and events now assumed an inexorable, inevitable logic, such that Wagner was in the following August compelled to leave Zurich for good. He separated from Minna, moving first to Geneva, then to Venice, where he continued work on *Tristan*. Soon after, Minna sold off their furniture by public announcement in the local newspaper, packed her bags for Germany, and left the Wesendoncks to cope with what by now was a more or less open scandal.

Wagner thus left Zurich hurriedly, alone, virtually penniless, dogged by scandal, and without any real hope of ever returning. The parallels with his flight from Riga as a young, penniless Kapellmeister twenty years earlier, and — even more so — with his flight from Dresden a decade after that, are striking. But the pattern was to be repeated yet again, less than eight years later. Just as Wagner had been unable to resist the urge in Zurich to betray the man who had paid his debts and given him a regular income, so too would he be compelled to leave Munich in late 1865, barely two years after having acquired, in Ludwig II of Bavaria, his richest patron yet. In Dresden, he had dabbled too much in politics; in Zurich, he had dabbled in other men's wives; and in Munich, he would double dabble in both. But in sheer creative terms, his years in Zurich were by far his most fruitful yet. It was there that he wrote his most important theoretical tracts, there that he composed *Das Rheingold*, *Die Walküre*, two thirds of *Siegfried*, half of *Tristan*, and the *Wesendonck-Lieder*, and wrote both the final version of the text to *Götterdämmerung* and the first prose sketch for *Parsifal*; and it was there that he first conceived the notion of a theater of his own. The remaining twenty-five years of his life would in large part be devoted to finishing what he had begun during those nine years in Zurich.

Notes

[1] See Joachim Köhler, *Der letzte der Titanen: Richard Wagners Leben und Werk* (Munich: Claassen, 2001), 292–304; see also Bernd Kramer, *"Lasst uns die Schwerter ziehen, damit die Kette bricht . . ": Michael Bakunin, Richard Wagner und andere während der Dresdner Mai-Revolution 1849* (Berlin: Karin Kramer Verlag, 1999), especially 59–70.

[2] Gustav Adolph Kietz, *Richard Wagner in den Jahren 1842–1849 und 1873–1875*, ed. Marie Kietz (Dresden: Carl Reissner, 1905), 94. For Minna's side of the story, see Eliza Wille, *Erinnerungen an Richard Wagner: Mit 15 Briefen Richard Wagners* (Zurich: Atlantis Musikbuch-Verlag, 1982), 30.

[3] Wagner, *Die Kunst und die Revolution*, in *Sämtliche Schriften und Dichtungen*, 6th ed. (Leipzig: Breitkopf & Härtel, [1911]), 3:8–41; here, 29–30. Since Wagner made certain alterations to his Zurich writings when editing them in later life (most notably to *Opera and Drama*), I have always consulted the first editions here when referring to the texts written during his Swiss exile. However, for consistency's sake, the page references of quotations are given, wherever possible, as in the sixth edition of his *Sämtliche Schriften und Dichtungen*, which is today still the edition most commonly available, and the standard reference edition.

[4] See Wagner's letter to Feuerbach of 3 December 1851, in *SB* 4:205–6.

[5] Emil Ermatinger, *Gottfried Kellers Briefe und Tagebücher, 1830–1861* (Stuttgart and Berlin: Cotta, 1916), 184.

[6] Wagner, *Das Kunstwerk der Zukunft*, in *Sämtliche Schriften und Dichtungen* 3:42–177; here, 150.

[7] Several letters from Liszt to Jessie are given in La Mara, ed., *Franz Liszts Briefe*, vol. 2: *Von Rom bis an's Ende* (Leipzig: Breitkopf & Härtel, 1893).

[8] Hans von Bülow, *Briefe*, vol. 4, ed. Marie von Bülow (Leipzig: Breitkopf & Härtel, 1900), 322.

[9] On MGB CD 6156.

[10] See, for example, Warren Darcy, "Creatio ex nihilo: The Genesis, Structure, and Meaning of the 'Rheingold' Prelude," in *19th-Century Music* 13, no. 2 (Autumn 1989): 79–100; here, 82.

[11] Quoted in Martin Gregor-Dellin, *Richard Wagner: Sein Leben. Sein Werk. Sein Jahrhundert* (Munich and Zurich: Piper, 1980), 304.

[12] Stewart Spencer, Review of *Wagner: Race and Revolution*, by Paul Lawrence Rose, in *Wagner* 16, no. 1 (January 1995): 46–48; here, 47.

[13] See Ulrich Drüner, *Schöpfer und Zerstörer: Richard Wagner als Künstler* (Cologne: Böhlau, 2003), 148.

[14] Such as J. C. Lobe; see Drüner, *Schöpfer und Zerstörer*, 144.

[15] For a brilliant elucidation of the history of Austro-German anti-Semitism after Wagner and its impact upon Adolf Hitler, see Brigitte Hamann, *Hitlers Wien: Lehrjahre eines Diktators* (Munich: Piper, 1996). Similar psychological mechanisms persisted elsewhere until the late twentieth century, as for example in apartheid

South Africa, where, however, the racism involved was not anti-Semitism but was determined by skin color.

[16] See Drüner, *Schöpfer und Zerstörer*, chapter 12.

[17] Richard Strauss, *Betrachtungen und Erinnerungen*, ed. Willi Schuh (Munich/Mainz: Piper/Schott, 1981), 94–97.

[18] Wagner, *Oper und Drama*, in *Sämtliche Schriften und Dichtungen* 3:222–321 and 4:2:229; here, 3:231.

[19] See Curt von Westernhagen, *Richard Wagners Dresdener Bibliothek, 1842–1849* (Wiesbaden: Brockhaus, 1966), 106–7.

[20] See Volker Mertens, "Wagner's Middle Ages," in *Wagner Handbook*, ed. Ulrich Müller and Peter Wapnewski (Cambridge, MA.: Harvard UP, 1992), 233–68; here, 247–48.

[21] Stanley R. Hauer: "Wagner and the 'Völospá,'" in *19th-Century Music* 15, no. 1 (Summer 1991): 52–63; here, 54.

[22] Ludwig Ettmüller, *Der Singerkriec uf Wartburc* (Ilmenau, Germany: Voigt, 1830).

[23] Ludwig Ettmüller, *Sigufrid: Schauspiel in fünf Handlungen* (Zurich: Bürkli, 1870).

[24] See, for example, Martin Gregor-Dellin, *Richard Wagner: Sein Leben. Sein Werk. Sein Jahrhundert*, 876.

[25] See Max Fehr, *Richard Wagners Schweizer Zeit* (Aarau and Leipzig: Sauerländer, 1934), 1:362.

[26] See Hans von Bülow, *Ausgewählte Schriften, 1850–1892*, ed. Marie von Bülow (Leipzig: Breitkopf & Härtel, 1896), 257–61.

[27] For more information on Max Seifriz, see Clytus Gottwald, " 'Herr Seifriz hält mit dem Jahrhundert Schritt': Max Seifriz (1827–1885) — Ein Dirigent der 'Neudeutschen Schule,'" in *Musik in Baden-Württemberg: Jahrbuch 2003* (Stuttgart, Weimar: Metzler-Verlag, 2003), 211–28.

[28] Communication from Evelyn Liepsch of the Goethe and Schiller Archive in Weimar, 9 November 2004.

[29] See Niklaus Meienberg, *Die Welt als Wille und Wahn* (Zurich: Limmat Verlag, 1988).

[30] See Eliza Wille, *Erinnerungen an Richard Wagner*, 30.

[31] See Max Fehr, *Richard Wagners Schweizer Zeit* 1:223.

[32] See Jürg Winkler, *"Ich möchte dir meine Heimat einmal zeigen": Biographisches zu Johanna Spyri, Autorin des "Heidi" und ihren Hirzler Vorfahren* (Hirzel: Jürg Winkler, 1982), esp. 121–28.

[33] See Hermann Schollenberger, *Geschichte des Sängervereins Harmonie Zürich, 1841–1921: Jubiläumsgabe zur Feier des achtzigjährigen Bestandes 12. Februar 1921* (Zurich: Harmonie, 1921), 300.

[34] *ML*, 512. See also Reinhard Wiesend's extensive discussion of the matter in "Die Entstehung des 'Rheingold'-Vorspiels und ihr Mythos" in *Archiv für Musikwissenschaft* 49, no. 2 (1992): 122–45.

[35] See John Deathridge, "Wagner's Sketches for the 'Ring': Some Recent Studies," in *The Musical Times* 118, no. 1611 (May 1977): 383–89; here, 387.

[36] See Hans Erismann, *Das fing ja gut an*, 169–74.

[37] See Chris Walton, "*Iphigenia* Lost and Found: A Newly-Discovered Gluck Arrangement by Richard Wagner," in *Fontes artis musicae* 45, nos. 3–4 (July–December 1998): 227–36.

[38] See Egon Voss, "Der Vergessenheit anheimgefallen: Der Musikdirektor Carl Ludwig Eberle," in *Im Dienst der Quellen zur Musik: Festschrift Gertraut Haberkamp zum 65. Geburtstag*, ed. Paul Mai (Tutzing, Germany: Schneider, 2002), 575–83.

[39] See Max Fehr, *Richard Wagners Schweizer Zeit* 1:275–77.

[40] Robert von Hornstein, *Memoiren*, ed. Ferdinand von Hornstein (Munich: Süddeutsche Monatshefte, 1908), 89–90.

[41] The ticket sales are given in Fehr, *Richard Wagners Schweizer Zeit* 1:326.

[42] Ermatinger, *Gottfried Kellers Briefe und Tagebücher, 1830–1861*, 386.

[43] Ermatinger, *Gottfried Kellers Briefe und Tagebücher, 1830–1861*, 407. Keller's terminology is not incorrect; Wagner's *Ring* is a trilogy with "a preliminary evening," though we use in this book the term "tetralogy," as it is both more concise and no less accurate.

[44] See, for example, *TB* 2:869, entry of 9 January 1882.

[45] See, for example, Fehr, *Richard Wagners Schweizer Zeit* 2:46–48.

[46] See Fehr, *Richard Wagners Schweizer Zeit* 2:54–55.

[47] See László Eösze, "Neue Aspekte eines Künstlerbundes" in *Studia Musicologica Academiae Scientiarum Hungaricae* 28 (1986): 195–200.

[48] In *Mein Leben* he gives the sum as Fr. 800; see 558 there.

[49] See Eva Rieger, *Minna und Richard Wagner: Stationen einer Liebe* (Düsseldorf and Zurich: Artemis & Winkler, 2003), 269–70.

[50] See Max Fehr, *Richard Wagners Schweizer Zeit* 1:225.

[51] For details on the history of these various bands — whose names are listed so variously that it is not always easy to know who played what, when, or with whom — see Roger Huber, *Im Reich der Töne erblüht das Schöne: Geschichte/Chronik der Stadtmusik Zürich von 1846 bis 1996; Jubiläumsbuch "150 Jahre Stadtmusik Zürich"* (Zurich: Stadtmusik Zürich, 1996); and Zimmermann, *Richard Wagner in Zürich: Materialien zu Aufenthalt und Wirken*, vol. 2, in particular 57–58. The "Harmoniemusik-Gesellschaft," formerly under the direction of the violinist Heinrich Honegger, was subsumed in 1854 into Bär's ensemble, which was variously called the "Bärsche-Musik" or the "Schiffländemusik." Philipp Fries, on the other hand, was the director of the "Dilettanten-Musikgesellschaft Harmonie."

3: Weathering Storms

> This Switzerland, with its nature, its air, makes the most miserable man healthy and full of the joys of life — I would willingly grant it to everyone I love.
>
> Wagner to Theodor Uhlig, 9 August 1849

WAGNER'S LETTERS AND AUTOBIOGRAPHIES offer us manifold examples of his love for nature. This love was never more ardently expressed than in his correspondence of the years 1849–50, immediately after his removal to Switzerland. They are all but overflowing with praise for the country, its nature, its air, its everything natural. As always with Wagner's own comments, of course, we must tread warily. The "healthiness" of Switzerland, for one, was a useful stick with which to beat unhealthy Paris, the scene of so many of his disappointments.[1] And when Wagner exclaimed "I am utterly homesick for Switzerland. Ah! Nature!" in a letter to his wife from Bordeaux on 17 March 1850, he was at the time actually contemplating an elopement to the Orient with Jessie Laussot (*SB* 3:306).

The best-known examples of nature inspiring Wagner's creative imagination are also those whose veracity must be doubted the most. There is the story of the storms he weathered on his sea voyage from Riga to London in 1839, of how his ship had to find shelter from the elements in the Norwegian fjords, and of how this provided not just the "poetic-musical color" for his future opera *Der fliegende Holländer* but also "the theme of the sailors' song" in it (*ML*, 172). While it is perfectly possible that his voyage might have influenced his depiction of the sea in the opera, we also now know that its Norwegian setting was an afterthought, presumably added in the hope that an "autobiographical" element to the plot would stimulate public interest in both him and his work. In the specific period with which we concern ourselves here, there is the equally famous moment of inspiration, in April 1857, when *Parsifal* was supposedly conceived:

> Now fair spring weather also arrived: on Good Friday I awoke for the first time in this house [the *Asyl*] to the full light of the sun: the garden had turned green, the birds were singing, and at last I could sit on the balcony of the little house, and enjoy the long-desired silence, full of promise . . . now the ideal form [of *Parsifal*] came to me in an overpowering manner, and with the thought of Good Friday as my starting point, I quickly conceived a whole drama, and in a few brush strokes sketched it immediately, in three acts. (*ML*, 561)

But as is also known today, Good Friday in 1857 fell on 10 April, more than two weeks before the Wagners moved into their new house. It has generously been postulated that Wagner must have visited the house some two weeks before moving in, and for some reason stayed overnight from the 9th to the 10th,[2] which would then allow for the veracity of the story. But the far simpler explanation, of course, is that he was lying in order to connect once more the events of his own biography with the content of his artworks. And this is more or less what he admitted to Cosima over twenty years later, on 22 April 1879:

> Richard pondered today the impression that inspired him to the "Good Friday Magic"; he laughs, and "really it is all far-fetched, just like my love affairs, for it wasn't a Good Friday, nothing, just a pleasant mood in nature of which I thought: This is how it ought to be on Good Friday." (*TB* 2:335)

There is another example of nature inspiring him during his months in the *Asyl*, though in this case it sounds more plausible, precisely because it is quite unspectacular: Wagner's claim in *Mein Leben* that it was his regular walks in the Sihl Forest, just a couple of miles from his new home, that provided him with the inspiration for the "forest murmurs" in *Siegfried*:

> In the fresh summer afternoon, I directed my daily walks to the quiet Sihl Forest, in whose woodland environment I listened often and attentively to the song of the woodbirds. I was thereby astonished to become acquainted with completely new tunes from singers whom I never saw, and whose names were even more unknown to me. What I brought home of their melodies I imitated in my art in the forest scene of *Siegfried*. (*ML*, 565)

We must naturally beware of letting Wagner's often casual handling of the truth lead us to discount all relationships between his work and his experiences of the natural world. In this case, some commentators have even found plausible, precise ornithological connections between Wagner's music and his environs.[3] In general, his preference is far more for half-truths than for downright lies, and, as intimated above, his extant correspondence indeed leaves us with no doubt as to how important to him his experiences of the Swiss countryside were. It is also a documented fact that Wagner's most extensive forays into nature took place during his years in Zurich. Since the late eighteenth century, the Swiss Alps had become increasingly popular with writers and painters, and in the mid-nineteenth century this led to the development of a thriving business. Large hotels began to spring up around the country in order to cater for the foreign guests who came to wander in the footsteps of Goethe, Shelley, and others. By the time of Mark Twain's Swiss sojourn, no self-respecting tourist could possibly visit Central Switzerland without sampling the delights of a sunrise from the top of the Rigi mountain.

Of all the places that Wagner visited in Switzerland, the Rigi is probably the one that he found most appealing, and to which he would later come back, again and again. Indeed, when he returned to Switzerland from Munich in the 1860s, he probably chose his house at Tribschen in part because he could see the Rigi from its windows. It was the sunrise over the Rigi that remained fused in his mind with the memory of his son's birth, in 1869, and it was this to which the original title of his *Siegfried-Idyll* referred (*Tribschener Idyll mit Fidi-Vogelgesang und Orange-Sonnenaufgang* [Tribschen Idyll with Fidi Birdsong and Orange Sunrise], "Fidi" being the Wagners' pet name for their son Siegfried).

Wagner made his first-ever visit to the Rigi in late August 1850, at the time of the world première of *Lohengrin* under Liszt in Weimar. Unable to attend himself, he at some point decided to spend the evening on the Rigi instead, just he and Minna alone (*SB* 3:383), rather than back in Zurich where he would, presumably, have had to deal with the commiserations of his friends for being so far from his opera. A gift of 100 thalers from the Grand Duke of Weimar, sent via Liszt, made the jaunt possible. Wagner and Minna accordingly left for the Rigi on 26 August, reached the summit on the twenty-seventh, spent one night on the mountain, but then decided to descend instead to Lucerne, where they spent the evening of the première in a Gasthof appropriately named "Zum Schwan" (The Swan), with Wagner noting the hour when the performance was due to start, and waiting until the moment when he was sure it was over — though in fact he grossly undercalculated (*ML*, 465). They returned to Zurich the next day. Wagner uses this episode in *Mein Leben* in order to cast Minna in a poor light, both physically and emotionally. Climbing the Rigi made what he termed her "heart condition" apparent for the first time, he says; and he goes on to complain of how she had no real understanding of how he felt while he sat in their hotel and watched the hours of his *Lohengrin* tick by in silence. One can hardly blame her, however, for a disinclination to spend an evening brooding mournfully with him when they were supposed to be enjoying a little holiday together — their first since they had patched things up after the Jessie Laussot episode.

This was merely the first of many trips that Wagner made into the mountains. As mentioned in chapter 2 above, it was just under a year later, in early July 1851, that he embarked on an extensive walking tour with Theodor Uhlig. They wandered through Appenzell and over the Säntis before returning to Zurich via the Toggenburg. Just a few days later, they were off again, spending the first week of August wandering in the footsteps of William Tell in central Switzerland. Wagner's longest walking holiday took place the following year, from early July to early August 1852, when he walked from Lake Lucerne to the Bernese Oberland, along the Gries Glacier, to Domodossola, then to the Lago Maggiore. He was joined in Bellinzona by his wife, Herwegh, François Wille, and one Johannes

Eichelberger. Together they took the short boat trip to the Borromeo Islands (which half a century later would attract the attention of numerous literati, from Rainer Maria Rilke to Graf Harry Kessler[4]) before they all parted company, with Wagner and Minna returning to Zurich by the highly circuitous route of the Simplon Pass, Martigny, Chamonix, and Geneva.

Wagner also took a great liking to Brunnen on Lake Lucerne — "mein alter Lieblingsort" ("my favorite place of old"; *ML*, 550) — where he would stay at the "Golden Eagle" Hotel of Xaver auf der Maur. Auf der Maur had in fact been a colonel on the losing side of the *Sonderbund* War, but he seems not to have objected to his guest's apparently liberal/ revolutionary tendencies. And when Wagner visited Brunnen with Liszt and Herwegh in July 1853, the three of them took the short boat trip across the lake to the Rütli Meadow, the semi-mythical founding spot of the Swiss Confederation in 1291, where Liszt and Wagner — already on first name terms — granted Herwegh the same privilege by drinking "Brüderschaft" at the springs found there (literally "brotherhood," though it refers specifically to the peculiarly German tradition of moving from the formal mode of address to the informal by means of a toast, usually with alcohol; thereafter, the parties involved call each other "du," not "Sie," and use their first names). A week after that, Wagner and Herwegh set out for the Engadine, traveling via Coire. The Engadine plateau lies at some two thousand meters above sea level. Its ambience is unique in Switzerland, and its landscape is remarkably bare, a fact that obviously made a deep impression on Wagner, for he remarks on it in *Mein Leben* (510). From here, they went on the Rosegg Glacier, of which Wagner later wrote of "the sanctity of its emptiness ['Heiligkeit der Öde'] and the almost violently soothing calm that the extinction of vegetation brings forth from the pulsating life of the human organism" (*ML*, 510). This was Wagner's last walking tour along a glacier. Indeed, his subsequent forays into the Alps were much less ambitious.

To what extent Wagner's nature music in the *Ring* might have been influenced, directly or indirectly, by his experiences of the Swiss Alps we cannot determine with precision. There are, of course, numerous examples of the Swiss landscape and its meteorological aspects being depicted in music, though the relationship is usually highly tenuous unless the composer deigns to imitate an alphorn or a herd of cowbells. Mountains and lakes are for the musical tourist largely interchangeable. If, for example, those idyllic works by Johannes Brahms written by the idyllic Lake of Thun had been written near the idyllic Lakes of Starnberg or Murnau in Bavaria, or in equally idyllic lake districts elsewhere, then the literature on the composer would, no doubt, still reflect at length on how the composer had found inspiration in a specific landscape. We would be more justified in claiming that the finest representations of Switzerland in music are in fact

Figure 5. The Rosegg Glacier (Wagner's "sanctity of emptiness"). Mid-nineteenth-century print. Used by permission of the Zentralbibliothek Zürich.

to be found in Wagner's music dramas of the 1850s, not least because almost his sole impressions of landscape and weather in these years were gained in and around the Alps — his only forays further than this were to Paris, to northern Italy just beyond the Alps and, once, for four months, to London (if only his *Ring* were full of stage smog, one could argue strongly for an English influence too). The notion is appealing that there might be direct parallels between, say, the storm at the opening of the *Walküre* and the extremes of nature that Wagner witnessed in the Alps, or between the "Heiligkeit der Öde" of the Rosegg Glacier and the "Selige Öde" ("blessed emptiness," thus Siegfried) of Brünnhilde's rock. And, as the present writer can testify, the parallels appear even more appealing when one has actually seen the vast emptiness of an Alpine glacier or experienced at first hand the fury of the weather in the Swiss mountains — be it from the midst of the tempest itself, or from a near vantage point in a lakeside town such as Zurich, with the Glarner Alps looming in the distance. An Alpine tempest has something unutterably primeval about it when compared to a storm in a big city such as Dresden (or Paris, or London). One might then deduce therefrom that the scenes of nature in the *Ring* in particular — which are indubitably elemental in their impact — are hardly the inventions of a city-bound mind, and must thus betray the direct influence of the Alpine countryside and climate. But this would also be to suppose that the imagination of a fine composer is bound wholly by his own physical space, and there is ample proof in the history of music that this is rarely the case. And a counter-argument could also point to the irony that the Rhine, so powerfully depicted in Wagner's *Ring*, had been most often experienced by the composer as the narrow river that runs through Coire, along the valley floor to Lake Constance, and thence, via the Rhine Falls of Schaffhausen, to Basel on the German border (in fact, if the prelude to the *Rheingold* depicts the "birth" of the Rhine along with everything else, then one could argue pedantically that the tetralogy itself begins in the Swiss Alps, since the source of the river lies there). The Rhine had become a particular focal point of German nationalist feeling since the French announced their own claims to it in 1840, but this most German of mighty rivers, placed center-stage in the most Germanic of stage works, was in fact, in the experience of its composer, a Swiss river of modest proportions. Wagner's imagination was thus — as if one did not know it already — more than capable of conjuring up nature in music when he wished it, without need of direct reference to the real world.

Nevertheless, one event of nature that we know Wagner to have observed does not feature in either his autobiographies or his extant correspondence, but it might have exerted a quite specific influence on his notions of operatic staging. The only record of this comes from Natalie, to whom either Minna or Wagner, or both, must have reported it just a day or so after its occurrence. Natalie wrote of it in a letter to Wagner's friend Gustav Kietz, who then quoted her in a brief article published in the *Richard Wagner-Jahrbuch* of 1907. It pertains to Wagner's first ascent of the Rigi, at the time of the *Lohengrin* première in late August 1850. Kietz/Natalie wrote about the trip as follows:

> After climbing up [the mountain], Wagner walked to the outermost edge of Rigi-Kulm, while Minna went into the house to order dinner. When she came out again and looked up at the sky, she saw Wagner's image quite clearly in it as if in a mirror, and in her surprise she called to him: "Richard, move your arms!," and every one of his movements was mirrored, too, in the sky again. Then Minna went up to his side and both of them made movements, happily like children, enjoying their heavenly mirror image as long as this atmospheric reflection lasted (known popularly as the "Rigi ghost," as they then found out).[5]

This "Rigigespenst" (Rigi ghost) is well documented, and is an atmospheric effect that is not confined to the Rigi but has apparently been observed on other mountains when the sun is low and there is low-lying mist.[6] It has, in fact, been most often referred to as the "Brockengespenst" (Brocken ghost), for it is on the Brocken mountain in the Harz Forest in Wagner's native Saxony that the effect seems most often to have been

Figure 6. Rigi-Kulm and its "ghost"; nineteenth-century postcard. From private collection.

observed — probably not only because this is the highest mountain in the Harz, but also because mists descend upon it for some nine months throughout the year. The Brocken accordingly entered folklore as a meeting place of demons and witches and was immortalized as the "Blocksberg" by Goethe in his *Faust*. Given Wagner's love of Goethe, and the fact that he visited the Harz when a youth, it is likely that he had heard of the phenomenon well before his ascent of the Rigi: a quarter of a century later, as Cosima recorded in her diary, he apparently even dreamed of being in the Harz and of seeing the Brocken — though there was no mention then of the "Gespenst" (*TB* 1:942). The phenomenon itself is the same, whether on the Brocken or the Rigi, and the report of Kietz and Natalie corresponds to all the usual accounts: one observes one's shadow projected massively onto a bank of mist or cloud. The shadow is usually ringed by a rainbow-like "halo" ("Glorie" is the word used by most writers in German), and this was featured on postcard depictions of the Rigi ghost from the later nineteenth century. Furthermore, when one looks at artists' impressions and photographs of both the "Rigi" and "Brocken" ghosts, it appears as if the figures are walking into the air, enveloped in a rainbow.

There are further accounts of the Rigi ghost that are roughly contemporary with Wagner's trip up the mountain. In G. Kemmler's *Liederklänge vom Rigi* of 1855, a poem entitled "Nebelbild" (Picture in the Mist) gives instructions in rhyme as how to experience the "Ghost":

> . . .Wann der Morgen träuft von Thau,
> Wandle durch des Berges Au,
> Kehr' der Sonne stets den Rücken,
> Darfst nur auf den Nebel blicken,
> Der am Bergesabhang steigt.
> Da, o Wunderanblick, zeigt
> Sich dein Bild auf Nebelgrunde,
> Schatten zwar, doch eine bunte
> Glorie kränzt es rings mit Licht . . .

> [. . . When the morning drips with dew,
> Wander through the mountain pastures,
> Keep your back turned to the sun,
> You may only look at the mist
> That rises at the mountain slope.
> There, o marvelous sight, is shown
> Your picture on the mist,
> A shadow to be sure, but a colorful
> Halo encircles it with light . . .]

Gottfried Keller, too, mentions the Rigi ghost in his narrative poem *Der Apotheker von Chamounix* (The Apothecary of Chamounix) — here it is a mountain goat whose "reflection" tricks a hunter into shooting, and he ends up killing his girl instead (this incident is, incidentally, not wholly unlike the ending of Weber's *Freischütz*, though there is no *Rigigespenst* there). Many years later, Wagner's son-in-law Houston Stewart Chamberlain would also relate in a letter to Gerhart Hauptmann how he had in his youth observed a "Brockengespenst" with a "fourfold halo" on the Monte Generoso in Italian Switzerland.[7]

The incident of the Rigi ghost of 1850 was, to our knowledge, the first time that Wagner had experienced such an optical illusion in nature. It is noteworthy that the stage directions for the close of *Das Rheingold*, written in its final form two years later, bear no small resemblance to the usual descriptions of the Rigi ghost:

> Froh has disappeared, too, in the mists. Suddenly, the clouds part: Donner and Froh become visible: at their feet, a rainbow bridge stretches out, brilliantly lit, over the valley to the castle that now, lit by the evening sun, is resplendent in the greatest brilliance.[8]

A bank of cloud and mist; a rainbow emerging from it in the evening sun; and the gods walking across the valley on that same rainbow: the similarities with reports of the Rigi ghost are undeniable.

One does not need to experience the Rigi ghost, however, to see Alpine objects as if suspended in the clouds. For even if one climbs the smaller mountains in Switzerland, the clouds often descend low enough for the wanderer to see before him nothing but a sea of white, with the summits of the Alps lying as if islands in its midst. In summer, when much of the snow has melted, those mountaintops can assume in the evening sun a bright, orange hue that makes them appear to be edifices of brick and stone, built by giants in the clouds. Such effects are common enough that Wagner must have experienced them several times on his wanderings, and the similarity of the effect to his description of Valhalla in the evening sun at the close of *Rheingold* is just as striking.

While we are probably justified in postulating a causal relationship between Wagner's experience of the Rigi ghost and his stage directions for the *Rheingold*, there is another case in which the "ghost" might have had a direct influence on the staging of one of his operas: *Der fliegende Holländer*, the first opera of his own that Wagner was able to put on in Zurich, in April/May 1852 (just six months after writing the prose sketch for the *Rheingold*). The original stage directions for the close of the opera state: "In the glowing red of the rising sun, we see over the wreck of the ship the transfigured shapes of Senta and the Holländer, embracing each other, rising out of the sea and floating upwards."[9] This was from the start intended to have religious connotations, of course, and the commentators of the early productions themselves used the vocabulary of Christ's ascension into heaven in order to describe the effect — "Himmelfahrt" and "Ascension" [*sic*], for example;[10] the same commentators mention that the lovers rose up surrounded by a flurry of clouds. In 1860, Wagner brought out a revised version of the opera, in which the close is now described thus:

> In the background, a cliff rises slowly out of the water, with the wreck of the ship on it; we see on it the Holländer, kneeling before Senta, both of them in transfigured form. A brilliant halo ["eine blendende Glorie"] lights the group in the background; Senta lifts up the Holländer, presses him to her bosom, and points with one hand, as with her glances, toward heaven. The cliff, which gently but constantly continues to rise, takes on

> imperceptibly the form of a cloud. At the last three bars, the curtain closes quickly.[11]

To the usual clouds is thus now added a brilliant halo; and again, there is a clear, if superficial, similarity to the usual descriptions of the Rigi ghost. We must acknowledge, however, that to add a "halo" is merely to realize more fully the religious connotations of the ascension of Senta and her Dutchman, for there are hosts of iconographical depictions of Christ's ascension in which he is completely enveloped in just such a halo, and Wagner will not have been unaware of them. And had he ever taken the trouble to visit the Swiss town of Beromünster on Ascension Day, he would even have been able to witness an old tradition — still continued today — of a church service that ends with a three-foot-high figure of Christ, placed in a circular "halo" lit by candles all around, being hoisted on a rope into the roof of the church.

As it happens, however, the *Allgemeine Theater Chronik* wrote of the Zurich production in 1852: "We saw in the final act the Holländer's ship with man and mouse sink before our eyes on stage and the Holländer and Senta float upwards to heaven in a halo ['Glorie'] at the same moment."[12] At the risk of indulging in philological hairsplitting, we are surely not wholly unjustified in suggesting that the stage picture of Senta's ascension in Zurich was perhaps already what Wagner then described in print eight years later. Since the Zurich production was naturally in greater chronological proximity to Wagner's experience of the Rigi ghost, this could in turn suggest that this had in some way altered his scenic conception of the close of the opera. We know from his correspondence to Uhlig and others at the time of the Zurich production that Wagner made some minor alterations to the end of the overture and to the instrumentation of the opera, but in a letter to Wilhelm Fischer of 2 January 1853, he also confirms that he had changed the ending of the last act for the Zurich run — though precisely how is not quite clear (*SB* 5:151–52). Sadly, no stage directions for Zurich have survived, nor have Ludwig Caësmann's set designs; but as we saw in chapter 2, we do know that Wagner paid particular attention to this aspect of the production, giving precise instructions and ensuring that they were carried out.

To argue that Wagner's experiences on the Rigi might have found direct expression in the *Rheingold* and in his *Holländer* is not without interest, but we also run the risk here of failing to see the wood for the trees. For what is of greater import is that the Rigi ghost, together with the other optical effects created by nature in the Alps that Wagner will have observed, might have played a major role in prompting the composer to expand the bounds of what was considered technically possible in the theaters of the day. If nature can use light and mist to create such theatrical illusions, he might have thought, so then must it be possible to recreate them in the theater itself.

Wagner was fully aware that the latest advances in technology were already making stage effects possible that would have been unthinkable just a generation before. The mid-nineteenth century saw the development of many new artificial optical effects intended to astonish the paying public. The most "low-tech" of these, and the most widespread, was the simple "panorama," beloved in the late eighteenth and well into the nineteenth centuries, in which spectators would be "enclosed" within a circular, 360° painting in a specially designed room that would give one the impression of actually being on a mountain top or high up in a city, with an all-round view. Later developments even provided for "moving panoramas," in which painted screens would be unrolled to convey to the spectators the impression of moving (Anno Mungen has drawn attention to the existence of a "virtual Rhine journey" of this type that was shown in Berlin in 1835, over thirty years before Wagner composed Siegfried's Rhine Journey in the opening scenes of *Götterdämmerung*).[13] Wagner will have been well familiar with the concept of the panorama (he actually referred to it several years later in his correspondence with King Ludwig[14]), but his walking tours in Switzerland in the early 1850s naturally provided him with the "real" thing instead.

In the first half of the nineteenth century technical progress in stage effects was achieved above all in Paris. It was there in 1822 that the "diorama" was first put on show by its creator Jacques Daguerre (the inventor of photography who was also, *nota bene*, a set designer). Huge paintings

Figure 7. A "Great Theater of Apes" from Paris recreates the Fall of Constantinople in Zurich, July 1851. From the *Tagblatt der Stadt Zürich*, 10 July 1851.

on partly transparent canvas were shown in darkened rooms and then lit from behind in a manner so as to give the impression of a sunrise or sunset, with incidental noises added from behind in order to impart *couleur locale* to the picture, be it an Alpine scene or the inside of a cathedral. We do not know for sure if Wagner visited a diorama in Paris, but we can be certain that he will have known precisely what they were. Nor was Zurich isolated from such theatrical innovations. It was a regular stopping-off point for traveling shows of all kinds, of which several came through Zurich in 1850 and 1851 alone — thus in the months immediately preceding Wagner's intensive work on the *Ring* libretto. On 13 September 1850, the *Tagblatt der Stadt Zürich* advertised the public exhibition of a "Sun microscope with a magnification of 1.5 million" at the Meise guild house (one of Wagner's regular haunts); throughout July 1851, it proclaimed the presence in Zurich of a "great theater of apes [*Affen-Theater*] from Paris," at which a number of performing apes and dogs gave a dramatic reconstruction of the Fall of Constantinople (which makes Wagner's notions of Siegfried's friendly bear, or of Brünnhilde's horse Grane leaping with her onto Siegfried's funeral pyre, seem positively modest in scope). Then, of more direct interest to us, on 25 August 1851 the *Tagblatt* announced: "The experimental physicist Heinz will today produce his dissolving views, mist pictures [*Nebelbilder*], and chromatrope in the hall of the Münsterhof Café"; this would thus seem to have been a kind of diorama show.[15] We do not know if Wagner attended; but we do know that he was in Zurich in late August 1851, and he will hardly have been unaware of this, or of other such touring oddities that visited the city to astound and entertain. There is documentary evidence of his having attended at least one of these traveling shows, for he bought his parrot Jacquot at one of them — namely from "Kreutzberg's great Menagerie" in October 1853[16] — and we can probably assume that this was not an isolated occurrence, but that he took the trouble to sample what other itinerant troupes had to offer.

The most famous optical effect in the theater of Wagner's day was undoubtedly the sunrise featured in the third act of Meyerbeer's *Le Prophète*. Wagner himself attended a performance of the opera when he was in Paris in February 1850, just six months before his ascent of the Rigi (*SB* 3:239). The opera had caused astonishment upon its world première on 16 April 1849 on account of its sunrise, which was the first-ever use of electric light at the Opéra (over two decades before Edison's invention of the filament bulb). There had been theatrical sunrises before, but none had hitherto achieved such a level of verisimilitude and its concomitant public sensation.[17] It is thus probably no coincidence that Wagner's draft libretto for *Wieland der Schmied*, written in early 1850 and originally intended for Paris, ends with the morning sun filling the stage as Wieland flies off, with his metal wings glittering in the early light.

It is tempting to postulate on the one hand that Wagner wished to recreate in the theater the spectacularly theatrical effects that he had observed in nature, and on the other hand that his experiences of the Paris Opéra and of traveling shows in Zurich might have served to convince him either that such effects were truly possible, or at least that the rate of technological progress was such that they soon would be. After all, if he was prepared to write for an orchestra that included six harps at a time when he barely possessed the means to hire a copyist, why should he not have taken the impossible into the realm of staging itself? He was to be disappointed, of course, when he finally came to stage his *Ring des Nibelungen* a quarter of a century later. Cosima's diary records his painful struggles with the machinery at the first Bayreuth festival: ". . . the rainbow bridge doesn't work (so far), and the steam fails . . ." (1:995). Today, matters are quite different. Our demands are far greater, not least thanks to our being spoiled by the visual splendor of cinematic tales inspired in part by Wagner's own — *Star Wars* and *The Lord of the Rings* being the two most obvious, though the *Superman* and *X-Men* trilogies also offer indestructible heroes of the Siegfried ilk. However unjustly, we today expect to enjoy spectacles of similar magnificence, live, in the theater. And while Brünnhilde's horse still proves unwilling or unable to bend to man's will in matters of self-immolation, Nature herself otherwise seems indeed willing to obey the instructions of our stage directors. Rhinemaidens swim, Valkyries fly, rainbow bridges lead the gods into Valhalla, views are dissolved and assembled, and worlds are created and destroyed before our eyes. It may have taken many decades after his death, but the Musician of the Future's obvious faith in the putative "stagings of the future" has at last been justified after all.

Notes

[1] See, for example, Wagner's letter of 1 December 1849 to his sister Kläre (*SB* 3:169).

[2] See the note by the editor (Martin Gregor-Dellin) on 817–18 of Wagner's *Mein Leben*.

[3] See, for example, Graham G. Hunt, "Wagner's Forest Bird(s): The Genesis of the Maternal Spirit in Act Two of Siegfried," in *Wagner* 25, no. 1 (April 2004): 19–47.

[4] See Walton, *Othmar Schoeck und seine Zeitgenossen* (Winterthur: Amadeus, 2002), 81.

[5] Gustav Kietz, "Das 'Rigigespenst,'" in *Richard Wagner-Jahrbuch*, vol. 2, ed. Ludwig Frankenstein (Berlin: Hermann Paetel, 1907), 431–32; here, 431.

[6] The *Tages-Anzeiger der Stadt Zürich* of 11 December 2004 mentioned an occurrence of the phenomenon on the Üetliberg on the day before, complete with rainbow rings. The author (one "jr") remarked: "The phenomenon is called the 'Brockengespenst.' Or is it the Flying Dutchman?"

[7] Letter to Gerhart Hauptmann from Bayreuth, 16 March 1918. See Houston Stewart Chamberlain, *Briefe, 1882–1924 und Briefwechsel mit Kaiser Wilhelm II*, vol. 2, ed. Paul Petzsch (Munich: Bruckmann, 1928), 53.

[8] Wagner, *Sämtliche Schriften und Dichtungen* (Leipzig: Breitkopf & Härtel, [1911]), 5:199–268; here, 266.

[9] See Richard Wagner, *Sämtliche Werke*, vol. 24, ed. Egon Voss, *Dokumente und Texte zu "Der fliegende Holländer"* (Mainz: Schott, 2004), 250.

[10] See the reviews of the early Dresden and Berlin productions in the *Berlinische Nachrichten für Staats- und Gelehrtensachen* and the *Allgemeine Wiener Musik-Zeitung* respectively, in Helmut Kirchmeyer, *Situationsgeschichte der Musikkritik und des musikalischen Pressewesens in Deutschland, dargestellt vom Ausgange des 18. bis zum Beginn des 20. Jahrhunderts*, part 4, vol. 2, "Dokumente, 1842–1845" (Regensburg: Bosse, 1967), columns 337 and 318.

[11] See Richard Wagner, *Sämtliche Werke* 24:250.

[12] *Allgemeine Theater Chronik*, 26 April 1852, reproduced in Helmut Kirchmeyer, *Situationsgeschichte der Musikkritik*, part 4: "Das zeitgenössische Wagnerbild," vol. 6, part 2: "Dokumente 1852 V — 1852 XII" (Regensburg: Gustav Bosse, 1984), columns 580–82.

[13] See Anno Mungen, "Entering the Musical Picture: Richard Wagner and Nineteenth-Century Multimedia Entertainments," in *Music in Art* 26, nos. 1–2 (2001): 123–29 for an extensive consideration of the panaroma, the diorama, and other forms of entertainment and their impact upon Wagner's work. The details on these inventions given here are taken largely from Mungen.

[14] See his letter of 17 May 1881 to the king, in Richard Wagner, *König Ludwig II and Richard Wagner, Briefwechsel*, ed. Otto Strobel (Karlsruhe: Braun, 1936), 3:210.

[15] The *Tagblatt*, oddly, uses the English words "dissolving views" to describe the show, then adds the German translation "zerfliessende Ansichten."

[16] See Werner G. Zimmermann, *Richard Wagner in Zürich: Materialien zu Aufenthalt und Wirken*, vol. 1 (Zurich: Hug, 1986), 72.

[17] For a precise description of how Meyerbeer and his designers achieved the sunrise, see Oswald Georg Bauer, "Zur Genese des Begriffes 'Effekt,'" in *"Schlagen Sie die Kraft der Reflexion nicht zu gering an,"* ed. Klaus Döge, Christa Jost, and Peter Jost (Mainz: Schott, 2002), 151–57; here, 152.

4: The Life Aquatic

From 15 September to 23 November 1851 Wagner undertook an extended "cure" at the Hydrotherapy Institute of Dr. Zacharias Brunner at Albisbrunn, some ten miles due south of Zurich. It was there, as outlined in chapter 2, that the notion of turning his "Siegfried" project into a four-part drama took on concrete form, and it was there, too, that he made the prose sketches of *Das Rheingold* and *Die Walküre*. As has often been pointed out, it is particularly appropriate that he should have conceived his *Rheingold* during a water cure — even more so, when one considers that the springs of the area all flow, albeit indirectly, into the Rhine, which just twenty-five miles to the north forms the border with Germany. Indeed, the very idea of a "festival" of his works as later practiced in Bayreuth has itself been linked to Wagner's fondness for taking the waters at the sanatoriums so beloved of the nineteenth century. As Matthias Theodor Vogt has observed, the "ideologies" of both the sanatorium and the Bayreuth festival provided for a carefully calculated daily regimen of "purification," the one physical, the other aesthetic, in a place of relative isolation where one's concentration would not be diverted (as was the case in the more commercial spas) by the worldly delights of casinos, luxury shopping facilities, and the like. And, as Vogt has also pointed out, the fact that the Festspielhaus was conceived without a proper foyer meant that its audiences were forced out into the fresh air for the long pauses between the acts.[1]

Albisbrunn was not, of course, Wagner's first experience of a spa. To "take the waters" had long been a popular activity for the upper classes throughout Europe, and he had been an eager spa visitor for some time in the hope of gaining relief from his recurring physical ailments. The most lasting of these were erisypelas — which had plagued him since the mid-1830s — and an assortment of bowel problems, ranging from constipation to hemorrhoids to flatulence (in both directions), which first surfaced in his late 20s, and from which he never wholly freed himself. It has even been suggested that he in fact suffered from irritable bowel syndrome[2] — which would allow us to make proper sense of Theodor Kirchner's favorite recollection of Wagner: "The most important thing," he told Kirchner at some point in the mid-1850s, "is that a man has good bowel movements. Everything else isn't so important."[3]

Wagner's first recorded visit to a spa was in the early summer of 1834, in Teplitz, together with Theodor Apel. He wrote to his sister Rosalie that they had visited the baths there "for serious reasons in Theodor's case, though for me it was more for pleasure," although it has been suggested that Wagner in fact went to help cure an early occurrence of his erysipelas.[4] Be that as it may, by his own admission it was during this cure that he sketched out his next opera, *Das Liebesverbot*.[5] In the summer of 1842, and again in 1843, Wagner went back for cures in Teplitz, this time not "for pleasure," but with the clear aim of improving his health. Neither visit brought him lasting relief from his ailments, but they were again profitable in creative terms. In 1842, he made his prose sketch for *Tannhäuser* there, and then during his cure of the following year he began the composition of the music for the same opera. It was during his 1843 cure that he also focused his attention for the first time on German mythology, for he there began to read Jacob Grimm's *Deutsche Mythologie* (German Mythology). By 1845, Wagner had obviously decided that it would be wise to try another spa. On 5 June 1845, he wrote to Karl Gaillard: "At the end of this month I will go to Marienbad in order to mend my awful abdominal complaint" (he uses here, as elsewhere, the word "Unterleib," which is usually translated as "abdomen," but can in fact mean anything from the reproductive organs to the intestines; when Wagner employs the word, it is usually a polite way of referring to his bowels). This cure, like the two in Teplitz, proved also of greater creative than palliative significance, for it was there that he completed the prose sketches of both *Die Meistersinger* and *Lohengrin*.

Apart from bathing at Marienbad and Teplitz, Wagner also on occasion resorted to other uses of water to try and alleviate illness. It was in Teplitz in 1843 that he preempted one of what he would later discover were Albisbrunn's principal therapeutic methods, by simply drinking large quantities of water. But he apparently gave it up very swiftly, for on 14 June he wrote to Minna: "drinking lots of water is no good — yesterday I almost sh — [*sic*] in the bed" (*SB* 2:332).[6] And when he complained of hemorrhoids in a letter to Minna from Hamburg on 17 March 1844, he remarked that he was following the example of a friend by pouring "ice cold water" over himself, and asked Minna to procure a nice "bath pail" for him to indulge in his "holy washings" every morning (*SB* 2:495). The theme of "water" also returns often enough for us not to be too surprised that Wagner should have resorted to the stuff once more, in more radical form, in the second half of 1851, in yet another attempt to mend his health.

He had just finished his extended summer walking tour with Theodor Uhlig, who was a keen adherent of hydrotherapy and had urged him to undergo a full-scale water treatment. Soon after this, Wagner wrote to Uhlig of how he was now reading "Rausse" (one of the main theorists of hydrotherapy) and had embarked upon a diet of much water and milk. His stomach and intestines, he maintained, were already showing signs of improvement (*SB* 4:99). His next letter to Uhlig then announces: "I'm going to the Water Institute . . . I can't bear half measures" (*SB* 4:101); his purpose, as he wrote to Wilhelm Fischer shortly afterwards, was "to wash my abdomen clean, as I have now washed my head clean with my theoretical writings" (*SB* 4:106). So it was off to Albisbrunn, where he found the therapy far more worthy of enthusiasm than the traditional cures he had hitherto undergone. Wagner described the daily regime of Albisbrunn as follows, in a letter to Uhlig of 18 September 1851:

> 1, at half past five in the morning, a wet wrap until 7am; then a cold bath and a walk. 8am breakfast: dry bread and milk or water. 2, immediately thereafter, one enema then another; another short walk; then a cold compress on the abdomen. 3, toward 12 o' clock: wet rub-down; short walk; new compresses. Then lunch in my room with Karl [Ritter] to prevent insubordination. Then an hour of lazing: then a brisk walk of two hours, alone. 4, toward 5pm: another wet rub-down and a short walk. 5, a sitting bath of a quarter hour at 6pm, with a walk afterwards to warm up. New compresses. At 7pm, dinner: dry bread and water. 6, after that: one enema, then another; then a game of whist until after 9pm. Then another new compress, and toward 10pm to bed. (4:270)

Albisbrunn was thus a spa altogether different from the run-of-the-mill, and intentionally so. It had been founded in 1839 by the Winterthur doctor Christoph Zacharias Wilhelm Brunner and proudly proclaimed itself the first of its kind in the whole of Switzerland. It was situated near Hausen in the southwest of the Canton of Zurich and lay at some 645 meters above sea level, affording its guests a view of both Pilatus and Wagner's beloved Rigi. Within just two years of opening its doors, the institute had become so popular that Dr. Brunner was able to build two extra wings. As early as 1840, patients were arriving from as far away as Berlin and England. The *glitterati* of the day followed in the years thereafter, including the painter Alexandre Calame and even Crown Prince Humbert of Italy.[7] So while the daily routine was puritanical, the patients themselves were no local yokels. Albisbrunn was also built close to one of the "sacred" spots of Swiss Protestantism, the site of the Battle of Kappel of 1531, where Huldrych Zwingli fell. The monument that marked the spot was only just over a quarter of an hour by foot from the institute, so presumably featured on Wagner's walks in the vicinity. Whether he felt at all inspired, one reformer by another, remains sheer speculation.

Dr. Brunner's "medical" aim was to expunge excess products from the body by making the patients increase vastly their intake of water. Given his strict regime of baths and the diet of water, water, water, milk, dry bread, fruit, and more water, it surprises us today that Wagner and his fellow patients did not perish altogether at Albisbrunn. Instead, he claimed to feel much better for it. He reported to Uhlig in the letter mentioned above that, for the first weeks of his cure, he had "sweated sulfur," and after that, he assured his reader, "mercury." Whatever he might truly have been excreting through his pores, and regardless of the degree to which autosuggestion played a role in his improved state of health, it was perhaps simply the enforced rest in the country air upon which Albisbrunn insisted that Wagner needed most of all. For Brunner rejected the entertainments often provided at other spas, believing in nothing intellectually more stimulating for his charges than a game of cards.

The cure at Albisbrunn — for whatever reason — seems to have had a more lasting effect than those of Marienbad and Teplitz, as Wagner's digestion seems to have remained untroubling for a while. However, in his letters to Minna from London in 1855, he again complained that: "My abdomen is very out of sorts" (*SB* 7:194). And a year later, he visited yet another hydrotherapy institute, this time near Geneva, where, however, the more flexible regime of its Dr. Vaillant succeeded both in curing him of his erisypelas and in alleviating his bowel problems to such an extent that he could write to Ignaz Heim ecstatically on 13 July 1856 of his "control over orifices of which I had no conception any more" (*SB* 8:114). Just two years later, however, his correspondence with Minna and others confirms that his orifices had wrested back that hard-won control, and his battles with them, which hardly need more detailed description here, continued to the bitter end, so to speak. As late as 1876, he was contemplating yet another stay at Marienbad on account of the problems of his "Unterleib"; when he did take the waters the next year, at Bad Ems, he was still complaining, in a letter to Carl Landgraf of 16 June 1877, of the "sluggishness" of his "Unterleib," bloating, and flatulence.[8]

Wagner's bowels and his muse seem to have existed in a strangely symbiotic relationship; indeed it seems almost as if his creativity was in some measure dependent upon his "control over his orifices" (or lack of it). During a discussion in a first-year undergraduate class on the famous, though probably spurious, "vision" of La Spezia in which Wagner, plagued by dysentery, sank into a half-sleep and supposedly dreamed the opening music of his *Rheingold* (*ML*, 511), one of my wittier students suggested that the notion of constantly rushing water might just as easily have been prompted by the uncontrollable movements of the composer's diarrhetic bowels. While such a notion might at first appear absurd, it is noteworthy that the summer of 1853, when Wagner was by his own admission wrestling with his decision to begin composing the *Ring*, was a time when he also complained of prolonged constipation ("seit mehreren Tagen bin ich verstopft"). In fact, this is almost the only time in his published correspondence when he mentions (in a letter to Minna) suffering from it (*ML*, 509; *SB* 5:390). Just a month later, in La Spezia, his bowels unblocked themselves with a vengeance; and this in his memory became linked with the release of his creative energies into *Das Rheingold*. Nor is this the only example in these years of Wagner discussing his music and his bowels in the same breath. It is an odd fact, but after he had completed *Rheingold*, his intestinal blockage returned. On 9 April 1854, he wrote to his sometime Parisian doctor Karl Lindemann: "[I have] composed Rheingold! This put me in a good mood. Now I am troubled most of all by a congestion of blood in the anus" (*SB* 6:106). Wagner also used the word "verstopfen" ("to be constipated") in a letter to Hans von Bülow, eighteen months later, to refer specifically to the latter's lack of productivity as a composer (*SB* 7:290). The notion of a "birth of the tetralogy out of the low E flat of flatulence" is unappealing, but hardly more absurd than the many myths that Wagner himself spun in and around his life and work. That there is a relationship between creativity and the act of sexual release is no invention of the "new musicology" but has been obvious for at least as long as composers have been portraying the act itself in their music (one of the first, and most graphic examples, of course, being found at the close of Isolde's "Liebestod" in Wagner's own *Tristan*). But for Wagner's musical imagination, the expunging of his other bodily products seems to have been of equally seminal importance.

Wagner's health problems were by no means confined to his erratic bowels. In *Mein Leben*, he also all but admits there is a psychosomatic factor in his repeated bouts of ill health, as, for example, when he describes his experiences during the week of his readings of the *Ring* libretti in the Hotel Baur au Lac in February 1853. His stomach had been plaguing him throughout the winter, and to cap it all, he had now gone hoarse after the first reading. But his doctor, Rahn-Escher, insisted with admirable common sense that canceling the remaining readings would undoubtedly have a far worse effect on Wagner's nerves, and his prescription of rest, quiet, keeping warm, and drinking tea did the trick. The subsequent success of the readings seems to have banished Wagner's ill health, at least for the moment. Nevertheless, such episodes aside, there is little doubt that Wagner was in regular physical pain that had real physical causes, and of a kind that must have brought considerable social embarrassment with it. Indeed, one cannot but marvel at his productivity as writer, composer, conductor, and organizer when one considers the chronic conditions from which he suffered. One can even sympathize with the immensity of his ego when one contemplates the degree of willpower and self-confidence that he must have developed in order to feel able to show himself in public, when his face was blotched with red and the air around him pungent with the flatulent odors of his discomfort.

If there is some causal relationship to be found between Wagner's physical ailments and his music, it is better documented less in the ailments themselves than in his repeated efforts to cure himself of them by means of various sanatoriums. Taking the waters never brought more than temporary relief, of course, neither in their traditional form as at Teplitz and Marienbad, nor even in the more rigorous regime of Albisbrunn, despite its slightly longer-lasting impact. We cannot rule out the possibility that Wagner, all too human, might have been able to convince himself from year to year that the next water cure, or the next, or the next, must surely prove more efficacious than the previous one. But it would be more logical to conclude that what drew him back to spas with such frequency over a period of more than thirty years was rather the creative stimulus that such watering holes obviously afforded him. His fate was, in fact, remarkably similar to that of Amfortas in *Parsifal.* While the parallel between Wagner's own water cures and Amfortas's healing bath is obvious, the real similarity lies in the fact that the waters gave lasting relief to neither of them.

When he came to record his experiences of Albisbrunn in *Mein Leben*, Wagner exercised a little economy with the truth, choosing — perhaps not surprisingly — to omit the details of his colonic irrigation. He does manage, however, a certain degree of self-irony in his descriptions, and minces no words about the fact that the therapy barely helped him, and that he lost a lot of weight there. But he does recall what his letters of the time in any case seem to confirm: the water therapy "had become a new religion for me" (*ML*, 488). Indeed, it was Wagner's evangelizing zeal that had led Karl Ritter to join him there (and he took offense when Karl surreptitiously sampled the delights of the local *confiserie* instead of restricting himself to water, cold milk, and dry bread). He also convinced his fellow Dresden exile, Hermann Müller, to take the Albisbrunn cure. And when he wrote to Liszt from Albisbrunn on 20 November 1851 to explain his new plan for the *Ring* tetralogy, Wagner ended by exclaiming (perhaps only partly in jest) that all the wrongs of politics, diplomacy, and art in society could be traced back to a bad digestive system (*SB* 4:192). He was even serious enough to engage in a bitter debate about the evils of the vine with the likes of Sulzer, whose ample wine cellars he had hitherto sampled without compunction (and would again, after his zeal had abated). We must ponder, of course, whether or not his "exalted" state of mind, induced by his religious fervor for the joys of water, was in fact a necessary preliminary to embarking upon the libretti for the *Ring.* But Wagner was by no means alone in his utopian praise for the power of water, as such ideas were at the time very fashionable. To what extent this was the result of a residual element of Christian symbolism surviving into an ostensibly less superstitious, more "scientific" age is difficult to determine with precision here; but the step from the baptismal "washing away" of sin to the washing away of more easily identifiable ills is an admittedly small one. Just three years before Wagner went to Albisbrunn, the author Henry J. Forrest published his *A Dream of Reform*, in which he postulated a future England cleansed of dirt, grime, crime, and stupidity, all thanks to the widespread use of water. A "Mr. Kindly" (whose name is perhaps intentionally reminiscent of John Bunyan's *Pilgrim's Progress*) explains:

> Water is the great purifier of everything; and to make a race of people healthy and happy, you must not fail to supply that element in profusion, rather than in a niggardly spirit. We have rivers, canals, ponds, baths, both open and under cover, for each sex, for all weathers, and of every description. We have hard and soft water available for each family, and at all times.[9]

We even find similar sentiments in Wagner's letters to King Ludwig of Bavaria, some twenty years later, when he urged the king to order the building of a channel all the way from the mountains in order to provide Munich with fresh drinking water.[10]

The claims made for hydrotherapy at Albisbrunn in the nineteenth century were not quite as far-reaching (or as far-fetched) as those of Henry J. Forrest, but it did recommend itself for patients with everything from migraine to epilepsy, claustrophobia, rheumatism, pneumonia, hemorrhoids, typhus, malaria, addiction to various substances, and even syphilis[11] (one can only hope that they washed their enemas in between patients). The promise of relief from manifold ailments may well have been what prompted the choice of hydrotherapy for Minna when she went on a cure, a week after her discovering the "Morning Confession" that Richard had written to Mathilde Wesendonck in early April 1858. The cure was ostensibly for her "Herzklopfen" (though given their domestic situation, she obviously had more reason than ever to complain of a "palpitating heart"). Wagner had originally contemplated sending her to Dr. Vaillant, but they decided instead on a cure much closer to home, at the institute of one Adolf Erismann at Brestenberg by the lake of Hallwyl, some twenty miles to the west of Zurich. A pamphlet exists that was published by Erismann in 1846 in which he detailed the results of his therapy, and there is one specific case of "Herzklopfen" that he recorded as having cured completely. Just like Brunner at Albisbrunn, Erismann too claimed the ability to heal a myriad of ailments through the power of water, from "monomania syphilitica" to "hysteria" and rheumatism — though his pamphlet does admit that a case of "nymphomania" required a particularly long cure before it was completely "healed," while in a case of "general weakness" as a result of eighteen months [*sic*] of masturbation, the cure was not wholly successful (one wonders how many cold showers the poor fellow was forced to take).[12] We do know that Minna had been taking laudanum regularly, and a letter to her from Wagner of 11 June 1858 suggests that Erismann's hydrotherapy was also intended to cure her of this: "Your body, which has been quite undermined by terrible amounts of opium and medicines, must first renew itself completely" (*SB* 9:298). But even the failure of this water cure did nothing to quell Wagner's belief in the stuff.

Water therapies were not the only medical fads of the age, of course. The man who employed Wagner at the Zurich theater in 1850, for example, Philipp Walburg Kramer, later became a devoted practitioner of another "natural" treatment, namely *Heilmagnetismus* ("healing magnetism," comprising a laying-on of hands and the application of "magnetized water"). This also promised alleviation of everything from typhus to paraplegia and "the English disease" (syphilis once again). But water itself was obviously the element closest to Wagner's heart, bowels, and muse. To be sure, Albisbrunn and its sister institutions promised the easing of symptoms rather than complete healing in every case. Nevertheless, their aims were hardly less utopian than those of Mr. Kindly above, and Wagner would appear to have fallen for hydrotherapy hook, line, and sinker (as it were). Water had already been the conduit for redemption in two of his operas — in the *Holländer*, Senta and the Dutchman at the close rise up out of the sea to ascend into heaven, while in *Lohengrin*, the swan/Gottfried, who redeems the plot at the close, arrives by swimming along the River Scheldt; and in his work-in-progress too, *Siegfrieds Tod/Götterdämmerung*, it is water — the Rhine — that by breaking its banks at the close is able to wash the world clean again. Given the magical, redemptive properties of water in his dramatic oeuvre, there is therefore an odd but undeniable logic in Wagner's having sought redemption from his own woes through the same element, by attending a cure at Albisbrunn; and by the same logic, it is fitting that it should have been there that he made the first draft for his libretto to the *Rheingold*, in which the golden treasure of the deep is revealed in the water that flows out, implicitly, from the bowels of the earth.

Notes

[1] Matthias Theodor Vogt, "Die Geburt des Festspielgedankens aus dem Geist der Bäderkur," in *Welttheater, Mysterienspiel, rituelles Theater "Vom Himmel durch die Welt zur Hölle,"* ed. Peter Csobádi, Gernot Gruber, Jürgen Kühnel, Ulrich Müller, Oswald Panagl, Franz V. Spechtler (Anif/Salzburg: Verlag Ursula Müller-Speiser, 1992), 343–64; here, 343–44.

[2] See Joachim Thiery and Dietrich Seidel, " 'I Feel Only Discontent': Wagner and His Doctors," in *Wagner* 16, no. 1 (January 1995): 3–22; here, 4.

[3] Letter from Kirchner to Friedrich Hegar, Dresden, 11 March 1886, quoted in Harry Joelson-Strohbach, "Theodor Kirchner bei Mathilde Wesendonck," in *Minne, Muse und Mäzen: Otto und Mathilde Wesendonck und ihr Zürcher Künstlerzirkel*, ed. Axel Langer and Chris Walton (Zurich: Museum Rietberg, 2002), 142–59; here, 159.

[4] See his letter to his sister Rosalie of 3 July 1834 (*SB* 1:156), and Vogt, "Die Geburt des Festspielgedankens," 350.

[5] See his *Autobiographische Skizze* of 1842, in *Sämtliche Schriften und Dichtungen* (Leipzig: Breitkopf & Härtel, [1911]), 1:4–19; here, 10.

[6] Wagner writes "gesch-," which is probably best translated as it is here.

[7] Julius Studer, "Albisbrunn: Eine geschichtliche Skizze," in *Neue Zürcher Zeitung*, 31 July 1889, no. 212.

[8] Carl Glasenapp, ed., *Bayreuther Briefe von Richard Wagner (1871–1883)* (Berlin and Leipzig: Schuster & Loeffler, 1907), 272.

[9] Quoted in John Carey, ed., *The Faber Book of Utopias* (London: Faber & Faber, 1999), 238. A near-contemporary, but more immediately practical, use of water to keep a city clean was the London sewer system of Joseph Bazalgette, completed in 1865.

[10] Wagner to King Ludwig, 25 November 1865, in *König Ludwig II and Richard Wagner, Briefwechsel*, ed. Otto Strobel (Karlsruhe: Braun, 1936), 1:225.

[11] See Julius Studer, "Albisbrunn: Eine geschichtliche Skizze," and E. Paravicini, *Die Wasserheil-Anstalt Albisbrunn* (Albisbrunn: Paravicini, 1886), esp. 14–18.

[12] These details of Erismann's successes and failures are listed in Adolf Erismann, *Über den gegenwärtigen Stand der Hydrotherapie: Ein Beitrag zur wissenschaftlichen Begründung des Priessnitz'schen Heilverfahrens. Nebst einem Anhange: Die Ergebnisse des hydrotherapeutischen Heilverfahrens in der Wasserheilanstalt Brestenberg am Hallwylersee* (Baden: J. Zehnder, 1846), 37–40.

5: Publishing in Zurich

When Wagner embarked upon his career as an author of political-cum-aesthetic tracts in Zurich, he was situating himself squarely in a tradition that already existed in his chosen city of refuge. On the last day of 1840, Julius Fröbel, a German-born professor of mineralogy at Zurich University, founded a publishing company by the straightforward name of "Das literarische Comptoir" (The Literary Office). Its purpose was primarily political, and Fröbel was soon publishing books by various renegades from north of the border. First among these was Fröbel's colleague Georg Herwegh — later Wagner's friend — whose *Gedichte eines Lebendigen* (Poems of a Living Man) in 1841 proved an immense success, with some twenty thousand copies sold in just a matter of months. The Comptoir even published Hoffmann von Fallersleben's *Deutsche Lieder aus der Schweiz* (German Songs from Switzerland), which included the first edition of "Deutschland, Deutschland über alles," in 1842. It is not a little ironic that what still serves as the German national anthem — though only its third strophe is sung today — was not just written outside the country, namely on the then English island of Helgoland, but also first published outside it, in Switzerland. The other authors promoted by the Comptoir included Karl Marx, the theologian David Strauss, and Ludwig Feuerbach. But when the German states, understandably peeved, banned its publications in 1845, the Comptoir lost its main market. It went into inevitable liquidation in 1846, just five years after it had begun its activities.[1]

When Wagner arrived in Zurich in 1849, there was thus no obviously political publishing house nearby where he might have considered placing his "revolutionary" writings. His largest theoretical works of his early years of exile were thus all published in Germany: *Art and Revolution* and *The Artwork of the Future* with Wigand of Leipzig, who (like the old Comptoir of Zurich) had a reputation for radical titles; and *Opera and Drama* with Weber, also in Leipzig (though as chance would have it, Weber himself came from Siblingen in northern Switzerland). The far less political *A Communication to My Friends* was then brought out by the music publishers Breitkopf & Härtel, again in Leipzig. Wagner's shorter articles that he considered necessary to put before a larger public were usually given to Franz Brendel of the *Neue Zeitschrift für Musik* (as, for example, "Jewishness in Music" of mid-1850). The fact that Wagner should have chosen to publish in Leipzig, the center of both the music and book trades in Germany, should hardly surprise us. But he soon found it useful to publish certain shorter tracts in Zurich itself. The *Eidgenössische Zeitung*, edited by his friend Bernhard Spyri, was where he allowed his more everyday utterances to be presented to the public. This paper was published by Schulthess, which was also the company that Wagner chose for the publication of his longer prose pieces for the Zurich market, such as *A Theater in Zurich* (1851) and his program notes to Beethoven's *Coriolanus* Overture and his own *Tannhäuser* Overture (both in 1852). Then, as now, Schulthess ran a book shop as well as a publishing company, and it was apparently there that Wagner made his regular book purchases, as his correspondence with Mathilde Wesendonck and others makes clear (he inevitably left Zurich still owing Schulthess money; his friend Ignaz Heim was engaged to sort the matter out [*SB* 10:98]). For his libretto to the *Ring*, of which only fifty copies were published, Wagner chose the small firm owned by Erwin Kiesling, who operated primarily as a printer but also, in modest fashion, as a publisher too. To the well-known Zurich publisher Orell Füssli, however, he never entrusted anything. The closest that they came to publishing Wagner was in the form of the lithograph portrait by Caspar Scheuchzer of 1851 (nicknamed the "Schlafrockbild" or "Dressing-Gown Picture").

Orell Füssli was in fact the biggest publishing house in Zurich; Schulthess occupied second place in the 1850s. Wagner's choice of the latter rather than the former seems at first rather incongruous, for Schulthess was hardly a progressive institution such as one would imagine Wagner would prefer. It had been founded in 1791 by Johannes Schulthess, a theology professor. In Wagner's day it was run by the founder's younger son, Friedrich, formerly a precocious army officer, who still had a passion for things military (he had reached the rank of lieutenant colonel by the age of only twenty-eight). Schulthess's principal publications included the collected works of Huldrych Zwingli and various military books. During the debate surrounding David Strauss's appointment to the university in the late 1830s — a good barometer of political opinion — Schulthess and Orell Füssli had been on opposing sides, each publishing booklets urging the public respectively to oppose and support the cause. In 1845, Schulthess had even produced a book that could have stood Wagner in good stead on the Dresden barricades, had he only known: *A Guide to Shooting with the Infantry Rifle*. It is not a little odd that Wagner, an exiled revolutionary, should have been welcome at a publishing house owned by a politically conservative lieutenant colonel; we can only assume that his path had been smoothed over by Bernhard Spyri himself. Indeed, Spyri's enthusiastic, partisan, even uncritical support for Wagner's cause offers us one of the earliest cases of the Wagner discipleship that the "Master" would in just a few years inspire among many others, and expect from as many more again. The *Neue Zürcher Zeitung*, the liberal competitor and rival of the *Eidgenössische*, was published on the other hand by Orell Füssli, which in turn offers us a possible reason for Wagner's never having published with them. While it would be an oversimplification to claim that anyone or anything supported by the one paper would be opposed automatically by the other, it does seem clear that Spyri's stance as the perfect Wagnerite helped to push the *Neue Zürcher* into criticism of Wagner's activities in the city, even though its politics were far closer to what Wagner was himself espousing upon his arrival there. While the two main factions in Zurich's political life were not devoid of points of contact (the liberal Jakob Sulzer, for example, seems to have got on perfectly well with the conservative Bernhard Spyri), we nevertheless have the absurd anomaly that Wagner, the supposed left-wing, revolutionary democrat, was supported on the one hand by the members of Zurich's liberal elite and on the other by the main paper in Zurich that opposed them. While this might have come about by mere chance, it does seem that it was in Zurich that Wagner truly learnt how to be quite different things to different people in order to further his social, economic, and artistic prospects — a talent that he would later put to excellent use in his relations with the malleable Ludwig II of Bavaria.

The firm of Kiesling, with whom Wagner published the limited run of his *Ring* libretto in early 1853, was named after its founder, Erwin Kiesling. He had been born in 1818 in Oppeln in Silesia and had then settled in Zurich in about 1846, working as a typesetter. In autumn 1848, he opened his own printing company at Schmidgasse 6, and by 1853 he had been successful enough to increase his capital from SF 1500 to SF 2500. Eleven years later, in 1864, he sold his business to a former vicar by the name of Johann Herzog. Kiesling then bought his own house and opened up a cigar and tobacco shop. In 1875, he married a woman thirty years his junior, started a family, and in 1885 moved with them all to Rotterdam. With that, he disappears from the records. A few years ago Kiesling's old company was still in existence, going by the name of "Buchdruckerei Leemann," but it has in the meantime closed its doors for good.

Some sixty titles survive from Kiesling's decade and a half as a small-time publisher (we do not know how many titles he printed in total, as his firm's records have not survived; furthermore, the borderline between "printer" and "publisher" was at the time vague in the extreme).[2] These sixty cover a huge spectrum of topics — volumes of poetry, doctoral theses, books for religious instruction, scientific and moral tracts, and so on. This should not surprise us, for a printing company, especially a new one founded by a foreigner relatively new to the city, would have to publish whatever was asked of it in order to survive. In 1850 and 1851, Kiesling published two titles by Wilhelm Rüstow (1821–78), a Prussian officer who had fled to Zurich in the wake of the 1848 revolutions.[3] Rüstow later worked for the Swiss Army, and, like Gottfried Semper, lectured at the ETH (if only briefly). He embarked on a publishing career too, bringing out a number of books on military history and contemporary military tactics (in the mid-1850s, his works began appearing with Schulthess). Although Rüstow belonged to the circle around François and Eliza Wille and through them came into contact with Wagner, he is not the most likely candidate for having introduced him to Kiesling. The company was in fact already working sporadically for the Zurich Theater. In 1849 Kiesling published the libretto of Flotow's *Martha oder der Markt zu Richmond* (Martha or the Market at Richmond) on the occasion of a production in Zurich, while in 1850 — at about the same time that Wagner began conducting at the theater (his debut being on 4 October) — he began publishing the *Journal des Aktien-Theaters* (Journal of the Aktien-Theater). In that same year he also brought out a historical play by the theater's director, Philipp Walburg Kramer: *Die Mordnacht in Zürich* (The Night of Murder in Zurich). Kiesling also had close contact with a more important colleague of Wagner's than Rüstow, Ludwig Ettmüller, the scholar and translator of old Nordic languages, two of whose works he published in 1852 and 1854.[4] It was also in 1852 that he first published something by Wagner, namely the text of his *Fliegender Holländer* upon its first performance at the local theater. We can assume that the commission for this came from the theater itself — after all, it was not the first time that Kiesling had published a libretto on the occasion of an operatic performance. Wagner was presumably not unhappy with the result, for early in the following year he commissioned Kiesling to publish fifty copies of his completed libretto to the *Ring*. Wagner explained the limited nature of the edition in a letter to August Röckel of 8 June 1853. It was "a private printing in just a few copies, only for my closest friends and acquaintances" (*SB* 5:313). Wagner indeed seems to have sold none, giving them all away instead. The contrast with his predicament two years earlier is clear; at that time he was in part dependent upon the sale of his writings in order to make ends meet. The fact that he now had other sources of income — not least his conducting engagements — does not wholly explain, of course, why he did not attempt to disseminate the text of his projected tetralogy as widely as possible. But he will no doubt have realized that his *Ring* libretto was not something that would immediately appeal to a commercial publisher, and he will have had neither the means to fund a large print-run nor any prospect of commercial success. He could, of course, have got his rich friends to fund the publication by subscription; but he seems to have had other reasons for acting as he did. In a letter to Louis Schindelmeisser of 13 August 1853, Wagner made it clear that he had wished to restrict knowledge of his libretti to the *cognoscenti*:

> Where my new poem *Der Ring des Nibelungen* is concerned, now I regret terribly that I had fifty copies of it printed, and for a lot of money to boot. Not only was I unable to prevent the book from coming into the hands of the completely uninitiated ["Unberufene"], but even for

> my friends, I feel it now, this poem really should not exist at all before it has been carried out in music, even — I almost want to say — before it has been performed. I now see more and more that what I am planning is something that one should do, not something about which one should speak or have spoken about . . . if its execution in music (and its scenic execution) is by necessity still my secret, which I can reveal only when everything is finished, there is now nothing more embarrassing to me than to hear others talk about this, my innermost artistic secret, and in public too. In short, I wish I could call back all the copies that I gave away. (*SB* 5:394–95)

Had he really wished to keep his text secret, one could argue, then he would not have had it published at all. And he had hitherto, of course, been more than keen to read his libretti to his friends, his acquaintances, and even the *Unberufene* themselves. Not only had he given private readings of his texts in Zurich — as we have seen, almost his first act upon arriving in the city in late May 1849 had been to read his *Siegfrieds Tod* (the *Ur-Götterdämmerung*) to his hosts — but he had even organized a public reading of the whole revised *Ring* libretto in February 1853. Perhaps this did not quite count as truly "public," for he had chosen as his venue the main hall of Zurich's finest hotel, the Baur au Lac, where only the city's elite would attend, and where the *hoi polloi* would not have got past the doorman. To be sure, Wagner had argued for the theater to be open and free for all — but that was one of his precepts that he never showed any qualms about abandoning (as I show in chapter 8 in this volume). It is possible, though, that Wagner had rushed into print with his *Ring* libretto merely in order to forestall any charge that his work had been influenced by others. For the *Neue Zeitschrift für Musik* had just recently — on 17 December 1852 — announced that Wagner's old enemy (in his eyes), Heinrich Dorn, was on the verge of completing a *Nibelung* opera, with its première planned for March 1853 (to make things even more embarrassing for Wagner, not only did Dorn enjoy the support of Franz Liszt, but Wagner's own niece Johanna was intended for the role of "Brunhild"). The report was somewhat premature, for Dorn's work was not premièred until 22 January 1854 instead.[5] But by publishing his libretto and reading it in public in February 1853, Wagner was perhaps just making sure to stake his own claim to the topic.

Wagner's *Ring* libretto was in any case the last title that he published with Kiesling. Just over a decade later, however, his "muse" Mathilde Wesendonck followed his example, for when she at last ventured into the public domain with her literary works — albeit at first only under her initials — it was Kiesling whom she chose for the task, with her *Gedichte, Volkslieder, Legenden, Sagen* (Poems, Folksongs, Legends, Myths) in 1862. She might well have chosen Kiesling on account of his Wagnerian credentials, but she would also have been more likely to retain a certain degree of anonymity with a small printing company than would have been possible with a larger company such as Schulthess or Orell Füssli.

Music publishing in Zurich was by no means in its infancy when Wagner arrived there — indeed, it was arguably the one aspect of music in which the city had excelled in the first half of the nineteenth century, thanks to the endeavors of Hans Georg Nägeli with his editions of Bach, Beethoven, and others. But the glory days of Nägeli were now long past, and Hug had published very little — and nothing of consequence — for a long time. Not until they began publishing the music of Wilhelm Baumgartner did any composer of note entrust his works to them again (and indeed, his song "Noch sind die Tage der Rosen," op. 24, no. 1, would later give Hug its first real "hit," with over ninety thousand printings in the fifty years after its first publication in 1857[6]). Wagner thus arrived in 1849 in a city rich in publishing houses, but none of them were involved in any real way in the publishing of music. This situation altered drastically in the 1850s, and although Wagner was not directly involved in the developments on the Zurich music publishing scene, he seems to have exerted an indirect influence that was highly beneficial.

Zurich's first new music publisher to set up shop after Wagner's arrival in the city was his principal oboist in the AMG Orchestra, Philipp Joseph Fries, whose art he so greatly admired (see also chapter 8). Fries was born on 24 February 1815 in Eltmann near Bamberg in Germany, the eldest of nine children of a farming family (he is not related to the Zurich family of the same name whose members included the prominent sixteenth-century musician Johannes Fries).[7] He received music tuition from a local teacher, and as a teenager he played the organ in the nearby church, and the flugelhorn in the village band. A friend of the family paid for him to study in Munich with Peter Streck, a well-known military musician of the day. It was there that Fries learnt to play the oboe, and it was on this instrument, at Streck's recommendation, that Fries was given a job in 1839 in the Zurich orchestra, after having completed his military service in Bavaria. Fries was appointed to teach music at the School for the Blind in Zurich in 1842, an institution that enjoyed remarkable status in the city and was one of the regular stopping-off points for prominent visiting musicians (among them Mendelssohn and Clara Schumann). As mentioned in chapter 2 above, Fries ran one of the main wind bands in the city, and in 1846 even set up a music shop. It was not until July 1851, however, that he began to publish music. In that month, he advertised for sale twelve four-part pieces that he had himself composed for military trumpets. This publication is makeshift in both its paper and the quality of its printing. By the time he published what appears to have been his second title, Wilhelm Baumgartner's Six Little Songs op. 4, Fries had acquired C. F. Leede of Leipzig as his representative in Germany; and by his fourth publication — Baumgartner's *Andantino grazioso* for piano, op. 3 — he had not only acquired another representative in André of Offenbach, but his title page features a lithograph by the famed Friedrich Krätzschmer of Leipzig. His fifth publication — Six German Songs op. 5, by Johann Jakob Nater — was even engraved by Röder, also of Leipzig.[8]

As a publisher, Fries restricted himself on the whole to piano pieces and songs, and in his early years of business, it was works by his friends and colleagues, many of them former pupils of Alexander Müller, that featured most in his catalogue. These included six songs by Fanny Hünerwadel, published posthumously; three volumes of songs by Felix Kündig, a former pupil of the School for the Blind and a sometime composition student of Xaver Schnyder von Wartensee; the Salon Pieces op. 21 by Johann Carl Eschmann, and assorted pieces by Wilhelm Baumgartner. Baumgartner's Six Little Songs op. 4, mentioned above, were in fact his first songs to be published by anyone. They were dedicated to Fanny Hünerwadel and comprise settings of texts by Novalis, Hoffmann von Fallersleben, Rückert, Mazerath, Eichendorff, and Gottfried Keller (the last of these might well also be the first-ever publication of any setting of Keller's poems). Fries was also the first to publish Baumgartner's piano music: after the above-mentioned *Andantino* op. 3, there followed his Scherzo op. 5 (dedicated to Alexander Müller), then a number of salon pieces. When Wagner published an article in the *Eidgenössische Zeitung* of 7 February 1852 in praise of Baumgartner's music, it was prompted by the publication by Senff of his six songs op. 10, though it was to the songs op. 4 with Fries that Wagner referred specifically. For he holds up Gottfried Keller as an ideal poet and collaborator for Baumgartner — and their hitherto only published song was in the op. 4 set (though Baumgartner had already been setting Keller's poetry to music since at least 1847[9]).

Wagner was more directly involved in the early activities of Switzerland's most important music publisher of the second half of the nineteenth century. His immediate contact seems to have come via Hector Berlioz, with whom he became more closely acquainted during their simultaneous visit to London in 1855. Wagner thereafter made a point of maintaining contact with him — indeed, his few letters to Berlioz display real warmth and admiration. He read Berlioz's *Soirées de l'orchestre* while on holiday at Seelisberg in July 1855 and now showed a particular interest in getting to know Berlioz's scores better. Wagner had first heard his *Romeo and Juliet*, *Harold in Italy*, and *Fantastic Symphony* fifteen years earlier in Paris, and the experience had at the time left its mark upon the very *Faust Overture* that he had just recently revised (*ML*, 202). He now wished to renew his acquaintance with these works and accordingly wrote to Berlioz on 6 September 1855 to request copies (preferably *gratis*) of his published orchestral music (*SB* 7:271–72). Berlioz was unable to comply, however, and so Wagner tried Liszt instead (in a letter of 3 October 1855 [*SB*, 7:284]), impressing upon him that he would like them soon (since he was about to embark on the scoring of the third act of his *Walküre*, we must assume that he anticipated being able to learn something from Berlioz's use of the orchestra). But Wagner had no luck until the following spring, when he turned to Jakob Melchior Rieter-Biedermann of nearby Winterthur, the man who was in the process of setting up Switzerland's newest music publishing company. Rieter's father had owned a spinning mill — of which several had sprung up in Canton Zurich during its industrialization in the early nineteenth century — and the son had originally been intended to follow in his father's footsteps. In 1833, he had gone to Paris to study engineering, and while there he became acquainted with Berlioz and Rossini. Rieter's passion for music proved greater than his engineering interests, and from 1835 to 1848 he acted as librarian of the Musikkollegium in his native Winterthur (the city's equivalent of Zurich's AMG); he also played timpani in the orchestra of the Musikkollegium. In 1848, he set up a music shop that became well known in the wider canton (Hans von Bülow, for example, praised it in a letter to his father of 16 April 1851[10]), and this was obviously the reason for Wagner to approach him. We can assume that the two men were already adequately acquainted, and in fact Wagner's first extant letter to Rieter, of 6 April 1856, makes it clear that they had been in contact, for Wagner wrote to thank him "for your kind offer . . . I would be grateful if you would, for the moment, lend me the scores of the three symphonies (*Fantastic Symphony*, *Harold*, *Romeo and Juliet*)." Rieter and Berlioz were in fact in close contact at this time, for the former was about to launch his publishing business and would just three months later bring out the first edition of the latter's song cycle *Les nuits d'été* in orchestral and vocal score (with plate numbers 2 and 3 respectively, and with a German translation, as it happens, by Wagner's colleague Peter Cornelius). When Liszt wrote to his lover Carolyne von Sayn-Wittgenstein in August 1856 that he had just met Rieter, he referred to him specifically as "éditeur de Berlioz"[11] (two years later, Rieter would also publish a vocal score of Berlioz's *Roméo*). It might thus have been Berlioz himself who had specifically suggested Rieter's shop to Wagner in his hunt for the scores. Rieter certainly seems to have been well-disposed to Wagner, for he had obviously already agreed to lend him the scores free of charge; we can be sure of this, for Wagner added in his above letter that he would gladly repay the "favor" if there were something that he could do in return. Wagner then kept the scores longer than Rieter had anticipated, however. His only other extant letter to Rieter dates from 18 November 1856. In it, he apologizes for his delay, adding that the scores would be in the mail the next day at the latest. This letter also makes it clear that Wagner was expecting to meet Rieter in St. Gall for the concert he would conduct there, together with Liszt, on 23 November.

Rieter's reasons for setting up a music-publishing house are not wholly clear, but it had probably been a pet idea for quite some time. We can, however, surmise his reasons for believing that it would be financially viable. He will have known the market well through his work as a music dealer; and in the years since he had opened his shop there had been a remarkable increase in professional musical activities in the canton of Zurich. The intellectuals who had fled there from their failed revolutions were in many cases men and women who were accustomed to a high level of music-making in their former countries, and who were either keen amateur musicians or keen listeners; and, of course, Wagner's presence in Zurich in the opera pit and on the concert podium had increased audience attendances, brought the musical activities of the city to the attention of a wider press than was the norm, and also attracted other competent musicians to the canton. Apart from the audience statistics for his Zurich performances, which are well documented, we cannot, of course, specify the "invisible" (musical) earnings that were the result of Wagner's presence and activities. But a perusal of the extant sources does make it clear that there was an upturn in the musical fortunes of Zurich and its environs during Wagner's years there, and this will not have gone unnoticed by Rieter, astute entrepreneur that he was.

Of particular interest to us is the fact that Rieter seems to have followed Wagner's advice on composers who might be suitable for publication. In the above-mentioned letter of 18 November 1856, Wagner recommends the music of Robert von Hornstein for publication, though in a manner that suggests Hornstein had already been a matter of discussion between them. Indeed, that same month, Rieter-Biedermann published Three Songs op. 6 by Hornstein. It is also noteworthy that several of the earliest works published by Rieter-Biedermann were by men who belonged to Wagner's circle of friends and colleagues. The first work that he published (with plate no. "1"), in July 1856, was Theodor Kirchner's nine *Albumblätter*, op. 7. It was on the previous 26 April that Kirchner had done Wagner the great service of accompanying him and Emilie Heim in the private world première of the first act of the *Walküre*. To suppose that Wagner might have repaid him by recommending the publication of his music to Rieter-Biedermann is not without a certain appeal — that April was, after all, the same month of his above-mentioned earliest extant letter to the publisher — but it would be sheer supposition on our part, not least since Rieter and Kirchner had lived in the same town for over a decade and thus needed no introductions from anyone. And a publication date of July 1856 would normally presuppose that the publication in question had been planned several months earlier. But it is not impossible; and there were indeed several other works published by Rieter in the coming months that further indicate a possible involvement on Wagner's part regarding his choice of repertoire. In November Rieter published not only Hornstein's songs but also Berlioz's *Corsair* Overture in a piano arrangement by Hans von Bülow, and Kirchner's superb Scherzo op. 8. The *Corsair* even appeared in print just a few weeks after Bülow had sent it to Rieter, which proves that swift publication was by no means an impossibility.[12] Other works by Kirchner followed in 1857, and in the course of the next few years Rieter-Biedermann would publish a number of works by other colleagues of Wagner, such as Wilhelm Baumgartner and Johann Carl Eschmann, as well as three piano arrangements of Berlioz by Liszt. But the publisher's bias toward the music of Schumann and his school soon became clear. The works of Kirchner and Eschmann (and even Baumgartner) naturally did not conflict with this aesthetic stance, and these were joined by music from Schumann himself, Woldemar Bargiel, Heinrich von Herzogenberg, Carl Reinecke, and others. The most important addition to the publisher's stable, however, was Johannes Brahms. It was almost certainly Kirchner who recommended the two to each other, for he had made Brahms's acquaintance at the Music Festival of the Lower Rhine in Düsseldorf in May 1856. Brahms visited Switzerland with Clara Schumann in the summer of that year, in an effort to distract her after the death of her husband Robert on 29 July. They apparently visited Rieter on their way back to Germany, for Clara now gave him her husband's Overture to *Hermann und Dorothea*, which duly appeared in early 1857. Brahms's first work with Rieter was his *Volks-Kinderlieder* of late 1858, and this was followed in the ensuing years by a number of works both small and large-scale, ranging from his First Piano Concerto op. 15 to his *Magelone* songs, op. 33 and his *German Requiem*, op. 45. It would thus be a wonderful irony if the publication of Brahms's early music had come about, if only indirectly, through Wagner — if not through the latter's presumed advocacy for Theodor Kirchner, then at least, of course, through his success in establishing a more professional music culture in the canton of Zurich, the very culture that had helped to make Rieter-Biedermann's publishing house a viable venture in the first place. Perhaps it is a little *too* wonderful to be really much more than wishful thinking on the part of a historian keen to find firm connecting links where there exist really only tenuous strands of synchronicity; but that it is not beyond the bounds of the possible makes it all the more engaging to contemplate.

Notes

[1] See Paul Leemann-van Elck, *Druck, Verlag, Buchhandel im Kanton Zürich von den Anfängen bis um 1850* (Zurich: Leemann, 1950), 118–19.

[2] For a list of Kiesling's known publications, see Walton, "Wagner-Quellen in der Zentralbibliothek Zürich: Verleger, Kopisten, Dirigate," in *"Schlagen Sie die Kraft der Reflektion nicht zu gering an,"* ed. Klaus Döge, Christa Jost, and Peter Jost (Mainz: Schott, 2002), 92–113; here, 107–9.

[3] Wilhelm Rüstow, *Was hat die Schweiz von einem Angriffe der heiligen Allianz zu fürchten?* in 1850, and the second edition of his *Der deutsche Militärstaat vor und während der Revolution*, in 1851. Rüstow commited suicide in 1878, when he failed to gain an appointment as professor at the ETH.

[4] *Das verhängnisvolle Zahnweh oder Karl der Grosse und der heilige Goar*, 1852, and *Bi Gibikingo cvalma*, 1854.

[5] See Werner Breig and Hartmut Fladt, *Dokumente zur Entstehungsgeschichte des Bühnenfestspiels "Der Ring des Nibelungen,"* in Richard Wagner, *Sämtliche Werke*, vol. 29/I (Mainz: Schott, 1976), 75; and Adelyn Peck Leverett, "Liszt, Wagner and Heinrich Dorn's 'Die Nibelungen'" in *Cambridge Opera Journal* 2, no. 2 (July 1990), 121–44.

[6] Thomas Meyer, *Hug Musikverlage 1807–2007* (Zurich: Hug, 2007), 31.

[7] See Walton, "Die 'Synopsis isagoges musicae' von Johannes Fries 1552," in *Zentralbibliothek Zürich: Alte und neue Schätze*, ed. Alfred Cattani, Michael Kotrba, and Agnes Rutz (Zurich: Verlag Neue Zürcher Zeitung, 1993), 66–69.

[8] See Walton, "Wagner's Peculiar Oboist: Philipp Joseph Fries" and "The Zurich Music Publisher P. J. Fries: List of Publications, 1851–ca. 1872," in *Fontes artis musicae* 49, no. 4 (2002): 271–84 and 285–95 respectively.

[9] See, for example, Emil Ermatinger, ed., *Gottfried Kellers Briefe und Tagebücher, 1830–1861* (Stuttgart and Berlin: Cotta, 1916), 153.

[10] Hans von Bülow, *Briefe*, vol. 1, ed. Marie von Bülow (Leipzig: Breitkopf & Härtel, 1895), 311.

[11] La Mara, ed., *Franz Liszts Briefe an die Fürstin Carolyne Sayn-Wittgenstein* (Leipzig: Breitkopf & Härtel, 1899), 309.

[12] See Hans von Bülow's letter to Richard Pohl of 7 September 1856, in von Bülow, *Briefe*, vol. 3, ed. Marie von Bülow (Leipzig: Breitkopf & Härtel, 1898), 55.

Figure 8. Wagner's friends and colleagues in Zurich, from left to right, top to bottom: Wilhelm Baumgartner, Theodor Kirchner, Hans Meyer-Stadler, Bernhard Spyri, Moritz von Wyss Wilhelm Heisterhagen, Alexander Müller. From Adolf Steiner, *Richard Wagner in Zürich*, vol. 3. Zurich: Orell Füssli, 1903.

6: Colleagues and Competitors: The Men Who Weren't There

WE HAVE HERE ALREADY HAD OCCASION to examine Wagner's often idiosyncratic interpretations of historical truth. But his selective approach to autobiography is perhaps never better illustrated than in the manner in which *Mein Leben* deals with the musicians whom he encountered during his years in Zurich. Alexander Müller and his pupil Wilhelm Baumgartner receive ample mention, but since they had assisted Wagner from his earliest days in the city, and since Baumgartner in particular had thereafter become one of his closest friends, they could hardly have been ignored in print. Besides, of the dozen-and-a-half copies of the first, private, printing of *Mein Leben*, one was destined for Jakob Sulzer, by then City President of Winterthur, and a man of high importance who would have been piqued by the absence therein of two men who had been his friends, too. All the same, Wagner could not resist the temptation to belittle even those closest to him; thus Baumgartner — who had died just months before Wagner wrote about him — was "a happy, life-loving chap without any powers of concentration" (*ML*, 473).

The German-born Franz Abt was also allotted space in *Mein Leben*. He was the most successful of the local composers in the 1840s, not least on account of the immense popularity of his song "Wenn die Schwalben heimwärts ziehn" (When the Swallows Fly Homewards) — but his function in the book is primarily to be a measuring rod by which Wagner can establish for the reader his own superior talent. On the other hand, Wagner's friend, the German-born Ignaz Heim (1818–80), who succeeded Abt as the leading choral conductor of the city, is accorded scant mention. As we saw in chapter 2, he was jointly responsible for preparing the chorus for Wagner's festival concerts in 1853, and he later attained national fame on account of his various collections of songs for choirs. For a while, he was even Wagner's neighbor on the Zeltweg. But he also helped to tidy up Wagner's messy finances after the latter's hurried departure from Zurich in 1858, and the embarrassment of this might have been the reason for his having been all but edited out of *Mein Leben*. His young wife Emilie (1830–1911), who was Wagner's soprano soloist on more than one occasion, hardly receives better treatment. The description of Emilie as "the wife of music director Heim" is as close as Ignaz gets to a mention at all, while Emilie herself offers another example of Wagner's gift for barbed praise: she "possessed a really beautiful voice and a warm tone . . .

but she was thoroughly unmusical, and I had great difficulty on account of her inability to hit the right notes or keep in time" (*ML*, 545). Furthermore, since he had at one time been physically attracted to her, and since he was dictating his memoirs to the ever-jealous Cosima, circumspection was no doubt wise.

Theodor Kirchner was another who could not be completely overlooked, as Wagner had needed him to play Karl Klindworth's absurdly virtuosic vocal scores of his operas. And at least Kirchner, unlike both Heims, actually gets his first name mentioned. But here too, Wagner cannot bear to offer unalloyed praise; thus Kirchner was for him a "Schumann disciple . . . who did not refrain from portraying himself in an eccentric manner" (*ML*, 553). Ignaz Heim's compositions hardly ever rose above the level of the average strophic choral song; Kirchner and Baumgartner's musical merits warrant closer attention. But of equal interest are several of those composers whom we know to have been important to Wagner's activities in Zurich, but whom *Mein Leben* nevertheless ignores completely.

One of the latter group was a pupil of Alexander Müller's, Fanny Hünerwadel, to whom we referred briefly in chapter 2 above, and who was the first woman composer to emerge from German Switzerland. She was born in Lenzburg in 1826, where she received her first music tuition, namely from the "Song Institute" of one Traugott Pfeiffer.[1] She was then sent for several months to Morges in French Switzerland — presumably to improve her French — before going to live in Zurich in 1846. There she stayed with her maternal uncle, a wealthy banker named Johann Jacob Speerli, who financed her studies of piano and composition with Müller. Fanny apparently also took occasional lessons on the organ and in strict counterpoint from Christian Gustav Gottlieb Rabe, a talented composer and violinist who fled to Switzerland after the Baden uprising of 1848, and who later married her sister Louise. Fanny took part in the first known Zurich performance of Wagner's music at which the composer was himself present, when on 20 November 1849 she sang the duet from the second act of *Der fliegende Holländer*, together with Karl Keller (the same Karl Keller who was later a professor of German at the Eidgenössische Technische Hochschule). Fanny even received a brief mention in Wagner's correspondence, half a year later, when he wrote to Wilhelm Baumgartner on 25 March 1850: "Dear brother Boom! . . . Our good spinster Fanny Hühnerwadel [*sic*] will give an answer to your question about London." The meaning of this, however, remains unclear; we know that Fanny visited London, but if our sources are correct, this was not until the following year, when she also visited Paris (the Hünerwadels did not want for money). Fanny later took part (as did Rabe) in the Zurich Wagner festival in May 1853, though she only sang in the chorus. She was still in Zurich in July 1853 when Liszt visited, for he at this time wrote a few bars in a music album that she had been compiling for several months.[2] That same summer, Fanny went to Rome. There she took singing lessons, went bathing, went on excursions, attended the opera, visited St. Peter's, admired the singing of the castrati in the papal choir, and mingled with foreign artists and the nobility. At Easter 1854, she took ill with a so-called "nervous fever" — which in this case apparently meant typhus. She died on the following 27 April and was buried near the pyramid of Cestius.

Fanny is of interest to Wagner scholarship, not least because he took her seriously enough to write out for her album the "aria" of Brünnhilde from *Siegfrieds Tod* — one of the very few extant sources for his fragmentary opera. Her own compositions, however, also confirm that she was more than a mere amateur. To perform her piano music today, admittedly, would be to do her a disservice, for it never leaves the realms of the naive and the sentimental (and in this it resembles the extant piano music of her teacher, Müller). But her songs are a different matter; they would be well worth occasional performance. Six of them were published by Philipp Fries shortly after her death and were in 2006 released on CD. Their texts are perhaps a little over-pious (those that are anonymous might well have been penned by the composer herself). But it is clear that Fanny knew her Schubert well, and setting words to music led her to indulge in more interesting harmonic nuances than she ever showed in her piano music.

The "good spinster Fanny" deserves a modest place in the annals of Swiss music history; but as a song composer, her friend Wilhelm Baumgartner (1820–67) is of greater interest. Baumgartner was born in Rorschach on the banks of Lake Constance, enrolled in 1839 at the University of Zurich, and while there also took private piano and composition lessons from Alexander Müller. He sang in two of the choirs that Müller conducted and was soon deputizing for him. In 1842 Baumgartner left for St. Gall, where he spent two years working as a pianist and piano teacher. In the autumn of 1844, he went to Berlin in order to broaden his horizons. It was there that he met Mendelssohn, who recommended that he study with Wilhelm Taubert, and even facilitated a meeting between them (as their extant correspondence proves).[3] Baumgartner indeed took lessons from Taubert, if only for a short time. We also know that on one occasion in Berlin Baumgartner accompanied the renowned Jenny Lind (the "Swedish Nightingale"). He did not stay there long, however — perhaps for lack of money — and he set off for home in February 1845. He took a circuitous route, presumably aware that he would not soon again have the funds for a major foreign trip, and determined to make the most of the time that he had. He accordingly traveled back via Leipzig, Dresden, and Munich, stopping off in the second of them to hear Wagner conduct Beethoven's Ninth Symphony and to pass on Alexander Müller's greetings.

Baumgartner's output consists solely of *lieder*, choral songs, and character pieces for piano. His piano works are more interesting than those of Müller or Hünerwadel, to be sure, though they are still admittedly weak.

Nor do his songs always rise above the level of the salon; but they do so often enough for him to be the subject of more serious investigation. Some — such as his "hit," "Noch sind die Tage der Rosen" (The Days of Roses Are still with Us) op. 24, no. 1 — prove that he had a considerable melodic gift and a knack for a certain *Schwung*. Several of his songs are still in print today, and a number have in recent years been recorded for CD.[4] Wagner went so far as to praise Baumgartner's songs in the *Eidgenössische Zeitung* on 7 February 1852, stating that, while they were "the products of purely musical invention," their musicality is in fact prompted by the content of the poem. It must be noted, however, that Wagner claimed in a contemporaneous letter to Theodor Uhlig that he had praised Baumgartner merely in order to cock a snook at the latter's song-writing rival, Franz Abt (*SB* 4:282). Such back-stabbing of a friend hardly endears Wagner to us; but the tone of his article in praise of Baumgartner seems genuinely warm. It is not impossible that he simply felt embarrassed at never having praised Uhlig's own music thus, and now sought to play the matter down. Wagner had in fact already asked Uhlig to write something positive about Baumgartner's songs (*SB* 4:209), and his later back-tracking seems in fact far more hollow than his praise.

Some proof that Wagner's laudatory words on Baumgartner were not purely hypocritical is offered by Baumgartner's friend and first biographer, C. Widmer, who related that Wagner had exhorted him to write for larger forces, but in vain.[5] Baumgartner did try, it seems. In a letter to Minna of 23 November 1854, Wagner wrote that "Boom won't show himself; he's composing a big sonata, and won't come out until it's finished" (*SB* 6:229–30). But it was never finished; and come out he did, all the same. When Wagner wrote in *Mein Leben* of Baumgartner's lack of concentration, it was perhaps to his inability to create larger forms that he was, in part, referring. He further claimed that Baumgartner was content to exercise his talents only so far as to earn enough money to live on, but little else. This is perhaps not too far from the truth, either. From 1854 to 1861, Baumgartner lived in a flat owned by the piano makers Hüni and Hübert, for whom he had the job of "playing in" their pianos. It was obviously a comfortable post, though hardly one that would necessarily inspire an up-and-coming composer to greater things (in fact, he later almost fell out with Hans von Bülow because of it, when the latter criticized the Hüni-Hübert piano on which he played at a concert in Zurich in 1862. Baumgartner took this as a personal affront, though Bülow then offered his apologies in writing, and did his best to patch things up[6]). Wagner also mentions Baumgartner's fondness for alcohol more than once, with the implication that therein lay part of his problem. Occasional references in Wagner's letters of the 1850s suggest that this fondness of Baumgartner's was not a figment of the Wagnerian imagination either. On 2 August 1859, for example, he wrote to Minna that he, Baumgartner, and Felix Draeseke had gone for a walk through the forest near Lucerne, and that "Boom discovered that the farmer had wine, and we couldn't get him away from the place. Then we had to find our way back through the forest in the dark" (*SB* 11:172). Some twenty years later Cosima noted in her diary that Cornelius had accused Wagner of dropping his friends without compunction; Wagner told her "that it was they who dropped him when he put his faith in them to achieve more than they could, thus Herwegh, Baumgartner [etc.]" (*TB* 2:573).

Baumgartner published his Six Little Songs op. 10 (dedicated to Robert Schumann) and his Six Songs for Four Men's Voices op. 11 with Senff of Leipzig, at his own expense. But with one notable exception — the song cycle *Eine Frühlingsliebe* (A Springtime Love), op. 12, dedicated to Wagner, which was published by Breitkopf and Härtel in late 1852 or early 1853 — he published all his later works in Switzerland. Baumgartner's other dedicatees range from Mathilde Wesendonck (for his salon piece "Abends" for piano) to Franz Liszt (Ten Songs op. 20), Theodor Kirchner (Three Songs op. 23), and Ludwig Stark (Six Little Songs op. 19). The dedication to Wagner was presumably a token of thanks for the latter's article of 1852, for in the extant manuscript, the set was originally "dedicated in true admiration to Miss Betty Schneeli."[7] It was also at first entitled "Eine Frühlingsliebe: Stille Lieder für Singstimme und Pianoforte op. 12" (A Springtime Love: Quiet Songs for Voice and Piano). How Betty felt about Baumgartner's "admiration" turning out to be not quite so "true," we do not know — or perhaps any hopes he might have harbored through the dedication had already been thwarted before he dropped her name. The dedication was not the only change that he made before publication. The name "Stille Lieder" was omitted, later to be assigned to his op. 30, and he now left out four songs from the original sixteen, grouped the remainder in two sets of six, and added the designation "Liederkreis" (Song cycle), which is not merely identical to the title of Schumann's songs op. 39 but also implies the existence of a larger-scale form that the work did not, in fact, possess. Some of the adjacent songs are in keys a third apart, suggesting an attempt to model the key scheme on that of Beethoven's cycle *An die ferne Geliebte* (To the Distant Beloved). But Baumgartner soon abandons this pattern, and there is no real sense of overall unity. Breitkopf and Härtel wrote to him on 25 September 1852, confirming their decision to publish the "cycle." This was his only opus that they published — indeed, they turned him down just over a year later when he sent them another batch of compositions to consider.[8] Perhaps they had felt that the dedication to Wagner, just a few months after they had published his autobiographical *Communication to My Friends*, would help to sell the songs (and perhaps Baumgartner had astutely thought the same). It seems that they all miscalculated, however, for their rejection letter of October 1853 states that "too short a time had elapsed" since the appearance of the *Liederkreis* — in other words, it had not sold well. Baumgartner's later works were published by either Hug of Zurich or Rieter-Biedermann of Winterthur.

Although Baumgartner's songs are finely crafted, and despite their advocacy by Wagner himself, they remain stylistically within the orbit of Mendelssohn and Schumann. The poets he set are in large part typical for the German song composers of the day — Heinrich Heine, Ludwig Uhland, Goethe, Joseph von Eichendorff, and so on — but they also include writers such as Eduard Mörike and Friedrich Hölderlin. The poems of his friends Gottfried Keller and Georg Herwegh are also well represented, and there are settings of poets from Keller's wider circle of acquaintances, such as Ferdinand Freiligrath and August Heinrich Hoffmann von Fallersleben (there are in fact over half a dozen settings of the latter's poems). Baumgartner's devotion to Keller's poetry in itself makes him something of a rarity among composers, for Keller's often knotty verse was found appealing by only a few (at least until their compatriot Othmar Schoeck set several dozen of his poems in the first half of the twentieth century). Baumgartner's extant oeuvre does not encompass even a single piece of chamber or orchestral music, nor is there anything from his pen for piano that is more substantial in form than a "scherzo" (op. 5). His oeuvre for the instrument is otherwise restricted to waltzes and character pieces. If there were ever sketches to the "sonata" in progress to which Wagner referred, then they have not survived — or at least not enough to allow one to recognize them as such. We know that he at least attempted to write chamber music, for his archives contain the opening of a piece for flute and piano. But it, too, breaks off after just a few bars.

Another "small-scale" composer active in the Zurich area during Wagner's years of exile was Theodor Kirchner — that "eccentric" disciple of Schumann. But while he may have devoted much of his time to writing miniatures, he is in matters of quality a case quite different from Baumgartner. If ever there were a competition for the most obscure composer with the most remarkable biography, Theodor Kirchner would undoubtedly reach the finals. He was Schumann's protégé, Mendelssohn's student, Wagner's accompanist, Brahms's friend, Dvořák's arranger, the dedicatee of Reger's Second Violin Sonata, a virtuoso organist and pianist, Clara Schumann's lover, Mathilde Wesendonck's would-be-lover, a gambling addict, and a womanizer; but today he is almost completely forgotten. Born in Neukirchen in Saxony in 1823, he displayed so much early promise that he was talked about in the same breath as the young Brahms. But he frittered away much of his energy and most of his money on gambling, and when he died in 1903, he was half blind, half dumb, half paralyzed, and wholly dependent on the charity of a former pupil. During the ensuing decades, a few of his piano pieces did remain in print (most of them of didactic nature), but to all intents and purposes his music disappeared from the repertoire. Since the 1990s, his works have been appearing in new editions,[9] while a number have now found their way onto CD. All the same, however, little remains known of Kirchner outside the German-speaking world (the newest *New Grove*, for example, devotes just half a column to him, with no worklist). This is to be regretted, for he was not just a friend of the famous but a composer, organist, and pianist genuinely admired by men whose views we must take seriously. Brahms in particular kept faith with Kirchner even when the latter's misanthropy left him, in the eyes of some, barely deserving of it. Of significance for us here, however, is the fact that Kirchner was by far the most gifted composer and musician active in the canton of Zurich during the years of Wagner's exile there, with the sole exception of Wagner himself. He was a man whom Wagner respected and admired and yet whose existence was largely erased from his memoirs.

Fürchtegott Theodor Kirchner received his first music tuition from his father, a teacher who played the organ in the local church. From his twelfth year onward, Theodor attended school in Chemnitz, where he was given a grounding in harmony and counterpoint. In order to gain advice on a possible career for his son, Kirchner Senior took him to see Schumann in 1837 and Mendelssohn the year after. Both were impressed, with Mendelssohn being particularly taken by Kirchner's improvisatory gifts. At his recommendation, Kirchner spent the next three years in Leipzig, where his principal teacher was Carl Ferdinand Becker, the organist of the Church of St. James. In April 1843, Kirchner was invited by Mendelssohn to become the first student on the books of the newly founded Leipzig Conservatory, with all his fees paid by a royal scholarship. However, it remains unclear as to the extent to which Kirchner received actual tuition from him. Kirchner had already become a disciple of Robert Schumann, whom he even resembled in outward appearance. The affection was mutual — in June 1843, Schumann wrote to his friend Johannes Verhulst that "only in Kirchner do I find a warm, musical soul . . . his is in any case the most significant creative talent of them all [at the Conservatory]. Mendelssohn has greatly praised the first movement of his new [string] quartet." Kirchner's Ten Lieder op. 1, to which Schumann gave a glowing review in the *Neue Zeitschrift für Musik* on 13 April, had also just been published. In autumn 1843, Kirchner was appointed — on the recommendation of Mendelssohn and Schumann — to the post of City Organist in Winterthur. Among the friends that Kirchner made there were the poet and artist August Corrodi (1826–85), and the composer Johann Carl Eschmann (1826–82).[10]

Since he was appointed to his organ post while still only nineteen, it is likely that Kirchner (and Mendelssohn and Schumann) had envisaged the job as primarily an early stepping-stone to better things. But he remained there for nineteen years instead. He displayed increasing weariness with his provincial existence as a church musician ("as boring as a mousetrap without the cheese," he once wrote),[11] but Winterthur society obviously provided something of a cushion for him. Furthermore, the town boasted a cultural life remarkably lively for a place so small. Hans von Bülow — though in admittedly polemical mood — praised it in the *Neue Zeitschrift für Musik* in 1853, singling out the contributions of Kirchner and Johann Carl Eschmann, and claiming that: "The little city of Winterthur . . . is several decades ahead of Munich, and is a musical Aranjuez compared to that dead Madrid."[12]

Kirchner soon acquired a goodly number of piano pupils to help supplement his income. He seems to have liked playing the dandy, and he proved particularly popular, at times notoriously so, with female pupils of an impressionable age. With the benefit of hindsight, Kirchner later described these as his "happiest years." In fact, he was continually in debt on account of his addiction to gambling. But in Switzerland he at least had friends — specifically the music-loving Basel banker Friedrich Riggenbach-Stehlin — who were prepared to pay his debts for him. Like many other musicians from Winterthur, Kirchner too traveled regularly to nearby Zurich in order to enjoy the (relatively) greater cosmopolitanism to be found there. He gave concerts and visited acquaintances, usually staying with his friend Wilhelm Heisterhagen, a former pupil of Spohr's who had led the Winterthur orchestra in the 1840s until moving to Zurich in 1850 to lead the AMG Orchestra instead. Kirchner and Wagner naturally came into frequent contact with each other. They did not become close friends, perhaps in part because of Kirchner's open admiration for Schumann and Mendelssohn, and Wagner's equally open dislike of them. Nevertheless, Wagner's few extant letters to him are warm in tone, and Kirchner himself always remembered the older man with respect, even fondness. Shortly after Wagner's death, Kirchner reminisced in a letter to Friedrich Hegar in Zurich as follows:

> Although, from my youth to the present moment, I have not altered my opinion as to his specifically musical importance and was unable to gain unalloyed pleasure from any of his works . . . I nevertheless have always regarded him as a giant when compared to his operatic peers . . . People who misunderstand his character have often accused Wagner of being petty in that he did not admire composers such as Mendelssohn, Schumann, and Brahms. I am not of this opinion. Wagner was thoroughly open and honest about it. He simply was incapable of understanding the goals of these composers, and always stated his opinion to me openly.[13]

Wagner himself admired Kirchner as a performer, referring to him in his letters more than once as a "capable pianist" (*SB* 8:312 and 331). The mention that he receives in Wagner's autobiography *Mein Leben*, however — that "Schumann disciple" who "did not refrain from presenting himself in an eccentric manner" — is obviously tinged with the condescension that

Wagner often showed in print toward those possessed of considerable gifts (*ML*, 553). Wagner pointedly fails to mention the single most important collaboration between Kirchner and himself, namely the fact that Kirchner accompanied the first, private, performance of the first act of the *Walküre* in Zurich on 26 April 1856, with Emilie Heim as Sieglinde and Wagner as both Hunding and Siegmund (*Mein Leben* mentions only the performance given later that year, accompanied by Liszt). Wagner employed Kirchner again in the first half of 1857, when he had him accompany other scenes from the *Walküre*, this time with Karoline Dressler-Pollert as the soprano soloist (a singer whom Wagner had known in Magdeburg and Riga back in the 1830s). Wagner even tried in May 1857 to interest Breitkopf and Härtel in his latest operas by inviting them to visit him and hear Kirchner accompany them (*SB* 8:332). Further proof that Kirchner had become something of a feature in Wagner's musical life is offered by a letter that Wagner sent in October 1857 to a young composer named Heinrich Gottwald in reply to a piano sonata that the latter had sent him: "Right after receiving it I was able to go through it once with Kirchner from Winterthur. We both recognized immediately that it is something significant" (*SB* 9:56).

It is odd, however, that Wagner comments not one whit on the obvious fact that Kirchner himself was far more significant as a composer than as a pianist. To be sure, Kirchner was hardly prolific in these years. His op. 2, comprising ten piano pieces, only appeared in 1852, nine years after his opus 1, though they were greeted by Schumann as being possessed of "genius."[14] Kirchner accordingly received a mention by name as one of the "new, significant talents" on the composing scene in Schumann's famous article "Neue Bahnen" in the *Neue Zeitschrift für Musik* of 28 October 1853, which is otherwise devoted to hailing the young Johannes Brahms. We know that Wagner read this article, for he wrote of it, disparagingly, just ten months later, in a letter to Hans von Bülow (*SB* 6:206). The next twenty years saw Kirchner publish nothing but three small sets of songs and five sets of piano pieces, though their quality of inspiration is undeniably impressive. The songs do have occasional Schumannesque reminiscences (as an example, "Im Rosenbusch die Liebe schlief," op. 4, no. 2 — "Love slept in the rosebush" — begins in a manner similar to Schumann's "Mondnacht"), but they must still be counted among the finest in the German language between Schumann and Brahms. The few songs that Kirchner published in the 1850s — his opp. 3, 4, and 6, with fourteen songs in total — show in their choice of poet similar preferences to other composers of the day, including Baumgartner, namely Emanuel Geibel (three songs), Carl Beck (four songs), and Hoffmann von Fallersleben (four songs). In one case, Kirchner and Baumgartner even published a setting of the same poem within just a year or so of each other: Hoffmann von Fallersleben's "Wie die jungen Blüthen leise träumen" ("As the young

Example 6.1. Theodor Kirchner: *Grüsse an meine Freunde*, op. 5, no. 4, bars 10–11.

Example 6.2. Wagner: *Die Walküre,* second act, first scene.

blossoms quietly dream"), published by Baumgartner in his *Liederkreis* op. 12 with Breitkopf in 1853, and then by Kirchner in his Four Songs op. 6, with Senff, in 1854. Baumgartner was the dedicatee of Kirchner's Scherzo for Piano op. 8, published by Rieter-Biedermann in 1856. This must rank as one of the finest piano works of its kind at the time; besides its veritably Beethovenian energy, it is typical in displaying Kirchner's delight in compositional dexterity — toward the close of its trio, melody and accompaniment are suddenly inverted.[15] Kirchner was in turn the dedicatee of Baumgartner's Three Songs op. 22, published by Hug in the early 1860s.

The fourth of Kirchner's *Grüsse an meine Freunde* op. 5 for piano (Greetings to My Friends), published by Senff at the end of 1854,[16] is notable not least because of a passage using a minor sixth chord with a major third, in a dotted rhythm, that bears a resemblance to the "Ho-jo-to-ho"s of the Valkyries from Wagner's *Walküre.* The two passages even resolve in a manner not wholly dissimilar; Kirchner's chord of G–B natural–E flat resolves onto a 6–4 chord of c minor, while Wagner's augmented triad of G–B natural–D# resolves naturally into C major (see examples 6.1 and 6.2). We have no idea as to the identity of the "friends" to whom Kirchner offers his "greetings," but it would be erroneous to suppose that this was a veiled reference to Wagner (or a "greeting" to him), for Wagner's "Ho-jo-to-ho"s are first heard in the opening scenes of the second act of his opera, which he began only in September 1854. We can thus safely assume that Kirchner's work came first, for a publication date of late 1854 probably means that it was submitted to its publisher several months previously. It is notoriously difficult to date Kirchner's works from these years, but we do know that Kirchner's op. 8 — not published until 1856, as mentioned above — had in fact been composed in at least 1851 or earlier, for in that year he wrote out its first forty-five bars as an *Albumblatt* for Robert Radecke.[17] It thus seems likely that his op. 5, too, was composed several years before its publication. When Liszt planned his visit to Wagner in the early summer of 1853, he wrote: "If it isn't a problem for you, let Kirchner and Eschmann in Winterthur know [about my coming], as it will please me to make their personal acquaintance." Wagner replied four days later: "I'll let Kirchner and Eschmann know."[18] We know that the men did indeed meet up in Zurich, and that Liszt played his latest works to the assembled company.[19] So it is not impossible that Kirchner, too, might have in return played his *Grüsse* and other works, though we have no proof of it. Wagner had already composed the dotted Valkyrie motive in b minor that we know best from the opening of his "Ride of the Valkyries," this being in fact one of his earliest musical ideas for the *Nibelungen*. If Wagner heard or saw Kirchner's piece in mid-1853, perhaps the similarity of its dotted rhythm to his own Valkyries drew his attention to the effect of Kirchner's augmented harmony; or perhaps the matter was in fact purely synchronicitous. The similarity, while not striking, is sufficient to warrant consideration here, and it is in any case but one of several examples of possible influence on Wagner's early music for the *Ring*, of which the others will be discussed below, and which in their entirety form more convincing proof of Wagner's susceptibility to outside influence in the mid-1850s.

Kirchner was certainly being encouraged in these years to write for forces other than just the piano and voice, and in genres bigger than the character piece or *lied*. In February 1854 Schumann complained to his friend Hermann Rollett that Kirchner should "work harder and use his powers to create higher artistic forms."[20] Clara Schumann, too, urged Kirchner to try his hand at larger-scale works, even suggesting a piano concerto.[21] After the death of her husband she began a career as a traveling virtuoso in order to support her family, and it was in this capacity that she met Kirchner, Wagner, and Mathilde Wesendonck in Zurich in December 1857, when she gave a concert there. Clara was back in Switzerland the following spring, when she and Kirchner together played Robert Schumann's Andante and Variations op. 26 for two pianos in Winterthur on 10 March. Their respective reaction to Wagner's ignominious departure from Zurich is not known. Kirchner all but fell silent as a composer in the ensuing years, though his private and professional lives were as turbulent as his creative life was calm. He even embarked on an affair with Clara Schumann herself, though the fact that she allowed him to consummate their relationship merely made her bitterness all the greater when he abandoned her just a few months afterwards. She had even paid his gambling debts, despite needing money herself. His promises that he would mend his ways were swiftly broken, with any further money lent to him being lost swiftly through yet more gambling. "Pull yourself together, dear Kirchner," she wrote to him on 13 July 1862,[22] extolling the virtues of hard work in a manner that was hardly going to appeal. It was in this same year that Kirchner finally decided to leave Winterthur and settle in nearby Zurich, in the hope of earning more money to help to pay off his debts (and also, it seems, to escape mounting criticism of his womanizing). As a member of the board that decided upon his successor in Winterthur, Kirchner was instrumental in ensuring the appointment of Hermann Goetz to the post. Kirchner was already well known in Zurich and was now offered the post of principal conductor of the AMG Orchestra. He accepted and took the matter seriously enough to engage Hermann Levi as his conducting teacher in the summer of 1863. Kirchner's subsequent conducting activities in Zurich seem to have been particularly successful, even impressing Theodor Billroth. But he was less convinced of his talents than were others, and so he decided in 1865 to pass the baton of the orchestra over to his friend Friedrich Hegar, at that time the leader of the orchestra. Hegar remained in charge of the orchestra for some forty years, dominating the city's musical life as has no single individual before or since. It was Kirchner who was primarily responsible for introducing the music of Brahms to the Zurich public,[23] but it was Hegar who now turned Zurich from what just a few years earlier had been a "Wagner city" into a thoroughly Brahmsian one.

As will be discussed in greater detail in chapter 10 below, Kirchner soon entered Mathilde Wesendonck's inner circle, becoming as devoted to her as had been Wagner in the 1850s. But he was just as unsuccessful as his predecessor, and he embarked instead upon a marriage to a singer, Maria Schmidt,[24] that proved disastrous (most of all, undoubtedly, to his wife). Two children survived, but both suffered from health problems, and money remained tight for years to come. Kirchner became the organist of St. Peter's in Zurich in 1871, but he disliked it, and in 1872 he left for Germany. He spent the next years in Meiningen, then Würzburg, Leipzig, and Dresden, by which time he was wishing himself back in Zurich. The last thirteen years of his life, from 1890 to 1903, he spent in greater comfort in Hamburg, thanks to the efforts of a well-to-do former pupil by the name of Mathilde Schlüter. Kirchner managed to alienate most of his colleagues but never lost the affection of Brahms, who was one of several who gave him regular financial assistance in his final years.

It is not a little ironic that the years when Kirchner mixed with Wagner, Gottfried Keller, and the leading intellectual lights of Zurich society were when he was least active as a composer. His years of depression and near poverty from 1872 onwards were his most productive. His opus 11 appeared only in 1870, when he was almost fifty, but by the time he died he had reached over a hundred opus numbers. More than a thousand piano miniatures date from these last three decades of his life, and their quality is as remarkable as their quantity. His chosen titles are often second-hand and Schumannesque in inspiration — for example, *Neue Davidsbündlertänze*, *Neue Kinderscenen*, *Florestan und Eusebius* — but the same can rarely be said of the music, which abounds in contrapuntal tricks, harmonic surprises, and many other brilliant displays of the composer's art and artifice. Elisabet von Herzogenberg, the wife of the composer Heinrich, wrote to their common friend Brahms on 27 March 1881 with regard to the piano pieces that Kirchner was churning out: "He is just like a rabbit, and he always brings forth such tubby little bunnies; but everything he does is so wonderfully musical and so graceful."[25] Kirchner also made a host of arrangements, many of them of works by Brahms. These range from a version for eight hands at two pianos of Brahms's First Piano Concerto to arrangements for piano trio of the two string sextets that are particularly fine; they are so idiomatic that if one did not know the originals, then one would never believe that they had been composed for any other ensemble. Kirchner's best works, however — apart from his songs, already mentioned above — are probably his Novelettes for piano trio op. 59 (published in 1881) and his Piano Quartet op. 84 (1888), whose scherzo alternates 5/4 with 3/4 time. Kirchner never wrote for orchestra — the biggest forces for which he wrote never had more than four players. Unlike, say, Hugo Wolf, Kirchner had no grand symphonic or operatic ambitions, but was apparently content to be a miniaturist. And yet, in his very preference for the non-organic, the epigrammatic, even the fragmentary, in a style that displays a mastery of contrapuntal and motivic working, Kirchner at times seems to be asserting a remarkably modern aesthetic.

The final composer from Wagner's circle whom we shall consider here was yet another who restricted himself mostly to limited forces and modest genres. Unlike Kirchner, however, Johann Carl Eschmann (1826–82) does not figure once in Wagner's autobiography, not even in an unflattering aside. Of course, an alternative musicology could easily produce a list of many other Swiss composers who do not figure either in Richard Wagner's autobiography or, for that matter, in anyone else's. And while it is true that he had studied with Alexander Müller and remained on friendly terms with others in Wagner's entourage, Eschmann did remain somewhat aloof, feeling more drawn to the aesthetic of Schumann and (later) Brahms. Of all the musicians working in Canton Zurich in the 1850s, he was closest, it seems, to Theodor Kirchner, who was himself by nature

Figure 9. Johann Carl Eschmann, portrait by August Corrodi ca. 1849. Used by permission of the Zentralbibliothek Zürich.

something of an outsider. All the same, Eschmann's absence from Wagner's autobiography is notable, not least because the latter once referred to him as his "friend" and seems to have employed his services on an occasion of no little delicacy. As Robert Münster has pointed out, the Bavarian State Library in Munich possesses a copyist's copy of the instrumental version of "Träume" from the *Wesendonck Lieder*, the version first performed for Mathilde Wesendonck on her birthday, 23 December 1857, while her husband Otto was away on business (see chapter 10). The score bears the autograph marking "Zürich 1857. Seinem Freunde Carl Eschmann zur freundl. Erinnerung R. W." ("For his friend Carl Eschmann, in friendly remembrance"), which unusually generous gesture Münster plausibly interprets as likely proof that Eschmann played in the ensemble that gave the first performance, possibly even the solo violin part. However, Johann Carl's first instrument was the piano, and although he also played the violin and the viola, he was never Wagner's first choice as a violinist — he instead preferred Wilhelm Heisterhagen and Johann Carl's cousin, Jean Eschmann.[26] If Johann Carl did not play the solo part, it must remain a mystery as to why Wagner would present him with a copy of the piece. We cannot rule out the banal possibility that it was in fact Jean Eschmann who played the solo part, that Wagner simply got his Eschmanns confused, and wrote the wrong name on the dedication. But this does not seem likely, either.

If Johann Carl Eschmann had indeed been involved in the first performance of the *Wesendonck-Lieder* and thus, by extension, implicated in Wagner's pursuit of Mathilde Wesendonck, then this might itself have prompted Wagner not to mention him when dictating his memoirs to Cosima. However, before considering in greater depth why Johann Carl Eschmann should have been ignored, and whether or not he deserved it, I ought to offer a brief sketch of his biography. Anyone attempting to collect biographical information on him rapidly discovers that Wagner was merely the first of many to ignore him. Eschmann's name did retain a certain currency after he died in 1882, though on account of his *Wegweiser durch die Klavierliteratur* (Guide to the Piano Literature), not his compositions. The *Wegweiser*, as the title makes obvious, was a didactic guide to the piano repertoire. It was first published by Hug of Zurich in 1871, then revised and extended in the ensuing decades, with Adolf Ruthardt taking on the task of editor from the fourth edition onwards. It is perhaps symptomatic of Eschmann's fate that, by the tenth edition of 1925, his name had disappeared from both the title page and the editor's foreword, while his music was also omitted except for his most basic didactic works. Eschmann's name does not figure in any editions of *Grove* until the most recent one; *Die Musik in Geschichte und Gegenwart* ignored him in its first edition, the entry in the new, second edition being apparently modeled on that in the latest *Grove*. Only in Riemann's *Musiklexikon* is Eschmann to be found consistently, though his name is in the first five editions given incorrectly as "Julius Karl." Such a mistake is easily made, as our Johann Carl came from a family of musicians who had the unnerving knack of giving their musically gifted progeny names that were at least similar, if not actually identical, and who in turn had the unfortunate habit of becoming proficient on the same instruments (though it must be admitted that there was, in fact, not a Julius among them).

While it is difficult enough to distinguish certain Eschmann cousins from each other, finding Johann Carl's music long proved most difficult of all, for the libraries of the world, be they in London, Munich, or Vienna, possessed next to nothing of his music until the composer's heirs donated their extensive collection of his manuscripts and published works to the Zentralbibliothek Zürich. This institution already possessed a number of documents from the estates of other members of the Eschmann family, plus the archives of several in-laws.

Johann Carl Eschmann was born on 12 April 1826 in Winterthur, where his father, Heinrich Eschmann (1802–82), was a music teacher and director of the Cantonal Military Band. Heinrich played the horn and bassoon in the Winterthur orchestra and was later required to do the same in the Zurich orchestra when Wagner needed to bring in extra forces. As mentioned in chapter 1 above, Johann Carl and his cousin Henriette both took piano lessons in Zurich with Alexander Müller. Johann Carl then studied from 1845 to 1847 under Mendelssohn, Ignaz Moscheles, and Niels Gade at the Leipzig Conservatory but thereafter moved back to Zurich to work as a music teacher. It seems, too, that he spent a brief time working in Kassel as a piano teacher. From 1850 to 1859, Eschmann lived back in Winterthur, but apparently suffered from the competition of the more talented Theodor Kirchner (which did not, however, prevent their becoming firm friends; it is not impossible that Kirchner had recommended Eschmann to Mendelssohn in the first place). So Eschmann moved to nearby Schaffhausen, where from 1859 to 1866 he worked as a piano teacher and choral conductor. In 1866, he moved back to Zurich, where he continued working as a piano teacher until his death on 27 October 1882 (just four days after the death of his father).

Johann Carl's cousin Jean (Henriette's brother, 1826–69) was a violinist and a member of the Zurich orchestra under Wagner in the early 1850s (he also played second violin in the Zurich String Quartet that was patronized by Wagner). But Johann Carl, too, occasionally played in the AMG's string section. To make matters even more complicated, there was a further cousin, Carl Eschmann (1835–1913) who, presumably to distinguish himself from the rest, termed himself "Eschmann-Dumur," no doubt according to the Swiss custom whereby a husband adopts the surname of his wife, placing it after his own. This Carl Eschmann-Dumur succeeded his father as organist in Wädenswil near Zurich then lived for several years in Geneva and Lausanne before becoming a professor at the *Institut de musique* in the latter city. In 1884, he published a *Guide du jeune pianiste*, a graded survey of the piano literature in French, very similar to that published in Zurich (in German) by Johann Carl thirteen years earlier.[27] Eschmann-Dumur in fact recommends the earlier book at the start of his preface, and writes that Johann Carl was his first teacher. By an odd quirk of history, yet another musical member of the extended Eschmann family was (co-)responsible for a guide to the piano literature, almost a century after Johann Carl's *Wegweiser*: Rudolph Ganz, the former Busoni pupil who in 1969 published a revised version of Ernest Hutcheson's *Literature of the Piano*.[28]

The Eschmanns thus form just one branch of what must be Switzerland's most impressive music dynasty, for through the marriage of Barbara into the photographer's family Ganz and that of Johann Carl's daughter Marguitta to the son of the composer Robert Radecke, the family includes over a dozen musicians, spanning some two centuries. The family tree given as table 6.1 is based on information garnered from the Eschmann and Ganz family archives in the Zentralbibliothek Zürich, cross-checked with similar documents in the possession of the Radecke family today.

Johann Carl's opus 1 — a set of four "romances" for piano entitled *Poesieblumen* (Flowers of Poetry) — was published by Breitkopf and Härtel in Leipzig in 1849. Numerous further publications of piano, chamber, and vocal works followed swiftly, published primarily by Breitkopf or Kistner in Leipzig or by Luckhardt in Kassel (the contrast to Wilhem Baumgartner, whose success with Breitkopf was short-lived, is thus as obvious to us as it probably was to Eschmann and Baumgartner themselves). Eschmann's understanding of himself as a composer in the school of Mendelssohn and Schumann is underlined by his cycle of piano pieces op. 8 (ca. 1849/50), *Was einem so in der Dämmerung einfällt* (What Occurs to One at Dusk), which is dedicated to his fiancée. In its postlude, Eschmann slips skilfully, almost imperceptibly, into a quotation from Schumann's song "Widmung" (Dedication): the passage whose words run "what you give to me makes me worth more."

In the years immediately after completing his studies, Eschmann indulged in a certain amount of technical and formal experimentation. Like Kirchner a few years before him, Eschmann wrote a single string quartet. It is undated, but its style seems to place it in the late 1840s, which would make it — again like Kirchner's — a "journeyman's" work written at the close of his studies with Mendelssohn. It is a technical tour-de-force abounding in inversions, canons, imitative entries, and the like. It is somewhat demonstrative in its technical expertise, which perhaps confirms our suspicion that it was designed to show off Eschmann's newly learnt skills after his years in Leipzig. But the technique always supports the musical

Table 6.1. Eschmann (-Ganz) family tree

Jakob Eschmann
Musican and cobbler

Heinrich Eschmann
1802–1882
Military Kapellmeister in Winterthur.
Played the French horn and bassoon

Rudolph Eschmann
Kapellmeister in Wädenswil

Hans Jakob Eschmann
1786–1846
Regimental Kapellmeister

One further brother, apparently a clarinetist in the French army

One further brother, apparently a trumpeter in the French army

Robert Radecke
1830–1911
Composer

Johann Carl Eschmann
1826–1882
Composer and conductor.
Married
Susanne Knus
1835–1918

Carl Eschmann-Dumur
1835–1913
Pianist and teacher. Pupil of Johann Carl Eschmann

Jean Eschmann
1826–1869
Violinist. Student of Johann Kalliwoda

Henriette Eschmann
1829–1896
Pianist and piano teacher. Pupil of Barbara Eschmann and of Wagner's friend Alexander Müller

Barbara Eschmann
1816–1878
Piano teacher; taught her sister Henriette.
Married
Johannes Ganz
1821–1886

Ernst Radecke
1866–1920
Music director in Winterthur

Marguitta Eschmann
1872–1944

Mathilde Eschmann
1853–?
Piano teacher. Studied at the Stuttgart Conservatory

Rudolf Ganz
1848–1928
Married
Sophie Bartenfeld

Ewald Radecke
1907–1979
Music director in Winterthur

Paul Ganz
1872–1954
Married
Béatrice Kern

Hans Ganz
1890–1957
Composer, author, painter

Rudolph Ganz
1877–1972
Pianist and composer. Studied with Carl Eschmann-Dumur and Ferruccio Busoni

Béatrice Ganz
*1915
Piano teacher

(Peter) Felix Ganz
1922–1990
Pianist and teacher in Chicago

invention, never hindering it, and there is nothing student-like about it. Astonishingly, this quartet was only discovered in the mid-1990s. It was published in 2000, recorded that same year, and — as can now be heard by the public at large — it can well bear comparison with any work in the genre from the mid-nineteenth century between Beethoven and Brahms.[29] Eschmann's only orchestral work also dates from this time: a *Grosse Conzert-Ouvertüre*, which, though charming, is very much a workaday effort when compared to the string quartet, and presumably preceded it. Where the quartet is concise and compelling, the overture is prolix — though a little judicious pruning could perhaps still make of it an effective concert piece. It was played once in a Zurich concert on 21 March 1848, then never again until the year 2002.[30] It was most recently performed in February 2005 by the Zurich Tonhalle Orchestra under Daniel Harding, but to mixed reviews. Peter Hagmann in the *Neue Zürcher Zeitung* of 25 February 2005 was damning, finding it "clichéd," and wishing it had been allowed to slumber on; Nick Liebmann in the *Zürichsee-Zeitung* of the same day found it "full of melodic inspiration, harmonic and rhythmic contrasts, and wonderfully orchestrated," while Sibylle Ehrismann in *Der Zürcher Oberländer* of 28 February found it "elegantly orchestrated and possessed of a certain *Schwung*, though it remains episodic in character."

There are only a few references to Johann Carl in the correspondence of his contemporaries. One of the most tantalizing is the letter of Liszt to Wagner, already mentioned above, in which he asks to meet Kirchner and Eschmann during his visit to Zurich in July 1853. Liszt's specific desire to make Eschmann's "personal" acquaintance suggests that they were already known to each other. Eschmann had in fact dedicated his op. 16 to Liszt: Twelve Studies for piano, of which the first two volumes (with four studies each) had been published by Luckhardt of Kassel in December 1852 and June 1853 respectively. Eschmann had presumably written to Liszt in advance, in order to ask for permission to make the dedication. While it is quite possible that Wagner might have played an intermediary role in the matter, we have no proof of it (although Eschmann's travels from Leipzig to Zurich in the mid-1840s might have taken him through Weimar, he could not there have become acquainted with Liszt, for the latter did not take up his post in the town until 1848. By that time, Eschmann was once more resident in Zurich).

The contact between Liszt and Eschmann is intriguing, not least because of their common interest in cyclical form at this time. Cyclical techniques were naturally nothing new — Eschmann and his contemporaries will have all been familiar with their use in Beethoven's later works such as *An die ferne Geliebte* and the Piano Sonata op. 101. In his own Piano Sonata in b minor of 1854, Liszt offered what is generally regarded as the hitherto most rigorous application of cyclical techniques. Nevertheless, one slightly earlier work of Eschmann's does deserve consideration here: his *Fantasiestücke* (Fantasy Pieces) op. 9 for clarinet and piano, written in late 1850 and early 1851. Eschmann evidently took as his model Schumann's *Fantasiestücke* op. 73 for the same instruments — even the introduction of Eschmann's first movement is reminiscent of the Schumann — and he published them with the same company, Luckhardt (Schumann's pieces had appeared in July 1849, bearing the plate number 124). Eschmann's work is essentially in two movements; a much shorter, third and final "movement" entitled *Schluss* (Conclusion) is in fact a recapitulation of the close of the first movement. While in Schumann's pieces the individual movements are separate but lead *attacca* into one another, Eschmann avoids a final cadence, leading without a break from one movement to the next. His two main movements were, however, originally intended to be separate, as is proven by the extant draft of the first movement, dated "30 Dec. 1850." A similar procedure to that used in these *Fantasiestücke* is to be found in Eschmann's four *Lyrische Blätter* (Lyric Leaves) op. 15 for piano, written shortly afterwards, in which previously heard material is brought back to form a coda to the whole set (the close of no. 4 recapitulates the opening of no. 3). This use of cyclical techniques might have been primarily a means for Eschmann to circumvent his own natural inclination to the small-scale character piece. Simply repeating a substantial section of material as a coda to a different movement can at least give the impression that the composer has mastered a "bigger form." However primitive such a procedure might seem, Eschmann's works of ca. 1850 — including his string quartet — do not just display a desire for musical unity and a dramatic trajectory on a larger scale but also prove that he had the technical ability to achieve what he wanted. This fact marked him off from his Swiss contemporaries, among whom the simple piano character piece, the salon *lied*, and the song for male-voice choir for the moment reigned supreme.

Eschmann's years of experimentation were also his finest. They were followed by a rapid decline of his compositional ambitions and a concurrent dimming of his creative spark (a sad pattern repeated time and again into the mid-twentieth century by Swiss composers who returned from studying abroad to devote their lives to teaching and conducting). After the early 1850s, Eschmann too wrote mostly solo piano music, much of it of a didactic nature. Apart from Three [Piano] Sonatas op. 23 "for instructive purposes" and a "Sonata in an Easy Style" for piano, op. 33 (they are all essentially easy sonatinas), Eschmann seems to have written no works of that title for any instrument (though there are three much later sonatinas for violin and piano, this time entitled thus). Nevertheless, there are still some charming character pieces from Eschmann's later years, such as *Licht und Schatten* op. 62 (Light and Shadow), six piano pieces dedicated to Brahms and published by Simrock. Their publication was apparently prompted by Brahms himself, who wrote to Simrock on 3 April 1878: "He [Eschmann] will already be known to you and does not need my recommendation, since you look with envy upon Luckhardt's many editions [of his works]."[31] Also in 1878, Eschmann published an easy piano duet arrangement of Brahms's Waltzes op. 39, made with the composer's permission and at the request of his publisher Rieter-Biedermann.[32] After Eschmann's death, Theodor Kirchner paid tribute to his friend by editing several volumes of his unpublished piano pieces for Siegel of Leipzig. While we sadly have no documentary evidence on Eschmann's part regarding his relationship to Wagner in the 1850s, there can be no doubt that he had in his final years moved wholly into the Brahmsian camp. In a letter to Joachim Raff as early as 6 December 1866, Hans von Bülow had referred to both Eschmann and Friedrich Hegar as 'ghastly Leaguists'[33] — that is, adherents to the anti-Wagnerian Manifesto published by Brahms and others in 1860. And in his *100 Aphorisms* published in 1878, Eschmann allowed himself a remarkable broadside against the New German School. In his 99th aphorism, Eschmann first rails against the fact that "these days, every musician and composer also wants to be a writer"[34] — quite obviously referring to Wagner, whose "Collected Writings" were appearing throughout the 1870s, one volume at a time, edited by the composer himself. He then praises Brahms for remaining instead true to his compositional gifts alone, but soon returns to his vitriol, criticizing bitterly "one" ["Einer"] who

> laboriously puts together a completely thought-out system full of contradictions, and only then composes out his works according to this template, seemingly without suspecting that in this manner, the work of the spirit sinks to the level of a machine's work; the reader will no doubt know whom I mean. The New German trends, as well as the compositions of the Frenchman Berlioz, who is in some ways related to them, are simply false paths on a large scale upon which real musicians such as a Brahms, Gade, J. O. Grimm, etc. are not tempted to tread and which, hopefully, will not be traversed by anyone again after the death of their discoverers.[35]

It was, and is, all too obvious whom Eschmann meant, and his vitriol was such that his son-in-law omitted it when he came to revise the book for publication a decade after the author's death.[36] Of course, Wagner's "theories" had been no secret to Eschmann or anyone else back in the 1850s, when the two men had associated often, and — to judge from the dedication of his copy of "Träume" — as friends. The dislike expressed here is so passionate as to suggest that Eschmann was in fact compensating for something — perhaps precisely for his earlier proximity to the object of his current dislike. Nor can we ignore the possibility that he might also have been informed of the existence of Wagner's autobiography (perhaps by a mutual colleague such as Sulzer) and of his own exclusion from it.

The simultaneous fondness of Eschmann and Liszt for cyclical procedures as mentioned above can naturally be explained as a product of both the *Zeitgeist* and the common influence of Beethoven. But there are in fact two instances in Eschmann's oeuvre where an influence on his part upon the music of Richard Wagner must be more carefully considered. Of course, resemblances between the music of the famous and the less-famous have long exerted an undeniable fascination. However, unless this tells us something about the way a composer's mind works, it really has more in common with train-spotting than with musicology. One can argue that it would have been surprising for Wagner *not* to have been influenced by those around him, as no composer works in a vacuum. Such resemblances only really promise to become interesting when they are pitch-specific.[37] This is more or less the case with the Kirchner passage mentioned above; but the two examples in Eschmann are arguably more interesting. The *Allegro* theme of Eschmann's *Fantasiestücke* op. 9 is a remarkable presentiment of one of the principal motives from the love scene in the first act of the *Walküre*, and it is heard at the same pitch on several occasions, most prominently in Siegmund's "Spring Song" (see examples 6.3 and 6.4). The energetic use of sequence in the coda of the *Fantasiestücke* is similarly reminiscent of the close of that act of the *Walküre*, where the same motive

Example 6.3. Johann Carl Eschmann: *Fantasiestücke* op. 9 for clarinet and piano, first movement, bars 12–19.

Example 6.4. Wagner: *Die Walküre*, first act, Siegmund's "Spring Song."

Example 6.5. Johann Carl Eschmann: *Fantasiestücke* op. 9, coda to second movement, bars 131–37.

Example 6.6. Wagner: *Die Walküre*, close of the first act.

is also used in sequence in order to achieve climax (see examples 6.5 and 6.6). Since Eschmann and Wagner were in regular contact, and since the latter was already a famous composer, we can assume that the former will have taken the trouble to show or play him his latest compositions, or at least give him a copy of his newest publications (the fact that the Richard Wagner Museum in Bayreuth holds no copies of any music by Eschmann is of little consequence, for Wagner's wandering existence between his departure from Dresden and his settling in Bayreuth made it impossible for him to build up and maintain a private library). The *Fantasiestücke* were also dedicated to a Zurich musician who was much admired by Wagner, Hans Conrad Ott-Imhof, the principal clarinetist in the AMG orchestra. It thus cannot be ruled out that Wagner heard or saw Eschmann's opus 9, and that it did indeed exert some influence on the first act of the *Walküre.*

Our final example of Eschmann's possible influence on Wagner is of greater potential significance. Eschmann's op. 34 is a set of six songs, for soprano or tenor and piano, with the composite title *Aus dem Liederbuch eines Malers* (From the Songbook of a Painter). All are to texts by the composer's friend August Corrodi, who was both painter and poet, and they are taken from a volume of poetry that he published in 1853, entitled *Lieder* (hence, presumably, the title of the song collection). Since the volume was published by Luckhardt, Eschmann's own principal publisher, it seems reasonable to assume that it might have appeared on the recommendation of the composer. Eschmann's devotion to his friend and his work is well documented. They had attended school together, and after their years of study in Germany (Leipzig for Eschmann, Munich for Corrodi) they both took up residence in Winterthur and there resumed their friendship; when Corrodi left in 1854 to work as a writer and journal editor in St. Gall, the two remained in close contact by letter. Eschmann had already set three of Corrodi's lyrics in his Four Songs op. 5 and had dedicated the set to his friend. Altogether, Eschmann set twenty of Corrodi's poems to music; and he was not alone in doing so. Heinrich Sczadrowsky, the music director of St. Gall who brought Wagner and Liszt to the city in November 1856, set three of Corrodi's poems for voice and piano as his op. 12,[38] Ludwig Liebe set his "Wem Gott ein braves Lieb beschert" for mixed choir as his op. 71, no. 5, while Arthur Sullivan in 1859 set "Ich möchte hinaus es jauchzen," also from Corrodi's 1853 collection. Over two decades later, Winterthur's long-time music director Ernst Methfessel set a libretto by Corrodi to music: *Die Entführung* (The Abduction), after a novella by Eichendorff,[39] while even the twentieth-century Swiss composer Armin Schibler set five of Corrodi's poems to music in 1985 — more precisely, five of his translations of Robert Burns — as a cycle entitled *Der Kiltgang.*

Eschmann's Corrodi songs op. 34 were published by Luckhardt, just like the volume from which their poems were taken. They bear the plate numbers 434–39 (i.e. one number per song); the dedicatee was Louis Spohr. Since Spohr, like Eschmann's publisher Luckhardt, was based in Kassel, this suggests that Eschmann had indeed spent some time there in around 1849–50 and had there made the acquaintance of the older man. Wagner himself was personally acquainted with Spohr and had resumed his own long slumbering correspondence with him on 17 November 1853. However, he makes no mention of Eschmann in it (*SB* 5:429–30 and 6:47–48).

The fourth song of Eschmann's op. 34 set, "Mittags" (At Midday) is remarkable because it bears a close resemblance to the passage early on in

Wagner's *Rheingold* in which the gold is seen for the first time. The key is identical (G major); the accompaniment figure in both cases is situated above the melody and comprises triplets (though Eschmann's are thirty-seconds as opposed to Wagner's eighth notes); the harmony of that accompaniment is identical (G major with an added major sixth); and the melody

Example 6.7. Johann Carl Eschmann: opening of "Mittags," no. 4 from *Aus dem Liederbuch eines Malers* op. 34.

Example 6.7. (continued)

Example 6.8. Wagner: "Rheingold" motive from the first draft of *Das Rheingold*, first scene.

itself begins on the dominant D, rising to its octave (see examples 6.7 and 6.8). The poetic context is also similar, the triplet accompaniment depicting the rippling of water.[40] Of course, it is not impossible that the two works — *Rheingold* and "Mittags" — were written independently, without their composers being cognizant of the other's music. But the similarities are so striking that it is difficult to believe that the one did not influence the other. Wagner began his draft of *Rheingold* in November 1853, completing it on 14 January 1854, so our passage was probably written down in mid- or late November 1853. As far as we are aware, he did not show the music of it to anyone in Zurich (except his copyist) until Klindworth had finished making the vocal score in early 1856 (see, for example, *ML*, 545).

Dating Eschmann's song is thus obviously essential in determining who might have influenced whom, if indeed an influence took place. But this is particularly difficult, for no manuscript of "Mittags" has survived in the composer's estate. It would appear that the op. 34 songs were only published in the latter half of 1857, for they first receive a mention in Hofmeister's monthly reports of recent music publications in November of that year.[41] Eschmann's opus numbers seven to twenty all appeared with Luckhardt, as did his op. 27 (two fantasy pieces for piano). But while Luckhardt published several of his works in the very early 1850s, they seem to have been in no hurry to publish his music from 1853 to 1857. His above-mentioned Studies op. 16 were published in three volumes over a period of some eighteen months, and for the next three or four years, Luckhardt all but ignored Eschmann's new works, instead bringing out individual numbers from his various existing sets of piano pieces, in particular from his twelve *Lebensbilder* op. 17, which they had first published entire in late 1852. This would all naturally suggest that sales were not particularly good. It is also noteworthy that Eschmann at this time swapped rapidly from one publisher to another, including Philipp Fries (op. 21), Hofmeister (opp. 22, 23, and 24) and Kistner (opp. 24, 26, 28, 29, and 30). Of importance for us here is the fact that Peters brought out Eschmann's *Sonata in an Easy Style* op. 33 in mid-1854. It appeared in Hofmeister's catalogue in August of that year, which means that it probably came on the market in June or July. Given that it could take up to a year between the submission of a work and its publication, it would be reasonable to postulate a date of composition of early 1853. It also proves, of course, that Eschmann — who in the early 1850s was highly prolific — was in his opus numbers well ahead of what he was actually publishing. It is also noteworthy that Eschmann's op. 35 (a set of eight preludes for piano), published at the same time as his songs op. 34, is in fact his first work to bear the dedication "To my dear wife," whom he had married in early 1853 (the marriage was presumably something of a hurried affair, for their first child was born in June of the same year). We can safely assume that Eschmann will not have waited almost five years before dedicating a work to his new bride; and thus we are surely justified in postulating that all his opus numbers in the early 30s — including the Sonata op. 33, the piano pieces op. 35 and the songs op. 34 — were indeed written in either late 1852 or the first half of 1853. Furthermore, the title of the op. 34 set (*Aus dem Liederbuch eines Malers*), with its allusion to the title of Corrodi's volume of 1853 from which its poems were taken, suggests that Eschmann had intended his songs and Corrodi's poetry to be coupled together, perhaps to provide publicity for each other. This, again, would make 1853 the most likely year of composition, with (economic?) circumstances intervening to prevent their publication until four years after. Eschmann might in fact have felt duty bound that his settings of poetry should be published by the same company that had just published the poetry itself, and for this reason did not seek another publisher for them in the meantime.

There is also, however, internal evidence that can help us to construct a chronology that would place "Mittags" before *Rheingold*. The opening of Eschmann's "Mittags" seems in both text and music to be indebted primarily to a yet older model, Franz Schubert's "Wohin?" the second song of the *Schöne Müllerin* (The Fair Maid of the Mill). Let us compare the text of each:[42]

Wilhelm Müller/Franz Schubert
"Wohin?"

Ich hört' ein Bächlein rauschen
Wohl aus dem Felsenquell,
Hinab zum Thale rauschen
So frisch und wunderhell.

Ich weiss nicht, wie mir wurde,
Nicht wer den Rath mir gab,
Ich musste auch hinunter
Mit meinem Wanderstab.

Hinunter und immer weiter,
Und immer dem Bache nach,
Und immer frischer rauschte,
Und immer heller der Bach.

Ist das denn meine Strasse?
O Bächlein, sprich, wohin?
Du hast mit deinem Rauschen
Mir ganz berauscht den Sinn,

Was sag' ich denn vom Rauschen?
Das kann kein Rauschen sein.
Es singen wohl die Nixen
Tief unten ihren Reih'n.

Lass singen, Gesell, lass rauschen,
Und wandern fröhlich nach!
Es geh'n ja Mühlenräder
In jedem klaren Bach.

["Where to?"

I heard a little brook murmuring
From out of the springs in the cliff,
Murmuring down to the valley,
Fresh and wonderfully bright.

I do not know what happened to me,
Or who told me to do so,
But I just had to go down too,
With my staff.

Downwards and ever onwards,
Always following the brook,
And it murmured ever fresher
And ever brighter.

Is this, then, my path?
O little brook, tell me where it leads!
Your murmuring
Has quite befuddled my senses.

What do I mean: murmuring?
That is no murmuring,
It must be the water nymphs singing
Their roundelay down in the deep.

Keep singing, my friend, keep murmuring,
And wander happily after!
There are mill wheels that spin
In every clear brook.]

August Corrodi/Johann Carl Eschmann
"Mittags"

Ich stieg von grünen Waldeshöhn
In's kühle Thal hernieder,
Ein Bächlein sang mit Lustgetön
Im Geh'n mir munt're Lieder.

Ich folgte froh des Bächleins Spur,
Um seinem Sang zu lauschen,
Doch als wir kamen auf die Flur,
Verstummete sein Rauschen.

Und als ich schaute, lag es tief
In bunter Blumen Decken,
Ob seinem Singen es entschlief
Ich mocht' es nicht erwecken.

["Midday"

I left the green heights of the forest to go
Down into the valley.
A little brook sang
Merry songs to me, happily, as I went on.

Example 6.9. Franz Schubert: "Wohin?" from *Die schöne Müllerin.*

I followed cheerfully the little brook's track,
In order to listen to its song,
But as we came to the valley floor,
Its murmuring fell silent.

And as I watched, it lay deep
Unter a blanket of colorful flowers.
It had sung itself to sleep,
And I did not wish to waken it.]

In each case, the narrator is wandering through the countryside and follows the sound of a brook down into a valley. While the poem by Corrodi is undoubtedly similar to Müller's in both its theme and vocabulary, one should beware of assigning any specific significance to the "rauschendes Bächlein" or "little murmuring brook," as there is barely a brook in German Romantic song that does not murmur in the diminutive (as an example: the first song in Schubert's *Schwanengesang*, to a text by Ludwig Rellstab, begins "Rauschendes Bächlein . . ."). Nevertheless, given Corrodi's firm friendship with Eschmann and his own wide cultural interests — he corresponded with Schumann, Eichendorff, and others, and was by all accounts a competent pianist and singer himself[43] — we can safely assume that he was as familiar with Schubert's song cycle as was his friend. Eschmann's response to Corrodi's poem was rippling triplets in G major and a melodic line strikingly reminiscent of Schubert's "Wohin" (see example 6.9). His song seems also to have been influenced by at least the next two songs in the *Müllerin* cycle. A broken chord in sixteenth notes on the tonic triad, plus an added major sixth, form the opening of the third song, "Halt!" (see example 6.10), while a rising G major triad on the word "rauschen" — with the major sixth as a subsequent passing note — is to be found in the sixth bar of the next song, "Danksagung an den Bach" (see example 6.11). While these resemblances are more tenuous, it does seem that certain characteristics from all three songs are conflated in Eschmann's setting. It is as if the "songs" (note the plural) that the brook is singing

Example 6.10. Schubert: "Halt," from *Die schöne Müllerin.*

Example 6.11. Schubert: "Danksagung an den Bach," from *Die schöne Müllerin.*

are, in fact, those by Schubert, now refracted through the memory of the narrator/singer/composer. In such a reading, then, the brook *is* Schubert himself, singing to the narrator, with "Mittags" not merely a song influenced by another composer, but a song about the act of being influenced — and it is noteworthy that at the moment when the "brook" (in our reading: "Schubert") falls silent, at the close of the second strophe, the music becomes distinctly less Schubertian. In any case, the resemblances are surely numerous enough for us to assert with confidence that Eschmann's response to Corrodi's poem was conditioned by his knowledge of the Schubert cycle as surely as Corrodi had been influenced by the poems that Schubert had set.

The debt owed here to Schubert should not, however, blind us as to the quality of Eschmann's song. It is no more a copy or a paraphrase of Schubert than one could claim that the above-mentioned passage from *Rheingold* might be a paraphrase of Eschmann. The added sixth is no passing note as in Schubert, but an integral, defining moment in Eschmann's opening harmony; the melody is at first placed below the accompaniment, not above; when the narrator follows the trail of the brook in the second strophe, the piano follows him in canon; in the first two stanzas, the voice avoids cadencing in a manner of which Wagner would undoubtedly have approved; and, finally, it is fascinating to observe how the descending chromatic figure of D–C#–C–(B), first outlined in the voice at "ein Bächlein sang" ("a little brook sang"), is taken up by the accompaniment and later given in retrograde when the brook falls silent, after the second strophe.

Our proposed chronology is thus as follows: Schubert's "Wohin?" conditions Eschmann's response to the poem "Mittags," resulting in the setting discussed here, presumably in the first half of 1853; shortly thereafter, Wagner hears or sees the music of this song, and this then influences, in turn, the passage in *Rheingold* given as example 6.8, which was composed in late 1853. The three examples together would seem to form the musical equivalent of those word puzzles, once common in schoolboy magazines, by which one has to transform one word into a quite different one in a given number of steps, changing only one letter at a time. The first and final stages of the puzzle — in our case, Schubert's "Wohin?" and the passage from *Rheingold* — have little or nothing in common, with only the in-between stage ("Mittags") making sense of the transition. There is one aspect of "Wohin?," however, that brings added interest to our little list of influences. Its penultimate strophe runs: "Es singen wohl die Nixen tief unten ihren Reih'n" ("It must be the water-nymphs singing their roundelay in the deep") — which here naturally brings to mind Wagner's own water nymphs, the Rhinemaidens. For Wagner's subconscious, it would not be a great step to misread (or mis-remember) "ihren Reih'n" as "im Rhein," thus: "It must be the water-nymphs singing their songs deep down in the Rhine." In our reading, then, the appearance of the Rhinegold glittering under the water was prompted by Wagner's acquaintance with Eschmann's song, which in its turn triggered off in Wagner a host of memories of Schubert's "Wohin?" with its water nymphs and rippling waters in G major. Thus Wagner perceived "Mittags" not on its own but already conflated with the song(s) "behind" it. Eschmann's song itself was quite possibly Wagner's principal source for the added major sixth, the basic shape of the melody in question, and the arrangement of accompaniment in the treble and melody in the bass.

When Liszt specifically invited Eschmann and Kirchner to meet him at Wagner's apartment during his visit of July 1853, they will surely have understood it as an exhortation to bring along their latest works. We also know for certain that Liszt did not just play his own music for the assembled company, for Kirchner remembered years later having played with him the piano-duet version of Schumann's D Minor Symphony.[44] Perhaps Eschmann took along his latest songs to play, just as we have supposed in the case of Kirchner and his *Grüsse an meine Freunde*. Wagner's memoirs — and here they are surely accurate — depict vividly how "anregend" (inspiring) he had found Liszt's music as played by its composer in July 1853, how it had stimulated his own imagination, and how he had hesitated and wrestled with himself that same summer before embarking upon the composition of the *Rheingold* (*ML*, 508–9). It is tempting to posit that Wagner's emphasis on the influence of Liszt is in part a ploy to deflect us from the influence exerted on him by the music of the "lesser" composers who were present (just as *Mein Leben*, as we mentioned above, also ignores the first performance of the *Walküre* accompanied by Kirchner, in favor of the later, more prestigious, performance accompanied by Liszt). Similarly, we can only suspect, but not prove, that Wagner's self-confessed inner turmoil of that summer might have left him particularly susceptible to outside musical influence. It is also a peculiar coincidence that the song in Eschmann's op. 34 set preceding "Mittags" is entitled: "Es sprang der gold'ne Ring" — which title, if one reads the whole poem, means "The golden ring broke" — this being a ringlet of hair from her boyfriend that the narrator had entwined around her finger, but that broke when he stopped loving her. When read alone, out of context, however, the title could also mean: "The golden ring sprang forth." If Eschmann indeed showed his songs to Wagner and Liszt, then this was, of course, at precisely the time when Wagner was preparing himself for the task of composing his *Ring des Nibelungen* (for the "springing forth" of his own "golden ring," so to speak), after a creative hiatus of several years. Given Wagner's penchant for the synchronistic and for "omens" of all kinds, the title of Eschmann's song (if indeed he saw it) would undoubtedly have attracted his attention.

If my general thesis is indeed correct, then the pitch-specific resemblances between *Rheingold* and "Mittags" are of particular significance, as they would seem to have led Wagner to introduce his "Rheingold" motive (that is, the instrumental fanfare) in G major, even though that motive is primarily associated throughout the *Ring* with the key of C (while examples of it occurring in other keys are not difficult to find, its general association with C major is undeniable). Werner Breig has pointed out that this passage only appears to be in G major because of the persistent use of the note G in the bass and the G-major triad in the harmony. In reality, however, this passage is a long dominant preparation for the C-major appearance of the "Rheingold" fanfare and the immediately subsequent cries of "Rheingold" by the Rhinemaidens. Breig rightly describes this passage as proof of Wagner's mastery of the "art of transition."[45] In our reading, however, both the motive and the key in which it first appears would also seem to have been prompted by Eschmann's work. If this is so, it by no means alters the significance as accorded to the passage by Breig, but provides further proof of Wagner's skill in adapting foreign influences to suit his own needs. If Wagner was even partly aware of having been influenced by such a "minor" composer as Eschmann, it might well have been his pride that prompted him to omit him from his autobiography, thus expunging him from history and preventing later generations from suspecting that Wagner's originality did not preclude adapting what he found best in others. If this is the case, then we must admit that Wagner's strategy was, until now, eminently successful.

There is a further aspect to this similarity between Eschmann and Wagner, however. Unlike his presumed Schubertian models, Eschmann's opening melody is a linear description of the accompanying harmony — a major triad with an added major sixth. Its contours are in fact not dissimilar to the opening vocal melody of the *Rheingold* (Woglinde's "Weia! Waga! Woge, du Welle!"), of which the earliest, brief sketch (without accompaniment) is believed to date back to mid-1852[46] — though Wagner's vocal line is not in Eschmann's G major, and it includes the supertonic as a passing note. Jean-Jacques Nattiez has remarked of how such pentatony is a "kind of *Urmusik*," regarded already in Wagner's day as "typical of *Naturvölker* ['primitive peoples']."[47] Nattiez further draws a parallel between this melody, as it later appears in *Rheingold*, and the passage in *Opera and Drama* in which Wagner describes the birth of melody out of harmony, namely as "[the] horizontal expansion as the surface of the harmony."[48] Nattiez continues: "The aquatic metaphors of *Opera and Drama* remind us of the opening of *Das Rheingold*, while the opening of *Das Rheingold* recalls the theoretical tract."[49] If Wagner indeed heard "Mittags" in July 1853, then its superficial similarity to his "Weia! Waga!" melody might well have haunted him as he returned to work on the *Rheingold*. But in any case, he would have found in the opening bars of "Mittags" ample confirmation of his aquatic metaphors of the birth of melody out of harmony. Woglinde, Flosshilde, and Wellgunde, so to speak, would thus have a grandmother in Schubert's Fair Maid of the Mill.

Notes

[1] For more information on Fanny Hünerwadel, see Walton, "'. . . Unsre gute jungfer Fanny Hühnerwadel [*sic*]. . .' — Eine Schweizer Komponistin in Wagners Zürcher Entourage," in *Bulletin der Peter-Mieg-Stiftung* 12 (1998): 21–26.

[2] The album is discussed in detail in Werner Breig, "Von Alexander Müller bis Richard Wagner und Franz Liszt: Das musikalische Album der Schweizer Sängerin, Pianistin und Komponistin Fanny Hünerwadel," in *Musikalische Quellen — Quellen zur Musikgeschichte: Festschrift für Martin Staehelin zum 65. Geburtstag*, ed. Ulrich Konrad, Jürgen Heidrich, and Hans Joachim Marx (Göttingen: Vandenhoeck & Ruprecht, 2002), 405–23.

[3] See Mendelssohn's letter to Baumgartner of 20 November 1844, held today by the Zentralbibliothek Zürich, shelfmark Ms Z II 351.1.2.

[4] The songs are published by Hug of Zurich. Some have been recorded by Zsuzsa Alföldi, accompanied by Christoph Keller, on the CD *Richard Wagner im Schweizer Exil*, MGB 6156; the set of songs op. 4 has been recorded by Yvonne Howard and Richard Edgar-Wilson, accompanied by Kathron Sturrock, on Guild Music GMCD 7293.

[5] C. Widmer (first name unknown), *Wilhelm Baumgartner: Ein Lebensbild* (Zurich: David Bürkli, 1868), 130–31.

[6] Letter from Hans von Bülow to Baumgartner of 21 December 1862, in the Zentralbibliothek Zürich, shelfmark Ms Z II 351.3.23.

[7] Manuscript in the Zentralbibliothek Zürich, shelfmark Mus Ms 606.

[8] These letters are held today by the Zentralbibliothek Zürich; both that of 25 September 1852 and the second, dated 10 October 1853, bear the shelfmark Ms Z II 353.1.

[9] Amadeus Verlag of Winterthur in Switzerland is publishing Kirchner's complete works in practical editions, edited by Harry Joelson-Strohbach, Bernhard Billeter, and the present writer. Most of Kirchner's manuscripts are held by the Brahms Institute in Lübeck.

[10] Two CDs from the Swiss label MGB offer a selection of music by Wagner and his contemporaries Kirchner, Eschmann, August Röckel, Wilhelm Baumgartner, Heinrich Schulz-Beuthen, Christian Gottlieb Rabe, and Fanny Hünerwadel, mostly from the 1850s: *Richard Wagner und seine Zürcher Komponistenfreunde*, MGB CD 6153, and *Richard Wagner im Schweizer Exil*, MGB CD 6156.

[11] Letter of 8 September 1861 to Friedrich and Margarethe Riggenbach-Stehlin, in Peter Otto Schneider, ed., *Theodor Kirchner: Briefe aus den Jahren 1860–1868* (Zurich: Hug, 1949). In the original, Kirchner writes of a "mousetrap without the bacon," which foodstuff I have altered in translation to conform to Anglo-Saxon rodent-catching custom.

[12] Hans von Bülow, "Die Opposition in Süddeutschland," reprinted in Hans von Bülow, *Ausgewählte Schriften, 1850–1892*, ed. Marie von Bülow (Leipzig: Breitkopf & Härtel, 1896), 79–100; here, 86.

[13] Letter from Kirchner to Hegar, Leipzig, 15 February 1883, quoted in Joelson-Strohbach, "Theodor Kirchner bei Mathilde Wesendonck," in *Minne, Muse und Mäzen: Otto und Mathilde Wesendonck und ihr Zürcher Künstlerzirkel*, ed. Axel Langer and Chris Walton (Zurich: Museum Rietberg, 2002), 143–58; here, 143.

[14] Robert Schumann, *Gesammelte Schriften über Musik und Musiker*, vol. 3, ed. Heinrich Simon (Leipzig: Reclam, 1888), 136.

[15] This work is today published by Amadeus Verlag of Winterthur (together with the Scherzo op. 54), BP 2213, and has been recorded by Christoph Keller on MGB CD 6153.

[16] The year of publication is often given as 1855, though it seems that the work was in fact published in the last weeks of 1854. The *Grüsse* were published in a new edition by Amadeus (Winterthur) in 2002, BP 1199.

[17] See Reinhold Sietz, *Theodor Kirchner: Ein Klaviermeister der deutschen Romantik* (Regensburg: Gustav Bosse, 1971), 29.

[18] Letters of 23 June 1853 from Liszt to Wagner, and of 27 June from Wagner to Liszt, in Erich Kloss, ed., *Briefwechsel zwischen Wagner und Liszt*, 3rd ed. (Leipzig: Breitkopf & Härtel, 1910), 1:243–44.

[19] See Wagner, *Mein Leben*, 507–8, and Max Fehr, *Richard Wagners Schweizer Zeit*, vol. 1 (Aarau and Leipzig: Sauerländer, 1934), 240.

[20] Unpublished letter to Hermann Rollett of 7 February 1854, quoted in Renate Hofmann, *Clara Schumanns Briefe an Theodor Kirchner* (Tutzing, Germany: Schneider, 1996), 15.

[21] Letter from Clara to Kirchner of 27 July 1859, published in Hofmann, *Clara Schumanns Briefe an Theodor Kirchner*, 57.

[22] Hofmann, *Clara Schumanns Briefe an Theodor Kirchner*, 80.

[23] See Werner G. Zimmermann, *Brahms in der Schweiz: Eine Dokumentation* (Zurich: Atlantis Musikbuch-Verlag, 1983); and Hans Erismann, *Johannes Brahms und Zürich: Ein Beitrag zur Kulturgeschichte von Zürich* (Zurich: Fretz, 1974).

[24] In some contemporary sources, her name is also spelled "Schmid."

[25] Quoted in Hofmann, *Clara Schumanns Briefe an Theodor Kirchner*, 31.

[26] Robert Münster, "Eine *Serenade* von Richard Wagner," in *Studien zur Musikgeschichte: Eine Festschrift für Ludwig Finscher*, ed. Annegrit Laubenthal (Wiesbaden: Bärenreiter, 1995), 614–21.

[27] Carl Eschmann-Dumur, *Guide du jeune pianiste: Classification méthodique et graduée d'oeuvres diverses pour piano* (Lausanne: E.-R. Spiess, 1884). As if matters did not need confusing even further, our "Johann Carl" is even given as "Charles Eschmann" on the first page of his op. 29.

[28] Ernest Hutcheson, *The Literature of the Piano*, second edition "revised and brought up to date by Rudolph Ganz" (London: Hutchinson, 1969).

[29] Johann Carl Eschmann, *Quartet in d minor*, ed. Bernhard Päuler (Winterthur: Amadeus, 2000). Recorded by the Ceruti Quartet for Guild Music on GMCD 7171.

[30] The first modern performance was given on 12 September 2002 by the University of Pretoria Symphony Orchestra under Lance Phillip.

[31] Johannes Brahms, *Briefe an P. J. Simrock und Fritz Simrock*, ed. Max Kalbeck (Berlin: Deutsche Brahms-Gesellschaft, 1917), 2:71.

[32] See Johannes Brahms, *Briefwechsel mit Breitkopf & Härtel, Bartolf Senff, J. Rieter-Biedermann, C. F. Peters, E. W. Fritzsch und Robert Lienau*, ed. Wilhelm Altmann (Berlin: Deutsche Brahms-Gesellschaft, 1920), 287.

[33] Hans von Bülow, *Briefe*, vol. 4, ed. Marie von Bülow, 160.

[34] Johann Carl Eschmann, *Ein Hundert Aphorismen: Erfahrungen, Ergänzungen, Berichtigungen, Anregungen, als Resultat einer 30jährigen Clavierlehrerpraxis* (Berlin and Leipzig: Luckhardt, 1878), 169.

[35] Johann Carl Eschmann, *Ein Hundert Aphorismen*, 170.

[36] Johann Carl Eschmann, *Ein Hundert Aphorismen*, second edition revised and ed. by Ernst Radecke (Berlin and Leipzig: Raabe and Plothow, 1899). See especially the editor's comments on page IV.

[37] For further discussion of pitch-specific quotations, conscious and unconscious, see Derrick Puffett, " 'Lass er die Musi, wo sie ist': Pitch Specificity in Strauss" and "A Notational Peculiarity in Webern," both in *Derrick Puffett on Music*, ed. Kathryn Bailey Puffett (Aldershot, UK: Ashgate, 2001), 661–86 and 488–97 respectively.

[38] See Hofmeister, *Musikalisch-literarischer Monatsbericht*, January 1856. http://anno.onb.ac.at/cgi-content/anno-buch?apm=0&aid=1000001&bd=0001856&teil=0203&seite=00000925&zoom=1, accessed July 2006.

[39] Rudolf Hunziker and Paul Schaffner, *August Corrodi als Dichter und Maler* (Winterthur: Literarische Vereinigung, 1930), 27 and 34.

[40] This excerpt from the complete draft ("Gesamtentwurf") is reproduced here by kind permission of the Richard Wagner Museum in Bayreuth, shelfmark A III a 1.

[41] See http://anno.onb.ac.at/cgi-content/anno-buch?apm=0&aid= 1000001&bd=0001857&teil=0203&seite= 00000171 &zoom=1, accessed July 2006.

[42] The texts are given here as printed with the music. There are several minor differences between the poem as set by Eschmann and the version printed in Corrodi's volume, though these are of no consequence for its content. I am greatly indebted to Harry Joelson of the Stadtbibliothek Winterthur for his assistance in procuring important source material.

[43] Hunziker and Schaffner, *August Corrodi*, 14–16.

[44] Adolf Steiner, *Richard Wagner in Zürich*, vol. 3 (Zurich: Orell Füssli, 1903), 23.

[45] Werner Breig, "Der 'Rheintöchtergesang' in Wagners 'Rheingold,' " in *Archiv für Musikwissenschaft* 37, no. 4 (1980): 241–62, especially 244–46.

[46] See, for example, Darcy, "Creatio ex nihilo: The Genesis, Structure, and Meaning of the 'Rheingold' Prelude," in *19th-Century Music* 13, no. 2 (Autumn 1989): 79–100; here, 88.

[47] Jean-Jacques Nattiez, *Wagner Androgyne*, trans. Stewart Spencer (Princeton: Princeton UP, 1993), 57.

[48] Wagner, *Oper und Drama*, in *Sämtliche Schriften und Dichtungen* (Leipzig: Breitkopf & Härtel, [1911]), 3:222–321 and 4:2–229; here, 4:142.

[49] Nattiez, *Wagner Androgyne*, 58.

7: Composing in Wagner's Footsteps

BY THE CLOSE OF THE NINETEENTH CENTURY, Wagner's operas had attained a popularity at the Zurich City Theater such as not even he could have envisioned. Not only did Wagner become the staple diet of the Theater, but its first Kapellmeister, Lothar Kempter, made a point of staging all of his dramatic works, even including his very first opera, *Die Feen*; only the early *Das Liebesverbot* remained elusive and unperformed. The crowning moment of Kempter's career came in 1913, when he conducted the Zurich première of *Parsifal*, the first legal production of the work outside Bayreuth since the end of its copyright protection.[1] However, there is no denying the fact that Zurich from the 1870s onwards was, for at least some three decades, very much a "Brahms city." As we have already mentioned above, the most prominent musicians in Zurich and its environs at the time of Wagner's arrival were in fact all, almost without exception, "Schumannites" and "Mendelssohnians": Eschmann, Kirchner, Baumgartner, Abt, and Oswald Lorenz had all either studied with Mendelssohn or had enjoyed personal contact with Mendelssohn and/or Schumann, and had been influenced decisively by their aesthetic. Yet they all, to a man, fell in some way under Wagner's spell, or at the very least participated willingly in his activities during his Zurich exile. And although Wagner made no secret of his dislike of Mendelssohn and Schumann, neither he nor his new-found friends and colleagues seem to have found their common convergence of interests in the 1850s in any way odd. But then, after Wagner's departure, they all — again, to a man (except for Abt, who had long since left) — gravitated back to a Schumannian/Mendelssohnian aesthetic, as personified by its newest, most compelling representative, Johannes Brahms. One could thus interpret Wagner's Zurich years as a decade-long interlude in which the "music of the future" briefly distracted the city from its natural inclinations to follow more "classical" aesthetic paths. This is well illustrated by considering the fate of the only two composers of note in Zurich who remained open advocates of the New German School in the two decades after Wagner's departure, one a native of the city, the other from Silesia.

Albert Rudolph Fäsy was the only Zurich-born composer of his generation who did not restrict himself to small-scale forms; but his oeuvre was completely ignored during his lifetime.[2] He was born in 1837 in the suburb of Enge (the same suburb where the Wesendonck's villa was later erected), the son of a well-to-do businessman who also served in the

Zurich parliament. Fäsy studied with both Franz Abt and Alexander Müller and enrolled in 1856 at the Leipzig Conservatory. We know that he was in Zurich in the summer of 1858, when Wagner was about to leave the city, because he was visited at the time by Wendelin Weissheimer, a fellow student from Leipzig, who later became a trusted friend of Wagner's. Weissheimer tells us in his memoirs that he made a point of visiting Wagner in his *Asyl*, so we can probably assume that Fäsy went along with him. The Prussian State Library in Berlin today possesses Fäsy's personal copy of the first edition of the score of *Tannhäuser*. Since this contains corrections in Wagner's hand, he and Fäsy must surely have had some direct contact. Fäsy moved to Vienna in 1859, where the minor publisher Albrecht brought out his first work: a song with piano accompaniment entitled "Sehnsucht." He moved in 1860 to Dresden, was back in Zurich in 1862, but apparently moved back to Dresden in 1868. In 1879, he took up residence in Constance, sixty kilometers northeast of Zurich, just across the border in Germany, where he died on 5 May 1891. Fäsy's extant oeuvre comprises several vast symphonic poems after the manner of Liszt (*Columbus, a Dramatic Suite*; *Prelude to Schiller's "Der Triumph der Liebe"*; *Prelude to Goethes "Götz von Berlichingen*," and *Sempach: A Symphonic Poem*). None of these were performed in the composer's lifetime — indeed, they have thus far only been recorded for CD, never performed in the concert hall.[3] While they are perhaps somewhat ungainly in their form, their instrumentation is highly effective. It remains a mystery as to why Fäsy wrote them — except, one presumes, as a private challenge — nor how he was able to calculate so accurately the effect of his huge orchestration without, it seems, ever hearing any of his works except those for piano or voice. Had his manuscripts not found their way into the Zentralbibliothek Zürich in his native city, they would no doubt have been lost entirely.

While Fäsy composed after the manner of Liszt, Zurich's second representative of the New German School, Heinrich Schulz-Beuthen, enjoyed the latter's active advocacy.[4] Born in 1838 in Beuthen (today "Bytom" in Polish Silesia), whose name he added to his own plain surname of "Schulz," he too studied at the Leipzig Conservatory, though from 1862 to 1864. He first drew attention to himself when his setting of the 29th Psalm was performed, at Liszt's instigation, at the 1865 festival of the Allgemeiner Deutscher Musikverein (ADM). He moved to Zurich in 1866 at the suggestion of a former fellow Swiss student from Leipzig, Gustav Weber, a native of Bern. Schulz-Beuthen worked briefly as a critic for the *Neue Zürcher Zeitung*, gave private lessons, and enjoyed an increasing reputation as a composer, with performances of his orchestral works and cantatas, not just in Zurich, but also, with regularity — and again, it seems, thanks to Liszt — at the festivals of the ADM. We know that Schulz-Beuthen met Wagner at least once in Zurich, for Hans Richter's diary notes that he was present at a quartet evening that Wagner attended there, along with the Wesendoncks and the Willes, on 17 February 1871.[5] He knew the Wesendoncks well, it seems, and is one of only two composers besides Wagner who are known to have composed a set of songs to poems by Mathilde (the other being Ödön von Mihalovich in 1891[6]). It was also Schulz-Beuthen who made it possible for Mathilde to realize her long-held dream of becoming a librettist. She had hoped that Brahms might oblige, though of course he did not. The only known opera to one of her texts is Schulz-Beuthen's *Der Zauberschlaf* (The Enchanted Slumber), written from 1868 to 1878, after Mathilde's play *Aschenbrödel* (Cinderella) from her collection of 1864, *Märchen und Märchen-Spiele* (Fairy Tales and Fairy-Tale Plays). It does not seem that she had any hand in preparing her text for operatic treatment. The world première in May 1879 at the Zurich Theater was not a great success, though the work does seem to have awakened the interest of both Liszt and Wendelin Weissheimer. Sadly, we cannot judge it for ourselves, as the score is lost. It was destroyed in the firebombing of Dresden, thirty years after the composer's death, as was the larger part of his oeuvre. However, to judge from contemporary accounts from both critics and the composer himself, Schulz-Beuthen had in his *Zauberschlaf* attempted to combine a Wagnerian leitmotivic technique with the world of the fairy-tale in a manner that sounds remarkably prescient of Humperdinck's *Hänsel und Gretel.* It is thus a strange irony that Mathilde Wesendonck, as the "librettist" of what seems to have been the first post-Wagnerian fairy-tale opera, thus became, in a sense, Wagner's "successor."

Schulz-Beuthen was an ardent supporter of the New German School throughout his Zurich years, and in a small act of homage he even managed to acquire one of Wagner's former pianos for his own use. He dutifully attended the first Bayreuth Festival of 1876, and he had an orchestral work performed at the World Exhibition in Philadelphia in that year: an "Indian Corn Dance," conducted by Theodore Thomas, the man who had commissioned Wagner's *Grosser Festmarsch* for the same event. In fact, Schulz-Beuthen's surviving music seems to our ears today less reminiscent of Wagner than of Grieg or Dvořák. But he still felt in the later 1870s that he was being persecuted by the reigning "Brahmsians" in Zurich. Admittedly, he suffered a series of family tragedies at this time, and he was also quite possibly slightly schizophrenic, so the persecution might have taken place more in his mind than in reality. Nevertheless, he felt compelled to leave the city and his "persecutors" and make a new start. He moved to Dresden, as had Theodor Kirchner just before him — the two misanthropists apparently got on well, with Schulz-Beuthen later even orchestrating four of Kirchner's piano works and an organ piece.[7] A two-year stint in Vienna in the 1890s was less successful, despite Schulz-Beuthen's written assurance to a friend in Zurich that Brahms had received him well.[8] But his Viennese years did at least result in two operas, both to texts by Friedrich Spigl: *Die Paria* (The Pariah) and *Die Verschollene* (The Girl Who Disappeared), the latter having apparently been originally intended for Spigl's friend, Anton Bruckner.[9] These are also the only operas by Schulz-Beuthen of which the music survives, albeit in each case only as a manuscript vocal score (and even these were considered lost until they were discovered amongst hitherto uncatalogued holdings in the Harvard University Library in 2006). In 1895, Schulz-Beuthen was back in Dresden once more, teaching at the conservatory, where he remained until his retirement. His mental health, however, broke down at the end, and he died in 1915 in an institution in nearby Löbtau.

We cannot know, of course, to what extent Schulz-Beuthen and Fäsy were actively sidelined in Zurich in the 1870s. Just because a man might be paranoid — as it seems Schulz-Beuthen was — does not mean *per se* that his paranoia is unfounded. But from what we know of Friedrich Hegar, the man who dominated Zurich's musical life for the last quarter of the nineteenth century, he was generous in spirit, and an unlikely candidate to engage in petty rivalries with those whose aesthetic was different from his own (he even attended the first Bayreuth Festival, despite his anti-Wagnerian misgivings). Rather does it seem that the general atmosphere in the city and its institutions (which were still dominated by the large choral societies) was so orientated toward the more "classicist" aesthetic of Mendelssohn and Brahms that any composer aligned with Wagner and Liszt must inevitably have felt a certain degree of exclusion. The influence of Brahms in Zurich was immense, which fact is all the more remarkable in that the composer himself never lived in the city for longer than a few weeks at a time.

Brahms's first contact with Switzerland had come about very early, when he was still in his twenties, through his friendship with Julius Allgeyer. Allgeyer had fled Germany in the wake of the 1848 revolutions, had settled for several years in the Catholic monastery town of Einsiedeln in Canton Schwyz, and then moved back to Germany, where he subsequently met Brahms. Oddly, perhaps, Allgeyer is not known to have cultivated close relations with any of the other German exiles who were active in nearby Zurich in the 1850s. As mentioned in chapter 6 above, Theodor Kirchner was Brahms's first real champion in Zurich, though the city's devotion to the composer only came about thanks to his close friendship with Friedrich Hegar. Brahms visited Hegar several times over the years, for business and for pleasure, and they even holidayed together on occasion. These visits culminated in the festivities for the opening of the new Tonhalle building in 1895, at which Brahms was the guest conductor. Brahms's long-standing fondness for Switzerland is well-documented, and has over the years been the subject of assorted articles and books.[10] Equally well documented, of course, is the general antipathy that he and Wagner felt for each other. Wagner took several sideswipes at Brahms in his writings, in a manner that even the most sympathetic commentator could not really describe as anything but downright mean,[11] and he took particular umbrage when he and Brahms were awarded the "Order of Maximilian" at the selfsame time (*TB* 1:772). But we would also do well to remember that it was really Brahms who had taken the first potshot at the New German School, when he, Joseph Joachim, Julius Otto Grimm, and Bernhard Scholz had published their "Manifesto" against it in the *Berliner Musik Zeitung* of May 1860. They had refrained from mentioning Wagner by name, though the latter rightly knew that he and Liszt were the joint targets.

Brahms's omission of Wagner's name from the Manifesto suggests, of course, that his feelings toward him were less antagonistic than ambivalent. Indeed, two years later, in late 1862, Brahms aided Peter Cornelius and Carl Tausig in preparing the parts for Wagner's series of concerts in Vienna. He is even reported to have attended all seventy-seven rehearsals for *Tristan* in Vienna in 1863, which suggests a fascination bordering on the obsessive.[12] And Friedrich Hegar later wrote that when Brahms visited the Wesendoncks in Zurich "he showed a lively interest in everything that one could learn about Wagner there."[13] There is yet more detailed evidence that Brahms was attracted by what he found in Wagner's scores, even to the point of envy. Through the offices of Peter Cornelius, Brahms had acquired the manuscript of the Paris additions to *Tannhäuser* for his private collection. Richard Heuberger reported in his memoirs how Brahms would page through it, fascinated, calling Wagner "a man possessed of a gigantic capacity for work, colossal industriousness, horrendous energy." Another time, he showed Heuberger the same manuscript again, once more leafing through it, page after page after page, then exclaiming of a B major passage that

> "Wagner has on every line, on every page, placed each of the five sharps in its place with meticulous precision, and yet despite this precision, it's written with such swiftness and fluidity!" . . . he leafed through the whole passage, pointing specifically, almost reproachfully, at every sharp sign.[14]

This fascination seems to have left its mark in ways both musical and biographical. There is no denying that Brahms, whether by intention or not, in many cases trod directly in Wagner's footsteps, ranging from the seemingly banal and coincidental to the uncannily synchronous. Wagner enjoyed a working holiday in Fluntern in 1852; Brahms did the same in mid-1866 (Wagner stayed in the Pension Rinderknecht on the Hochstrasse, while Brahms resided on the Toblerstrasse, just a couple of hundred yards up the hill); Wagner visited the Gasthaus Sonnenberg on the Seelisberg, opposite Brunnen, in July 1866 (a favorite haunt of his since the mid-1850s); and Brahms did so just a week later. As Max Fehr has documented, the hotel's guest book bore the names of both on the same page, the former on 13 July, the latter on the twentieth. Both men shared a love of Central Switzerland, with Wagner preferring the region around Lake Lucerne, while Brahms was most fond of the lake district around Thun and Spiez (though Wagner in fact had at one time considered looking for a summer house in or near Thun [*SB* 11:152–53]). Their love of the Swiss Alpine region even found musical expression in their respective oeuvres, for they each featured an alphorn melody prominently in one of their compositions. On 9 July 1859, Wagner wrote as follows to his wife from Lucerne:

> I have profited from my Rigi trip. Early in the morning, at 4 am, the servant woke us with his alphorn. I sat up, saw that it was raining, and so remained in bed in order to sleep on. But the funny tune went round and round in my head, and from it there came a very merry melody that the shepherd now plays when he announces Isolde's ship [in the third act of *Tristan und Isolde*], which has a surprisingly jolly, naïve effect. (*SB* 11:261–62)

When Brahms visited Lauterbrun in Central Switzerland in 1868, he too noted down a melody that he heard played on the alphorn, and this later became the main theme in the slow introduction to the fourth movement of his First Symphony.[15] The two tunes are both in C, and are not dissimilar (though this is hardly odd, given the limited range of the instrument). Since he knew *Tristan*, Brahms will already have been familiar with Wagner's own "alphorn tune."

It is amusing that the two men who became the "leaders" of the progressive and "classical" schools of the late nineteenth century should each have found inspiration in the alphorn, not least because this was rare apart from salon pieces intended to convey a Swiss *couleur locale* (of which even Liszt included an example in his *Album d'un voyageur*). But the most intriguing point of intersection between the two men lies neither in their choice of holiday hotel nor in their music. For it is a fact, odd but undeniable, that Brahms also later "acquired" Wagner's Zurich acquaintances and friends, one by one. There is the manner in which, as discussed above, Brahms more or less replaced Wagner in the affections of Mathilde Wesendonck, who even offered him the use of the *Asyl* (though he in this case declined); it is also well known that Hans von Bülow, in his youth an ardent Wagnerian, in later years became just as ardent a Brahmsian. In von Bülow's case, of course, the fact that Wagner stole his wife, while Brahms did not, might well have played a not insignificant role in the realignment of his affections. But then there were also Gottfried Keller, Johann Carl Eschmann, and Theodor Kirchner, all of whom had close contact with Wagner, but who later became keen supporters of Brahms; the same is true of certain later close associates of Wagner, such as Hans Richter, who was, off and on, part of the Wagner household in Tribschen, and later conducted the *Ring* at the first Bayreuth festival. He, too, would later also turn instead to Brahms. (Another Tribschen friend who dallied with the Brahmsians was Friedrich Nietzsche, and it is not a little ironic that it was supposedly his advocacy of Brahms's *Triumphlied* that was the catalyst for his break with the jealous Wagner, for that work celebrated an event for which both Wagner and Brahms were united in their demonstrable enthusiasm: the victory of Prussia in its war with France.) There are two more Zurich figures who deserve at least a peripheral mention in our list of Wagner-to-Brahms converts, both real and putative, namely the composer and piano virtuoso Robert Freund (1852–1936), who taught piano at the Zurich Conservatory upon its founding in 1876, had studied with both Wagner's protégé Carl Tausig and Franz Liszt himself, but later also became a good friend of Brahms; then there was the most obviously "Brahmsian" composer active in Zurich in the late 1860s and early 1870s, Hermann Goetz (1840–76), who had studied with Hans von Bülow in Berlin, long before the latter's own "conversion" to Brahms. Of course, one's natural inclination is to assume that this must surely all be a mere matter of chance, devoid of cause or intent. But we must not forget that it was not the first time that Brahms had acted thus toward one of his composing elders. Even before Robert Schumann's death in 1856, Brahms had in effect "acquired" his idol's wife and family. Seen in this perspective, the manner in which Brahms became friends with Wagner's former colleagues seems less a matter of happenstance than an almost methodical process of appropriation.

Perhaps it was Brahms's well-documented fascination with Wagner the artist that prompted him to court the attention of those who had once been close to Wagner the man; or perhaps those men and women in fact discerned something in Brahms that reminded them subconsciously of Wagner, and this then prompted a similar response on their part; or perhaps — more likely — the truth lies somewhere in the middle. But regardless of what all this friend-swapping might tell us about the psyche of Brahms and his circle, the ease with which men of intellect and integrity in Zurich were able to modulate their aesthetic alliances merely serves, of course, to remind us of what has now long been acknowledged: that the supposed gaping chasm that lay between Brahmsian "Classicism" and the New German "Progressivism" was in fact not really so vast after all.

Notes

[1] See Walton, "*Parsifal* in Zurich," in *Wagner Society of Scotland: Journal* 2 (2005): 7–16.

[2] See Hans Erismann, "'Albert R. Fäsy, Enge': Ein unbekannter Zürcher Komponist des 19. Jahrhunderts," in *Neue Zürcher Zeitung*, 20/21 March 1976.

[3] They have been recorded by the Moscow Symphony Orchestra, under the Swiss conductor Adriano, on Marco Polo, CD no. 8.225134.

[4] For more information on Schulz-Beuthen, see Chris Walton, *Heinrich Schulz-Beuthen (1838–1915): Eine biographische Skizze* (Zurich: Hug, 2003), or "Lost Without Trace: Hunting for Heinrich Schulz-Beuthen," in *The Musical Times* 147, no. 1895 (Summer 2006): 25–38.

[5] *King Ludwig II and Richard Wagner, Briefwechsel*, vol. 5, ed. Otto Strobel (Karlsruhe: Braun, 1939), 166.

[6] See Inge Pechotsch-Feichtinger, "Briefe von Ödön von Mihalovich an Mathilde Wesendonck," in *Studia Musicologica Academiae Scientiarum Hungaricae* 40, no. 1 (1999): 249–301; here, 268.

[7] Op. 43, no. 2; op. 64, no. 1; op. 29, no. 1; all for orchestra; and op. 13, no. 1 and op. 82, no. 2 for wind band.

[8] Letter from Schulz-Beuthen to Johannes Wolfensberger, from Oberdöbling, Vienna, 17 December 1893. Held by the Zentralbibliothek Zürich, shelfmark Ms Z II 438.1.

[9] See Alois Zosel, *Heinrich Schulz-Beuthen, 1838–1915: Leben und Werke; Ein Beitrag zur Geschichte der neueren Programmusik* (Würzburg-Aumühle: Triltsch, 1931), 25.

[10] See, for example, Werner G. Zimmermann, *Brahms in der Schweiz: Eine Dokumentation* (Zurich: Atlantis Musikbuch-Verlag, 1983); and Hans Erismann, *Johannes Brahms und Zürich: Ein Beitrag zur Kulturgeschichte von Zürich* (Zurich: Fretz, 1974).

[11] For example in "Über das Dirigieren" or the "Offenes Schreiben an Herrn Friedrich Schön in Worms," in *Sämtliche Schriften und Dichtungen* (Leipzig: Breitkopf & Härtel, [1911]), 8:261–337 and 10:291–96 respectively.

[12] See Kurt and Renate Hofmann, "Johannes Brahms als 'Autographensammler,'" in *Bunte Blätter: Klaus Mecklenburg zum 23. February 2000*, ed. Rudolf Elvers and Alain Moirandat (Basel: Moirandat, 2000), 99–123; here, 114.

[13] Quoted in Zimmermann, *Brahms in der Schweiz*, 28.

[14] This, and the previous quote from Heuberger, are given in Kurt Hofmann and Renate Hofmann, "Johannes Brahms als 'Autographensammler,'" 114.

[15] See Zimmermann, *Brahms in der Schweiz*, 37–39.

8: Wagner Conducts

When Wagner wrote to Liszt in the autumn of 1849 begging him to help him escape from his current state of penury, the latter declined, claiming temporary financial embarrassment himself. Instead, he suggested: "Couldn't you organize some concerts in Zurich, the proceeds of which could serve to keep you adequately through the winter?"[1] It was sensible advice, and Wagner was sensible enough to follow it. As mentioned in chapter 2 above, he made his debut with the orchestra of the Allgemeine Musikgesellschaft on 15 January 1850, in the fourth program of its concert season. He conducted only Beethoven's Seventh Symphony; the rest of the program was the responsibility of the AMG's nominal conductor, Franz Abt. Wagner conducted no more in that season, but he had made such an impression that when he did return to the podium later that year, he was allowed more or less to pick and choose what he wished to conduct, and when. As we have already seen, he made a similar arrangement in the autumn of that year with the small city theater. Neither institution ever demanded that he bind himself with a written contract.

Wagner's influence on Zurich's concert life was considerable. In 1849, the paid orchestral staff on the AMG's books comprised five violinists, one violist, one cellist, one double bass player, and thirteen woodwind players. But Wagner wanted more. The number of orchestral musicians employed by the AMG accordingly was doubled during the next five years. A further sign of Wagner's preferential treatment was his salary. In the 1849–50 season, Franz Abt was paid SF 107.32 for seven concerts, whereas for conducting that single Beethoven symphony, Wagner received SF 37.20. The next year, Abt was paid SF 107.05 for seven concerts, while Wagner received SF 128.23 for a total of three symphonies and two overtures. One can hardly blame Abt for leaving Zurich in the autumn of 1852. By 1854, Wagner was being paid SF 100 for each concert he conducted, which was no mean sum by any standards (it was equivalent, for example, to over a month's rent for an apartment).

In his *Art and Revolution*, Wagner had recently declared that the public should have free entry into the theater.[2] However, the Zurich audiences were a far cry from his expressed ideal. Most of the tickets for the AMG's concerts in the Casino were sold on a subscription basis, and since the hall seated only some four hundred people, entrance was restricted *de facto* to the city's upper classes. The theater next door seated about twice as many, to be sure, but entry there was also at a price. Zurich may have been a republic in which refugees from the various uprisings of the time were made welcome, but it was still run by elites, albeit of a far more liberal disposition than in most of the remainder of western Europe. Wagner's theoretical scorn for such elitism was presumably alleviated by the practical fact that those same upper classes were paying him extremely well.[3] Not until the Tonhalle Society was founded in 1868 and the old Kornhaus converted into a spacious concert hall was "high art" in Zurich democratized to any degree.

Wagner had a lasting impact on concert programming in Zurich. Although Casimir von Blumenthal had introduced the symphonies of Beethoven to the Zurich public, they were hardly a common occurrence. Until the 1840s, if a Beethoven symphony was played it was likely to be set aside for ten years before being heard again. Thanks to Wagner, the Zurich public now heard Beethoven's orchestral works on a regular basis. But there was more than this. Before Wagner's arrival, the AMG concerts usually consisted of a merry medley of mostly small pieces, mixing chamber music and song with the occasional symphony or overture. Under his direction, they assumed a format closer to what remains today the "norm," namely an overture to begin with, then a concertante work, and then, to close the evening, a symphony. This format was admittedly not adhered to with any rigidity, nor did the old ways die out immediately; but the shift in programming policy under Wagner was obvious and undeniable. It is thus not without irony that Wagner's theoretical writings of this time condemned absolute music as passé at the same time that he was introducing to Zurich the principal means of its future propagation: the new concept of the "symphony concert." Another of Wagner's innovations was the introduction of program notes to enlighten his concert-going public. These were not always printed separately, probably for reasons of cost, but they were at least published in advance in Bernhard Spyri's *Eidgenössische Zeitung*.

While the bibliography on Wagner is huge, his art of conducting and rehearsing has, until recent years, rarely been the object of sustained musicological interest.[4] His own writings and the reports of others can, however, throw some light on his methods. The Zurich composer Wilhelm Baumgartner apparently esteemed Wagner most as a conductor, saying: "He knew how to rule and inspire the orchestra like a military leader, full of life, spirit, clarity, and fire, with a clear conception of the work to be conducted."[5] Of the Zurich *Tannhäuser* production of 1855 the ever-enthusiastic Bernhard Spyri wrote: "The rehearsals took place under the baton of the composer himself, and anyone who has ever attended a rehearsal of Wagner's will know what that means."[6] Sadly, Spyri does not say "what that means." But other sources are somewhat more precise. In his autobiography *Mein Leben*, Wagner himself writes about the Zurich orchestra of early 1852 as follows:

> Since the existing orchestral forces were very small in number, I only consented to conduct on the condition that capable players were brought in from outside to strengthen the string section. I restricted my participation in each case to a single Beethoven symphony. Since I always demanded three rehearsals just for the symphony, and a number of the musicians came from far away especially for the occasion, these events took on something of a solemn character. Because I was able to spend a whole rehearsal exclusively on a single symphony, I was able to devote much time to the more minute details of execution. And since the purely technical difficulties were not great, I achieved a freedom of interpretation that I had not hitherto attained — a freedom of which I became even more aware upon observing the surprising results that it brought with it. (*ML*, 470)

As ever, *Mein Leben* is here to be treated with caution on account of its virtuosic blend of poetic and empirical truth. In light of this passage, one might think that Wagner had graciously condescended to bring High Art to the boys from the backwoods of Zurich, whereas in fact it was he who had been more or less rescued in his hour of (financial) need by the AMG's willingness to engage him. Nevertheless, the substance of what he wrote is confirmed by a letter he sent to Hans Conrad Ott-Imhof of the AMG committee on 23 November 1854:

> I hear that a large number of the musicians that you intend to place at my disposal are due to come from Winterthur and will not attend all rehearsals, but only the last one. Once and for all I wish to explain that I am no longer able to rehearse if musicians are not present, and I must demand that all participants should attend the three rehearsals necessary for the concert. (*SB* 6:283)

Since Wagner found it necessary to demand the attendance of all musicians at all three rehearsals, this had clearly hitherto been an uncommon occurrence. As we have seen in chapter 2 above, Wagner's various proposals in the 1850s to reform the Zurich music scene came to nothing. But there is no doubting Wagner's commitment to bettering the state of the AMG orchestra. He himself wrote countless letters to engage musicians from the outlying towns and cities whenever he needed to boost his forces for his orchestral programs, and on one occasion — as is proven by a letter to Moritz von Wyss of 13 November 1853 — he even caught a double bassist by the name of Weber, just as he was about to leave the city by post coach, and guaranteed him a modest but steady income in the AMG and theater orchestras if he would only stay, because "we can't let the man slip away so easily" (*SB* 5:463).

Despite the modest state of the orchestra, Wagner did in fact find there a few local orchestral musicians who were, he claimed, as fine as he had ever heard elsewhere. In *Mein Leben*, he singled out Hans Conrad Ott-Imhof and the horn player Rudolf Bär. The latter is described as "vorzüglich" — "excellent" — while Ott, a clarinetist in the orchestra (and the dedicatee of Johann Carl Eschmann's Fantasy Pieces op. 9 — see chapter 6 above) receives more attention, being "finely educated . . . a rich, patrician friend of the arts and an amateur musician; not very energetic, but extraordinarily tender and gentle in his clarinet-playing" (*ML*, 471). It is to the oboist and bandmaster Philipp Joseph Fries that Wagner devotes the most attention, however:

> I even discovered in the orchestra several truly talented musicians who were capable of being trained with rare success. Of these, I wish to mention by name Fries the oboist, whom I raised from a subordinate position to play the first part. In the Beethoven symphonies, he had to rehearse his highly important part privately with me as if it were a vocal line. When we performed the c minor Symphony for the first time, I managed to get this peculiar man to play the small "song" passage marked *Adagio* in the first movement in a marked and gripping way such as I have never heard equaled since. When I later withdrew from the orchestra [in 1855], he left it immediately and became a music-seller. (*ML*, 470–71)

The extent to which Fries made an impression would seem to be confirmed by the very absence of his name in an essay that Wagner wrote at approximately the same time as the above passage from *Mein Leben* (that is, mid- or late 1869). In *Über das Dirigieren* (About Conducting), Wagner discusses the oboe "cadenza" from Beethoven's Fifth Symphony in a manner that is remarkably similar:

> I received the best guidance with regard to the tempo and the performance of Beethoven's music from the soulful, carefully accentuated singing of the great *Schröder-Devrient*; thus it was impossible for me since then to let the inspiring oboe cadenza in the first movement of the c-minor symphony [here Wagner gives the "cadenza" as a music example] be so embarrassingly blown in that same manner in which I have otherwise always heard it . . .[7]

It is probable that this reference was prompted by Wagner's memories of Fries, even though the latter remains unmentioned. The above quotation actually includes an implicit *non sequitur* — why should a general description of the art of Schröder-Devrient lead directly to a specific discussion of how bad oboists play a passage from Beethoven's Fifth Symphony? However, if one conflates this passage with the one from *Mein Leben*, one arrives at a version — albeit "invented" — that seems to make better sense than either of the sources:

> I received the best guidance with regard to the tempo and the performance of Beethoven's music from the soulful, carefully accentuated singing of the great Schröder-Devrient. When we performed Beethoven's c minor Symphony for the first time in Zurich, the oboist Fries had to rehearse his highly important part privately with me as if it were a vocal

> line sung by her. I thus managed to get this peculiar man to play the small "song" passage marked *Adagio* in the first movement in a marked and gripping way such as I have never heard equaled since.

Our two sources were quite possibly written concurrently, in which case our "invented" passage could actually be closer to Wagner's original intentions. As his mind strayed from the one text to the other, his embarrassment at the thought of praising a provincial music-seller in a serious tract on the conductor's art was probably coupled with a desire not to copy a passage wholesale from one work into another. As a result, he seems to have left each text with only one half of the information necessary for the reader's full understanding. If our invented passage does indeed approximate to an "Urtext" that was first "divided" before being committed to paper, then it is not impossible that the two halves in fact remained a whole in Wagner's imagination, so that he was never really aware of their individual incompleteness.

We can probably take Wagner's praise of Fries as sincere, since he could expect neither financial nor social gain from it. However, his praise is undeniably self-reflecting. It was Wagner (according to Wagner) who recognized Fries's talent and raised him to the post of first oboist, and it was to Wagner's didactic gifts (according to Wagner) that Fries owed the secret of his success. In one respect, however, Wagner strays demonstrably from the truth. Fries actually began his career as a publisher in 1851, the year in which Wagner first conducted Beethoven's Fifth Symphony in Zurich (on 28 January), and a full four years before Wagner left the Zurich orchestra. In fact, as we have seen in the above chapter on Zurich's publishers, Fries had been an "instrument-seller" since 1846, and had presumably also been selling printed music as a sideline since then. But Wagner's error can be interpreted as underlining his praise, as it suggests that Fries was important enough a "discovery" for him to have developed a belief in certain proprietary rights concerning the man. When Wagner left the orchestra, then his protégé could, in his eyes, no longer function as a musician: the only future for Fries *après* Wagner could be in abandoning high art for small-time capitalism instead, with all its negative connotations. Fries did indeed leave the orchestra shortly after Wagner, though he in no wise ceased to play, and Wagner specifically asked for his participation when he conducted Beethoven's *Eroica* Symphony in St. Gall in November 1856, and again when he conducted a program of individual movements from Beethoven symphonies for Otto Wesendonck at Easter 1858.

The impression one gains from the extant anecdotal sources is that Fries was promoted from second to first oboe as soon as Wagner had taken up his baton for the AMG. One of the stories recorded by the Fries family is of Wagner exclaiming after his first rehearsal: "As long as I direct these concerts, Fries must sit at the first oboist's desk."[8] The man whom Fries replaced was one Karl Schmidt, though in fact the orchestral lists in the archives of the AMG suggest that Schmidt remained first oboist, at least in name, up to and including the 1850–51 season, after which he left the orchestra. It therefore seems more likely — given that Wagner conducted only one work in the 1849–50 season — that Fries's promotion occurred during the rehearsals for Wagner's first concert of the following season, on 28 January 1851, when the principal work on the program was, as it happens, Beethoven's Fifth Symphony. It is not known whether Wagner consulted Franz Abt before swapping the two oboists, but such consultation would have been unlikely, given the rivalry between them (or, at least, between their respective supporters), and given the fact that the former will have been the very man responsible for Fries's sitting at the second desk in the first place. It does, however, seem unlikely that the difference in quality between the two oboists would have been as startling as Wagner suggests. To be sure, the orchestra did contain a number of prominent citizens from Zurich's oldest families who were aware of their privileges, but Karl Schmidt was not one of them, and so did not owe his position in the playing hierarchy to his social standing. Nor can one really believe that Franz Abt was so incompetent as to place a bad musician above a fine one. It is thus possible that Fries's rapid promotion was a means for Wagner to establish his authority immediately at the beginning of the new concert season, and thereby to lessen the authority of Abt. However, Wagner's later insistence on employing Fries as his first oboist in St. Gall and in the Villa Wesendonck suggests that the decision was not merely one of cynical political expedience. Furthermore, Wagner's insistence on strict rehearsal discipline and his obvious attempts to raise musical standards, all well documented, would hardly have allowed him to favor a lesser musician above a better one (the very thing of which Abt is implicitly accused). Perhaps — as *Mein Leben* suggests — Wagner's support for Fries and his individual "tuition" did in fact spur Fries on to interpretative heights that surprised them both. Nor does Wagner seem to have soured relations between Fries and Abt. For in 1852, in his capacity as music publisher, Fries brought out a choral song cycle by Abt, the text of which had been penned by J. J. Leuthy, the godfather of Fries's daughter Maria (*Ein eidgenössisches Sängerfest: Cyclus von 12 Gesängen und einem Quodlibet* [A Swiss Singing Festival: Cycle of 12 Songs and a Quodlibet]).

With regard to Wagner's conducting activities in the Zurich theater, we are largely reliant on contemporary reviews, for almost all other traces of his work were lost when the theater burnt down on 1 January 1890, along with its library and archives. However, the library of the AMG has survived largely intact and has been deposited for the last eighty years in the Zentralbibiothek Zürich. Among the holdings from the nineteenth century are scores and orchestral parts of works performed by Wagner during his career as guest conductor of the AMG orchestra. But none of these bears any markings in the hand of Wagner himself, who probably conducted from his own scores anyway. Furthermore, the orchestral parts used under his baton were never treated as relics but were used repeatedly by various orchestras until the early 1990s, when a veto was at last placed on lending them out.

The AMG's library contains but two fragments in Wagner's own hand. There are twelve bars of the double-bass part to Beethoven's *Egmont* music[9] and a fragment, discovered in the late 1990s, of Wagner's "lost" version of Mozart's *Don Giovanni*, made for the Zurich theater in the autumn of 1850.[10] This comprises nine bars of backstage music for the first trumpet, plus the necessary dialogue cues. This may not seem much — but the only other known fragment comprises just two bars and is held by the University Library in Leipzig. According to Wagner himself, the score and parts were taken by Zurich's theater director, Philipp Kramer, when he left to take up a post at Trier in Germany in 1851. In his correspondence with Theodor Uhlig, Wagner remarked that his changes to the work had been few in number. He had "added careful nuances" to the orchestra, amended the layout of scenes in order to reduce the number of scene changes, written a single new recitative for Donna Anna and Don Ottavio, and made new translations of the dialogue (*SB* 4:298–99; in Wagner's day, it was usual for the text of Mozart's recitatives to be spoken, not sung). Wagner's account is supported by a letter from Hans von Bülow to his father, written the day after the first performance of 8 November 1850.[11] As Egon Voss has remarked, Wagner used the word "Nüancierung" almost certainly to denote little more than alterations to the dynamics, phrasing, and such like, certainly not any far-reaching changes to the musical text.[12] Despite his claim to have "translated" the dialogue, Wagner's grasp of Italian was in fact no better than the educated tourist's average smattering. He would not visit Italy himself until mid-1852, and when he met Italians, his natural reaction would always be to speak to them in French (as was the case, for example, with Francesco De Sanctis — see chapter 10). Furthermore, the dialogue cues on the Zurich fragment do not differ greatly from the wording of the then current German translations by Neefe, Schroeder, Rochlitz, and others, which suggests that the "new translation" consisted of little more than minor revisions of an existing German text, perhaps with the aid of an occasional glance back at the Italian original.

The notion that Wagner had made considerable alterations to the score most probably originated with Kramer as a mere publicity ploy. On 7 November 1850, an ad in the *Tagblatt der Stadt Zürich* urged the public to support the theater, since Kramer, it said, had lost more than a thousand gulden (over SF 2000) in the course of the previous October; and just one day later, the first performance of *Don Giovanni* was announced, with noticeable space allotted to the mention of "Wagner's recitatives" — the use of the plural naturally being more attractive to the potential audience than would the singular. Once in the theater, of course, there will have been hardly anyone except von Bülow who would have recognized the hype for what it was. Perhaps the most conclusive proof that Wagner's emendations and additions had indeed been peripheral is the fact that he seems not to have made any attempt to prevent Kramer from taking his "arrangement" with him, and when the two men were briefly in contact once more, in early 1858 (albeit indirectly), when Kramer was back in Switzerland, running the theater of St. Gall, there is no record of Wagner having made any serious effort to retrieve it.[13]

Of the orchestral parts made for the series of concerts that Wagner organized around his fortieth birthday in May 1853, only those for the "March of Peace" from *Rienzi* have survived (and even these were considered lost, but for a sole tuba part, until the summer of 2006; by a curious irony of fate, they might well have been preserved only because in 1858 the empty space on the back of them was used to write out the parts for a "Scene and Cavatina" from Verdi's *Il Trovatore*).[14] As for the remaining orchestral parts in the AMG library that might have been used under Wagner, they bear many expression marks added by orchestral musicians over the past hundred and fifty years, with the result that it is difficult to ascertain who added what, and when. However, in the case of four works, we can indeed trace certain expression marks back to Wagner himself, and these can help us to understand Wagner's conducting and rehearsal methods in the early 1850s. The works in question are Mozart's Symphony no. 41, the *Jupiter*; Haydn's Symphony no. 104 in D; Beethoven's Fifth Symphony; and the Overture to Gluck's *Iphigenia in Aulis*. Our proof lies in handwritten copies of orchestral parts made for the AMG in the 1850s.

It has long been known that Adam Bauer worked as a copyist for Wagner in Zurich, for he is mentioned in Wagner's correspondence. He was born in Bavaria in 1821 and first surfaces in Zurich on 31 December 1841, upon taking rooms on the Obere Kirchgasse in the old city. Within a month of arriving he was playing in the AMG's orchestra (his first salary receipt is dated 31 January 1842), and it is possible that he came to Zurich precisely because he was confident of getting a job there. During the 1840s, 1850s and 1860s, Bauer played viola, and occasionally violin or clarinet, in the orchestra. From January 1843 onwards, he also worked as its copyist, though he was at first not alone — other orchestra members, such as Jean Keller, Rüegg Senior, and a certain Weixlstorfer, also copied parts. Bauer married a Swiss girl in 1844, became a citizen of Zurich in 1867, and died there in 1878. Judging from the receipts in the AMG archives, he had by the early 1850s advanced to being the orchestra's main copyist. His work was apparently much admired by Wagner, at least until 1855, when the latter complained — wrongly, as it happened — about mistakes that Bauer was supposed to have made in a copy of the revised version of his *Faust* Overture[15] (though since Wagner had completed the score on 17 January and the first rehearsal took place on the twentieth, giving Bauer just two full days to do his job, this suggests both that Wagner must have had great confidence in his efficiency and that there were mitigating circumstances for any mistakes that did creep in). Two of the parts for the *Faust Overture* (for cello and double bass) were not copied by Bauer but by a man who from now on became increasingly important as a copyist for the AMG: Carl Gisler, a clarinetist in the orchestra. He was born in 1827 in Winterthur, and moved to Zurich on or around 26 April 1852 (perhaps he had come in time to play in the first performance in the Zurich Theater's run of the *Holländer*, on 25 April); he died in Zurich on 22 September 1867. Wagner himself now turned instead to Karl Schmidt for his copying work, specifically for the music to his *Nibelungen* — a man Hans Bélart tells us was a fellow Saxon immigrant[16] (and who was also, it seems, the same Karl Schmidt whom Wagner had five years earlier replaced as first oboist for the AMG).

Wagner performed Mozart's *Jupiter* Symphony in Zurich on 14 February 1854. The AMG's orchestral parts for this symphony are not complete. Some were probably pilfered by musicians over the years or simply borrowed and never brought back. Of the extant parts some are printed, some the work of copyists. The printed parts were published by André in Offenbach around 1806. One cello and one double-bass part are the work of an unknown copyist, and — to judge by the paper used — they predate Wagner's performance by many years. Three parts for cello and double bass together, and eight sides of a second-violin part, were written out by Adam Bauer. Both printed and manuscript parts contain various handwritten annotations, and all contain rehearsal letters in Bauer's hand. Of particular note is the fact that the cello parts copied by Bauer include expression marks in his hand that are not Mozart's, and which I have not found in any contemporary editions (see figures 10 and 11). Furthermore, these exact same marks were added by Bauer to our extant printed cello part. It would thus seem natural that the source for the expression marks copied by Bauer was also the source for those added to the printed part. The very fact that extra cello parts had to be copied suggests that several new string players were drafted in for a particular performance — a practice we know to have been common under Wagner, but not before him. And the fact that the same expression marks were added to all the parts suggests a punctilious approach to rehearsing, such as was by all accounts also hitherto unknown to the orchestra. Lastly, since Bauer was Wagner's own copyist, the natural conclusion is that these expression marks were made at Wagner's request. We find convincing proof for this in the bills and receipts in the AMG's archives. There is a bill from Adam Bauer of 7 April 1854 in which he lists his copying work for the AMG of the past months:

Figure 10. Adam Bauer's hand-written cello part for Mozart's *Jupiter* Symphony (no. 41).

Figure 11. A printed cello part for Mozart's *Jupiter* Symphony (no. 41), with expression marks and rehearsal letters added by Adam Bauer.

> For Mozart's C major Symphony, 3 cello and double-bass parts, 2 violin parts . . . all expression marks and rehearsal letters added in all the orchestral parts

Further we find

> for Haydn's D major Symphony, 1 first-violin part, 1 second violin, 1 viola, 2 cello and double-bass parts . . . and in the score and all orchestral parts, the rehearsal letters and all expression marks added

and

> For the Iphigenie Overture by Gluck, Herr Wagner's ending added in all the parts and all the expression marks added.
>
> For the above overture, 2 clarinet parts, 2 bassoon parts and 4 cello and double-bass parts written out anew.

It is thus beyond any reasonable doubt that Bauer's copying work was done at Wagner's behest, and that the expression marks added to all these orchestral parts were his.[17] Adding the rehearsal letters to the parts too might seem a minor matter, but if the letters are the same in all parts and the conductor's score, much rehearsal time can be spared. If the conductor stops in the middle of a phrase to rehearse some detail or other, the rehearsal letters mean that everyone can start together at an easily definable point. This in turn confirms the picture that Wagner paints in *Mein Leben* of his careful rehearsal technique. The fact that Bauer added precise expression marks naturally means that Wagner had a clear picture of his ideal interpretation in advance. He also will have known that orchestral players in rehearsal are loath to put hand to pencil and pencil to paper in order to register the wishes of the man in front waving his baton at them. So someone (in our case Bauer) had to be authorized — and paid — to make sure that everyone had all the necessary expression marks to facilitate a uniform interpretation.

It may seem odd, however, that the number of expression markings added is by no means excessive. If Wagner was in a position to have orchestral parts copied at someone else's expense (for it was the AMG who paid Bauer, not Wagner), then we might expect a conductor as supposedly meticulous as he to have had everything copied that he could possibly wish for, in order to attain his ideal performance. This apparent paradox dissolves, however, when one considers the circumstances of rehearsal and performance in Zurich, where about half of the orchestra members were amateurs. As is well known to anyone who has ever conducted an amateur or semi-professional orchestra, the greatest challenge is always getting the players actually to look at the conductor in performance, instead of disappearing behind their music stands. The playing of an amateur orchestra inevitably deteriorates into a grey *mezzo-forte* unless the players pay close attention to the conductor. Furthermore, in an amateur orchestra, it is usually the less capable string players who sit at the back, where their chances of being able to see the conductor properly, or of being noticed by him, are vastly reduced.[18] Wagner was surely aware that, had he filled his orchestral parts to the brim with expression markings, then his players would have spent most of their time with their heads in the music and would have been unable to pay proper attention to him. The expression marks in the parts thus provide the skeleton of his interpretation, but would not have distracted from whatever he might have wished to convey in the spirit of the moment.

Of the parts mentioned in Bauer's bill above, one second-violin part for the *Jupiter* has been lost, while of the manuscript parts to Haydn's symphony no. 104 in D only one viola part has remained. As for Gluck's overture, we are somewhat luckier in that we possess a complete set of parts, only discovered in the late 1990s, of which some are in Bauer's hand and the remainder printed, but with his handwritten rehearsal letters and annotations added (this hitherto unknown arrangement of the whole overture was given its first modern performance by the Zurich Tonhalle Orchestra in 1999).[19] The AMG's parts for the *Adagio* of Beethoven's Fifth Symphony also feature a few handwritten expression marks that we can be certain originated with Wagner. The scores that Wagner must have used are no longer extant, having survived neither in Zurich nor in the library he had later in Bayreuth.[20]

The existence of annotated parts for just these few works prompts the question: why do we not find similar expression marks elsewhere? The AMG's library today possesses parts for the overtures to Weber's *Freischütz* and Spontini's *Vestale* that were most probably the ones used under Wagner; furthermore, its parts for the symphonies of Beethoven are also all either first or very early editions, presumably acquired during Casimir von Blumenthal's tenure, and almost certainly the same that were used by the orchestra under Wagner's baton. We must therefore assume that they do not bear any added expression marks (with the sole exception of the *Adagio* from the Fifth), simply because Wagner regarded the composer's own as adequate.

It is noteworthy that Wagner did not conduct Beethoven's first two symphonies in Zurich — in fact, it seems he never conducted them at all.[21] In his introduction to the *Eroica* written for a performance in Zurich, Wagner described this as "the work in which Beethoven first began his own individual development" — which suggests that he regarded the preceding two symphonies as immature by comparison. This is underlined some years later in his article *About Conducting*. There, he draws a dividing line between two types of allegro movement, calling the "genuinely Beethoven" type *sentimental* (meaning here "emotive" or "Romantic"), and the older, Mozartian type *naive*. His terminology is taken from Friedrich Schiller's essay *Über naive und sentimentalische Dichtung* of 1795 (On Naive and Sentimental Poetry), in which the poet divided up writers into the "naive" ones who "imitated nature" and the "sentimental" ones who "reflected upon the impression" that events and objects made upon them. Wagner's opinion on the "newness" of the *Eroica* is confirmed by a remark he made many years later to Cosima. He asked, rhetorically: "Do you know the name of the note of the whole of modern music? It is C sharp, it's the C sharp of the first theme of the *Eroica*" (*TB* 1:401).

Wagner says that the *naive* allegro (or *classical* allegro, as he also calls it) is characterized in its dynamics by the simple alternation of *piano* and *forte*, soft and loud, and by its stable rhythmic-melodic forms. The *sentimental*, Beethovenian type is, however, distinguished by the use of *crescendi* and *diminuendi* — that is to say, by a more flexible, differentiated approach to dynamics. Wagner states many times that the first movement of the *Eroica* belongs to the *sentimental* type of allegro, as do the allegros of all the later symphonies. Beethoven's first two symphonies remain unacknowledged, and thus by implication belong to the earlier, *naive* type.

Wagner's article on conducting also calls for fidelity to the text in Beethoven. He tells how he removed the expression mark *piano* that his colleague Reissiger had added in the last movement of the seventh symphony, and replaced it instead with Beethoven's original *forte*.[22] Wagner also complains that a particular section in the first movement of the Ninth Symphony (bars 116–22) is usually played with a crescendo instead of *pianissimo* all the way through, as marked. The music should be performed, he says, "as the Master intended" (273). Beethoven wrote many expression marks into his music, whereas Mozart and Haydn wrote very few. The main difference between them is that Beethoven made much use of *crescendo* and *diminuendo*, while Mozart and Haydn rarely did. Wagner's expression marks for the *Jupiter* Symphony, for his Gluck overture, and for Haydn's Symphony no. 104 indeed comprise mostly *crescendi* and *diminuendi*. Where the original parts feature a sudden *forte*, it is as often as not prepared for by a hairpin *crescendo* added by Bauer. Thus those sharp differences between loud and soft that Wagner says are characteristic of the older, "naive," Mozartian style, are dissolved. This annulling of simple contrasts — the addition in other words of "transitions" of dynamics — in effect brings about a "Romanticization" of the works in question, and suggests that Wagner regarded them as already belonging to the "sentimental," "Beethovenian" style. In order to achieve a correspondingly "sentimental" interpretation, Wagner had to add those expression marks — above all, *crescendi* and *diminuendi* — that the composer had "failed" to add himself. This implies a certain criticism of the composers in question, who had lacked the insight necessary to realize that they had crossed the boundary into a "new" compositional style — albeit a style defined only retrospectively by Wagner himself. In *About Conducting*, Wagner writes the following about the second movement of Mozart's g minor symphony No. 40:

> If the expression marks do not suffice, then the feelings inspired by the wonderful course of this piece do their work, and our fantasy tells us how we might give expression to these feelings in our actual interpretation. It then seems as if the Master wished to leave this completely to us, for the expression marks he gives as binding are of the utmost paucity. (305)

Thus the g minor symphony implicitly belongs to the "sentimental" type, and this is obviously why Wagner insists that it calls for differentiated dynamics, even if Mozart did not know it himself. Wagner makes it clear that he expects the conductor to add them. As for our *Jupiter* Symphony, Wagner expressly mentions that it is in matters of style "already not far" from the *Eroica* Symphony (287) — and thus, by implication, also latently "sentimental." And Wagner "sentimentalized" Haydn's Symphony no. 104 perhaps not least because the opening of its first movement is somewhat prescient of Beethoven's Ninth, a work that he adored. This Haydn symphony was, as it happens, one of the few works that Wagner copied out in score for study purposes when he was a teenager.[23]

The "sentimental," "Beethovenian" style does not merely require a differentiated treatment of dynamics. Just as the *crescendo* was an innovation in Mozart's day, says Wagner, so the use of *rubato* belongs to the interpretation of music from the mature Beethoven onwards. This is the so-called "espressivo" conducting style that was practiced above all by Wagner's successors in the German tradition, from Arthur Nikisch down to Wilhelm Furtwängler.[24] It is first mentioned by Wagner in his article from 1846 on Beethoven's Ninth Symphony, but it is not described in detail until *About Conducting*:

> Since Beethoven, a quite fundamental difference has occurred in the treatment of musical material and its performance compared with earlier times. Elements that once, thanks to single, closed forms, were kept apart to lead their own separate lives, are here . . . placed together in the most contrasting forms possible and developed together and against each other. Of course, the performance of the work should correspond to this too, and above all, the tempo should not be any less fluid than the thematic web. (290–91)

Beethoven applies a "fluid" treatment to the thematic content of a work and its dynamics, and the conductor of the work should apply the same treatment to its tempo. The art of interpretation is thus, in effect, an art of transition. However, we must not forget that when Wagner is talking either about the work of others or about his own earlier works, he is often referring obliquely to a compositional matter with which he is wrestling in the present. It is surely no coincidence that Wagner wrote *About Conducting* just as he resumed work on the *Ring* after a hiatus of several years. His desire to treat all parameters of a Beethoven symphony in a fluid, flexible manner thus finds its corollary in his own symphonic web of leitmotifs in that work.

To explain Wagner's interpretative practices in Zurich with reference to an article written over ten years later is no mere musicological sleight of hand. For although *About Conducting* was first published in 1869, it was in fact planned back in the 1850s, when Wagner was working on the *Ring*, and its content is clearly — at least in part — the result of experiences that he made during his Zurich years. After all, that was the last time that Wagner conducted the staple classics with a regular ensemble over a prolonged period. In the excerpt from *Mein Leben* quoted above, he claimed that his performances with the semi-professional orchestra of Zurich allowed him "a freedom of interpretation that I had not hitherto attained," and it is surely this very freedom that he later described, in detail, in *About Conducting*, though without mentioning either the city or its orchestra. It is significant that this article was written at the same time that Wagner was dictating his reminiscences of his Zurich years to Cosima, for as we have already seen in the case of Philipp Fries, there are passages in both texts that are too similar to be coincidental.[25] And while the AMG had its firm place in Wagner's autobiography, he might have felt it wise to leave out any mention of a semi-amateur orchestra in an article intended to be a serious study of the art of the conductor.

The orchestral parts in the AMG library naturally cannot reveal Wagner's precise manner of interpretation or his conducting technique. Any attempt to perform Mozart's *Jupiter*, say, or Haydn's 104th Symphony using Wagner's expression marks would be of purely academic interest and would fly in the face of his own belief in the flexibility of interpretation. But the AMG parts do provide us with modest information on Wagner's conducting and rehearsal methods and on his interpretation of the late works of Mozart and Haydn. They also support the notion that Wagner's claim to be the master of the "art of transition" must also be extended to include his work as an interpretative artist. There is, however, one further correlation here between Wagner as conductor and composer. If the notion of the "unified work of art" that we know from Wagner's Zurich writings is a fantasy of control (albeit understandable on the part of a man who has only recently lost everything), then we must acknowledge, too, that this desire for control is no less evident in Wagner the conductor. Aside from the meticulousness with which his rehearsals were prepared, as evinced by the precise annotation of the orchestral parts, his "espressivo" method of conducting is more specifically born of an authoritarian temperament. For if the tempo is in a constant state of flux, then the orchestra must devote its complete attention to the conductor if the performance is not to disintegrate. It must, in effect, be subservient to him. Let us not forget Baumgartner's description of Wagner the conductor as "like a military leader." The flexibility of interpretation extolled by Wagner is thus the prerogative of the conductor, not of the individual players. If the AMG's holdings can reveal any single truth to us, then it is surely this indivisibility of Wagner the creative artist: the uniform face that he presents to us, both as composer and conductor.

Table 8.1. Wagner's public concert performances in Zurich

The venue of all these concerts was the Casino, with the exception of the "festival concerts" of 18, 20, and 22 May 1853, which were given in the City Theater.

Composer	Work	Date of Performance
Beethoven, Ludwig van	*Coriolanus* Overture	17 February 1852
	Egmont (complete)	20 January 1852
	Egmont: Overture	30 March 1854
	Egmont: Overture and Interlude	13 December 1853
	Piano Concerto no. 5	21 February 1854 30 March 1854 Soloist in each case: Alexander Müller
	Leonore Overture no. 3	14 February 1854
	Septet op. 20	30 January 1855
	Symphony no. 3	25 February 1851 8 March 1853 9 January 1855
	Symphony no. 4	27 December 1853
	Symphony no. 5	28 January 1851 17 February 1852 29 November 1853 23 January 1855
	Symphony no. 6	16 March 1852 7 March 1854
	Symphony no. 7	15 January 1850 18 March 1851 15 February 1853 21 March 1854 6 February 1855
	Symphony no. 8	20 January 1852 17 January 1854 30 March 1854
Bériot, Charles de	Violin Concerto no. 7	20 February 1855 Soloist: *Niklaus Gall*
Gluck, Christoph Willibald von, arr. Wagner	*Iphigenia auf Aulis*: Overture	7 March 1854 21 March 1854 20 February 1855
Haydn, Joseph	Symphony no. 104	13 December 1853
Mozart, Wolfgang Amadeus	*Don Giovanni:* Aria "Ich grausam? O mein Geliebter!"	20 February 1855 Soloist: Katharina Hoffmann
	Symphony no. 41 (*Jupiter*)	14 February 1854
	Die Zauberflöte: Overture	23 January 1855

Table 8.1. (*continued*)

Composer	Work	Date of Performance
Rossini, Gioachino	*Semiramide*: Aria for soprano	20 February 1855 Soloist: Katharina Hoffmann
Spontini, Gaspare	*La Vestale*: Overture	25 February 1851
Wagner, Richard	*Der fliegende Holländer*: Overture; Senta's Ballade; Song of the Norwegian sailors	18, 20, & 22 May 1853 Soloist: Emilie Heim
	Faust-Ouvertüre, revised version	23 January 1855 20 February 1855
	Lohengrin: Elsa's Bridal Procession	20 February 1855
	Lohengrin: Prelude to the third act and Bridal Chorus	18, 20, & 22 May 1853
	Lohengrin: "Men's Scene" ("In Früh'n versammelt uns der Ruf") and Elsa's Bridal Procession	18, 20, & 22 May 1853
	Lohengrin: Prelude	18, 20, & 22 May 1853 20 February 1855
	Rienzi: "March of Peace"	18, 20, & 22 May 1853
	Rienzi: "March of Peace" (with a slightly revised close) and Chorus of the Messengers of Peace	27 December 1853
	Tannhäuser: Entrance of the guests, with the chorus "Freudig begrüssen wir die edle Halle"	18, 20, & 22 May 1853
	Tannhäuser: Entrance of the guests and "Festive March"	30 March 1854
	Tannhäuser: Overture	16 March 1852 18, 20, & 22 May 1853 21 March 1854 20 February 1855
	Tannhäuser: Tannhäuser's "Journey of Repentance" (Prelude to the third act) and Song of the Pilgrims	18, 20, & 22 May 1853

Table 8.1 (*continued*)

Composer	Work	Date of Performance
Weber, Carl Maria von	*Der Freischütz*: Overture	21 February 1854 6 February 1855
	Euryanthe: Overture	28 January 1851 17 January 1854

Table 8.2. Wagner's operatic performances in Zurich

The venue of all these operas was the City Theater.

Composer	Work	Date of Performance
Beethoven, Ludwig van	*Fidelio*	4 April 1851
Bellini, Vincenzo	*Norma*	21 October 1850
Boieldieu, François-Adrien	*La dame blanche*	11, 18 October, 6 December 1850 7 February 1851
Mozart, Wolfgang Amadeus	*Don Giovanni* (with minor alterations by Wagner)	8, 18 November 1850 26 March 1851
	Die Zauberflöte	29 November 1850
Wagner, Richard	*Der fliegende Holländer*	25, 28, 30 April, 2 May 1852
	Tannhäuser	23 February 1855
Weber, Carl Maria von	*Der Freischütz*	4, 27 October 1850

Table 8.3. Wagner's house concerts in the Wesendonck Villa

Composer	Work	Date of Performance
Beethoven, Ludwig van	Movements from the symphonies: no. 3: Finale no. 4: Adagio & Scherzo no. 5: Andante no. 7: Andante & Scherzo no. 8: Menuetto & Scherzando no. 9: Scherzo & Adagio	31 March 1858
Wagner, Richard	**Rienzi*: "March of Peace"	23 December 1857
	**Tannhäuser*: Entrance of the guests	23 December 1857
	Träume (WWV 91 B), for solo violin and small orchestra	23 December 1857

*It would appear that these were played by an ensemble brought in from outside (probably that run by the Bär brothers; see chapter 2). It is not clear if Wagner conducted, or whether this was left to the ensemble's own director.

Notes

[1] Letter of 28 October 1849 from Franz Liszt to Wagner, in Richard Wagner, *Briefwechsel zwischen Wagner und Liszt*, ed. Erich Kloss, 3rd ed. (Leipzig: Breitkopf & Härtel, 1910), 1:40.

[2] Wagner, *Die Kunst und die Revolution*, in *Sämtliche Schriften und Dichtungen* (Leipzig: Breitkopf & Härtel, [1911]), 3:8–41; here, 40.

[3] Wagner, *Die Kunst und die Revolution*, 40.

[4] Besides my own articles on the topic (see the Works Consulted), Wagner's conducting has also been the subject of Norbert Heinel's *Richard Wagner als Dirigent* (Vienna: Praesens Verlag, 2006) and Laurenz Lütteken, "Wagner dirigiert Mozart," in *Musikalische Quellen — Quellen zur Musikgeschichte: Festschrift für Martin Staehelin zum 65. Geburtstag*, ed. Ulrich Konrad, Jürgen Heidrich, and Hans Joachim Marx (Göttingen: Vandenhoeck & Ruprecht, 2002), 425–37.

[5] C. Widmer, *Wilhelm Baumgartner: Ein Lebensbild* (Zurich: David Bürkli, 1868), 131.

[6] Spyri in the *Eidgenössische Zeitung*, 16 February 1855.

[7] See Wagner, *Über das Dirigieren*, in *Sämtliche Schriften und Dichtungen* 8:268.

[8] Willy Fries, *Ein Zürcher Musiker unter Richard Wagner*. Typescript, 3.

[9] Shelfmark AMG I 310.

[10] Shelfmark AMG XIII 313y. The discovery is explained in Walton, "Flickarbeit oder Bearbeitung?" in *Neue Zürcher Zeitung*, 14/15 December 1996. The fragment is also published in facsimile in Walton, "Richard Wagner als Dirigent in Zürich" in *Tribschener Blätter* 55/56 (1998): 2–45; here, 44.

[11] Hans von Bülow, *Briefe*, vol. 1, ed. Marie von Bülow (Leipzig: Breitkopf & Härtel, 1895), 272–73.

[12] Egon Voss, "'*ein göttliches, unvergleichliches Werk*' — '*leider alles unkonzentriert*': Richard Wagner und *Don Giovanni*," in *Festschrift Christoph-Hellmut Mahling zum 65. Geburtstag*, ed. Axel Beer, Kristina Pfarr, and Wolfgang Ruf (Tutzing, Germany: Schneider, 1997), 1463–73.

[13] A letter from Wagner to Wilhelm Heisterhagen of 25 March 1858 mentions negotiating with "Dir. Kramer" in St. Gall regarding musicians he needed for a concert in Zurich — presumably the house concert for the Wesendoncks just before Easter (*SB* 9:222).

[14] See Walton, "Wagner-Quellen in der Zentralbibliothek Zürich: Verleger, Kopisten, Dirigate," in *"Schlagen Sie die Kraft der Reflektion nicht zu gering an,"* ed. Klaus Döge, Christa Jost, and Peter Jost (Mainz: Schott, 2002), 92–113; the tuba part is reproduced on p. 111. I discovered the remaining parts in June 2006 when consulting various recently catalogued manuscript parts from the old Tonhalle Library that had been given to the Zentralbibliothek Zürich. They are held in shelfmark TMs 339.

[15] See Richard Wagner, *Sämtliche Werke*, vol. 18, part 3, ed. Peter Jost (Mainz: Schott, 1995), 272.

[16] Hans Bélart, *Richard Wagner in Zürich (1849–1858)*, vol. 1 (Leipzig: Hermann Seemann, 1900), 14.

[17] For a precise listing of the orchestral parts in the AMG library that might have been used under Wagner, see Walton, "Richard Wagner als Dirigent in Zürich" in *Tribschener Blätter* 55/56 (1998): 18–30.

[18] I can confirm this from my own experience.

[19] See Walton, "*Iphigenia* Lost and Found: A Newly Discovered Gluck arrangement by Richard Wagner," in *Fontes artis musicae* 45, nos. 3–4 (1998): 227–36.

[20] Communication from Günter Fischer of the Richard Wagner Museum in Bayreuth.

[21] See Norbert Heinel, *Richard Wagner als Dirigent*, 544.

[22] Wagner, *Über das Dirigieren*, in *Sämtliche Schriften und Dichtungen*, 8:303–4. Further references to this work in this chapter will be given in the text using the page number alone.

[23] The copy bears the date "1831" and is held by the Huntington Library, San Marino, California. See John Deathridge and Carl Dahlhaus, *The New Grove Wagner* (London: Macmillan, 1984), 10.

[24] See Hans Curjel, "Espressivo und objektivierter Ausdruck," in his *Synthesen: Vermischte Schriften zum Verständnis der neuen Musik* (Hamburg: Claassen, 1966), 149–54, and Chris Walton, "Furtwängler the Apolitical?" in *The Musical Times* 146, no. 1889 (2004): 5–25. The "rubato" tradition is also discussed at length in Ray Holden, *The Virtuoso Conductors: The Central European Tradition from Wagner to Karajan* (New Haven and London: Yale UP, 2005).

[25] See Walton, "Wagner's Peculiar Oboist: Philipp Joseph Fries," in *Fontes artis musicae* 49, no. 4 (2002): 271–84.

Figure 12. Wagner's friends and colleagues in Zurich, from left to right, top to bottom: Eliza Wille, François Wille, Johann Jakob Sulzer, Mathilde Wesendonck, Otto Wesendonck, Franz Hagenbuch, Emilie Heim, Ignaz Heim. From Adolf Steiner, *Richard Wagner in Zürich*, vol. 3. Zurich: Orell Füssli, 1903.

9: Otto's Family Ways

Otto Wesendonck ought to be the object of our envy, for few patrons of the arts have attained his degree of immortality. But while no one has ever doubted the importance of his wife Mathilde in Wagner's biography, scholars have long regarded Otto himself as largely unworthy of closer attention. Polite commentators — taking their cue from Wagner's own barbed flattery — note his being the model for Pogner in the *Meistersinger*, the more truthful ones identify him as the model for Hunding in the *Walküre* and for King Mark in *Tristan*. Otto is thus known to the world through his operatic portrayal by the very man who deceived him. As "the husband of Wagner's muse," his reputation is essentially that of the cuckolded husband: a stock figure of fun, as old as the comic stage. That is surely a high price to pay for immortality, by any standards.

But this supposed figure of fun ran jointly one of the most profitable textile import businesses in New York. He was a hard-headed businessman who would later shock Cosima Wagner by asking for advance quotes when requested to help fund the Bayreuth Festival (*TB* 1:746). He was rich and powerful enough to consolidate his social position by building a neo-Classical villa on a hill outside Zurich, from where he could look down upon his neighbors geographically, just as he was presumably accustomed to looking down upon them socially (though we naturally cannot rule out the possibility that he needed to look down on them precisely because he himself felt otherwise looked-down-upon). Otto Wesendonck was no fool who would pour money unthinkingly into a venture without first calculating potential gains and losses; he will surely have guessed from the start that any "loan" given to Wagner might never be repaid. And yet, as Egon Voss has pointed out, Otto's assistance was, relative to his own means, far greater than that ever given to Wagner by King Ludwig II.[1] Why should a successful capitalist have given such massive support to a semi-plebeian would-be revolutionary with designs on his wife? Why did he tolerate that same composer's penchant for writing operas in which the heroine repeatedly abandons a rich husband of high standing for the charms of a man more charismatic but lower in the social hierarchy? And why, when that composer had humiliated him by allowing private passions to become public knowledge, did Otto continue to support him? This surely went far beyond any patronage of the arts that Otto might have considered his upper-middle-class duty. The answer cannot lie in Otto's musical tastes, for these were both Classical and non-Wagnerian — Wagner once even wrote mockingly to Mathilde, promising to compose a cadence every eight bars to satisfy her husband (*SB* 11:44). Nor did Otto approve of Wagner's anti-Semitism, as the composer himself later acknowledged.[2]

Historians have hitherto sought to provide one definitive answer in the person of Mathilde, who, it is implied, must have exerted an overpowering influence on her husband, cajoling him into supporting the very man with whom she is supposed to have betrayed him. Perhaps Otto does fit the cliché, beloved of Hollywood and the tabloid press, of the older man powerful in the world, yet ruled at home by his younger wife. But such a simplistic explanation also runs the risk of turning Otto yet again into little more than a cipher. If we try to explain the relationship between Otto, Wagner, and Mathilde as a "love triangle" determined purely by the ebb and flow of sexual attraction, then that is tantamount to seeing it as a mirror of *Tristan und Isolde* or the first act of the *Walküre* — in other words, what is purported to be Wagner's own dramatic portrayal of their relationship. We would do well to remember that this "Wagnerian" interpretation is fatally flawed, for the "battle" for Mathilde was one that Otto won decisively. After all, she stayed with her rich husband rather than abandoning him for a debt-ridden composer. In the world of Wagner's music dramas, love conquers all. In the real world, the power of capital would seem to have been triumphant. But this, too, is a cliché. If we wish for a closer understanding of Wagner's biography in the 1850s, more differentiated than hitherto, then we must first undertake a more thorough investigation of Otto's biography *avant* Wagner. There is in fact remarkably little historical evidence to be found, so concrete conclusions can be but few. But a strange, compelling web of coincidences does unveil itself, one that can alter our perception of both Otto and Mathilde and thereby shed new light on the gestation of Wagner's music dramas in the 1850s and beyond.

If "Mathilde Wesendonck as Wagner's muse" was essentially an "invented" figure, it is one of history's ironies that she had in fact, long before, already been invented by her husband. Otto Wesendonck was born in 1815 in Elberfeld (today a suburb of Wuppertal) into a bourgeois family of merchants, mayors, lawyers, and Protestant vicars. His father ran a silk-dying business, while his uncle Johann Schramm (the husband of his paternal aunt Wilhelmine) ran a silk factory in Krefeld. Otto emigrated to America in ca. 1833, having apparently been sent there by his father to help run the silk importing firm of "Loeschigk, Wesendonck & Co." together with one William Loeschigk, a fellow native of Elberfeld. By the 1850s it was counted among the most successful in New York. Since all sources mention Otto's strong business links with Krefeld, it is not impossible that these were in fact with the firm of his uncle, who might well have exported from Germany the very silk that Otto imported into the United States. At some point, Wesendonck was made his company's European representative; in any case, he seems to have spent a good deal of his time commuting between New York and Europe. During one of his trips to Germany, the current literature tells us, Otto married Mathilde Eckhard, the daughter of a Frankfurt textile merchant, on 15 October 1844. She died in Florence just weeks later, on 8 December, while they were still on their honeymoon. In late 1847, back in Germany once more, Otto met Agnes Luckemeyer, born in 1827 in Elberfeld, and the daughter of Karl Luckemeyer, founder of the German-Dutch Steamship Company. Agnes had received her education partly in Germany, partly in Dunkirk, where she had learnt French. They married on 19 May 1848. Otto apparently began to refer to her as "Mathilde" even before that date, and she seems to have accepted willingly his suggestion to change her name permanently (there is little doubt that the suggestion was his). Thus did Agnes Luckemeyer become Mathilde Wesendonck. According to Marie-Luise Baum, a noted historian of the region where both Otto and Agnes were born, Agnes knew nothing of Otto's first wife until after his death in 1896 (though Baum also states that Otto's and Agnes's respective fathers were old acquaintances, which would surely have made such secrecy difficult to maintain).[3] While Mathilde would later prove highly independent, her early acquiescence to Otto makes it unlikely that she could just five years later have been able to coerce him against his will into supporting a potential rival for her affections.

Straight after their marriage in Düsseldorf, Otto took his new Mathilde to Frankfurt — an odd choice for a honeymoon, perhaps, given that it was the city where he had married his first wife. The new German parliament was in session in the Church of St. Paul, and Otto's younger brother Hugo — cofounder of a "Society for Democratic Monarchy" — was a member for Düsseldorf. Hugo was a particular admirer of Robert Blum, considering him

> the best man in the German Parliament. He was a Socrates in both body and features, but broader, fatter, more stocky, with prominent shoulders and a bulging chest. He stood on the rostrum like the trunk of an oak tree . . . he was the best example of the liberal bourgeoisie — even, if you will, of the German *petite bourgeoisie*."[4]

Just a few months later, Blum was executed in Vienna on account of his political activities.

In his reminiscences of the Frankfurt Parliament, Gustav Schwetschke called Hugo "Hugo Schnickschnackius ICtus [*sic*] Rhenanus . . . a lawyer from Düsseldorf, with a lively Rhineland temperament and a pleasant appearance; a democratic word-hero of the purest water, though it wasn't very deep."[5] Despite Schwetschke's inference that he was a man of words, not deeds, Hugo was in fact no passive member of the parliament. In its early stages he had suggested that all the German armies should swear it an oath of allegiance and that parliament itself should nominate the commander-in-chief. Fifty years later Hugo wrote in his memoirs: "I still see clearly before me the horror on the faces of my family when they heard that I sympathized with the leftists."[6] Since Otto and Mathilde were staying with him at the time, it is probably their "horror" to which he is referring. As it happens, Otto's new father-in-law was a personal acquaintance of the current nominal commander-in-chief of the Prussian army, King Friedrich Wilhelm IV. It was Friedrich Wilhelm's subsequent rejection of the emperorship that meant the death of the Frankfurt legislature. Hugo remained a member of the rump parliament that met in Stuttgart in June 1849, but when Prussia demanded the arrest of all its citizens still involved in it, he fled to Paris. He was formally accused of high treason in Stuttgart and condemned to death in his absence. France decided to expel him, so he and his family took the schooner "Splendide" to New York, where they landed on 5 December 1849. The property of some members of parliament was confiscated by the state. Whether or not this was also the case with Hugo, we do not know; but it seems that he was indeed dependent on his brother's help upon his arrival in New York.[7]

According to Friedrich Wilhelm von Bissing, the grandson of Otto and Mathilde, his newly wed grandparents settled first in Düsseldorf on account of Otto's contacts with the textile industry in nearby Krefeld. Given his job, and the necessity to spend time on both sides of the Atlantic, we must presume that it was no less convenient for Otto to live in Germany than in New York (especially since the establishment in 1847 of the "Hamburg-Amerikanische Packetfahrt-Actien-Gesellschaft," the first German transatlantic steamship line, running from Hamburg to New York in roughly two weeks). But when Hugo had to flee Europe, writes von Bissing, Otto and Mathilde left too in order to help him establish himself in the New World.[8] Hugo had married their cousin Johanna Wilhelmine Schramm in 1844, the daughter of their silk-exporting uncle Johann (who had died in 1840). Besides any fraternal duty that he must have felt toward Hugo, Otto might also have decided that the onus was now squarely on him to aid the family of the man who (as we suggested earlier) had most probably helped him in business. Given the significance that Otto seems to have attached to names, it was perhaps not unimportant to him that Johanna was named after her father (and had already given one of her own sons the name "Otto").

Otto and Mathilde did not arrive in New York until six months after Hugo, though this should not be taken as a lack of interest in his fate. Mathilde was heavily pregnant when Hugo had departed, and she bore a son, Paul, on 27 November 1849. The child died the following March, after which she and Otto left for New York. Their help for Hugo was evidently successful, for he soon moved to Philadelphia, set up a profitable business there, and became active in the anti-slavery movement. By the late 1850s he had moved back to New York, where in 1860 he founded and was appointed first president of the life insurance company "Germania," which had a starting capital of $200,000. It opened its first branch in San Francisco in 1862, and within twenty years was the ninth-biggest insurance company in the country (it still exists, as the "Guardian Life Insurance Company," having changed its name during the First World War. It is today, according to its own figures, the fourth-largest mutual life insurance company in the United States).[9]

Hugo soon mixed in high political circles, becoming a good friend of Carl Schurz, another political refugee from Germany. Schurz had fled from Germany in 1848 but had returned to free his friend Gottfried Kinkel from prison in Spandau. (In 1866, Kinkel moved to Zurich, where he became friendly with both Otto Wesendonck and Wagner.) Schurz became a prominent supporter of Abraham Lincoln, was made a general in the Civil War, and later became a US senator. According to Cosima's diaries, he even attracted the admiring attention of Wagner in the 1870s: "Schurz is an example of what a proper German can be," he declared (*TB* 2:509). When Hugo Wesendonck's wife died in 1889, it was Schurz who gave the official speech at her grave.[10]

Mathilde did not take to America as had her husband and in-laws and seems to have pressed Otto into returning to Europe as soon as possible. They arrived back in autumn 1850, stopping off to see Mathilde's family, then moving south to pay a visit to Zurich. They were presumably looking for a new city of residence, for it was to Zurich that they then returned on a permanent basis in April 1851. The reason for settling there, rather than returning to Düsseldorf, is usually given as being Zurich's importance in the silk industry and its relatively equidistant position between Krefeld and Lyon, two textile centers that were of particular importance to Otto (though if geography had been the major determining factor, it would have made more sense to move to a town on the Rhine, such as Basel in Switzerland or Freiburg im Breisgau in southern Germany). While Zurich was a long way from any seaport that would facilitate Otto's occasional trips to the USA, the journey was by no means unusual — the *Tagblatt der Stadt Zürich*, for example, ran regular adverts for the Atlantic crossing (such as that of "Ouzelet & Comp." on 1 June 1850, listing the departures from Le Havre in northern France that would connect with the steamers to New York leaving from either Southampton or Liverpool).

The Wesendonck's move to Zurich was apparently recommended by Henri Bodmer, a native of the city who had also emigrated to New York and had there become one of the world's biggest silk magnates. He established a friendship with Otto before returning home to Zurich in 1842; their friendship has an unusual footnote, for Bodmer's son-in-law, as it happens, would many years later become the owner of Otto's Zurich villa.[11] The most likely reason for choosing Zurich, however, was political. After the victory of the anti-liberal forces in 1849, Mathilde's father had become deputy mayor of Düsseldorf. He cannot but have been embarrassed to learn that his daughter and new son-in-law had given succor to the very man who had represented his city for the opposing liberal faction in parliament, and who now stood under sentence of death for high treason. Since Zurich had become a haven for many German liberals and revolutionaries after the events of 1848 and 1849, it was presumably a compromise place where Otto and Mathilde could still mix with their own kind and converse in their native High German (as opposed to the local patois). Otto collected paintings; Mathilde had literary interests; but they both enjoyed music, and it was this that brought them together with Wagner in early 1852. Given the fact that the musical life of Zurich was decidedly small-scale, it might seem odd that they should not have met him before this. However, the Zurich concert season was short, and they had, it seems, arrived after Wagner's last appearance on the podium in the previous season (on 18 March 1851). And since Mathilde was again pregnant, she will not have been keen to have a full diary of cultural events and social functions. She gave birth to a daughter, Myrrha, on 7 August 1851. For much of the rest of this year, of course, Wagner was in any case out of the city, taking the waters at Albisbrunn.

Wagner did not direct the local orchestra again until 20 January 1852, when he conducted the music to Beethoven's *Egmont* and the same composer's Eighth Symphony. The Wesendoncks were in the audience, as they were again for the next subscription concert, on 17 February, when Wagner conducted Beethoven's *Coriolanus* Overture and Fifth Symphony. Shortly after this concert, the Wesendoncks were introduced to Wagner by a leading figure from the Dresden uprising who had also settled in Zurich, Hermann Marschall von Bieberstein. The meeting-place was his apartment — one that Wagner himself had rented until recently. As chance would have it, Wagner's final orchestral concert of the season was on Otto's birthday, 16 March, when he conducted his own *Tannhäuser* Overture and Beethoven's *Pastoral* Symphony.

Friendly relations between the Wagners and the Wesendoncks were soon established. This is usually ascribed to the power of Wagner's personality, his immediate infatuation with Mathilde, and hers with him. But again, this means seeing matters through Wagner's eyes, for it was he who emphasized Mathilde's "Schwärmerei" for him (an expression conveying a mixture of enthusiasm and passion) when he first mentioned the Wesendoncks in his correspondence, in a letter of 26 February 1852 to Theodor Uhlig (*SB* 4:301). In that letter Wagner stresses his indifference to Otto, while at the same time gloating over his riches and the "luxury" with which he surrounds his family. The real reason for their rapid rapprochement might in fact lie with someone who was not even present: Hugo Wesendonck. Wagner had fled from Dresden just a few weeks before Hugo had left Stuttgart, and both had taken the route to Paris via Switzerland. While Hugo had moved on to the United States, Wagner had returned to Zurich. We know that Wagner was acquainted with Hugo's fate, for in his letter to Uhlig, he referred to Otto as "the brother of the Reichstag member" — "des Reichstäglers Bruder" (*SB* 4:301). We cannot rule out the possibility that Wagner sought out the Wesendoncks precisely because he knew of their connection to Hugo, and that he from the very start intended to emphasize the superficial similarities to his own fate in order to profit from their wealth. It is a noteworthy coincidence that Otto's eldest brother, Moritz Reinhard (born 11 May 1812), died just three months later, on 20 May 1852 (while Otto had gone west, Moritz had gone east, setting up business in Moscow. He died, however, in his native Rhineland). Otto had now lost two brothers: one through death, the other through exile. At some point, though we do not know when, he lost another to America, his youngest brother, August. Of him we know nothing except what is recorded on the family tree: that he was born in 1820 in Elberfeld and died a "land owner" ("Gutsbesitzer") in Virginia in 1902. In Wagner Otto found a revolutionary outcast whose fate was uncannily similar to that of his own brother Hugo but who was a needy case that could be helped on the spot. Perhaps Wagner was able to slip into the position of an *ersatz* brother just at a time when Otto was bereaved and thus particularly vulnerable.

Otto's first major act of generosity to Wagner was to help fund the "Wagner festival" held in Zurich in 1853, as mentioned above in chapter 2, when Wagner conducted three concerts of bleeding chunks from his operas *Rienzi*, *Der fliegende Holländer*, *Tannhäuser*, and *Lohengrin* (on 18, 20, and 22 May). Commentators have never failed to mention that the last of the concerts was scheduled for Wagner's fortieth birthday. However, it has hitherto been overlooked that the first concert also took place on the fifth anniversary of the opening of the Frankfurt Parliament that had, in effect, sealed Hugo Wesendonck's fate; and the second concert fell on the first anniversary of the death of Otto's elder brother. Given Wagner's near-obsession with the significance of dates,[12] it is highly likely that he was as aware of all these synchronicities as was Otto. As it happens, the first concert also fell on the anniversary of the death of Otto's uncle Johann. Of this fact Wagner can hardly have been aware, though Otto presumably was. But there was one final anniversary that fell in the middle of the festival and that might in part have determined Wagner's choice of program: the Wesendoncks' fifth wedding anniversary on 19 May. The last items of the concert, appropriately, were excerpts from the third act of *Lohengrin*, the Prelude and Bridal Chorus, followed once more by the Prelude, to which Wagner had written a new close. The program book for the evening ends with this brief explanatory paragraph from the composer:

> The guests have left the lovers to their quiet happiness; when they again enter the brilliantly lit hall, joy and festive jubilation break out once more among them: this is in celebration of the highpoint of human life, the

> happiness of a couple united in love — a happiness that we today, regardless of the deeper seriousness of our drama, will gladly think of as never to be sullied![13]

By finishing with a repeat of the prelude, Wagner did not just provide a rousing finish to the evening, but also — as his note suggests — implicitly reversed the fate of his lovers. In the opera, the bridal music is partly ironic in intent, for Lohengrin and Elsa will in fact never consummate their union. But if Wagner indeed meant the evening to flatter Mathilde and Otto on their anniversary, it would naturally have to end "united in love" — no matter how much he would have preferred to be united with Mathilde himself.

Mathilde's brother Eduard Luckemeyer (born 1830) also crossed the water, probably in around 1850 or slightly later. He is mentioned in the literature as having tried to arrange an engagement for Wagner in America in 1859 (*SB* 11:47). A letter Wagner wrote to Mathilde tells us that Eduard ran a "dry-goods" company together with one Gustavus Kutter, whom Wagner met, through the Wesendoncks, in Zurich in June 1857 (*SB* 8:365). "Kutter and Luckemeyer" was registered under the same New York address as the firm of Loeschigk and Wesendonck. When the latter moved twice in the 1850s, Kutter and Luckemeyer moved each time to the same new address, which suggests that the two firms were closely linked. It seems likely that Otto Wesendonck had offered the same helping hand to Mathilde's brother that he had to his own — perhaps even as a conciliatory gesture to his wife's family, if relations between them had indeed been disturbed by the events of 1849. If Mathilde's brother was in some way economically dependent on Otto, then we would have an added reason why she would have been loath to leave her husband in the crisis of 1858, when Wagner's love for her became common knowledge and made his departure from Zurich inevitable. To have abandoned Otto could have jeopardized her brother's business position and thus completely ruined any chance of future support for her, moral or financial, from her own family.

Whatever Wagner's precise role was in the Dresden uprising, he arrived in Zurich as a wanted man, and his supposedly revolutionary activities no doubt served to ingratiate him to the larger German exile community. But, as outlined in chapter 2 above, he also made sure to cultivate the local political establishment, and in doing so displayed a remarkable talent for playing to both sides of the fence, both liberal and conservative. Wagner's political ambivalence might even have endeared him all the more to Otto Wesendonck, who seems not to have embraced his brother's overtly democratic ideals and was quite possibly torn between his fraternal duties and his own conservative leanings. During the Franco-Prussian war the Wesendoncks made their support for Prussia plain, while German-Swiss opinion remained largely on the side of the French. The wrath that the Wesendoncks incurred when organizing a German victory celebration in the Zurich Tonhalle in March 1871 resulted in a near-riot, during which a mob tried to burn down the Wesendonck villa. They did not succeed, but the incident prompted the Wesendoncks into a rapid, permanent exit from Zurich.

As we have already noted, contact between Wagner and Otto did not cease after the former left Zurich in 1858. After a cooling-off period of several months, Otto seems to have displayed remarkably little rancor: he not only continued to offer his support but also wrote off Wagner's debts to him, and even, at Wagner's request, gave up the manuscript score of the *Rheingold* when Wagner told him that Ludwig II of Bavaria wanted it; Otto also figured later among the patrons of the first Bayreuth Festival. There are, however, a number of possible reasons, besides their political links, for their enduringly cordial relations. As chance would have it, Otto's family came from Xanten on the Rhine, the town that German legend tells us was the birthplace of Siegfried. Non-causal relationships were of great interest to Wagner; perhaps he was able to convince Otto that he, as a son of Xanten, had been chosen by fate to support Wagner's musico-dramatic recreation of the Siegfried myth. A remark by Otto's grandson von Bissing provides a further possible clue to their relationship. He writes that, since Otto had emigrated at an early age, he had "worked tirelessly to educate himself, since his education had not been completed while at home. The English classics, but above all Goethe and Beethoven, were his companions."[14] Wagner himself made repeated reference to Wesendonck's supposed cultural ignorance, as, for example, in a letter to Mathilde of 21 December 1861 ("reading cannot help him much; he is missing too much of what one has to acquire in early youth, and which one cannot catch up with later").[15] The villa that Otto had built in Zurich was in fact a copy of the villa built for Jean-François Bartholoni (1796–1881), a rich businessman and patron of the arts in French Switzerland. The art collection that Otto assembled also suggests someone keen to collect rather than someone with particular taste.[16] Perhaps, then, he suffered from a cultural inferiority complex that he tried to counter by using the only means richly available to him: money. Wagner's broad knowledge would thus have seemed all the more imposing to Otto and his wife — let us not forget that they first met Wagner when he conducted the Zurich orchestra in works by Wesendonck's beloved Beethoven.

But Otto's remarkable patience with Wagner might have an even deeper reason. Our "Mathilde Wesendonck" was in fact not the second but the third in Otto's life. His only sister, whose year of birth is given by the most reliable sources as 1814, also bore that name.[17] Otto's mother Sophie died in 1824, when he was nine. As his only sister, Mathilde could have slipped easily into the role of an *ersatz* mother; what we know for certain, however, is that she too died early, in 1838. Family documents in the

Frankfurt City Archives prove that Otto's first wife was actually named Julia Johanna Mathilde Eckhard. Since it was not unusual in mid-nineteenth century Germany for children to be called by their second or third name, it is possible that any of the three was the name by which she was known in her family. Other documents in the Frankfurt Archives refer to her only as "Johanna Mathilde Eckhard," suggesting that she was perhaps called after her father, Johann (though "Johanna" was also the first name of an elder sister). Perhaps the decision to ignore Julia's first two names was in fact taken by Otto, though we have no evidence to support or disprove it. There is, incidentally, a further peculiar coincidence in that Julia Johanna Mathilde's mother bore (almost) the same name as Otto's deceased mother: Sophie (Otto's mother was "Sophia," though the final vowel is of little significance). We can only speculate as to Otto's feelings when his new Mathilde died within weeks of their wedding. As Oscar Wilde might have said, to lose one Mathilde-born-of-Sophi(e) may be considered unfortunate, but to lose two smacks of carelessness. If Otto was indeed plagued by guilt at having lost a second Mathilde, it still did not stop him from taking yet another, in the shape of Agnes Luckemeyer. A letter exists from Otto to his former mother-in-law (they obviously kept in contact after Mathilde Eckhard's death) in which he writes that his new fiancée, "Mathilde," looks remarkably like his deceased first wife.[18] To what extent Sophie the mother-in-law was an *ersatz* for Sophia his own dead mother we cannot tell, but it seems that Agnes Luckemeyer, alias Mathilde Wesendonck the Third, was an *ersatz* not merely for a first wife lost in tragic circumstances but also for a deceased sister and a deceased mother. Otto's family history is thus a strange mesh of latently incestuous relationships.

Scholars have been discussing incest in Wagner's works since the early twentieth century,[19] though it has been a topic of comment among critics and wits for longer than that. Incest features large in one of the early Wagner parodies, Paul Gisbert's mini-tetralogy *Der Ring, der nie gelungen*, which first appeared shortly after the Bayreuth Festival of 1876 (parody always being a good barometer of how an artist is judged by his contemporaries).[20] A favorite theme among the "incest commentators" is Wagner's close relationship with his adored elder sister Rosalie. She had died in 1837, just a year before the first Mathilde Wesendonck (it is naturally possible that Wagner and Otto might have become aware of their similar loss, and that this could have helped to cement the bond between them). The incest theme is already to be found in *Rienzi* and *Lohengrin*. But in the *Walküre*, the incestuous act between brother and sister is positively glorified, with the plot of the whole *Ring* hingeing upon it (this union results of course in the birth of Siegfried, Otto's fellow citizen of Xanten). However, the incest of Siegmund and his sister is already present in the *Volsunga Saga* that was one of Wagner's medieval sources, and it featured too in both his prose sketch for a Nibelung drama in 1848 and in his *Siegfrieds Tod.* His first prose sketch for the *Walküre* was completed in late 1851, just a few weeks before he met the Wesendoncks. So, just as we cannot prove conclusively that Otto Wesendonck had incestuous tendencies, we also can not claim that Wagner might have discovered their existence and scripted the plot of the *Walküre* in a manner likely to appeal to the tendentially incestuous. It is unlikely that Otto was aware of the latent incest in *Lohengrin et al.*, but he might have become aware of Wagner's implicit — if theoretical — acceptance of incest in his latest literary work, *Opera and Drama*, published in November 1851.[21] This contains a remarkably frank discussion of incest in Greek myth. Wagner asks:

> Did Oedipus offend human nature when he married his mother? Most certainly not . . . Oedipus and Jocasta did not *know* [Wagner's emphasis] in what social relationship they stood to one another: they had acted unconsciously, according to the natural instinct of the purely human individual. Their union was an enrichment of human society in that two strong sons and two noble daughters sprang from it.[22]

Of the love of Antigone for her brother Polynices, he wrote: "From out of the ruins of sexual, parental, and sibling love, which society had disowned and the State had negated, there grew — nourished by the indestructible buds of all these loves — the richest flower of *pure human love* [his emphasis]."[23] There is, of course, no proof that Otto had read *Opera and Drama.* However, we know from Wagner's letter to Uhlig of February 1852 that Mathilde had read his recent autobiographical sketch *A Communication to My Friends*, and we know from other sources that Wagner read to her from his later works. So it is in fact quite probable that Otto, too, will have learnt of Wagner's apparent liberality toward incestuous passions.

While Wagner himself seems in the case of his *Walküre* to have equated the characters of Siegmund, Sieglinde, and Hunding with himself, Mathilde, and Otto respectively,[24] it is just as possible that Otto saw the opera as an allegory of *his* own position, though with himself as Siegmund — after all, the latter's final words in act 1 are: "Braut und Schwester bist du dem Bruder, so blühe denn Wälsungen Blut!" ("Bride and sister art thou to thy brother, so let the blood of the Wälsungs flourish!"). If, during the process of composition, Wagner became even partly aware of the possibility of such an interpretation on the part of his patron, then this naturally makes the relationship between his operatic characters and their supposed real-life models more complex than has hitherto been supposed. It was, of course, the first, private, performance of the first act of the *Walküre* on 26 April 1856 that prompted Otto Wesendonck to offer Wagner an increase in his "salary" in order to provide him with the freedom to complete the work. He had cleared Wagner's debts two years before and, together with Jakob Sulzer, had endeavored to help Wagner put his financial affairs in order. It had been a frustrating experience, not least because Wagner's figures did not always add up, and Wesendonck had written to Sulzer: "I will in future not get involved in anything more. There has been enough annoyance"[25] — sentiments that he expressed more than once. But on 28 April 1856, two days after hearing the first act of the *Walküre*, Wesendonck changed his opinion completely:

> Dear friend!
>
> I have the heartfelt desire that you should be able, untroubled by the worries of material existence, to finish in magnificent fashion your great work, so magnificently begun. Last Saturday evening gave me great pleasure and I am pleased that you wish to repeat the performance of that act before my departure for Düsseldorf.
>
> You tell me that in order to be granted the necessary quiet to finish the *Nibelungen* you need, besides the annual monies of Fr. 3000 from the Ritters, the same sum from another source, without being bound to the income from performances of your operas.
>
> I wish to take this on, and I am instructing our friend Sulzer to pay out to you Fr. 250 on a monthly basis.[26]

Thus were Wagner's financial worries solved, at least for the moment. The incest theme by no means disappears from Wagner's work after the *Ring*. At least one commentator has identified an incestuous trait in Pogner's paternal love in the *Meistersinger*.[27] Wagner was himself the first to suggest that Pogner was loosely based on Otto, with an appropriately flattering reference in a letter to Otto himself of 26 July 1862 (*SB* 14:219). His correspondence with Mathilde from the same time suggests that she was the model for Pogner's daughter Eva (*SB* vols. 13 and 14). Was there, perhaps, an ironic intention on Wagner's part by thus making Otto the "father" of his own wife? *Parsifal* was also conceived during Wagner's months of geographical proximity to the Wesendoncks, though it is surely stretching things too far to suggest that the example of Otto and his Mathildes might in any way have influenced the combination of mother and lover in the figure of Kundry.

It is easy to speculate where sexual matters are concerned and where concrete proof is lacking. In this murky realm one can swiftly be misled into reading significance into what might, in fact, be banal coincidence. There is little doubt that names, and the act of naming, were for both Wagner and Otto Wesendonck of symbolic import. So if the name "Sophie/Sophia" was dear to Otto, did he find out that it was the name of Wagner's grandmother too (and would it matter if he had)? Are there shades of Siegfried and his aunt Brünnhilde when Wagner refers to Mathilde as his "Tante" or "Muhme" in letters of 1855 (both meaning "aunt")? At the same time, he writes to Otto as his "lieber Onkel" or "liebster Onkel" — "Dear/dearest Uncle" — and adds: "Fahren Sie so fort, so werden Sie bald zu meinem 'Vater' avanciren" — "If you carry on like this, you'll soon advance to being my 'father'" (*SB* 7:61, 87, and 92). But before we let ourselves be carried away by increasingly unlikely speculation, we would do well to remember a remark made by Wittgenstein in his criticism of Sigmund Freud's fondness for recognizing phallic symbols: sometimes a top hat is just a top hat.[28] Many of the correspondences listed here — perhaps even most of them — might have been the result of innocent coincidence. However, what we can assert with confidence is that the relationship between Wagner and the Wesendoncks was marked by a host of synchronicities that are surely too many and too striking for them all to be written off as the result of mere chance. The questions that they raise, though, are far more numerous than any answers we can offer. If Otto did carry a burden of (sexual) guilt regarding his deceased mother, sister, and wife (a "wound that would not heal"), perhaps he hoped for some form of catharsis by assisting Wagner to bring that guilt to consciousness though artistic expression. But why did Otto commission a portrait of Wagner in 1862, to be hung in his own home, a constant reminder of the man who had publicly humiliated him (sexually) just four years before? Perhaps we must also consider the possibility that Otto tolerated his wife's infatuation because, in fact, he shared it. While there are no indications of any homosexual tendencies on his part — and despite the obvious fact of his two marriages and the conception and birth of his children — the extant sources somehow give the impression of a man barely sexual at all. But perhaps, again, we have simply been too influenced by the sexual passivity of King Mark and are projecting this back onto Otto himself.

The fundamental questions here are not new. To what degree was Wagner prepared to mould his persona and his work in order to win financial security and social acceptance, and at what point did his natural inclination merge into cynical self-interest? While this, of course, is impossible to answer, it is a sign of his success as self-publicist that Wagner research has so long ignored the history of the man whose patronage proved so crucial to him. If we can appreciate the complexity of Otto Wesendonck's biographical context, then we might find new things to say about Wagner's own biography, his political affiliations, and the works that he composed during his period of Zurich exile.

Notes

1 See Egon Voss, "Die Wesendoncks und Richard Wagner," in *Minne, Muse und Mäzen: Otto und Mathilde Wesendonck und ihr Zürcher Künstlerzirkel*, ed. Axel Langer and Chris Walton (Zurich: Museum Rietberg, 2002), 117–29; here, 119.

2 See the letter from Wagner to Otto Wesendonck of 4 December 1870, in Richard Wagner, *Briefe Richard Wagners an Otto Wesendonk, 1852–1870*, ed. Wolfgang Golther, neue, vollständige Ausgabe (Berlin: Alexander Duncker, 1905), 129.

[3] Marie-Luise Baum, "Mathilde und Otto Wesendonck," in *Wuppertaler Biographien*, vol. 3 (Wuppertal: Born Verlag, 1961), 135–48; here, 137.

[4] Hugo Wesendonck, *Erinnerungen aus dem Jahre 1848* (New York: n.p., 1898), 14–15.

[5] Gustav Schwetschke, *Jubiläums-Ausgabe der Novae epistolae obscurorum virorum: Zum ersten Male mit Erläuterungen versehen; Erinnerungen aus den Frankfurter Parlamentstagen* (Halle: G. Schwetschke'scher Verlag, 1874), 49.

[6] Hugo Wesendonck, *Erinnerungen*, 5.

[7] See Wolfram Albrecht, "Hugo Wesendonck," in *Wuppertaler Biographien*, vol. 7 (Wuppertal: Born-Verlag, 1967), 99–110; here, 106–9.

[8] Friedrich Wilhelm Freiherr von Bissing, *Mathilde Wesendonck: Die Frau und die Dichterin* (Vienna: Anton Schroll, 1942), 13.

[9] Anita Rapone, *The Guardian Life Insurance Company, 1860–1920: A History of a German-American Enterprise* (New York and London: New York UP, 1987), 3. See also www.guardianlife.com, accessed September 2006.

[10] Carl Schurz, *Worte gesprochen am Sarge von Frau Wilhelmine Wesendonck geboren zu Crefeld am 10ten April 1820, gestorben zu Ems am 24sten August 1889 und auf Greenwood Cemetry* [*sic*] *zur Ruhe bestattet am 16ten September 1889* (New York: s.n., 1889).

[11] See Jürg Wille, "Rieter im Rietberg," in Langer and Walton, *Minne, Muse und Mäzen*, 168–73; here, 171.

[12] As an example: Wagner wanted to have his son Siegfried christened on 28 August 1870, which was both the anniversary of the first performance of *Lohengrin* and Goethe's birthday; only the decision of King Ludwig to become godfather delayed the act.

[13] Wagner, *Programm zu den Musikaufführungen am 18. 20. und 22. Mai 1853 in Zürich* (Zurich: Kiesling, 1853), 16.

[14] Von Bissing, *Mathilde Wesendonck*, 12.

[15] See *SB* 13: 339. See also Wagner's mocking of Otto's "now favorite language," namely Latin, in his letter to Mathilde of 2 May 1860, in *SB* 12: 137.

[16] See Walter Cohen, *Katalog der Gemäldegalerie vorwiegend Sammlung Wesendonk* (Bonn: Kommissionsverlag Friedrich Cohen, 1914); and Ingeborg Krueger, ". . . fast nur Gutes und einiges ganz Treffliche . . . Zu Otto Wesendoncks Gemäldesammlung," in Langer and Walton, *Minne, Muse und Mäzen*, 100–113.

[17] One family tree drawn up by the Wesendoncks of the twentieth century, and held by the Zurich City Archives, gives the date of birth of Otto's sister Mathilde as 1821; however, that source contains so many verifiable inaccuracies (e.g. the dates of Otto's marriage to Agnes/Mathilde and of the birth of their first son) that it cannot be regarded as trustworthy.

[18] I have been unable to see the original letter, owned by the Wesendonk family, though it is too important not to be mentioned here. It is quoted by Judith Cabaud in her *Mathilde Wesendonck ou le rêve d'Isolde* (Arles: Editions Actes Sud, 1990), 46.

[19] See, for example, *Das Inzest-Motiv in Dichtung und Sage*, by Otto Rank, a pupil of Sigmund Freud (Leipzig: Deuticke, 1912). See also Isolde Vetter, "Wagner in the History of Psychology," in *Wagner Handbook*, ed. Ulrich Müller and Peter Wapnewski (Cambridge, MA. and London: Harvard UP, 1992), 118–55.

[20] Paul Gisbert (pseudonym of Paul Pniower), "Der Ring, der nie gelungen," in *Wagner-Parodien*, ed. Dieter Borchmeyer and Stephan Kohler (Frankfurt am Main: Insel, 1983), 87–139; here, 107–8.

[21] Wagner, *Oper und Drama*. Three volumes (Leipzig: J. J. Weber, 1852 [*recte*: November 1851]).

[22] Wagner, *Oper und Drama*, in *Sämtliche Schriften und Dichtungen* (Leipzig: Breitkopf & Härtel, [1911]), 3:222–321 and 4:2–229; here, 4:110–11.

[23] Wagner, *Oper und Drama*, in *Sämtliche Schriften und Dichtungen*, 4:122.

[24] See Egon Voss, "Die Wesendoncks und Richard Wagner," in Langer and Walton, *Minne, Muse und Mäzen*, 117–29; here, 121–22.

[25] See Max Fehr, *Richard Wagners Schweizer Zeit*, vol. 1 (Aarau and Leipzig: Sauerländer, 1934), 406–7.

[26] See Max Fehr, *Richard Wagners Schweizer Zeit*, vol. 2 (Aarau and Frankfurt am Main: Sauerländer, 1953), 38.

[27] See James M. McGlathery, *Wagner's Operas and Desire* (New York: Peter Lang, 1998), 205.

[28] Ludwig Wittgenstein, *Lectures and Conversations on Aesthetics, Psychology and Religious Belief*, ed. Cyril Barrett (Oxford: Blackwell, 1978), 44.

Figure 13. Mathilde Wesendonck. Portrait by Carl F. Sohn, 1850. Used by permission of the Stadtmuseum Bonn.

10: Voicing Mathilde: Wagner's Controlling Muse

MATHILDE WESENDONCK MAY BE one of the most famous women in the history of Western music, but hers is undeniably a fame by default. It rests, of course, not on any concrete achievements of her own but on her role as "muse" of Richard Wagner. Not only did he set five of her poems to music — the "Wesendonck Lieder" are one of the highpoints of German Romantic song — but, according to his own testimony, he also monumentalized his love for her in his music dramas *Die Walküre* and *Tristan und Isolde*. But here already, we arrive at the heart of the problem in the reception history of Mathilde Wesendonck: *Wagner's* testimony, *Wagner's* monument, *Wagner's* love, *Wagner's* music dramas. Popular music history rapidly established his relationship with her as a "love tragedy" wherein the pressures of society and its mores forced Tristan/Wagner to lose Isolde/Mathilde (an interpretation that still lives on today).[1] But the apparent certainties of the tale let us forget all too easily that almost everything we know about their relationship is through Wagner's own words. Nearly all of Mathilde's letters were destroyed on the wish of his second wife, Cosima. In the first edition of the correspondence between Wagner and Mathilde, published in 1904, two years after her death, her few surviving letters were not even placed in their chronological context (which would have disturbed the flow of the Master's musings), but relegated instead to an appendix.[2] This book thus offers hardly a "correspondence," but really little more than an inner monologue on the part of the composer. Mathilde was, to all intents and purposes, "silenced" posthumously. She underwent a mythologizing process that left her little more than a disembodied, de-voiced muse of the composer, with no identity except what his words and music deigned to give her. Only through him do we know of her supposed feelings for him. But we can hardly understand a "love story" if we only know half of it, nor can we hope to place Wagner and his work properly in context if we know only the concrete results of his "inspiration" — his music — but almost nothing of its source. It is time to give Mathilde her voice back.

There is always a certain satisfaction in being able to postulate a direct relationship between the life and work of an artist, though the results are usually too simplistic to be convincing, for they tend to ignore the complex dialectic in which the two are engaged. The loose ends one wishes to tie up thus remain stubbornly unknotted. However, composers can be far more susceptible to straightforward correlations than their commentators. As mentioned in chapter 9, Wagner was himself the first to draw a parallel between the triangular relationships of Siegmund, Sieglinde, and Hunding in his *Walküre* and himself, Mathilde, and Otto. Before he gave the composition draft of its first act to Mathilde, he covered it with cryptic references to his love for her, as for example: "I.l.d.g.!!" — which scholars usually decipher as "Ich liebe dich grenzenlos" ("I love you boundlessly") — and "W.d.n.w., G.!!!" — "Wenn du nicht wärst, Geliebte" ("[What would I do] if you were not [here], beloved").[3] In mid-1857 Wagner put aside his *Siegfried* in order to work on *Tristan und Isolde* — the story of yet another love triangle. On 18 September he presented Mathilde with the finished libretto. A year later he wrote in his diary: "You led me to the sofa, embraced me, and said: 'Now I can wish for nothing more.'"[4] Between late 1857 and spring 1858 Wagner set five of Mathilde's poems to music, one of which, "Träume" — as outlined in chapter 2 — he arranged for violin and small orchestra to play to Mathilde on the morning of 23 December 1857, her birthday. This "serenade" was, so Minna Wagner maintained, in lieu of a Christmas present for Mathilde (let us not forget that the two women had begun as friends, too).[5] There were others who acknowledged its real significance, however. In a letter to Emma Herwegh, Cosima von Bülow remarked, somewhat facetiously: "He [Wagner] has thus composed a serenade for his pretty Mathilde."[6] Otto was on his way home from the USA at the time, having struggled with a business crisis that had apparently threatened his very liquidity, and he was not a little perturbed to find upon his return that Wagner — whose financial wellbeing naturally depended upon his own — had in the meantime acquired the freedom of his villa. The two families nevertheless celebrated Christmas together.

Precisely what happened next remains unclear, but on 31 December 1857 Wagner finished the draft of the first act of *Tristan* and sent it to Mathilde together with an effusive dedicatory poem that declared: "[Tristan's and Isolde's] tears and kisses I place at your feet, that they might praise the angel who raised me up so high!" Whether or not Otto saw this, he obviously understood that Wagner was encroaching dangerously on his territory, and now at last he seems to have attempted to reaffirm his authority. But his task was not an easy one. According to the reminiscences of François Wille, Otto had confessed to him that he had wanted to expel Wagner from the *Asyl*, but that Mathilde had threatened to throw herself off the balcony if he did. Asked for his advice, Wille replied: "The next time, say: *Over you go, Mathilde.*"[7] Otto was right to be worried, for it seems that Wagner was now seriously contemplating an elopement with her. A letter exists from Wagner to Franz Hagenbuch of 26 December in which he begs for a passport to allow him to travel to Paris, very soon (*SB* 9:85); there is another to Franz Liszt written at some point between 9 and 12 January, in which he passionately declares that he is "at the end of a conflict that encompasses everything that can be holy to a man: I have to make a decision, but every choice that lies before me is so terrible that I have to have my friend by my side to make the decision." He continues that he feels compelled to leave Zurich in order to take that decision, and begs Liszt to meet him either there or in Strasbourg. There is also, however, an odd letter that Wagner sent to Emilie Ritter on 25 December 1857, in which he mentions Jessie Laussot for the first time in a year. Indeed, he does not merely mention her, but asks Emilie "Could you believe that I could ever forget J., and that she could become indifferent to me?" and begs for information, not just about her activities, but about her "inner life." He fantasizes about "putting her mind at rest" — implicitly by resuming contact, now that he knows she has long left her husband. It was not wholly uncommon for Wagner's mind to wander passionately from one woman to another, though it is probably a sign of his general emotional confusion with regard to Mathilde that he should now be grasping at straws from his previous life. It was perhaps the very notion of running away with Mathilde — and the near impossibility of it — that prompted him to remember his similar attempt at elopement with Jessie seven years earlier.

Wagner indeed left for Paris on 14 January, explaining to those around him that it was in order to sort out legal matters pertaining to his copyright in France. He borrowed the money for the trip from Gottfried Semper but wrote to Liszt begging for more. Liszt wrote back on 15 January 1858, offering to travel to Strasbourg to meet Wagner if he needed to discuss things in person, and then asking cryptically "is your wife remaining in Zurich? Do you perhaps plan to go back there later? Where is Mme. W.-[*sic*]?"[8] Since he refers to Minna just two sentences before, we can assume that Liszt did not here mean "Mme W[agner]." "Mme W[esendonck]," of course, was still in Zurich, now busy learning Italian with her handsome new Italian professor, Francesco De Sanctis. Wagner calmed himself in Paris, as his further correspondence shows, and returned to Zurich on about 6 February 1858. He thus established a pattern of behavior that was repeated over the coming months. Whenever conflict was provoked through the geographical proximity of the two families, one or more of the involved parties would simply leave the city for a few weeks.

Of course, Wagner's absence did nothing to alleviate his infatuation with Mathilde. On the evening of 6 April the Wesendoncks visited the Wagners, on which occasion Wagner and Mathilde had an argument about Goethe's *Faust*. The next morning, Minna intercepted a letter that her husband had instructed their servant to take next door to Mathilde: the so-called "Morgenbeichte" or "Morning Confession" (*SB* 9:228–31). Minna interpreted its rambling arguments about *Faust* as concrete proof of marital infidelity (she had probably been waiting for such proof for some time and now seized on the best thing she could find). She took this "proof" first to Richard, who tried to play the matter down. But then, after an interval of several days, she went to show the letter to Mathilde herself.[9] Mathilde in turn now informed her husband, presumably because preemptive action was the only way she had of protecting herself. As long as Minna possessed the letter, Mathilde would have to assume it might be used against her; and if Otto were to find out about it later, he would also find out that she had kept the matter from him, and that would probably suffice for him to assume infidelity on her part. Wagner tried desperately to find a solution to the escalating crisis. On 15 April Minna was shipped off to a water cure for several weeks, while the Wesendoncks left for Italy. Things had now gone too far for any damage-limitation exercise to be of lasting effect, though a letter of 13 May that Wagner wrote to Carolyne von Sayn-Wittgenstein almost suggests that he was actually pushing matters to their awful, but logical conclusion as a means of stimulating his muse:

> God knows what will become of my Zurich *Asyl*. Wesendoncks have now left on their travels; they want me to stay here, but I could only do that if I refrain from any and all contact with them, which, given our neighborly proximity, would be so difficult and obvious to all. Here, probably, only a *coup de force* could help, and I fear that the dear "white rose" is destined to be a victim, as she always felt she would, and saw it in advance! Enough now of this deep feeling of apprehension, which makes me lonely before all the world and pushes me into solitude! I have at last been able to begin work on *Tristan* again. (*SB* 9:271–72)

The "white rose" seems to have been the name given to Mathilde by Carolyne's daughter Marie, presumably when she visited Zurich in October 1856 together with her mother and Liszt, according to a letter from Wagner to the latter (*SB* 8:258).

The Wesendoncks returned home on 2 June 1858. As Wagner's letter to Mathilde of the following 6 July makes evident, he had now decided to gamble everything by attempting to convince her to run off with him. A letter to his sister Kläre tells us that he knew of her earlier threat of suicide to Otto (*SB* 10:28), and he seems to have interpreted it as proof that she might indeed be prepared to leave her husband. She was not, of course, as she obviously made clear to him. But it speaks much for her powers of persuasion that both the men in her life seem to have taken seriously what was almost certainly an empty threat. After Minna came home on 15 July, relations between the two houses deteriorated such that Otto sent Mathilde away on her own: "My health has really changed so much that my husband finds it wise to procure for me a change of air" she wrote to Francesco De Sanctis on 26 July, just before departing for Munich. It seems that she joined her parents in August, though precisely where is uncertain, and her absence is not mentioned by Wagner in his autobiography.[10] He himself did write in *Mein Leben*, however, of how he had said his farewells to Mathilde just before he left the city (*ML*, 584), so it would appear that Mathilde had returned by the middle of that month. On 17 August, Wagner traveled alone to Geneva, and thence to Venice, where he resumed work on *Tristan*. Minna soon left for Dresden, though not before causing the Wesendoncks much embarrassment by advertising her furniture for sale, thus publicly announcing her departure and, by implication, the rift between the two families and all that it entailed. Although she and Wagner made a brief attempt at reconciliation over a year later, the events of August 1858 essentially ended their marriage for good.

It is difficult to pinpoint precisely when relations between the two families became so untenable that one of them had to leave. The "Morgenbeichte" was undoubtedly the catalyst for the catastrophe, though Wagner's last-ditch attempts in July to woo Mathilde away from Otto, coupled with Minna's behavior in July and August, seem to have been the final straw. The scandal had certainly become public by late August. In a letter of 27 August 1858 one Caroline Streuli-Maurer of Horgen (a few miles down the lake from the Wesendoncks) wrote to her son Emil, who at the time was working for the silk merchant Aschmann in New York:

> In Zurich there is apparently a great scandal regarding the wife of Wesendonc [*sic*] & Richard Wagner. Wagner's wife is supposed to have deposited letters with the courts and wants to get divorced. Mr Wesendonc, too, is said to be doing the same. But such neighborly relations always end badly, just like pride and foolishness.[11]

There is no record of Otto or Minna having officially filed for divorce (indeed, Minna seems in general never to have favored the idea), and this letter was probably just the result of local gossip having magnified matters beyond what was true. But for the members of the upper classes such as Otto Wesendonck, of course, if everyone who mattered in Zurich was of the opinion that his wife was about to run off with Wagner, then this was almost as embarrassing as if she had actually gone ahead and done it.

Nor did Wagner give up so easily his notions of a "union" with Mathilde. In late 1858, he endeavored to push their mutual friend Eliza Wille into the role of go-between, and apparently he even envisaged returning to Zurich at Christmas 1858 with a view to a surreptitious meeting with Mathilde. But now François Wille stepped in at his wife's request and wrote a letter that is impressive in its admixture of tact and bluntness, admonishing Wagner for his extreme selfishness, not least in wilfully bringing shame on the Wesendoncks by the public manner of his departure from Zurich. He made it clear that he would inform Otto Wesendonck if Wagner dared to return.[12] Nevertheless, as we saw in chapter 9, regular contact was indeed resumed between Wagner and the Wesendoncks, once a certain interval had elapsed. Visits were made on both sides over the next two decades, and the Wesendoncks were in later years regular guests at the Bayreuth Festival. The dream of one day reclaiming his *Asyl* was one that Wagner did not abandon for many years after his departure from Zurich, nor did his feelings for Mathilde disappear any more rapidly. All the same, when he wrote to Eliza Wille in June 1863 that "she [Mathilde] is and remains my only love," and swore his "eternal love" for her,[13] we should perhaps take his exclamation not quite so seriously. Both statements harbor an undoubted element of selfish pathos. And let us not forget that, in the same year, Wagner was involved in an affair with the actress Friederike Meyer and also began a relationship with both the notary's daughter Mathilde Maier (it almost seems as if Otto's fascination with the name had become infectious) and with Harriet von Bissing, the widowed sister of Eliza Wille (through a strange coincidence, Harriet's son Moritz later married Mathilde Wesendonck's daughter Myrrha; had he married Harriet, Wagner would thus have become the [step]father-in-law of Mathilde's daughter). And, according to *Mein Leben*, this was also the year in which he and Cosima von Bülow confessed to each other that they "would belong to each other only" (*ML*, 746). Thus Wagner's "only," "eternal" love, Mathilde, seems already to have become less than only or eternal, and more a now never-to-be-attained ideal alongside several far more real rivals of flesh and blood.

After the Wesendoncks' rapid departure from Zurich in March 1871, after the "Tonhalle riot,"they moved first to Dresden, then in autumn 1882 to Berlin. During their last years they spent much time in the Salzkammergut at their villa "Traunblick," which they had bought in 1878. All but one of their children died before their parents: besides Paul and Guido, who died in early childhood, Hans died in early 1882, Myrrha in 1888. In 1896 Mathilde felt compelled to publish her account of Wagner's years in Zurich, in order to counter the biography recently published by Houston Stewart Chamberlain.[14] In line with official Bayreuth policy, Chamberlain had played down the importance of Wagner's Zurich experiences and friends, claiming that the latter group had not really understood the greatness of the man whom they had harbored among them.[15] Mathilde had Albert Heintz publish her reminiscences in the *Allgemeine Musikzeitung* on 14 February 1896. A few months later, on 18 November 1896, Otto died. Mathilde thereupon retired to her Austrian villa, living long enough to see her son Karl raised to the aristocracy in 1899. She died in Traunblick on 31 August 1902. Two years later, as she had herself determined, Wagner's letters to her were published.

Friendly relations with the Wagner family were maintained to the last. When Siegfried Wagner studied in Berlin in the early 1890s, he was a regular and welcome guest in the Wesendonck home. Just a few months before her death, Mathilde was asked by Cosima to give her support to the campaign to keep the performance rights of *Parsifal* restricted to

Bayreuth. In addition, receipts in the Wesendonck archive prove that Mathilde gave cash donations to the Bayreuth Festival in 1898 and 1899. All the same, as mentioned before, Cosima remained passionately jealous of her. Even Wagner's surviving letters to Mathilde exist only in manuscript copies. But this is not the only loss to the would-be Wesendonck scholar, for remarkably few documents from Mathilde's pen have escaped oblivion (of her apparently voluminous correspondence with Theodor Kirchner and Ödön von Mihalovich, for example, only the composer's letters to her have survived in each case).[16] There exists only one comprehensive first-hand source of information on Mathilde: her poetic oeuvre. But even this has been largely ignored. Not only were her works published in small print runs during her lifetime, so that few copies have survived, but even those scholars who have taken any notice of them have done little but pour scorn. Ernest Newman remarked, mockingly, that we should be grateful to Mathilde that Wagner did not rely on her to write the libretto of *Tristan*.[17] The extent of this scorn is matched, however, by the degree of ignorance of her works displayed by most critics. For these have tended merely to repeat the mockery of their predecessors, without taking the trouble to pay due attention to its object.

By ignoring Mathilde's own creative and intellectual capabilities, commentators have inevitably explained away Wagner's attraction to her as primarily erotic in nature. It has naturally remained a matter of intense speculation as to whether the relationship between the two crossed the boundaries of the purely platonic; nor can the issue be ignored here, if only because the speculation in fact seems misplaced.[18] For when Wagner wrote to her on 6 July 1858, just a few weeks before he left Zurich, that "I felt that only a complete separation or a complete union ['Vereinigung'] would make our love safe from the terrible tribulations to which we have seen it subjected in recent times," he is presumably thinking not just of a geographical union (that is, living together) but of a sexual one. This naturally suggests that such a union had never taken place. And when he related these turbulent times to his second wife Cosima in 1873, he said (according to her diary entry of 14 March):

> "at that ghastly time, when Mathilde Wesendonck was jealous of my wife, I proposed that I should leave my wife, Mathilde her husband, and that we should marry. She replied: that would be a sacrilege ['Sakrilegium']. Anyway" — he added, laughing, "the word I didn't understand suited my suggestion perfectly, for deep down, subconsciously, I wasn't serious! . . . 'Sacrilege,' why not 'sin' ['Frevel'] or something. It had to be a word that one doesn't understand." (*TB* 1:653)

Even though Wagner here projects Mathilde into the role of the jealous woman and plays down the seriousness of the situation — all, no doubt, to guard himself against the jealousy of Cosima — the word "Sakrilegium" (derived from the Latin or the French, as opposed to the Germanic "Frevel") is undoubtedly something he will have remembered exactly. And if Mathilde found the idea of leaving her husband "sacrilegious," then we can probably assume that adultery would have been equally unacceptable to her. According to the memoirs of her grandson Friedrich Wilhelm von Bissing, Mathilde was in general a woman unwilling to ignore the norms of bourgeois society; he stressed her "Prussian nature" and her need for "order and cleanliness in every way."[19] In his letter to Mathilde of 6 July 1858 quoted earlier, Wagner wrote further:

> Thus the feeling that our separation was a necessity confronted the possibility — in thought, though not in volition — of our union ["Vereinigung"]. In this lay the cause of the awkward tension that we two could not bear. I went to you, and it stood before us, clear and definite, that that other possibility contained a sin ["Frevel"] that could not even be thought of. (*SB* 9:334)

Wagner's superficial renunciation of a "union" with Mathilde — something that "could not even be thought of," even while he is thinking it and describing it to her — seems here more a desperate attempt to nudge her into suggesting precisely such a union; this possibility hovers constantly between the lines of his text. We can be sure, given his biography before and afterwards, that Wagner himself found nothing "sinful" in such a notion; it must be Mathilde's own words that he is here quoting and twisting in order to convince her to reconsider them. "Frevel" means "Sakrilegium," of course — as Wagner himself mentioned all those years later — so we probably have here the origin of the anecdote that he told Cosima in 1873.

Wagner's use of the word "Vereinigung" ("union") in that letter of 6 July also deserves further investigation. The word naturally allows for a broad interpretation, as does the word "union" in English. However, it is notable that, besides his occasional use of it in general terms, Wagner also employed it repeatedly to mean two quite specific things: the union of man and woman (that is, an implicitly sexual union) and the union of the arts in his "vereinigtes Kunstwerk" ("unified work of art"), as he himself termed his music drama.[20] The sexual use of this word is well documented with regard to all the four women who were arguably the most significant for his sexual life, namely Minna, Jessie Laussot, Mathilde, and Cosima. Thus he wrote to his future wife Minna Planer on 23 May 1836, during several weeks of separation: "I wouldn't know what should become of me if heaven delays yet longer my union with you" (*SB* 1:266); he uses the same word to mean the same thing in another desperate letter to her just a few days later, on 3 June, and again on 26 June (*SB* 1:283 and 312); in his letter to her of 16 April 1850, when he announces their separation in the midst of his affair with Jessie Laussot, he uses the word "Vereinigung" once more to state that, when their relationship had begun a decade and a half before, "you only out of necessity gave in to my urge for union" (*SB* 3:276); but he had used the word just four weeks before this (three times, no less) in a brief letter to Emilie Ritter of 26 March 1850 from Bordeaux in which he announced, if rather obliquely, that he had found a new partner in Jessie (*SB* 3:262). In Wagner's letter of 20 August 1858 to his sister Kläre Wolfram, in which he explains the situation with Mathilde, "Vereinigung" reappears, almost as a mantra, in the same context as in his letter of six weeks earlier to Mathilde herself: "Since there could be no talk of a union between us . . . but we recognized immediately that there could be no thought of a union between us . . . since there could be no thought of our union . . ." (*SB* 10:27–32). This passage is so obviously a rehashing of his letter to Mathilde that it seems as if the word in question had been carefully chosen, presumably for its "innocent" manner of connoting something less than innocent. A decade later, "Vereinigung" was also the word that Cosima herself wrote in the margin of *Mein Leben* to signify the date when she joined Wagner, for good, in Tribschen.

As regards the use of the word "Vereinigung" (and the verb "vereinigen") to signify the union of the arts, it appears more or less as a "red thread" through his aesthetic tracts of the immediate post-Dresden period, first in *Art and Revolution*,[21] then in *The Artwork of the Future*[22] and in *Opera and Drama*[23] (the word "Gesamtkunstwerk," which has achieved the greatest currency among commentators, is in fact used only four times throughout the Zurich tracts, and only in *Art and Revolution*; even there, its first two mentions refer specifically to the tragedy of Ancient Greece, not to Wagner's own music drama[24]). While we should beware of venturing too far in our speculation, it is not impossible that Wagner made use of the word "Vereinigung" in his letter to Mathilde precisely because of its connotation for his music drama. His correspondence seems to confirm that the word was chosen with great care, and since his letter of 6 July to Mathilde reads as a summing up of a conversation between the two of them, we can probably assume that the word was also employed by Wagner more extensively on that occasion, with the letter intended to jog Mathilde's memory. We know that Mathilde was well-versed in Wagner's writings — she herself acknowledged in later life that she had either read them herself or allowed Wagner to read them to her[25] — so we can assume that she was aware both of the term "vereinigtes Kunstwerk" and of Wagner's extensive sexual metaphors in *Opera and Drama*, in which "music as woman" was to be penetrated by "poetry as man" in order to create [music] drama. Wagner had completed the latest (and, as it would turn out, the last) of his Wesendonck settings just over eight weeks before; did he, perhaps, in their conversation play on the union of music and poetry in their joint songs and use his undoubted rhetorical skill to suggest to Mathilde that the two artists should themselves now follow the example of their art? Did he perhaps even dangle the possibility of further artistic "unions" between them in exchange for a promise of the other form of "union"? And does the implicit reversal here of the roles postulated in *Opera and Drama* — for in the *Wesendonck-Lieder*, music is the "man," poetry the "woman" — reflect Mathilde's primacy in their relationship, with Wagner taking the more subservient, ostensibly "feminine" role?

Whether or not our suppositions here are close to the truth, or divergent from it, we do have further proof that Mathilde remained defiantly unattainable for Wagner in a sexual sense, and it is to be found in his *Tristan und Isolde*. As has often been remarked, the whole opera — the libretto and its music — is a tale of unfulfilled yearning. In the second act, at the close of the love duet, the lovers do not reach their musico-sexual climax, for the music breaks off at precisely that moment (that is, when King Mark enters). It is as if Wagner here distils into a single moment all the sexual frustrations that he has suffered through years of longing for Mathilde. Just like Tristan, he could not meet his (would-be) lover without an "envious watcher" in the background (Brangäne in the opera, Minna in real life; Minna herself told how Wagner and Mathilde would meet on the second floor of their house, while she remained on the first floor).[26] Nor was he able to meet his lover without King Mark/Otto Wesendonck appearing. As is well known, the music of the duet returns at the close of the final act, as the so-called "Liebestod" or "Love-death" of Isolde. This time, the climax is reached, though by Isolde on her own, for Tristan already lies dead at her feet. This music, written by Wagner after the separation from Mathilde, is essentially a voyeuristic, male depiction of a woman's onanistic fantasy: it is Wagner imagining how his lover fantasizes about him while he watches from afar. Isolde's musical orgasm is also a thoroughly masculine cliché: after a few minutes of foreplay, she reaches a single climax, then straightaway falls asleep (in this case, of course, the metaphorical, permanent sleep of death). There is no "union" in *Tristan*, and it is perhaps for this reason most of all that Wagner saw his own life reflected in his opera. In fact, as Roger Scruton has rightly pointed out, Isolde implicitly dies still a virgin.[27] The fact that Wagner was also, by his own later admission, practicing sexual abstinence in his final months in Zurich, merely underlines the autobiographical implications of this most "sexless" of erotic operas. Wagner had abandoned his wife's bed, presumably in constant anticipation of a "union" with Mathilde, though it was a union that was constantly being deferred to some future date and then never came about at all.

The fact that in *Tristan und Isolde* sexual love is portrayed directly in music, even including a graphic depiction of sexual climax, has led to the relationship between Wagner and Mathilde being understood as erotic in character, with little intellectual component. Commentators have often repeated Mathilde's own words, written forty years later, "thus I came to Zurich *quite unlearned*. Wagner himself called me a 'white sheet of paper' and took it upon himself to write on it."[28] But we do Mathilde an injustice if we take as literal truth her hagiographical description of the "Master," who had, after all, died thirteen years earlier. It is all too easy to see her as a passive object of inspiration, whose role was to listen to what Wagner would play to her and to react with appropriate feminine enthusiasm, but who otherwise should be seen and not heard. When Ferdinand Praeger published his controversial book *Wagner as I Knew Him* in 1892, he drew a parallel between Mathilde's relationship with Wagner and the latter's affair with Jessie Laussot in 1850.[29] However, in the story as Praeger tells it — and as related to him by Wagner, it would seem — Jessie had cast herself on Wagner's mercy, and he had sent a telegram to her husband requesting him to come and fetch his wife. Praeger implies that Mathilde had in 1858 acted in a similar manner to the Jessie of his (and Wagner's) imagination. We do not know how Jessie reacted to this, if she ever read it (her mother tongue, of course, was English, and we can assume that she will not have remained in the dark about such a well-publicized book). Mathilde, however, was furious, and on 26 March 1892 she wrote as follows (in English) to the Wagner scholar William Ashton Ellis:

> The tie that bound him to Mathilde Wesendonck, whome he then called his "Muse," was of so high, pure, nobel and ideal Nature that, alas, it will only be valued of those, that in their own noble chest find the same elevation and selfishlessness of Mind![30]

Mathilde was angry, not least because Praeger had suggested that she was possessed of the same subservience toward the opposite sex with which he imbued Jessie. For a "muse" — as Wagner did indeed describe her,[31] and as she liked to see herself — is no passive creature, let alone subservient. Rather is she the driving force behind the artist's creativity; she is responsible for his art; in a sense, she controls it. Indeed, the more closely one examines Wagner's relationship with Mathilde, the less she appears to have been a passive observer. Nor should we underestimate her intellect or her understanding of musical matters. She even seems to have studied some music theory under Wagner's watchful eye (which would make her his only known pupil). As early as 1852 he had asked Otto in a letter from Pallanza how her "studies in general bass" were progressing. And in a letter from London, three years later, he wrote: "Thank her most kindly for the bass theme" (*SB* 4:413 and 7:175). Mathilde was very well read and an unusually gifted linguist. Besides German, her mother tongue, she was fluent in French and English and later learned Italian, Greek, and Middle High German (her archives include her numerous translations into German of writings from all those languages). Her interest in the Germanic myths and legends that also occupied Wagner is proven in her later writings. Wagner's surviving letters to her discuss the authors that they read together — Calderón, Lope de Vega, Cervantes, and others —

and testify to their common interest in philosophy (in particular that of Schopenhauer). They also tell of visits made to the theater (together with Otto, of course). Even the famous "Morning Confession," as mentioned before, in large part comprised Wagner's reaction to a dispute about Goethe and to Mathilde's supposedly erroneous interpretation of the character of Faust in the play of that name. A glance through the list of correspondents whose letters survive in her archives can suffice to prove that Mathilde was taken seriously by her contemporaries and obviously expected this as a matter of course. Nor were her interests confined to music. There are some fifty letters from Otto Benndorf, professor in archaeology and later Director of the Archaeological Institute in Vienna; twelve letters from Theodor Billroth, the leading surgeon of the day and a friend of Johannes Brahms; twenty-six from Ludwig Ettmüller, who was reputedly responsible, along with Wagner, for Mathilde's first excursions into creative writing (he even dedicated to Mathilde his three-volume popular history of German language and literature[32]); there are more than twenty letters from the politician, revolutionary, and art historian Gottfried Kinkel; over one hundred letters from Franz Koppel-Ellfeld, arts editor of the *Dresdner Zeitung*; over thirty from the art historian Wilhelm Lübke; some forty letters from the writer Conrad Ferdinand Meyer; and sixteen from the architect Gottfried Semper. Her other correspondents included ambassadors, professors, and men and women active in various artistic and intellectual pursuits — music, poetry, the visual arts, antiquities, and so on. All in all, the extant letters to Mathilde testify to a mind keen to remain in touch with what is happening in the most varied fields of human endeavor.[33] The fact that many of these friends and acquaintances (such as Semper, Kinkel, Billroth, and others) were at some point resident in Zurich is also proof of the lively intellectual climate in the city in the third quarter of the nineteenth century.[34]

Even before they first met, as we have already seen, Mathilde had taken the trouble to read Wagner's latest book, *A Communication to My Friends* (which also contained the libretti to *Der fliegende Holländer*, *Tannhäuser*, and *Lohengrin*), and her claim to have been well acquainted with his other writings is confirmed in a statement made later by Natalie Planer (*RWB*, 641). We must surely entertain the possibility that Cosima wanted Mathilde's letters destroyed, not just out of sexual jealousy but also on account of intellectual envy. Our supposition that her attitude toward Mathilde was not just a matter of mere feminine, sexual rivalry is also confirmed by a close reading of Cosima's diaries. On one occasion, Cosima wrote of a dinner at the Wesendoncks, during which she and Wagner both attacked the latest book by David Friedrich Strauss (*Der alte und der neue Glaube*), while Mathilde defended it (*TB* 1:638). Another time she wrote: "Evening, letter from Frau Wesendonck, who did not understand me and now enlightens me as to world history" (*TB* 1:464). Of particular interest is the entry of 20 December 1873, which she made after receiving a volume of poetry that Mathilde had just published:

> One thing I cannot understand is that a woman can present herself to the public of her own accord, to please herself. It seems to me that the experiences of life would have to make her ever quieter, and lead her more and more back to her principal task: to bring up dutiful men and good women. (*TB* 1:765)

While Cosima herself was not averse to manipulating her husband behind the scenes with her womanly wiles,[35] she was demonstratively upset that Mathilde obviously would not have been prepared to play the role of quiet feminine appendage to a great genius, whose "principal task" would consist of bringing up his dutiful sons and good daughters. Rather did she wish to prove herself in the intellectual world of men, and in conversation did not even shy away from maintaining a different opinion from the one that Wagner espoused. However, Cosima was by no means alone in her apparent subservience. Even Mathilde's friend Eliza Wille, who was widely read, a master of three languages, and herself a published author, did not interfere in the conversation of men:

> When I was present, I sat busy with my handiwork, listening to everything but rarely saying anything. Neither my father nor the other men whom I admired would have been pleasantly touched by my making my knowledge known . . . so I preferred not so speak, but wrote down what I thought.[36]

The fact that Mathilde was a woman possessed of an independent will is proven not least by her actions in the year 1858, when she refused to give in to Wagner's desires, remaining with her husband instead (to be sure, in late 1858 Minna wrote to their common friend Jakob Sulzer that Wagner had claimed that Mathilde "could not stand me, was jealous of me and definitely wanted us to separate"[37] — a claim that was repeated by her daughter Natalie more than thirty years later [*RWB*, 675] — but, even if these words were indeed Wagner's, then this was almost certainly a case of wish fulfillment on his part). However unlikely it might seem to us, it was perhaps precisely this decision of Mathilde's to deny Wagner what he wanted that Cosima found so threatening. For she had left her husband Hans von Bülow in order to follow Wagner and suffered pangs of conscience on this account for years to come. Otto Wesendonck, however, had fought for his wife, and won. Mathilde had had the courage to say "no" to Wagner, which was something that Cosima was almost incapable of doing. As Cosima's diaries repeatedly confirm, she felt it her duty to submit to him in everything[38] — and yet still he dreamed of Mathilde.[39] Just after Wagner's death on 13 February 1883, Cosima's daughter Daniela wrote the following postscript to an entry in her mother's diary:

> One of the dreams that he had in his last two nights was that he had received letters from women, one from Frau Wesendonck, [and another] from a woman whom Papa or Mama had forgotten; [he dreamed] that he opened neither, but put them on each side of the table and said to himself: "If only Cosima doesn't get angry." (*TB* 2:1114)

We know next to nothing of Mathilde's feelings toward Cosima. Only once does she seem to have let her guard down. In her reminiscences of Wagner, published in 1896, which — as mentioned above — were essentially a reply to the "official" Wagner biography by Chamberlain, Mathilde wrote of Hans von Bülow as follows: "The gratitude, selflessness, and pleasure in sacrifice on the part of von Bülow knew no bounds"[40] — and since this selflessness naturally resulted in sacrificing his own wife to the needs of the Master, one might be forgiven for detecting here a hint of sarcasm. For Mathilde will also have known what Hans had said to Eliza Wille in September 1857: "I would not hesitate for a moment to give up my new wife, if it were necessary to inspire the Master."[41]

Mathilde was perfectly aware of the fact that she was attractive to the opposite sex. In later life she even remarked to her grandson "with a quiet smile" that people kept falling in love with her.[42] It should not surprise us if she used this to develop a strategy whereby she might be able to break through the social norms of which Eliza Wille wrote. For if a group of men at dinner are competing for the attention of a woman — no matter how sublimated or harmless this competition might seem — then her silence will hardly be desired by them; rather will they draw her into conversation. Where social circumstances restrict the freedom of an intelligent, determined woman, she will inevitably develop roundabout methods of asserting herself (it is perhaps not insignificant that Mathilde granted her only daughter, Myrrha, more independence than she had herself enjoyed, when she let her enter the Dresden Conservatory in 1868 at the age of only 17 — at the time not a common step for a girl from the upper classes).

There can be little doubt that Mathilde will have been flattered by the romantic attentions of the already famous composer Wagner and by the music that he wrote in her honor. Nor can we doubt that she was fully aware of her position of power in their relationship. For over six years she was able to play Wagner, her husband, and Wagner's wife off against each other, without herself becoming a victim of the jealousies of any one party. Her husband cleared Wagner's debts and paid him an allowance that kept him financially afloat; Wagner dedicated his music to her; and Wagner's wife more or less accepted this complicated situation (at least until 1858). One could even claim with some justification that Minna's silence had been "bought" in a calculating manner. For Mathilde ensured, through her husband, that Richard, Minna, and Minna's illegitimate daughter Natalie were able to live together in considerable comfort. Minna had not ceased to regret that Wagner's participation in the Dresden uprising had deprived them of a relatively high social and economic status, and she will have known that their new domestic and economic stability would last only as long as she turned a blind eye to her husband's infatuation with the wife of their patron.

Natalie played a not insignificant role in this drama, though she probably did not realize it. She had been born when Minna was only 15, and — as mentioned in chapter 2 above — she had been brought up to believe that her mother was in fact her sister. While it is usually assumed that she remained under this misconception until her death, it is surely likely that she at least suspected the truth but maintained the existing lie to escape the stigma of being officially acknowledged as illegitimate. She lived in the Wagner household for several years after her mother's marriage, and although it seems that she did not follow the Wagners to Riga, she did join them in Paris in late 1840. After their move to Dresden she lived for a while with Minna's sister Charlotte Tröger in Zwickau before moving back in with the Wagners in 1845. We also know that Natalie arrived in Zurich with Minna in autumn 1849. At some point in late 1852 or early 1853 she moved to Leipzig and took up work in the Hôtel de Pologne (*SB* 5:473) but then at Wagner's request returned in early 1854 to run the household in Zurich. She was apparently also responsible for looking after Wagner when Minna visited Germany in the autumn of that year. On occasion she was invited along to the Wesendoncks, and apparently she lived briefly in the *Asyl*. There was, however, frequent friction throughout these years between her and Minna (*SB* 8:83). Given the close relationship between Wagner and Mathilde, it is not unreasonable to assume that the latter either guessed or was told of Natalie's real parentage, for it was not a secret that he kept from his friends (for example, *SB* 11:335–38). Perhaps, then, Natalie became a kind of "ransom." For as long as Wagner was financially dependent on the Wesendoncks, then so were Minna and Natalie, and as long as Minna was confronted daily by the illegitimate product of her own sexual indiscretion, she might have hesitated to criticize openly an extramarital passion on the part of her husband. It is noteworthy that Natalie was no longer in Zurich during the months of crisis in the second half of 1857 and in 1858 but living with Charlotte and Adam Tröger in Zwickau (*RWB*, 603–4, 606, 653, 660, 674, etc.).

Mathilde thus exercised with great success, and for several years, a subtle art of control on the people around her. Here we also have a further possible reason why she would not have overstepped the boundaries of the platonic in her relationship with Wagner. Only by denying him the physical consummation that he desired was she able to juggle him, his wife, and her own husband with such success. If she had granted Wagner the "union" that he wanted, the delicate balance in this network of relationships would have been upset for good. Her power over him resided precisely in her never letting him (as it were) grasp the carrot that she dangled.

But Wagner had himself, no doubt unwittingly, handed her a philosophical basis for her very denial of him with his own (if superficial) demonstrative adherence to Schopenhauerian values and their concomitant disparaging of the sexual urge. It seems that Mathilde also used sexual denial as a weapon in her own marriage. Wagner himself implies that she did, in the letter to his sister of 20 August 1858, already quoted above, in which he adds that she insisted that her husband "abstain [or 'refrain'] from her" ("von ihr abstehen"), and that Otto had been compelled to adopt an "entsagende Stellung," a "position of renunciation" (*SB* 10:28) (or perhaps Wagner was himself now merely projecting onto Otto the passivity with which he was himself imbuing King Mark). The fact that Mathilde could write of herself, many years later, as having been a "white sheet of paper" when she met Wagner — implicitly a virgin, though she had already borne two children — sounds more like an attempt to divert our attention from the truth, for she was obviously a strong-willed personality who took delight in controlling others. Only a few people recognized this trait in Mathilde; one of them was Natalie. In a letter to Mrs. Burrell of 24 November 1892, Natalie wrote the following:

> This cold snake, slippery as an eel, this Wesendonk [*sic*] . . . this flirtatious, heartless creature, devoid of a sense of duty, this Mathilde . . . so deliberate and cunning . . . this celebrated, pious-as-a-lamb, sweet little devil, this pretty little Mathilde . . . a despicable, shameless creature . . . such a poisonous reptile . . . this self-serving, calculating woman . . . (*RWB*, 603–4)

It is not surprising that Natalie's stream-of-consciousness ragings have never been treated seriously. We know very little of her — even the date and place of her death remain a mystery[43] — so it has been all too easy to accept as true Wagner's description of her in his autobiography. She had, he maintained, "remained slow in the development of both body and mind; small and with a tendency to physical strength, she was clumsy and naive" (*ML*, 464) — this being the longest of just four references to her in the whole of *Mein Leben*. In a letter of 8 April 1843 to his half-sister Cecilie Avenarius, Wagner does mention Natalie's faulty prose style, which would seem to confirm her lack of learning. But her extant letters, though hardly literary in quality, are far from being as clumsy as one would expect from Wagner's later damning descriptions of her intellectual ability.[44] Furthermore, it was to Natalie that he turned in July 1849, after his flight from Dresden, writing her a long letter in the hope that she would intercede with Minna for him and convince her to join him in exile (*SB* 3:92–97). He wrote to her again in December 1858, when he needed her to keep him informed — "secretly" — about Minna's state of health (*SB* 10:174) and also required her to organize Minna's elaborate Christmas present. This she obviously did to Wagner's satisfaction, for he wrote on 3 January

1859 to Minna that she should "say my very best thanks to the excellent Natalie for her ingenious procuring of your Christmas present" (*SB* 10:221) And in *Mein Leben* he also mentions having corresponded with Natalie in the early 1860s, once more using her as a go-between for him and Minna, after their last estrangement (*ML*, 737). This all naturally suggests that Wagner indeed regarded Natalie as possessing not merely the wherewithal to conduct a correspondence but also, by implication, a certain degree of tact in interpersonal relations. Precisely why Wagner should have effectively "erased" from his life a woman who had lived in his household for many years remains something of a conundrum. Perhaps her very presence was the reason, and she had to be discredited because she was in fact the only regular witness, besides Minna, of the events of his private life during the first twenty years of his marriage. Minna had died in early 1866, while Wagner was dictating the early portions of his autobiography to Cosima. His disparaging description of Natalie several months later coincides with his attempts to acquire from her the letters that he had sent to Minna over the years — for Minna had declared her "sister" her only heir. Wagner might well have known that Natalie had also inherited the original "Morning Confession." In any case, the somewhat desperate tone in his correspondence with Natalie, for example in his letter of 27 November 1868, makes it clear that he was worried about sensitive documents coming into the public domain (*RWB*, 729). Wagner might also have feared that the issue of Minna's will and inheritance would have clarified for Natalie (and, more important, for everyone else) the facts surrounding her parentage; and if, as is always claimed, she had indeed been kept in complete ignorance thereof, then Wagner could also have feared a backlash on her part against him. He was, after all, a coconspirator of some thirty years' standing in keeping the truth from her. Cosima had just borne him his first child, Isolde, a few months earlier, so his private life was undoubtedly complicated enough already without the prospect of further complications from a "newly found" stepdaughter. Natalie did indeed send him a large number of the letters he had written to Minna, though the fact that she secretly kept many of them back would seem to prove that she was not quite as "naive" as Wagner maintained in his memoirs. Her reluctance to return all of them was indeed justified, for within months of receiving the letters, Wagner informed Natalie that he would be discontinuing her allowance (*RWB*, 730).

It seems not unlikely that Natalie — if she had not long guessed it — was by the 1870s aware of who her mother really was, though in her later correspondence with Mrs. Burrell she admittedly did maintain what must surely by then have been a mere charade, presumably for appearance's sake. Wagner obviously now felt confident enough to mention Natalie's real parentage in print, in the first edition of *Mein Leben* — and although it admittedly was restricted to less than twenty copies, he distributed these to enough friends for word of its contents to reach many more. So he must have either known that Natalie knew the truth, or been unafraid that someone would now tell her. A letter does exist, however, from Cosima, written four years after Wagner's death, in which she assures Natalie that she has arranged for the necessary repairs after weather damage to the grave of "her mother" (*RWB*, 585). If Cosima was still pretending that Natalie and Minna shared the same mother, it would be odd if she felt any responsibility for seeing to the woman's grave (Minna's mother — Natalie's grandmother — had been dead for forty years already); she would, however, undoubtedly feel beholden to ensure that Minna's grave was not ravaged by the elements. So Natalie probably did know the truth, after all.

Natalie wrote the letter quoted above to Mrs. Burrell (who then purchased the "Morning Confession," saving it for posterity) when she was sixty-five and living in considerable poverty (*RWB*, 17–18). She was the stepchild of the composer and had spent the early years of her life in his household, but she was now largely dependent on what financial crumbs her new "stepmother" Cosima gave her, while Wagner's biological children and his other two stepchildren (Hans von Bülow's daughters) were being brought up knowing all the comforts of the upper middle classes. The fact that Cosima was younger than her by more than a decade might well have rankled, too. In any case, one cannot be surprised that Natalie should ooze bitterness, and we would do well to hesitate before dismissing the content of her letter merely on account of its tone. After all, Cosima — who was also an observer from afar of the events of 1858 — harbored a dislike of Mathilde that can have been no less intense, for she would otherwise not have endeavored to erase the latter's existence by destroying all available written records of her. For Mathilde to inspire the hatred of one woman might be considered unfortunate, but to inspire it in three (Minna, Cosima, and Natalie) surely confirms that she was by no means a woman devoid of personality. A woman who is a mere "white sheet of paper" is hardly a threat to the fellow members of her sex.

It thus seems likely that Natalie's description of Mathilde contains at least a grain of truth. Emilie Heim, for example, who sang the part of Sieglinde at the first, private performance of the *Walküre* (with piano accompaniment) in 1856, mentioned many years later in a letter to Wilhelm Kienzl that Mathilde was a "richly attired lady," "who liked to let famous men burn incense to her" and "let herself be courted by other important artists afterwards," that is, after Wagner. Emilie also maintains, however, that Mathilde "hardly had any deep love for Wagner," though her opinion is perhaps not quite objective. As her contemporary Berta Roner once mentioned, she was herself rumored to have been Wagner's "first female redeemer in Zurich" (though we must here be careful not to lose ourselves in a maze of reciprocal jealous gossip; Berta's sympathies were decidedly with Minna, and she also took a dislike to Mathilde, whom she described — perhaps not without a hint of jealousy herself — as a "small, insignificant . . . silly, vain goose").[45] All the same, what we know of Mathilde's relations with other "famous men" tends to support Emilie's claim.

When Brahms visited Switzerland in 1866 to work on his *German Requiem*, he began to attract Mathilde's interest. As already mentioned, she even offered him Wagner's former *Asyl* as temporary living quarters (one wonders how Wagner might have reacted, had he heard of that). But Brahms warily declined her offer of hospitality. He was supported in his decision by Clara Schumann, who feared it might make him beholden to the Wesendoncks — or perhaps she was also motivated by jealousy, and by the fear that Mathilde was on the hunt for the next great composer to "inspire." After all, they were personally acquainted, and Clara will have observed in December 1857 the attraction that Mathilde had exerted upon Wagner. Mathilde remained persistent for several years, though when she wrote to Brahms on 30 December 1868 that "I would not like to have lived in this century without having at least asked you, in friendly but urgent fashion, to rest at our hearth," Brahms might well have noticed that she was paraphrasing the opening of Wagner's *Walküre* ("To whomsoever this hearth belongs, here I must rest"), which might not have endeared her further to him.[46] She subsequently tried, to no avail, to encourage Brahms to use one of her dramas as the basis for an opera, or at least to set her poems to music, and finally even suggested that he might want to set to music a "Cremation Cantata" whose words she had penned (she and Otto were among the most prominent of the early advocates of this method of burial). But Brahms found it hilarious, and sent it straight to his friend Theodor Billroth. He in turn told Wilhelm Lübke, who told Julius and Clara Stockhausen — and it seems likely that word of the general hilarity that she had caused now filtered back to Mathilde, for there exist no further letters from her to Brahms. There is a postscript to Mathilde's "courting" of him, however, for when her play *Alkestis* was performed in aid of charity in Dresden on 16 April 1881 (the only performance of any of her works that she saw on stage), Brahms is reputed to have accompanied several of his *Liebeslieder* Waltzes as part of the event. The why and how of this, however, remain a mystery.[47] In his later years, Brahms took to spending his summers in Ischl, not far from the Wesendonck residence of Traunblick. After Mathilde's death in 1902, the local *Gmundner Zeitung* reported that Brahms had made a habit of visiting her each summer — but again, we have precious little evidence of it.[48]

We should not be too surprised that Brahms was relatively immune to Mathilde's charms. Their friendship began in the mid-1860s when she was almost forty years old and he was five years her junior (though, given his infatuation with Clara Schumann, Mathilde had perhaps suspected that he might in general prefer older women). But besides this age difference, Brahms's friend Theodor Kirchner was at the same time developing a far stronger interest in Mathilde. This could in part explain Brahms's determination to keep his distance, if — as we might assume — he was aware of his friend's infatuation. After he moved from Winterthur to Zurich in 1862, Kirchner began making music frequently *chez* Wesendonck (as also *chez* Wille). His attraction to more or less unattainable women of status did not cease after the messy end of his affair with Clara Schumann in 1864 (who in the end had proven far from unattainable, to her subsequent regret). Just three months later, in October 1864, Kirchner began visiting the Wesendonck villa on a regular basis in order to give their thirteen-year-old daughter Myrrha piano lessons. "Wesendoncks give him special support," wrote Eliza Wille to her mother in January 1865. That means, presumably, that Otto will have given him support at the request of Mathilde (as in the case of Wagner). Over the coming months, he seems to have become at least as infatuated with Mathilde as Wagner had been just a decade before him, and his relationship to her seems to have followed a not wholly dissimilar pattern.[49] In 1867, Kirchner summoned up the courage to begin penning passionate letters to her. On 6 July (which, in an odd case of synchronicity, was nine years to the day since Wagner had written to Mathilde in an attempt to woo her away from Otto), Kirchner wrote:

> Really, you unique, wonderful woman, you cannot expect anything other than that one has to love you. That it is finally put into words is only human and the only means of not going insane. . . . That's how it is and I've told you. Grant me the happiness of a never-to-be-fulfilled yearning for you.[50]

Five days later he continued:

> Oh, how happy it would make me if I could have the happy feeling, just once only, that your wounds would hurt you less if you knew that there is a human being who so very much — so unutterably — loves you and whose lifeblood depends only — on you![51]

Mathilde's replies are sadly no longer extant, though Kirchner's next letters make it clear that she committed herself to nothing. Nevertheless, despite the obvious nature of his feelings toward her — far more obvious than Wagner had dared to express in his "Morning Confession" — Mathilde by no means broke off contact with him. She seems rather to have played with his feelings. Thus she sometimes made him wait for her replies; on 7 October 1868 he wrote to her: "Now I have finally also experienced what it is like to wait for a letter from day to day, from hour to hour — but always in vain . . . what in heaven has happened?" Kirchner was well known for his philandering — this was one of the reasons why he had left Winterthur. Perhaps, then, Mathilde was here exercising a degree of "vengeance" on the part of her sex. On 11 May 1868, Kirchner for the first time uses the intimate "Du" in a letter. But just six weeks later, he surprised everyone by becoming engaged to a young singer by the name of Maria Schmidt, whom he then married on 15 October 1868. One day before the official engagement, he wrote the following to Mathilde:

> Tomorrow, dear friend, you will receive notice of my engagement to Miss M. Schmidt. I have no choice, in order at least on the one hand to free myself from an embarrassing situation. I hope to speak to you soon, calmer and more reasonably that I was able to recently. In the hope that all of life's turmoil will not let us lose sight of each other, but that we will even remain dear to each other still,
>
> I send you warm, but painful, greetings,
> Your Th. Kirchner[52]

What this "situation" was, remains unclear. Since the Kirchners' first child was not born until 1870, it does not seem that Maria was simply pregnant and that marriage had become a necessity. If Kirchner rushed into marriage in order to spite Mathilde, or to forget her, or even in the hope that she might at the last minute be convinced of the need to achieve a "complete union" with him, then he remained without success. And if Mathilde had intentionally left Kirchner for months on end in an emotional no-man's-land in the cynical hope that he would be spurred on to creative work (as was Wagner), and that she would then be immortalized in his music, she was wrong, too. Apart from a single song "Sei mir gegrüsst, mein Edelweis" ("I greet you, my edelweis"), Kirchner's love for Mathilde did not find concrete musical expression. Whatever his reasons, Kirchner's reaction to his new situation seems to have been not a little cynical. He wrote to Julius Stockhausen after his engagement that his fiancée's only fault was that she was "stupid enough to love me."[53] His wife Maria sang only twice more at the City Theater, her Margarethe in Gounod's *Faust* in November 1868 receiving high praise from the composer-turned-critic Heinrich Schulz-Beuthen. He praised both her voice and her apparently considerable dramatic talent, writing that she was in particular "made for the tragic and the demonic."[54] It is not impossible that Schulz-Beuthen, as someone who knew Kirchner's character well, wrote with ironic intent. Kirchner's marriage soon proved to be the disaster that most of his friends had feared (though Clara Schumann's oblique references to the Kirchners' domestic situation in her letters to Brahms suggest that she, at least, was not utterly free of *Schadenfreude*). Mathilde's reaction to Kirchner's changed situation is not known.

On one occasion, however, Mathilde misjudged completely the impact that she had on the opposite sex. This was when she allowed Francesco De

Sanctis into her inner circle in the mid-1850s. De Sanctis is usually mentioned in the Wagner literature — if at all[55] — as Mathilde's "good-looking" Italian teacher,[56] as if he were some kind of Mediterranean flirt. In fact, he was one of the leading Italian intellectuals of the day. He was born in 1817, had studied law, then had taught philology, philosophy, and various other subjects at a private school in Naples. It was there that he became actively involved in the revolt against the Bourbons in 1848. Because of his support for Mazzini, he was imprisoned in 1850. After more than two years in the Castel dell'Ovo in Naples, he was sentenced in July 1853 to permanent exile. A passport was procured for him to emigrate to the United States and he was placed, under guard, on a steamer named the "Hellespont." But when the boat stopped at Malta, he succeeded in escaping, and returned to Italy, this time to Piedmont. He taught in Turin until being appointed in 1856 to a professorship at the newly created Eidgenössische Technische Hochschule in Zurich. In 1860 he returned to Italy, where he became, in succession, governor of the province of Avellino, editor of the daily newspaper *L'Italia*, education minister in Cavour's government, and professor at the University of Naples. He published much, his principal oeuvre being his *Storia della letteratura italiana* (1870–71), a history of Italian literature.

De Sanctis arrived in Zurich to be hailed by the *Neue Zürcher Zeitung* as the "reformer of Italian literature," and it seems that he rapidly made a great impression on the intellectual circles in the city. Among those who attended his lectures were his famous colleagues Friedrich Theodor Vischer and Jacob Moleschott.[57] The memoirs of the latter offer us one of the most colorful accounts of De Sanctis's rhetorical gifts. Moleschott writes that, although his knowledge of Italian was limited, he wished "for once in my life to have heard a series of public lectures in the Italian language."[58] He accordingly decided to attend De Sanctis's lectures on Ariosto at the ETH:

> How I was rewarded! If Tieck were to speak about Goethe, if Goethe or Schlegel were to speak of Shakespeare, the figure of the poet in question could not blossom more into life than under the malleable hand of De Sanctis. I understood every word, I saw every picture, I felt the whole magic of that bubbling jubilation in battle and love that the poet echoes out, with him always in full control of his material. This was a cornucopia that Cervantes and Wieland had listened to.
>
> De Sanctis did not treat his heroes as someone who stands before them admiringly. He was intertwined with them, united with them, so that the poet seemed to speak out of him. This was no longer a creative critic, for you forgot the man in front of you, believing that you could hear the breath of Ariosto himself.[59]

Moleschott continues to wax lyrical about De Santis's gifts for another two pages.

De Sanctis had realized in the first half of 1857 that he would never be united with the woman he loved — his former pupil, the teenager Teresa De Amicis.[60] He did find temporary solace elsewhere in the coming months (see below), but was still essentially "on the rebound" when Mathilde decided in late 1857 to engage him as her private Italian teacher (whether or not she was in any way aware of the state of his love life, we do not know, though it is not impossible that such gossip existed among the intellectual circles of what was, after all, a very small city). Precisely why Mathilde wished to employ De Sanctis in this capacity is not clear, for there would have been more than enough potential teachers of the language in Zurich at the time. Given his general popularity, not least among his female students (one of his prominent colleagues, Antoine-Elisée Cherbuliez, even tried to marry off one of his daughters to De Sanctis[61]), we can suppose that Mathilde was curious about him. Perhaps engaging the city's leading Italian intellectual for basic Italian conversation and writing practice was also intended as a display of economic and social power. De Sanctis, of course, did not need such a post — he was by all accounts financially comfortable on his professorship. So we can only assume that what drew him in turn to the Wesendonck villa was the person of Mathilde herself.

Mathilde first wrote to De Sanctis on 13 December 1857, stating a long-held wish to learn Italian, and hoping that he might be prepared to give lessons outside his duties at the ETH. (This was also, of course, at precisely the time when Otto was away on business). Mathilde added that she "does not know if you would accept a pupil for whom this language is still like a white sheet of paper [une page blanche]."[62] This is strangely reminiscent of her later recollection of how Wagner had originally described *her*; it seems almost as if this expression were in fact her own, and no more than a flirtatious means of establishing her supposed innocence and ignorance in order to gain the attention of (male) intellectuals to whom she was drawn. The lessons duly began, but De Sanctis wrote to her (in French) on 2 February 1858 — just a few weeks later — to put an end to them. He did so curtly, in no more than fifty words, maintaining that his "occupations" prevented him. It would seem that he realized that his purpose for her was more social than educational, and it is clear that Mathilde's company was not adequate recompense for him. Mathilde replied on 4 February, contrite that their last lesson had ended on something of a sour note, and imploring him to have more patience with her, and continue the lessons. "It's impossible for me to leave it like this!," she wrote (*E*, 437). (She had never had to beg like this with Wagner.) He acquiesced, and the lessons continued. Mathilde obviously liked De Sanctis. We must also surely assume — given the apparent virtuosity with which she usually carried out her relations with the opposite sex — that she will have known the degree of jealousy that her behavior would provoke on the part of Wagner.

We have a witness to Wagner's jealous passion in the shape of Robert von Hornstein, the young German composer (mentioned in chapter 5 above) who was in these years an occasional visitor to the Wagner household. In his memoirs, he later remarked how "the presence of Mrs. Wesendonck always made Wagner excitable. It seemed he could not bear it if she did not give him her attention."[63] He then gives a specific example from 1856 — thus well before matters had reached boiling point. Wagner, he wrote, insisted on leading the conversation whenever dining with the Wesendoncks and others. But on one occasion, the conversation at table became something of a noisy free-for-all, at which Wagner let forth a high-pitched scream, and in the ensuing astonished silence announced that he would read aloud E. T. A. Hoffmann's "Der goldene Topf," which he did from start to finish, until the hour was exceedingly late. Otto thereafter made a mildly critical remark of some sort, at which Wagner flew into a rage; it was then Otto once more who had to calm things down (*M*, 139).

Perhaps, then, Mathilde now took some strange pleasure in making Wagner share her attention; perhaps she needed it in order to reassure herself of her own position of power in their relationship; or perhaps she intended to "punish" Wagner for becoming too familiar in Otto's absence at the turn of the year, which had made relations somewhat frosty between the two families (and, presumably, between Mathilde and Otto too). However, it would seem that Mathilde had underestimated the effect that her new-found friend would have on Wagner.

Mathilde's first letter to De Sanctis after the resumption of lessons was written on 13 February 1858, asking him to lunch the next day (Sunday). She added: "Only Wagner will be there and it would please me in particular to get you better acquainted with him" (*E*, 440). Given Wagner's previous behavior, it was surely a recipe for disaster to put him together with another strong-willed man, and one who was to boot her current object of fascination. The lunch took place, and while we must assume that Wagner did not take to De Sanctis, we know for certain that the latter was not impressed with him. One topic of conversation, however, proved later to be of considerable significance: Arthur Schopenhauer. Wagner was proud of having introduced Mathilde Wesendonck to his writings. Mathilde retained a deep admiration for Schopenhauer throughout her life, and it seems to have been she who drew the attention of De Sanctis to the philosopher. On 20 February 1858, De Sanctis wrote to Virginia Basco of the "filosofo curioso" to whom "una signora di qua" had just introduced him, and whose watchword was renunciation (*E*, 445). But just a few days later, on 26 February, De Sanctis wrote to his friend Angelo Camillo De Meis in Turin that he was busy reading

> the great Schopenhauer, who proclaims his greatness to the four corners of the world, and the great Wagner, the genius of the future, as he modestly

> calls himself, while disparaging the men of the present, who do not understand him. With these charlatans before me, how must I appreciate you, Camillo! (*E*, 447)

This, we can be sure, was De Sanctis's impression of Wagner after their lunch together. As for the philosopher, it was perhaps merely his own enforced "renunciation" of Teresa De Amicis that had temporarily turned De Sanctis against him, for he in fact soon became engaged in a much closer investigation of Schopenhauer's thought. In March 1858 he wrote a dialogue on Leopardi and Schopenhauer in which he drew attention to the similarities between them, and even — in contradiction of his earlier statement — placed in the mouth of one of his protagonists the sentence: "Schopenhauer non è ciarlatano."[64] Given that he owed his knowledge of Schopenhauer to Mathilde, it is probable that De Sanctis told her of this dialogue at the time (he announced its completion to De Meis in a letter of 1 April). If he did, then she will surely not have waited to tell Wagner in turn. How he might have reacted to his muse having "his" philosopher explained to her by his perceived rival must remain a matter of supposition, but it is noteworthy that it was just a few days after De Sanctis finished his Dialogue that Wagner's jealousy reached the point where he felt compelled to write his "Morning Confession."

When De Sanctis's article was published in the *Rivista Contemporanea* later that year, it drew praise from no less a figure than Schopenhauer himself. Wagner had attempted just four years earlier to elicit such admiration from the old man by sending him a copy of the first, limited, edition of his libretto to the *Ring des Nibelungen*, and had at least three people convey his greetings: François Wille, Robert von Hornstein, und an unnamed third, but all to no avail. To von Hornstein, Schopenhauer said of Wagner: "The fellow is a poet but no musician" and also told him that he preferred by far the music of Rossini, which he himself played every day between midday and 1pm in arrangements that he possessed for solo flute (*M*, 108–10). When Hornstein returned to Wagner in Zurich, he did not mention Schopenhauer's negative comments, but noted in his memoirs that Wagner had obviously already heard from another party of the philosopher's disdain for his work (*M*, 147–48). Wagner's failure to impress Schopenhauer still rankled more than two decades later, and it had obviously become in his mind a symbol of his defeat in competition with De Sanctis. The latter is mentioned only once in Cosima's diaries, on 30 March 1878, in connection with Schopenhauer:

> Walking home through the Hofgarten, [Richard said]: "It is not a good sign for Schopenhauer that he paid no attention to my *Ring des Nibelungen*" . . . [later that evening:] We laugh at Schopenhauer's mistaken belief that De Sanctis was his follower. "One just mustn't labor under such illusions," says R., "then one can be truly happy." I tell R. that

> I think he is the only one to have really absorbed Schopenhauer's philosophy. (*TB* 2:73)

Wagner tended to read his philosophers superficially, in order to distil just what he needed for his musico-dramatic purposes. According to *Mein Leben*, he had begun to read Hegel toward the end of his time in Dresden, and it is commonly accepted that his writings of 1849–51 are heavily influenced by left-Hegelian dialectics. But De Sanctis knew Hegel's work too: he had apparently even translated a large part of his *Wissenschaft der Logik* (Science of Logic) into Italian during his years in prison, though the manuscript was subsequently lost.[65] Another interest that Wagner shared with Mathilde was Dante. While in London for his conducting engagements in April 1855, Wagner wrote to her that he was reading Dante every morning, and that it was beneficial to his work on the second act of the *Walküre* (*SB* 7:123–24 and *ML*, 539). But Dante was yet another field in which De Sanctis was far more of an expert than he, and one in which he lectured while in Zurich.

There were other similarities between the two men that might have caused discomfort to Wagner. He had established himself in Zurich not just as an artist but as a "man of action," someone who in Dresden had manned the barricades in the name of democracy and freedom. But, as discussed elsewhere in this volume, his wife claimed that he had in fact kept well away from any danger during the uprising.[66] Dashing De Sanctis, on the other hand, was known to have fought and suffered in the name of liberty.

Wagner thus saw himself now confronted with an intellectual on his own level who did not need to elaborate his revolutionary credentials, who seemingly understood Schopenhauer's world of ideas quicker then he, and who was presumably able to explain these ideas far better in conversation with Mathilde (after all, De Sanctis had studied law and will have been no stranger to the thrust and parry of intellectual debate). Although De Sanctis understood German, he and Mathilde corresponded mostly in French (two letters from him in Italian have also survived), and it seems that French was their principal language of communication. Wagner had lived in France, and he spoke and wrote the language adequately. We can thus safely assume that he also spoke it at that first lunch meeting with De Sanctis and Mathilde. De Sanctis had been reading French newspapers since 1841, but he had never been to France, and did not acquire any active knowledge of the language until his stint in Turin in the mid-1850s. Upon being offered his professorship in Zurich, he offered to lecture in French, as his German was, he said, not yet adequate.[67] When his appointment was confirmed in early 1856, he accordingly took French lessons with one Giuseppe Poerio in Turin. As it happens, it seems that De Sanctis was in fact allowed from the start to teach in his native Italian. Nevertheless, when he arrived in Zurich in March 1856, he was apparently both fluent and accurate in speaking and writing French.[68] He will have had enough opportunities to practice, for he took up lodgings with a Frenchman, Marc Dufraisse — another lecturer at the ETH, and like him a political exile (Dufraisse had fled France after Napoleon III's coup d'état of 1851).[69] To judge from Wagner's letters written in French, his linguistic gifts were not a match for those of De Sanctis. It is thus also possible that he felt sidelined in the conversation during their lunch with Mathilde, which naturally would only have exacerbated his frustration with his new "rival." The "Morning Confession" in fact makes specific reference to French as being a common language of conversation, with what could perhaps also be an ironic undertone: "Next Monday I shall come to tea after your lesson and will be properly pleasant to De Sanctis for the whole evening, and will speak French, so that everyone should be happy."

There are also a number of banal coincidences between De Sanctis and Wagner. They both loved pet birds; Wagner usually had a parrot and took pains to train it; De Sanctis on the other hand kept up to fifty canaries at a time in his flat, training them to know his voice, to peck breadcrumbs from his lips, and so on. While Wagner favored pet-like names for his birds such as "Papo," De Sanctis gave his artistic ones such as "Boccaccio" or "Manzoni."[70] One final matter that brings together Wagner and De Sanctis is peripheral, yet a fascinating case of coincidence. In mid-1857 De Sanctis embarked on an affair with a local German Swiss girl named "Mina," from whom letters to him survive from May 1858. In Zurich dialect, as in Italian, the names "Mina" and "Minna" (that is, of De Sanctis's lover and of Wagner's wife) would be pronounced in a not dissimilar manner (the first vowel being prolonged in the latter name despite the double consonant). It is naturally temping to speculate how Wagner, consumed with jealousy at De Sanctis's proximity to Mathilde, might have reacted if he learnt that his rival was also having an affair with "Min[n]a."

In his "Morning Confession" of April 1858, Wagner writes that he is angry with De Sanctis because the latter had been visiting Mathilde two days earlier when he, Wagner, had wanted to see her; and then, when Wagner indeed got to see her the day after, he became embroiled in an argument with her (that he now regrets) about the character of Goethe's Faust. But if one allows for the possibility that Wagner was jealous of De Sanctis, not just because he was younger and better looking, but also because he was his intellectual equal, then one can interpret this letter in a manner different from what has hitherto been customary:

> But no! No! It's not De Sanctis I hate, but *me*, that I surprised my poor heart again and again in such a weak state! . . . I could not hold it against him that he takes things so seriously with you — everyone does who has anything to do with you! And how seriously I take it! So seriously that it becomes painful for you! But why does she pay attention to this pedantic set of shackles? What importance does Italian have to her? Well, I easily

> answered that. But the better I did, the more morose I became about that bothersome chap . . . whenever I really desired to be with you, our boring pedant always came between us, he who robbed me of you, and I could not do anything except admit that I hated him. But oh, poor me! I had to tell you. Nothing else was possible. But it was really petty all the same, and I deserved to be punished for it. What kind of punishment shall I get? . . .
>
> What kind of silly argument was it again yesterday about Goethe? A construal of Goethe so that he is suited for the Philistine's view of the world is in the end only possible if it is based on a misunderstanding of the poet. But that it is *possible* keeps me in a state of watchful anxiety with regard both to him and also to those who would interpret him or dress him up as they will. Well, you know, I did not complain about anything yesterday, in particular your great pleasure in *Faust*. But finally to have to hear again and again that Faust is the most important type of human being that has yet been created by a poet — that made me (very stupid though it was!) — angry. I can't let my people be in error . . .

There follows a long discussion about the meaning of *Faust*. This play was something that united Wagner and Mathilde, at least in his eyes, for he had wanted to dedicate to her the second version of his *Faust Overture* that he had composed in early 1855. But De Sanctis too had occupied himself with Goethe's *Faust* — he had translated the first three scenes of the second part during his imprisonment.[71] We may safely assume that the "[Philistines] who would interpret [Goethe] or dress him up as they will," and against whom Wagner must remain "in a state of watchful anxiety" are in fact to be found, for him, in the person of the "boring pedant," Francesco De Sanctis, who it seems had convinced Mathilde of the rightness of *his* interpretation of the play. At the very end of his *Opera and Drama*, Wagner had railed against "the Philistine" as "the most heartless, the most cowardly product of our civilization . . . the most willful, the cruellest, the dirtiest bread-giver of the artist," and since Mathilde was familiar with his writings, it is possible that he intended her to understand his description of De Sanctis in these terms.[72] The "Morning Confession" reads less like a love letter than an attempt after the event to justify oneself with regard to an argument that one has lost badly. In fact, Wagner seems almost to talk *past* Mathilde in this letter, as if he is really arguing with a third party who is not named. He is here reduced to the level of an adolescent boy in a schoolyard squabble: since he cannot counter his opponent's reasoning, he calls him names. When Wagner describes De Sanctis as a "boring pedant," he essentially confirms that the latter had proven the cleverer in their dispute (Wagner even uses the word "pedant" or "pedantic" twice). Wagner sinks so low as to hope for "punishment" from Mathilde, as if even a (metaphorical?) spanking would be desirable if it means he gets her attention. Further on in the letter, Wagner seems to project onto De Sanctis what he regards as the negative aspects of Faust:

> Faust is no more than a fantastical academic who really has not yet experienced the world. This is because he is a cripple who is not properly developed, and he really deserves to be sent to learn the ways of the world . . . but how can one claim that [Goethe's] lamentable Faust is one of the most noble human character types? Get ready to be tortured for eternity by that mendacious spirit once that beautiful redeeming woman, that wonderful Gretchen, painfully uplifted, has turned her back on you . . .

Wagner's intention was obviously to attack a quite specific "fantastical academic," whom he regarded as an "undeveloped cripple" who had "not yet experienced the world"; and one can just as well interpret this letter as complaining that a "beautiful redeeming woman" had now "turned her back" on Wagner because she now only listens to a "mendacious spirit." Wagner's vocabulary is highly subjective; it is that of a man who has been personally wounded. A strange statement at the close of his letter serves to confirm that he cannot find the words necessary to wrest back control of the dispute:

> But what silly things am I driveling on about? Is it the pleasure of speaking alone, or the pleasure of speaking to you? — Yes, to you! But if I look into your eyes, then I can't speak any more. Then, everything I could say becomes trivial!

In other words: it is Mathilde herself and her feminine wiles that are to blame for Wagner's losing the argument against De Sanctis. And it is surely for this reason that he decided to defend himself in the only manner in which he could present his arguments in a well thought-out way, without any danger of anyone else contradicting him: in a letter. Why else would Wagner send such a long text to someone who lived next door, whom he was accustomed to seeing almost every day, and to whom he in the very recent past had explained Schopenhauer's philosophy verbally, not in writing? As mentioned earlier, the "Morning Confession" was intercepted by Minna and interpreted by her as being proof of her husband's infidelity. Because of her actions, this letter destroyed for ever the precarious equilibrium that existed between the Wagners and the Wesendoncks, and this in turn led inexorably to Wagner's leaving his beloved *Asyl*.

In a letter of 3 October 1859 to Minna's doctor, Anton Pusinelli, Wagner admitted that he had at some point stopped having sexual relations with her, and that her jealousy had increased "more than ever" from this moment onwards (*SB* 11:273). An educated guess would probably put this at some point in 1857, after the move into the *Asyl*, for this was when the Wagners took separate bedrooms for the first time. Wagner's "chastity" was ostensibly on account of Minna's ill health, though it was more likely in order to convince both himself and Mathilde that she alone was the true object of his affections. Minna's ill health itself has also been used as a possible reason for her erratic behavior in early 1858, as has her apparently immoderate use of laudanum. There is no doubt that she used this opiate, for Wagner mentions it as early as 1854 in a letter to the Parisian doctor Karl Lindemann, when he says that it gave her relief from her gout (*SB* 6:106). In a letter to Anton Pusinelli of 1 November 1858 — after the "catastrophe" — he even wrote of Minna's having used "several times twenty" drops of laudanum per day (*SB* 10:126). If Minna was indeed living in a cloud of opium in the first half of 1858, it would help to explain her somewhat self-destructive behavior. Wagner's concern about her laudanum use does seem a little hypocritical when one considers that he himself used it for medicinal purposes on several occasions, from the early 1850s to the early 1880s, as is confirmed by his letters, *Mein Leben*, and Cosima's diaries (*ML*, 518 and *TB* 2:593) — though it hardly seems likely, as Joachim Köhler would have us believe,[73] that Wagner was a laudanum junkie who composed in some kind of psychedelic haze. We must therefore also entertain the possibility that Wagner emphasized Minna's (supposed) dependence upon laudanum in order to undermine her sanity in the eyes of others (specifically Otto Wesendonck) when he realized that she might well be prepared to sacrifice their house and home on the altar of her jealousy. Furthermore, since we know that Minna used laudanum to help her sleep, it is not impossible that Wagner might even have encouraged her in its use, in order to keep things quiet at home and give him the space necessary to pursue his passion for Mathilde (in which case his repeated criticism of her laudanum use might then have been primarily to assuage his own conscience). And perhaps Minna suddenly feared, too, that she was being plied with drugs for that very reason, not unlike Gretchen's mother in *Faust*, who is administered a sleeping draught in order for Gretchen and Faust to continue with their assignations (and was this, then, in part why the "Morning Confession" with its mention of *Faust* prompted her into such an extreme reaction?).

However, just as we must beware of jumping to all the far-fetched but possible conclusions about these last months in the *Asyl*, so too must we beware of following too closely Wagner's own interpretation of the events of that year, seeing them as the result of a drama of jealousies in which only he remained innocent. It is noteworthy that Wagner himself detects feelings of jealousy only in all the other three participants in the drama: in Mathilde ("at that ghastly time, when Mathilde Wesendonck was jealous of my wife," he said to Cosima fifteen years later [*TB* 1:653]), in Minna (who, he wrote to his sister Kläre Wolfram on 20 August 1858, was "often jealous, mocking, and disparaging" [*SB* 10:28]), and in Otto (who, as he wrote to Kläre, was "devoured by jealousy" [*SB* 10:28]). It should not surprise us that Wagner himself claimed in these same sources that he had remained calm and devoid of base feelings, for in reality, he himself was the one person who was so obviously devoured by jealousy. While this is not to deny that the other players in our drama were subject to some degree to that same emotion, it does seem clear that Wagner, in order to protect himself, did project his own feelings onto everyone else. It is thus all the more regrettable that — with the exception of Minna's letters already quoted, in which she is hardly a model of objectivity — we know the events of the years 1857 and 1858 almost only through Wagner's eyes alone.

The matter of De Sanctis has a small postlude. In his letters to Mathilde of April 1859, Wagner refers several times in glowing terms to Goethe's *Tasso*, even comparing it to his own work. He also asks Mathilde to send him a German translation of Tasso's own *Jerusalem Liberated*, and refers obliquely to "Herrn 'von Heiligen,'" namely "De Sanctis" (*SB* 11:37–57). As it happens, De Sanctis was that very semester lecturing on Tasso at the ETH;[74] furthermore, he had himself written a play entitled *Torquato Tasso*, which was inspired by Goethe, but which he had not managed to have performed.[75] It is certainly possible that Wagner's praise of Goethe's *Tasso* was an oblique means of criticizing the play by his own rival, though we cannot know for sure, not least because Mathilde's letters, to which those of Wagner refer, are all lost.

After his return to Italy, De Sanctis seems to have followed Wagner's career from a distance, for an undated letter from him to Mathilde from early 1861 mentions that she might be "a little angry at Paris." This she took (no doubt rightly) to be a reference to the failure there of *Tannhäuser* in March 1861.[76] By this time, Wagner's sense of self-interest was enough to overcome his earlier dislike of the Italian, for in a letter to the publishers Ricordi of 14 November 1861 in which he urged the performance of his works in Italy, he dropped shamelessly the name of his "friend De Sanctis, currently Minister of Public Education."[77] The two men did meet one more time, when Wagner was at the height of his fame. In the winter of late 1876, after the exertions of the first Bayreuth Festival, Wagner and his family went on a trip to Italy, spending much of the time in Rome. The *Neue freie Presse* of Vienna wrote on 2 December:

> On 1 December [*recte*: 30 November, according to Cosima's diary], Wagner appeared at an evening reception of the international artists' society. The society's venue had been festively decorated to receive him and adorned with the bust of the "musician of the future." When he appeared, De Sanctis greeted him with a speech in French, to which Wagner also replied in French. He entered the hall accompanied by his wife Cosima and by Professor Sgambati, and they were followed by the German ambassador Baron Keudell.[78]

In Cosima's diary for their Italian trip, however, there is no mention of De Sanctis at all (*TB* 1:1016–17).

The only possible source of more detailed information on Mathilde is to be found in indirect form in her own writings. It is not clear precisely when she began to write, though it is clear that it was primarily Wagner who encouraged her to do so, probably in around 1856; it seems that Ludwig Ettmüller also offered encouragement in her literary endeavors. In his letter to Otto and Mathilde of 22 December 1856, Wagner wrote: "Since you are always sending me such beautiful verses, I have to answer with music" (*SB* 8:231), which could mean either that the Wesendoncks were giving him poetry books as gifts, or — more likely — that Mathilde had already begun to send him her own poems. In any case, they each now figured as the other's inspiring "muse." Mathilde seems to have wanted Wagner to be the first to see her verses, and he remained for a long time her most important reader, even after his departure from Zurich (though she was then forced to send her poems by mail). Mathilde's decision to publish her works (albeit at first under the initials "M.W.") was made only after her relationship to Wagner had taken a decisive negative turn in late 1861. Wagner and Mathilde had seen each other twice, briefly, since his departure from Zurich in August 1858: on 3 April 1859 and on 22 May 1861 (the latter date being his birthday). In autumn 1861 a reunion was planned in Vienna on the coming 20 October, as they were both due to be in the city at that time. But the meeting did not happen. Wagner expressed his intense disappointment in a letter that has not survived today, but to which Mathilde replied on 23 October 1861:

> Your recent lines made me very sad. I was for a long time unable to answer them. The prospect of our meeting in Vienna was so close and had become so certain to me. I had for a long time not believed it possible, and now believed, only to be disappointed again. What was placed in the hands of the future has been taken away from us for this moment, perhaps for ever. The moment belongs to us, but what the dark mother bears in her womb for us, who knows? Our meeting made me think first of the difficulties that would face the birth of a Tristan, and if we had known that you would only remain a short time in Vienna, then we would surely have come earlier. It was not to be! But I cannot sleep now.

Shortly after this strange letter — on or about 6 November 1861 — they did indeed meet, but in Venice (in the presence of Otto, of course). Wagner found the two of them "in very happy circumstances" (*ML*, 683) as he later wrote in his autobiography. This meeting was for Wagner, and perhaps also for Mathilde, a sobering experience. It seems that he had entertained fresh hopes — however absurd it might appear to us — that Otto and Mathilde might save him from his most recent financial disasters by letting him return to the *Asyl*. Indeed, a long letter he had written to Minna on 19 October (just a day before that planned meeting with Mathilde) seems to wish to prepare her for that possibility, for he castigates her once more for having "lost" him the *Asyl* in the first place and dangles the prospect of a permanent solution to his wanderings, but a solution in which she implicitly will not have a part (*SB* 13:251–58). It was not to be, of course, and in late December 1861, Wagner wrote again to Mathilde, as follows:

> One thing I had never given up, and thought I had won it after a long fight: to find my "Refuge" once more, to live again near you. One hour with you again in Venice was sufficient to destroy this last, dear vision for me!
>
> I had to realize swiftly that the freedom that you need, that you need to survive, is something that you cannot maintain as long as I am near you. Only my being distant from you can give you the power to move freely according to your will. Only when you have nothing to buy must you pay no price.
>
> I cannot bear to see you stifled and in distress, so self-controlled and dependent, as the price of my being near you: I cannot make recompense for this sacrifice, because my nearness cannot offer you anything any more, and the thought that the miserably small reward I can be for you under such circumstances — at the cost of all the freedom that is necessary for true human dignity — this makes me feel this nearness myself as a torment . . . You have long known this, before me, for I remained an incorrigible optimist for a long time, in secret.

However, if one switches the "I" and the "you" in this letter, one probably comes much closer to Wagner's true feelings:

> I had to realize swiftly that the freedom that [I] need, that [I] need to survive, is something that [I] cannot maintain as long as [you are] near [me]. Only [your] being distant from [me] can give [me] the power to move freely according to [my] will. Only when [I] have nothing to buy must [I] pay no price.
>
> I cannot bear to see [myself] stifled and in distress, so self-controlled and dependent, as the price of [your] being near [me]: [you] cannot make recompense for this sacrifice, because [your] nearness cannot offer [me] anything any more, and the thought that the miserably small reward [you] can be for [me] under such circumstances — at the cost of all the freedom that is necessary for true human dignity — this makes me feel this nearness myself as a torment.

At the time of this meeting, Mathilde must have been some eight weeks pregnant (her son Hans was born on 16 June 1862). Whether this was the reason for the "very happy circumstances" of her and Otto, we cannot be sure, but it seems likely. We can certainly assume that the Wesendoncks will have hoped that a new baby might banish the memory of the loss of their son Guido, who had died in October 1858 aged only three, just a few weeks after Wagner's departure from the *Asyl*. If Otto already knew of this new pregnancy, then this might also be a reason why he would allow another meeting between his wife and Wagner. Her pregnancy would have been a clear signal of her dependence on her husband (both sexual and financial). And if Wagner knew of the pregnancy, or even merely suspected it, then this will have contributed greatly to his disappointment. While he might still have fantasized that Mathilde would yet give up everything for him, even he will have realized that she would never contemplate such a risky undertaking while expecting a child. The pregnancy naturally also meant that Wagner's beloved still shared her bed with his rival, her husband — or, perhaps more precisely, that she was once again sharing her bed with him. The "renunciation" that she had ostensibly practiced during Wagner's final months in Zurich, and which he, perhaps, had fantastically imagined that she had maintained in his absence, was obviously at an end, and visibly so to all and sundry. It is not impossible that Mathilde had even encouraged Wagner in such an assumption, for it would have allowed her to maintain some semblance of power over him. The loss of so many of her letters, of course, prevents us from claiming this with any certainty. Mathilde's children in general seem to have been a sore point for Wagner. Already at Guido's christening in 1855 — when he had turned down Otto Wesendonck's offer to become godfather — Wagner had commented in an aside to Robert von Hornstein that the event was like "attending one's own execution."[79] When one reads Mathilde's letter to Wagner of 23 October 1861 in this light, its allusions to pregnancy and birth seem intended to prepare him for these new circumstances: "what the dark mother bears in her womb for us . . . the birth of a Tristan. . . ." For Mathilde will also have known clearly that having another child with Otto would destroy all hope that Wagner might have harbored that they might yet share a common future. This in turn would mean the certainty of losing her last vestiges of control over him. She seems to acknowledge precisely this in a letter to him of 16 January 1862:

> Our relations to one another came to mind, and I saw the whole, rich world before me that you had opened up to this childlike spirit. My eyes lingered with delight on the wonderful works, my heart beat faster and faster out of deep-seated gratitude, and I felt that nothing of it could ever be lost! As long as I breathe, I shall strive onwards, that is thanks to you . . . our fate is to gaze into loneliness!

After this, Mathilde continued to send Wagner her poems from time to time (a letter of his from 9 June 1862 says "The poem that you sent me today is very beautiful, really masterful I think"). But she now obviously needed a broader public, and so she decided to publish a selection of her works. This was a courageous step. Although she already had in Eliza Wille a close female friend who was a published novelist, Mathilde will have known very well the prejudice against women writers that was prevalent at that time. But the catalyst for her decision might well have been Wagner himself. He had published his settings of Mathilde's poems in mid-1862, but without naming the poet. Whether or not Mathilde was angered by the silence regarding her part in the work we cannot know, but she must have thought that if Wagner found her poems good enough to publish with his music, then she need not shy away from publishing them herself. And she cannot but have been pleased when the critics assumed that Wagner was himself the author of his song texts, noticing no difference between the quality of her poetic diction and his own. We should thus regard Mathilde's first slim volume of poems as at one and the same time a monument to her relationship with Wagner and a declaration of independence from him.

This first book of Mathilde's, entitled *Gedichte, Volkslieder, Legenden, Sagen* (Poems, Folksongs, Legends, Myths) was published by Kiesling in Zurich in late 1862. It presumably included several texts that Mathilde had shown to Wagner in the years before, though we only know this for certain in very few cases. We know from his letter to her of 23 May 1859 that Mathilde had sent him her "Soldier's Song" (as a birthday gift, no doubt). It is tempting, but probably wishful thinking, to assume significance in the fact that this poem is in the book printed opposite one called "Erinnerung" — "Memory" — in which she writes, "Viel [*sic*] Jahre sind nun schon vorbei, Seit ich dich scheiden sah, Und seltsam, mir ist stets, als sei Dein Wesen doch mir nah" ("Many years have elapsed since I saw you leave, and it is strange, but it seems constantly to me that you are still near to me"). We again have no proof, but we can probably assume, that she sent a copy of her book to Wagner straightaway when it appeared. It was five years since Wagner had arranged for their song "Träume" (Dreams) to be played on her birthday, 23 December 1857; is it also by chance that the aforementioned poem "Memory" tells at its close of a dream about the poet's beloved ("The dear hand still lies upon the breast like balsam, when sleep carries it, unknowing, in the land of dreams"), and is it also by chance that Wagner wrote to Mathilde on 21 December 1862: "I had a beautiful, lovely dream of you last night, just after falling asleep," or that Mathilde wrote to him two days later: "I knew it well: Dreams are faithful. The more reality withdraws from us, the more our dream becomes like waking")? But this can all serve, too, as an example of the kind of speculation into which we can be drawn when firm facts are largely absent.

Simply the fact that commentators have paid little attention to Mathilde's writings does not mean that they should now be celebrated as the fruits of an unjustly neglected talent. Let us be clear: if it had not been for Wagner, no one would pay much attention to her poetry, prose, and dramas. These also help to confirm the current picture of her as an appendage to Wagner, and it is easy to read them as a kind of autobiography *manqué*. One cannot deny that her writings, from the very first published poems to her late dramas, tell repeatedly of love lost or renounced. Whether this is merely a literary motive, or in fact a reflection of her own experiences, we cannot say. Nor can one ignore the presence of Wagnerian resonances in her work. His influence is most strongly felt where she uses the alliterative Stabreim, or in the vocabulary she uses to wax lyrical about "noble heroes" ("hehre

Helden") and the like. Even the literary themes she chooses are reminiscent of Wagner's music dramas. In her writings, one finds water nymphs, Valkyries, Norns, and the whole panoply of Germanic gods, just as in Wagner's works. While they obviously had common sources in the original legends and sagas — Mathilde also enjoyed occasional instruction from Ludwig "Eddamüller" in Middle-High German — her main source seems to have been Wagner. In her own drama *Siegfried* it seems almost as if she had taken the ingredients of Wagner's *Ring*, thrown them in a hat, shaken it, and then taken them out and arrayed them in the manner of a Dadaist poem. For the dwarfs at the beginning are reminiscent of those in the *Rheingold*, though their vocabulary is closer to that of Mime from *Siegfried*. In Mathilde's sword-forging scene, Siegfried invokes Loge in a manner similar to that of Wotan at the close of Wagner's *Walküre*, though her hero splits his anvil with his sword just as does Wagner's Siegfried. Her Stabreim naturally reminds one of Wagner's own *Ring* libretto, though sometimes it is as if she has kept just the rhythm of his text, not the actual words. She has Wieland the Smith appear in *Siegfried*, singing "Balmung! Balmung nenne dies Schwert!" ("let this sword be called Balmung"), while Wagner's Siegfried instead sings "Notung! Notung, neidliches Schwert!" ("Notung, desirable sword"; "Balmung" was the name of the sword in the original myth and in Wagner's first prose draft). When Siegfried kills the dragon Fafner (called "Fafnir" by Mathilde), he puts his blood-stained fingers in his mouth and sings "Wie Feuer brennt das Blut" ("the blood burns like fire"), while Mathilde's Siegfried says: "Wie Feuer brennt des Drachen Blut" ("The dragon's blood burns like fire"). In the third scene of her second act, Mathilde's Wodan gives more or less a synopsis of Wagner's *Walküre*. And his last words after being defeated by Siegfried are: "Zieh' hin! Ein Held bist Du — Dich halt' ich nicht!" while Wagner's Wotan sings: "Zieh hin! Ich kann dich nicht halten!" The last scene of Mathilde's drama is particularly interesting. She has Siegfried discover, not Brünnhilde on a fire-encircled rock, but Sleeping Beauty "under blossoming rose bushes in the midst of babbling fountains." Instead of resisting the imminent loss of her maidenhood as does Wagner's Brünnhilde, Sleeping Beauty gives herself to Siegfried without demur. Here, the woman places herself gladly and without hesitation at the will of her man — just as do almost all of Mathilde's heroines. It is noteworthy that Mathilde dated her *Siegfried* when she published it (something she very rarely did): 25 November 1863. Since Wagner had visited her and Otto in Zurich on 23 and 24 November 1863, it would be natural to presume that her naming the twenty-fifth was in order to make a statement of some kind; but if so, the nature of that statement remains a mystery.

We should perhaps list just a few more similarities between Mathilde's works and Wagner's own. In her short prose story *Walküren* (Valkyries), Wieland the Smith tries to keep his wife, the Valkyrie Schwanenweiss

("Swanwhite"), with him but she cannot resist the call of her sisters, and at the close she turns into a swan, to fly away for ever. In *Melusine*, the heroine named thus has to keep a secret from her husband — that she is in fact a mermaid. When he begins to doubt her and discovers her secret, she too has to leave for good. In both cases, there are obvious similarities to the libretto of Wagner's *Lohengrin*, in which Elsa doubts her husband, insists on knowing where he comes from, and thereby ensures that she loses him.

In *Gudrun* there is a scene on board a ship that seems closely modeled on the first act of Wagner's *Tristan und Isolde*; in *Genovefa*, the heroine and her husband Siegfried (!) part from each other in a manner not dissimilar to that of Brünnhilde and Siegfried in the prologue of Wagner's *Götterdämmerung*. And one inevitably must ask whether it is by chance that in Mathilde's plays *Genovefa*, *Gudrun*, *Odysseus*, and *Edith* a woman has to give up the man she loves; or whether it is perhaps an attempt over many years to overcome through creative means the (Wagner) crisis of 1858. We do know that Mathilde's career as a writer only really became a serious matter for her after Wagner's departure, so it seems that this loss provided the necessary impetus for her own creativity — indeed, there is a decided parallel between them, in that they each figured most powerfully as a "muse" to the other when they were in fact far apart. Mathilde certainly developed a healthy sense of her own worth. When she published her *Gudrun*, the poet Gottfried Keller remarked to his friend Ludmilla Assing in a letter of 12 June 1868 that "Madame Wesendonck now sets sail for the open sea of literature," adding "under her own name," as if to emphasize the courage involved. Keller found the air around Mathilde somewhat too rarified for his liking, but he took her seriously enough to offer forthright, detailed criticism of her *Edith* before it appeared, and advised against its publication. She in turn wrote back to defend herself, but received a reply tinged with sarcasm, mocking her "female logic," which Keller later admitted she had not taken kindly ("I'll stick with Mrs. Heim," he wrote to Theodor Vischer, referring to Wagner's sometime soprano soloist, for "I believe she doesn't write books").[80]

A closer knowledge of Mathilde's writings is undoubtedly desirable if one wishes to understand Wagner's life and work. For one can regard her writings, together with Wagner's letters to her, as a reflection of and testament to their discussions in the years when they lived in the same city. The similarities in their poetic diction and in their choice of topic should not be dismissed merely as the influence of the one (Wagner) upon the other (Mathilde), but also as proof of common interests. Mathilde's letters to him were almost all destroyed, her voice silenced, but in her writings and in his extant letters we can perhaps perceive at least an echo of the dialogue that she and Wagner had enjoyed, and in the course of which he must have discussed his dramatic and musical plans as well as his general cultural interests. As Egon Voss and others have remarked, it is only thanks to

Wagner's letters to Mathilde that we learn of the conception of *Parsifal*, of the *Meistersinger*, and of the Paris version of *Tannhäuser*.[81] In his letters to her, Wagner discusses numerous aesthetic matters, and he even mentions there for the first time his "art of transition" (*SB* 11:329). Only rarely did he engage in such a detailed correspondence about his art, and he did not allow such deep insights into his work to those whom he regarded as intellectually inferior. Nor does such a correspondence come about in a vacuum. In other words, it seems sensible to regard Wagner's extant letters to Mathilde as the written continuation of the regular conversations that they had held while Wagner lived in Zurich. If Wagner indeed discussed such matters with her in person, then we must drastically revise our estimation of Mathilde's importance as Wagner's conversation partner during his years of Zurich exile. When Wagner first met Mathilde, he was largely cut off from his fellow artists. His confidant Theodor Uhlig, with whom he had discussed by letter the aesthetic matters that were most important to him, died in January 1853 — just at the time when Wagner's contact with the Wesendoncks intensified. Is it possible that Mathilde became for Wagner not just his would-be lover, his muse, and his patron, but also, thanks to her intellectual curiosity in artistic and literary matters, a kind of *Ersatz* for Uhlig? The letters that Wagner wrote to her after his departure from Zurich indeed suggest that she had long before slipped into such a role. Just because she stands before us today "in silence," so to speak, does not mean that she was silent in her personal relationships. This is far more significant than Mathilde's writings themselves. It is surely time to regard her — despite her own words — not as Wagner's "white piece of paper," his passive object of inspiration, but as a strong, self-assured personality who was capable of holding her own in a man's world and who became an important sounding board for Wagner's plans and theories. In this reading of their relationship, Mathilde was his most significant conversation partner during the most crucial years of his artistic development — a conversation partner whom Wagner himself took far more seriously than his biographers have ever done since.

Notes

[1] Hans Bélart's 1912 study of the relationship was entitled: *Richard Wagners Liebestragödie mit Mathilde Wesendonck* ("Richard Wagner's Love Tragedy with Mathilde Wesendonck") (Dresden: Reissner, 1912). But see also, for example, Martha Schad, *"Meine erste und einzige Liebe": Richard Wagner und Mathilde Wesendonck* (Munich: Langen Müller, 2002), 18, where Mathilde is described as Wagner's "eternal beloved."

[2] Wolfgang Golther, ed., *Richard Wagner an Mathilde Wesendonk* [*sic*]*: Tagebuchblätter und Briefe, 1853–1871* (Berlin: Duncker, 1904).

[3] See Egon Voss, "Die Wesendoncks und Richard Wagner," in *Minne, Muse und Mäzen: Otto und Mathilde Wesendonck und ihr Zürcher Künstlerzirkel*, ed. Langer and Walton (Zurich: Museum Rietberg, 2002), 117–29; here, 121–22.

[4] Wolfgang Golther, ed., *Richard Wagner an Mathilde Wesendonk*, 44–45.

[5] See Eva Rieger, *Minna und Richard Wagner: Stationen einer Liebe* (Düsseldorf and Zurich: Artemis & Winkler, 2003), 269–70.

[6] Letter of 9 April 1858, quoted in Fehr, *Richard Wagners Schweizer Zeit*, vol. 2 (Aarau and Frankfurt am Main: Sauerländer, 1953), 121.

[7] Quoted in Sibylle Zehle, *Minna Wagner: Eine Spurensuche* (Hamburg: Hoffmann & Campe, 2004), 406.

[8] Richard Wagner, *Briefwechsel zwischen Wagner und Liszt*, ed. Erich Kloss, 3rd ed. (Leipzig: Breitkopf & Härtel, 1910), 2:188.

[9] Minna's letters to her friend Mathilde Schiffner, detailing her actions, are quoted in Eva Rieger, *Minna und Richard Wagner*, 278–81.

[10] Francesco De Sanctis, *Epistolario (1856–1858)*, ed. Giovanni Ferretti and Muzio Mazzocchi Alemanni (Turin: Einaudi, 1965), 496; in an undated letter (though obviously of August 1858) to Mathilde, De Sanctis mentions her continued absence and offers his best wishes to her parents.

[11] Letter in private hands in Switzerland.

[12] See Fehr, *Richard Wagners Schweizer Zeit*, 2:402–3. Only Wille's draft letter is extant, though Wagner's reply makes it clear that the letter was indeed sent.

[13] See Wolfgang Golther, ed., *Richard Wagner an Mathilde Wesendonk*, 309–11.

[14] Houston Stewart Chamberlain, *Richard Wagner* (Munich: Bruckmann, 1895).

[15] See Chamberlain, *Richard Wagner*, 75–82 in the 8th edition of 1933.

[16] See Harry Joelson-Strohbach, "Theodor Kirchner bei Mathilde Wesendonck," in *Minne, Muse und Mäzen: Otto und Mathilde Wesendonck und ihr Zürcher Künstlerzirkel*, ed. Axel Langer and Chris Walton (Zurich: Museum Rietberg, 2002), 143–58, and Inge Pechotsch-Feichtinger, "Briefe von Ödön von Mihalovich an Mathilde Wesendonck," in *Studia Musicologica Academiae Scientiarum Hungaricae* 40, no. 1 (1999): 249–301.

[17] Ernest Newman, *The Life of Richard Wagner*, 2: 1848–1860 (Cambridge: Cambridge UP, 1976), 570.

[18] The fact that Martha Schad left this question unanswered in her book *"Meine erste und einzige Liebe"* was cause for criticism on the part of Christine Lemke-Matwey in her review for *Die Zeit* of 2 October 2002.

[19] Friedrich Wilhelm von Bissing, *Mathilde Wesendonck: Die Frau und die Dichterin* (Vienna: Anton Schroll, 1942), 10.

[20] Wagner, *Oper und Drama*, in *Sämtliche Schriften und Dichtungen*, 6th ed. (Leipzig: Breitkopf & Härtel, [1911]), 3:222–321 and 4:2–229; here, 4:3.

[21] Wagner, *Die Kunst und die Revolution*, in *Sämtliche Schriften und Dichtungen* (Leipzig: Breitkopf & Härtel, [1911]), 3:8–41; here, 3:11, 20, 35, 37.

[22] Wagner, *Das Kunstwerk der Zukunft*, in *Sämtliche Schriften und Dichtungen* 3: 42–177; here, 3:96, 119, 150, 156, 157, 158, 161.

[23] Wagner, *Oper und Drama*, in *Sämtliche Schriften und Dichtungen* 4:3, 96.

[24] Wagner, *Die Kunst und die Revolution*, in *Sämtliche Schriften und Dichtungen* 3:12, 29 and 60 (twice).

[25] Albert Heintz, "Richard Wagner in Zürich," in *Allgemeine Musikzeitung* 23, no. 7, 1896.

[26] A letter of Minna of 23 April 1859 to an unnamed friend, published in John N. Burk, ed., *Richard Wagner Briefe: Die Sammlung Burrell* (Frankfurt am Main: S. Fischer Verlag, 1953), 499. Further references to this work will be made in the text using the abbreviation *RWB* and the page number.

[27] Roger Scruton, *Death-Devoted heart: Sex and the Sacred in Wagner's "Tristan and Isolde"* (Oxford: Oxford UP, 2004), 131.

[28] As related by Albert Heintz in "Richard Wagner in Zürich."

[29] See Ferdinand Praeger, *Wagner as I Knew Him* (New York: Longmans, Green, 1892), 196–97 and 299. Praeger refrains from naming Jessie specifically.

[30] This letter is given as a facsimile on the inside cover of Martha Schad's *"Meine erste und einzige Liebe."* The orthography is original.

[31] E.g. "Und meine liebe Muse bleibt mir fern?" ("And my dear muse stays away from me?") in Wagner's letter to Mathilde of May 1857. See *SB* 8:339.

[32] Ludwig Ettmüller, *Herbstabende und Winternächte: Gespräche über Deutsche Dichtungen und Dichter* (Stuttgart, Cotta, 1865–67).

[33] Mathilde's papers are held by the Zurich City Archives.

[34] For further information on Zurich's intellectual elite in the mid-nineteenth century, see Gordon A. Craig, *The Triumph of Liberalism: Zürich in the Golden Age 1830–1869*. New York and London: Collier, 1990.

[35] See, for example, Joachim Köhler's description of the power play between Cosima and Wagner in 1868, in his *Der letzte der Titanen: Richard Wagners Leben und Werk* (Munich: Claassen, 2001), 623.

[36] Eliza Wille, *Erinnerungen an Richard Wagner: Mit 15 Briefen Richard Wagners* (Zurich: Atlantis Musikbuch-Verlag, 1982), 32–33.

[37] Letter of Minna Wagner to Jakob Sulzer, Dresden, 15 December 1858, published in Max Fehr, *Richard Wagners Schweizer Zeit* 2:148.

[38] See for example the entry of 7 March 1872: "I ask R. to be certain that I have no will of my own at all and that my only happiness lies in striving to understand him in the tiniest, small thing, and to stand by his side" (*TB* 1:497–98).

[39] See for example, *TB* 2:425, entry of 14 October 1879: "We talk of the dreams; recently, Mrs. Wesendonck has often appeared in them, but always in a strange, unpleasant fashion."

[40] As related by Albert Heintz in "Richard Wagner in Zürich."

[41] See Jürg Wille: "Das 'Asyl' Richard Wagners (Frühling 1857–Sommer 1858) in der heutigen Villa Schönberg," in *Richard Wagner in Zürich: Eine Chronik*, ed. Werner G. Zimmermann. Second, expanded edition (Zurich: Präsidialabteilung, 1987), no page numbers.

[42] Friedrich Wilhelm von Bissing, *Mathilde Wesendonck*, 22.

[43] According to research carried out by Peter Jost and Christa Jost of the Wagner Gesamtausgabe, Natalie died, not in an old-people's home in Leisnig as previously thought, but probably in Dresden some time after 1899. Since many of the city's records were destroyed in the Second World War, no later proof of her residence there is extant (personal communication to the author, 1999).

[44] Several are published in Burk, *Richard Wagner Briefe.*

[45] See Roner's memoirs in Werner G. Zimmermann, *Richard Wagner in Zürich: Materialien zu Aufenthalt und Wirken*, vol. 1 (Zurich: Hug, 1986), 7–17; here, 8 and 10.

[46] See Erich H. Müller von Asow, *Johannes Brahms und Mathilde Wesendonck: Ein Briefwechsel* (Vienna: Luckmann, 1943), 83.

[47] See Langer and Walton, *Minne, Muse und Mäzen*, 179.

[48] See Renate and Kurt Hofmann, "Zu den Beziehungen zwischen Johannes Brahms und Mathilde Wesendonck," in Langer and Walton, *Minne, Muse und Mäzen*, 130–40; here, 140.

[49] For detailed information on the relationship between Kirchner and Mathilde, see Harry Joelson-Strohbach, "Theodor Kirchner bei Mathilde Wesendonck," in Langer and Walton, *Minne, Muse und Mäzen*, 143–58.

[50] Harry Joelson-Strohbach, "Theodor Kirchner bei Mathilde Wesendonck," 151.

[51] Harry Joelson-Strohbach, "Theodor Kirchner bei Mathilde Wesendonck," 152.

[52] Harry Joelson-Strohbach, "Theodor Kirchner bei Mathilde Wesendonck," 158.

[53] See Reinhold Sietz, *Theodor Kirchner: Ein Klaviermeister der deutschen Romantik* (Regensburg: Gustav Bosse, 1971), 44.

[54] See Chris Walton, *Heinrich Schulz-Beuthen (1838–1915): Eine biographische Skizze* (Zurich: Hug, 2003), 33. This volume contains all of Schulz-Beuthen's known writings on music. Schulz-Beuthen also arranged a number of Kirchner's piano pieces for orchestra; see 98–99 in the above-mentioned volume.

[55] For example, he is not mentioned by name in the 870 pages of Joachim Köhler's biography *Der letzte der Titanen*; he is referred to as the professor who gave Mathilde Italian lessons (535).

[56] See, for example, Martin Gregor-Dellin, *Richard Wagner: Sein Leben. Sein Werk. Sein Jahrhundert* (Munich and Zurich: Piper, 1980), 433.

[57] Pierre Antonetti, *Francesco De Sanctis (1817–1883): Son évolution intellectuelle, son esthétique et sa critique* (Aix-en-Provence: Edition Ophrys, 1963), 117.

[58] Jacob Moleschott, *Für meine Freunde: Lebens-Erinnerungen* (Giessen: Emil Roth, 1894), 302–3.

[59] Moleschott, *Für meine Freunde*, 303.

[60] Pierre Antonetti, *Francesco De Sanctis*, 112.

[61] Pierre Antonetti, *Francesco De Sanctis*, 113.

[62] Francesco De Sanctis, *Epistolario (1856–1858)*, 427. Further references to this work will be given in the text using the abbreviation *E* and the page number.

[63] Robert von Hornstein, *Memoiren*, ed. Ferdinand von Hornstein (Munich: Süddeutsche Monatshefte, 1908), 139. Further references to this work will be given in the text using the abbreviation *M* and the page number.

[64] Francesco De Sanctis, *Scelta di scritti critici e ricordi*, ed. Gianfranco Contini (Turin: Unione Tipograficao, 1969), 133.

[65] See the introduction by Gianfranco Contini to Francesco De Sanctis, *Storia della letteratura italiana* (Milan: TEA, 1989), 43. Also Pierre Antonetti, *Francesco De Sanctis (1817–1883): Son évolution intellectuelle, son esthétique et sa critique*, 68.

[66] Eliza Wille, *Erinnerungen an Richard Wagner*, 30.

[67] Francesco De Sanctis, *Lettere dall'esilio (1853–1860)*, ed. Benedetto Croce (Bari: Laterza & Figli, 1938), 40–41.

[68] For a discussion of De Sanctis's knowledge of the French language, see Pierre Antonetti, *Francesco De Sanctis et la culture française* (Florence and Paris: Edizioni Sansoni/Librairie Marcel Didier, 1964), 82–86.

[69] Pierre Antonetti, *Francesco De Sanctis et la culture française*, 114.

[70] De Sanctis, *Lettere dall'esilio (1853–1860)*, 221.

[71] Carlo Muscetta, *Francesco De Sanctis* (Rome: Laterza, 1975), 4.

[72] Wagner, *Sämtliche Schriften und Dichtungen* 4:226.

[73] Joachim Köhler, *Der letzte der Titanen*, 394–95.

[74] Antonetti, *Francesco De Sanctis et la culture française*, 118.

[75] Antonetti, *Francesco De Sanctis et la culture française*, 70–72.

[76] De Sanctis, *Lettere dall'esilio*, 245–49.

[77] De Sanctis, *Lettere dall'esilio*, 251.

[78] Ute Jung, *Die Rezeption der Kunst Richard Wagners in Italien* (Regensburg: Gustav Bosse, 1974), 95.

[79] See Hornstein, *Memoiren*, 143, and Wagner, *Das braune Buch: Tagebuchaufzeichnungen, 1865 bis 1882*, ed. Joachim Bergfeld (Zurich: Atlantis Musikbuch-Verlag, 1975), 125.

[80] Emil Ermatinger, ed., *Gottfried Kellers Briefe und Tagebücher, 1861–1890* (Stuttgart and Berlin: Cotta, 1916), 13–14, 24–26, and 36–37.

[81] See Egon Voss, "Die Wesendoncks und Richard Wagner," in Langer and Walton, *Minne, Muse und Mäzen*, 117–29; here, 123.

Figure 14. The Villa Wesendonck, early twentieth century. Used by permission of the Zentralbibliothek Zürich.

Epilogue

We have here investigated the impact of Zurich, the place and its people, on Wagner and his art, during and beyond the nine years that he spent there. But what of his long-term impact on Zurich itself? The immediate effects of his presence, both direct and indirect, have been discussed above, ranging from the transformation of the local, lackadaisical orchestra into a more streamlined ensemble with a rigorous rehearsal discipline to the generally stimulating effect that his manifold energies exerted on the musical life of city and canton. Yet, on the face of things, it would seem at first glance that Zurich itself attained no lasting benefit from his presence, and that his public achievements there were all short-lived. His repeated, detailed plans to establish concrete structures for the betterment of local music education, the orchestra, and the theater were all turned down by the authorities; one could thus be forgiven for perceiving a certain logic in the fact that, three years after his death, even his beloved *Asyl* was torn down, to make way for the "Villa Schönberg" that still stands today. But it is a fact that within less than twenty years of his departure much of what he had proposed had come about, and through the offices of the very people who in the 1850s had been his friends and supporters. The AMG Orchestra gave way in 1868 to the newly formed Tonhalle Orchestra, thanks in large part to the active support of the Wesendoncks, as also to Wagner's other old friends Moritz von Wyss, Franz Hagenbuch, and Karl Keller. It was housed in the former city cornhouse — which allowed for far bigger audiences than had the Casino — until a new, purpose-built concert hall was unveiled in 1895. The Tonhalle Orchestra flourishes still today, and the acoustics of its concert hall remain among the finest in Europe (though its magnificent mock Byzantine exterior was dismantled in the first half of the twentieth century). The year 1876 saw the founding of the Zurich Conservatory under the auspices of Friedrich Hegar, the conductor of the Tonhalle Orchestra, who had in the 1860s played in string quartet performances for Wagner in Tribschen. The Conservatory was a joint undertaking of the AMG, the Tonhalle Society, the Theater, the Gemischter Chor, the Harmonie Chorus, and the Music Commission of the Zurich School Synod. This was just the kind of collaboration that Wagner had dreamed of more than twenty years earlier, and it, too, had been driven onwards by Wagner's erstwhile cohorts: Karl Keller, von Wyss, Heim, and Hagenbuch (no doubt the Wesendoncks would have played their part too, had they not already left the city).

Hagenbuch himself served as the first president of the Conservatory Board and remained in office until his death.[1] A large donation from the estate of Heinrich Bodmer-Stockar had helped to make the Conservatory financially viable — the same Bodmer-Stockar with whom Wagner had negotiated in the 1850s with a view to buying a little house near the Zurich Lake. The Conservatory staff in its first years even included Johann Carl Eschmann.

It took the ravages of fire, however, to convince the city of the need to erect a new, purpose-built theater. On the evening of 1 January 1890, during a performance of Birch-Pfeiffer's play *Der Leyermann und sein Pflegekind*, the Zurich theater caught fire. Since the men in charge kept their cool, there was no stampede of theatergoers, and neither death nor injury. A new theater was erected swiftly, on a new plot near the lakeside. The city of Kraków had recently abandoned its own proposed new theater, and so, to save time, Zurich now simply bought up its plans, hired its architects, and built it instead. The new *Stadttheater* (today the "Opernhaus") was opened on 30 September 1891 with a gala performance of Wagner's *Lohengrin*. The new theater continued as it had begun, with Wagner's operas and music dramas proving the most popular over the ensuing decades. He was thus, ironically, largely responsible (if posthumously so) for most of the income that the theater needed to survive. Had he himself seen but a fraction of those monies in his lifetime, he would not have needed to beg so much (but there again, given his talent for living beyond his means and needs, he would most likely still have allowed his debts to grow in direct proportion to his income, however high that might have been). Although city subsidies for the theater remained for many years a matter of fierce debate, as they had in Wagner's day, the opening of the new building was the catalyst for an increase at last in public support — support that grew steadily over the ensuing decades.

There is, in fact, one Swiss building that owes its very existence to Wagner, albeit indirectly. When the "Bundeshaus," the Swiss Federal Parliament, was built in the 1890s, its architect Hans Wilhelm Auer drew heavily on the plans that his teacher, Gottfried Semper, had made in the 1860s for Wagner's proposed theater in Munich. The debating chamber for the *Nationalrat*, the upper chamber of Parliament, thus takes the inside shape of a theater, proscenium arch and all. Wagner's *Festspielhaus* in Bayreuth drew equally on Semper's plans, but thanks largely to Wagner's own intuitive changes, the Bayreuth acoustic is exemplary, while that of the *Nationalratsaal* is notoriously poor. By a happy Wagnerian coincidence, the latter hall features, instead of a stage, a vast panorama (by the Genevan artist Charles Giron) in which the view is that from Wagner's beloved Seelisberg.[2] There is, of course, a delightful irony in that the erstwhile left-wing democrat Wagner should have unwittingly contributed to the establishment of a home for one of the world's oldest democracies, long after he himself had converted to a monarchical, Bismarckian German nationalism. (In this context, however, we must mention that those same nationalist sympathies were not without resonance, even in neutral Switzerland — for when Adolf Hitler came to Zurich to drum up support for the Nazi Party in September 1923, he gave his main speech on the site of Wagner's former *Asyl.*[3])

While Wagner's legacy to Switzerland and Zurich was open-ended, his sojourn in Zurich ended more or less as it had begun: in penniless flight, and in disgrace. Wagner's biography has on occasion been interpreted as a series of "escapes," of one flight after the next, be it from creditors (in Riga, Vienna, and just about everywhere else), from the police and army (in Dresden), or from the consequences of illicit love affairs (in Zurich and Munich). Yet his biography is perhaps less a matter of "escapes" than of "escapism." From his participation in the May uprising in Dresden in 1849 and his ignominious flight therefrom to his equally ignominious departure from Zurich nine years, three months, and one week later, his life can perhaps best be interpreted as a flight, not merely *away* from things or people, but *to* a series of different utopias. The pursuit of a utopia of inclusion that dominated his actions in his last weeks in Dresden — a utopia of social revolution that would redeem mankind — led to another, inextricably linked with it, namely an equally revolutionary utopia that would also "redeem" us, but this time through the "artwork of the future." These inclusive utopias led — perhaps just as inevitably — to one of *ex*clusion, to a notional world "ethnically cleansed" of Jews in which both "they" and "us" would be redeemed by their *Untergang*, which utopia would somehow also work retrospectively in order to "purify" Wagner's art from the omnipresent traces of his undeniably Jewish, "operatic father," Giacomo Meyerbeer. From here, Wagner moved on to a prospective utopia of domestic bliss with Jessie Laussot in the Middle East (the most distant geographical Other he would ever contemplate), then to one of health and cleanliness through water at Dr. Brunner's Hydrotherapy Clinic in Albisbrunn, then to yet another notion of domestic utopia with Minna in a little house of his own in Zurich, and thence to a utopia of an all-consuming, unconsummated love for Mathilde Wesendonck (for the only love that is truly utopian is a love that has not experienced the disappointments of fulfillment). And all the while, of course, he was postulating an aesthetic utopia of his own creation, in which he would not only create a world on stage but would also implicitly recreate the world itself, with his stage at the center of it. It should not surprise us that he abandoned his plans of the early 1850s for an opera based on the legend of Wieland the Smith, for Wieland ends by flying away from his captivity into the sunrise. Given that Wagner was constantly "flying" from the threat of captivity — from the police in Germany, from his creditors, and from unsympathetic, cuckolded husbands — the character of Wieland was perhaps too close for comfort to be entertained further. But more than this: Wagner at this time did not really want to fly away from the world: he wanted it to fly to him. And the only place where this might happen was in his imagination, in his art.

The most astute comments on Wagner's theoretical writings come, perhaps not surprisingly, from the pen of Friedrich Nietzsche. In his *Unzeitgemässe Betrachtungen* (Thoughts Out of Season), he offered praise where he felt it due, but also (referring to *Opera and Drama* in particular) criticized the "irregular rhythm" of Wagner's prose, adding that "it seems to me as if Wagner often speaks as if to an audience of enemies — for the style of all these writings is of the spoken word, not the written."[4] In a recent study, James Treadwell has commented that these writings from Wagner's "revolutionary" period, "however much [they] may look like statements of intent . . . [are] essentially . . . admissions of incapacity, always deferring the future they anticipate so eagerly."[5] These writings, no less than Wagner's slowly germinating plan for a tetralogy on the *Nibelungen* myths, are admittedly utopian, a dream of having everything that can perhaps only truly be dreamt by one who has nothing. Most men and women, when confronted with the loss, real or potential, of career, income, home, friends, family, and marriage, would content themselves with any means to eke out an existence, however modest. Wagner, however, used his "nothing" as a mental springboard to create a world of his own in which he would have everything, indeed in which he would (one could argue) *be* everything, *be* everyone. This was surely one of the reasons for his fondness for reciting his *Ring* libretto, both in private and in public, for it allowed him to play every character in a world of his own creation — indeed, its language and gestures probably derived at least in part from Wagner's imagining, during the very act of writing, how he would then declaim his text out loud afterwards (and herein lies too, perhaps, another reason for his rejection of ensembles and choruses, if a reason of utter banality: he could naturally only be one character — could only recite one voice — at a time). Wagner's singing and acting out of the roles of both Hunding and Siegmund in his private performances of the *Walküre* — the betrayed husband and his betrayer — was on the one hand a tactless gesture toward Otto Wesendonck, the man in his audience whom he would dearly like to have cuckolded, but on the other hand it was merely another sign of the composer's desire to control "his" world. Had he had the vocal capacity to sing the part of Sieglinde too, he would surely have had no compunction in dispensing with the services of Emilie Heim.

As I have discussed above, to write a work such as the *Rheingold* in which gods ascend into a heavenly castle across a rainbow bridge to the sound of a huge orchestra (with six harps) while mermaids swim and sing in a river in the valley below (to the accompaniment of a seventh), was to challenge everything that was considered theatrically feasible at the time. It did not just postulate a theater of both limitless possibilities and near-limitless funds; it also ostentatiously proclaimed what everyone would assume was impossible, precisely because the impossible was what Wagner wanted. We cannot prove that he would never have written the *Ring* had he remained a Kapellmeister in Dresden, but we can be all but certain of it. Writing the *Ring* necessitated placing an unbridgeable gap between himself and current theatrical practice that he would have found impossible to contemplate were he still working in the profession. Its stage directions, especially in the *Rheingold*, are — literally — "over the rainbow [bridge]" in terms of what could be achieved in its day. It is significant that, when Liszt arranged for the commissioning of *Siegfrieds Tod* from Weimar in 1850, Wagner turned it down, even though he needed the money. For how could he have contemplated creating the utterly impractical for an indefinitely deferred future, had he been consigned to composing the immediately practicable in and for the here and now? The very fact, then, that Zurich possessed neither the venue, nor the musicians, nor the singers that his tetralogy would require seems to have spurred Wagner on to ever grander, ever more improbable conceptions, in a constantly repeating pattern of deferral of gratification; and it is naturally apposite that it was during these years that he should have conceived *Tristan und Isolde*, in which that deferral is raised to a harmonic and formal principle.

Elements of utopianism have naturally existed throughout the history of Western art, not least in the writings of the early German Romantics of whom Wagner was the heir, such as E. T. A. Hoffmann. But utopias in music were something new — the first, arguably, being Beethoven's vision of universal brotherhood as expressed in his Ninth Symphony. Wagner's postulation of a "Gesamtkunstwerk" (or, rather, a "vereinigtes Kunstwerk"), with its massive, accompanying theoretical-cum-philosophical scaffolding, now opened up the world of music for the first time to incorporate not just "all the arts," but also a whole Pandora's box of other ideas, from his own Schopenhauerian philosophy to the overtly political ideologies of the next century, with their concomitant utopian (and dystopian) visions of the future.

But there were, as we have seen, concrete examples too of Zurich, its citizens and its environs, acting as a catalyst to Wagner's imagination in what they possessed, not in what they lacked. Be it his experience of the natural world, his conversations with the myriad of intellectuals whom politics and revolution had placed on his doorstep (as he on theirs), the material and creative stimulation offered by his patrons Otto and Mathilde Wesendonck, or even his first real encounter with the hagiographical adoration he would later cultivate to such effect: his years in Zurich proved of central importance to his development as man and artist. And on a personal level, the relationship that was able to blossom in Zurich between him and Hans von Bülow — as it had not blossomed when they were acquainted in Dresden — was to have immense repercussions for Wagner's life and art, through von Bülow's advocacy as an interpretive artist, and more obviously through von Bülow's relations with Franz Liszt and his daughter Cosima.

Wagner's utopianism existed in counterpoint with an undeniably common-sensical, down-to-earth, instinctive knowledge of the practicalities of the world of music. His proposals for the reorganization of Zurich's musical life provide ideal testimony to this: eminently practical in their detail — so much so that, as we have seen, his principal suggestions were all realized, many years later — and yet as a whole impossibly utopian, given the reigning attitudes toward the arts in Zurich in the 1850s. Wagner's Zurich years show us with greater clarity what we can already observe *in ovo* in his last year in Dresden, namely how his ideas and his actions would be dominated increasingly by this oscillating between the practical and the utopian, with each of these aspects ruling in turn in a manner that from our perspective seems obsessively compulsive. Seen in this light, his notion, expressed in these years in a letter to Theodor Uhlig, of building a theater to stage his *Siegfried*, and thereafter tearing it down and burning the score (*SB* 3:426), seems less of a whim than a logical expression of his psyche. Indeed, whenever he did achieve, after immense struggles with himself and others, the practical means of ensuring some form of permanence in his life and art — with the support of Otto Wesendonck and, later, of King Ludwig II — then his need for impossibly more would thwart all that he would seem to have achieved. Perhaps, as Ulrich Drüner has postulated, Wagner needed such "destructive" acts to prompt his muse. But it was in any case surely thanks to the steely resolve of Cosima, and his need to provide a concrete legacy both for her and for their new family, that Wagner did at the last, in Bayreuth, realize several of his "Zurich utopias" — private and public, domestic and artistic — with the building of both Wahnfried as the seat of his newly founded dynasty and the Festspielhaus for the staging of the *Ring des Nibelungen* in 1876. That Wagner found his domestic bliss often less than blissful, and was deeply dissatisfied with his own production of the *Ring*, should hardly surprise us. Gratification is only ever perfect when deferred indefinitely. All utopias naturally cease to be, always, when they are faced with their realization.

Ironically, then, the greatest significance of Zurich for Wagner's life and oeuvre lies arguably in just what he said of it in his derogatory comments in *Mein Leben*, quoted at the very beginning of this book: "a place of refuge that had nothing to attract me, except precisely the complete and utter hopelessness of achieving anything there along the lines of what had thus far been the path of my life" (*ML*, 435). As I have proven here, Zurich was a city far from empty of intellectual and artistic interest, as Wagner would have us believe; it was, in fact, quite the opposite. But the self-styled "Athens on the Limmat" was a mere tiny, republican city on the edge of the Alps, and it was never going to be Wagner's new "Athens" for the staging of his own immense "vereinigtes Kunstwerk." Wagner found in Zurich in the 1850s what the Dadaists, James Joyce, Vladimir Illyich Lenin, Ferruccio Busoni, and many others would discover some sixty years later, during the next wave of refugees to seek asylum there: a place able to provide the material security, the political freedoms, and the intense intellectual stimulation that are all necessary in order to construct vast castles in the air (and the rainbow bridges that lead to them), while at the same time manifestly unable to provide the concrete means for them to be constructed in reality. For all the multifarious complaints of its provinciality, from Wagner to Busoni, and for all the complaints from its artist-residents of the restrictions that it imposed upon them, Zurich attained through them all a significance that is perhaps unique in the history of music of the past two hundred years: a city that would let fly the imagination, but only of those who were ready, and able, to soar beyond it.

Notes

[1] See Friedrich Hegar, "Brief an den Verwaltungsrat und an die Direktion des Konservatoriums für Musik in Zürich," in *Festschrift zum fünfzigjährigen Jubiläum des Konservatoriums für Musik in Zürich, 1876–1926*, ed. Hans Jelmoli (Zurich: Orell Füssli, 1926), 6–11.

[2] See Dorothea Baumann, "Wagners Festspielhaus: Ein akustisch-architektonisches Wagnis mit Überraschungen," in *Festschrift Hans Conradin zum 70. Geburtstag* (Bern and Stuttgart: Paul Haupt, 1983), 123–50; also Urs Staub, untitled presentation given in the Bundeshaus on the building's 100th anniversary, at http://www.parlament.ch/ab/frameset/f/v/4612/56958/f_v_4612_56958_56959.htm, accessed September 2006; and Martin Fröhlich, *Le Palais Fédéral à Berne* (Basel: Société d'Histoire de l'Art en Suisse, 1979), 18. I am grateful to Dorothea Baumann for bringing the matter of Semper, Auer, and the Munich plans to my attention.

[3] Raffael Scheck, "Swiss Funding for the Early Nazi Movement: Motivation, Context, and Continuities," in *The Journal of Modern History* 71, no. 4 (December 1999): 793–813, here 805.

[4] See Friedrich Nietzsche, "Richard Wagner in Bayreuth," in *Unzeitgemässe Betrachtungen*, ed. Peter Pütz (Munich: Goldmann, 1992), 225–89; here, 283.

[5] James Treadwell, *Interpreting Wagner* (New Haven and London: Yale UP, 2003), 75.

Works Consulted

Works by Richard Wagner

Programm zu den Musikaufführungen am 18. 20. und 22. Mai 1853 in Zürich. Zurich: Kiesling, 1853.

Sämtliche Schriften und Dichtungen. Sixth edition (*Volksausgabe*). Leipzig: Breitkopf & Härtel, [1911].

Sämtliche Werke. Edited by Egon Voss, Carl Dahlhaus, *et al.* Mainz: Schott, 1974–.

Das braune Buch: Tagebuchaufzeichnungen, 1865 bis 1882. Edited by Joachim Bergenfeld. Zurich: Atlantis Musikbuch-Verlag, 1975.

Mein Leben. Edited by Martin Gregor-Dellin. Munich: List Verlag, 1977.

Where relevant, the first editions of the following of Wagner's Zurich writings were also consulted:

Die Kunst und die Revolution. Leipzig: Wigand, 1849.

Das Kunstwerk der Zukunft. Leipzig: Wigand, 1850.

Ein Theater in Zürich. Zurich: Schulthess, 1851.

Drei Operndichtungen nebst einer Mittheilung an seine Freunde als Vorwort. Leipzig: Breitkopf & Härtel, 1852.

Oper und Drama. Leipzig: Weber, 1852.

Wagner's Correspondence

Richard Wagner an Mathilde Wesendonk: Tagebuchblätter und Briefe, 1853–1871. Edited by Wolfgang Golther. Berlin: Duncker, 1904.

Briefe Richard Wagners an Otto Wesendonk, 1852–1870. Edited by Wolfgang Golther. Neue, vollständige Ausgabe. Berlin: Duncker, 1905.

Bayreuther Briefe von Richard Wagner (1871–1883). Edited by Carl Glasenapp. Berlin and Leipzig: Schuster & Loeffler, 1907.

Familienbriefe von Richard Wagner. Edited by Carl Glasenapp. Berlin: Duncker, 1907.

Briefwechsel zwischen Wagner und Liszt. Edited by Erich Kloss. 3rd ed. Leipzig: Breitkopf & Härtel, 1910.

König Ludwig II. und Richard Wagner: Briefwechsel. Edited by Otto Strobel. Karlsruhe: Braun, 1936–39.

Sämtliche Briefe. Edited by Gertrud Strobel, Werner Wolf, Hans-Joachim Bauer, Johannes Forner et al. Leipzig: Deutscher Verlag für Musik, later Wiesbaden: Breitkopf & Härtel, 1967–.

Other Primary Works

Wagner, Cosima. *Die Tagebücher.* 2 vols. Munich and Zurich: Piper, 1976–77.

Other Literature

Albrecht, Wolfram. "Hugo Wesendonck." In *Wuppertaler Biographien,* 7:99–110. Wuppertal: Born Verlag, 1967.

Antonetti, Pierre. *Francesco De Sanctis (1817–1883): Son évolution intellectuelle, son esthétique et sa critique.* Aix-en-Provence: Edition Ophrys, 1963.

———. *Francesco De Sanctis et la culture française.* Florence and Paris: Edizioni Sansoni/Librairie Marcel Didier, 1964.

Asow, Erich H. Müller von. *Johannes Brahms und Mathilde Wesendonck: Ein Briefwechsel.* Vienna: Luckmann, 1943.

Baedeker, Karl. *Die Schweiz nebst den angrenzenden Teilen von Oberitalien, Savoyen und Tirol: Handbuch für Reisende.* 34th edition. Leipzig: Karl Baedeker, 1911.

Bauer, Oswald Georg. "Zur Genese des Begriffes 'Effekt.'" In Döge, Jost, and Jost, *"Schlagen Sie die Kraft der Reflexion nicht zu gering an,"* 151–57.

Baum, Marie-Luise. "Mathilde und Otto Wesendonck." In *Wuppertaler Biographien,* 3:135–48. Wuppertal: Born Verlag, 1961.

Baumann, Dorothea. *Vom Musikraum zum Konzertsaal: Auf den Spuren von Zürichs Musikleben.* Zurich: Hug, 2002.

———. "Wagners Festspielhaus: Ein akustisch-architektonisches Wagnis mit Überraschungen." In *Festschrift Hans Conradin zum 70. Geburtstag,* 123–50. Bern and Stuttgart: Paul Haupt, 1983.

Bélart, Hans. *Richard Wagner in Zürich (1849–1858).* Two vols. Leipzig: Hermann Seemann: 1900 and 1901.

———. *Richard Wagners Beziehungen zu François und Eliza Wille in Mariafeld bei Zürich (1852–1872) und sein Asyl auf Mariafeld (1864): Ludwig Geyer, der Schauspieler und Maler, als leiblicher Vater Richard Wagners.* Dresden: Carl Reissner, 1914.

———. *Richard Wagners Liebestragödie mit Mathilde Wesendonck.* Dresden: Reissner, 1912.

Bissing, Friedrich Wilhelm Freiherr von. *Mathilde Wesendonck: Die Frau und die Dichterin.* Vienna: Anton Schroll, 1942.

Borchmeyer, Dieter. *Drama and the World of Richard Wagner*. Translated by Stewart Spencer. Princeton and Oxford: Princeton UP, 2003.

Borchmeyer, Dieter, and Stephan Kohler, eds. *Wagner-Parodien*. Frankfurt am Main: Insel, 1983.

Brahms, Johannes. *Briefe an P. J. Simrock und Fritz Simrock*, ed. Max Kalbeck. Berlin: Deutsche Brahms-Gesellschaft, 1917.

———. *Briefwechsel mit Breitkopf & Härtel, Bartolf Senff, J. Rieter-Biedermann, C. F. Peters, E. W. Fritzsch und Robert Lienau*, ed. Wilhelm Altmann. Berlin: Deutsche Brahms-Gesellschaft, 1920.

Breig, Werner. "Der 'Rheintöchtergesang' in Wagners 'Rheingold.'" In *Archiv für Musikwissenschaft* 37, no. 4 (1980): 241–63.

———. "Von Alexander Müller bis Richard Wagner und Franz Liszt: Das musikalische Album der Schweizer Sängerin, Pianistin und Komponistin Fanny Hünerwadel." In *Musikalische Quellen — Quellen zur Musikgeschichte: Festschrift für Martin Staehelin zum 65. Geburtstag*, edited by Ulrich Konrad, Jürgen Heidrich, and Hans Joachim Marx, 405–23. Göttingen: Vandenhoeck & Ruprecht, 2002.

———, ed. *Wagner-Briefe-Verzeichnis: WBV: Chronologisches Verzeichnis der Briefe von Richard Wagner*. Wiesbaden: Breitkopf & Härtel, 1998.

Bülow, Hans von. *Ausgewählte Schriften, 1850–1892*. Edited by Marie von Bülow. Leipzig: Breitkopf & Härtel, 1896.

———. *Briefe*. Edited by Marie von Bülow. Seven vols. Leipzig: Breitkopf & Härtel, 1895–1908.

Burk, John N., ed. *Richard Wagner Briefe: Die Sammlung Burrell*. Frankfurt am Main: S. Fischer Verlag, 1953.

Cabaud, Judith. *Mathilde Wesendonck ou le rêve d'Isolde*. Arles: Editions Actes Sud, 1990.

Carey, John, ed. *The Faber Book of Utopias*. London: Faber & Faber, 1999.

Chamberlain, Houston Stewart. *Briefe 1882–1924 und Briefwechsel mit Kaiser Wilhelm II*. Vol. 2. Edited by Paul Petzsch. Munich: Bruckmann, 1928.

———. *Richard Wagner*. Munich: Bruckmann, 1895; also the 8th edition of 1933.

Cohen, Walter. *Katalog der Gemäldegalerie vorwiegend Sammlung Wesendonk*. Bonn: Kommissionsverlag Friedrich Cohen, 1914.

Corrodi, August. *Reisebriefe aus der Schweiz und Mailand*. Lucerne: Kaiser, 1857.

Craig, Gordon A. *The Triumph of Liberalism: Zürich in the Golden Age, 1830–1869*. New York and London: Collier, 1990.

Curjel, Hans. "Espressivo und objektivierter Ausdruck." In his *Synthesen: Vermischte Schriften zum Verständnis der neuen Musik*, 149–54. Hamburg: Claassen, 1966.

Dahlhaus, Carl, and Egon Voss, eds. *Wagnerliteratur — Wagnerforschung: Bericht über das Wagner-Symposium München 1983*. Mainz: Schott, 1985.

Darcy, Warren. "Creatio ex nihilo: The Genesis, Structure, and Meaning of the 'Rheingold' Prelude." In *19th-Century Music* 13, no. 2 (Autumn 1989): 79–100.

Deathridge, John. "Wagner's Sketches for the 'Ring': Some Recent Studies." In *The Musical Times* 118, no. 1611 (May 1977): 383–89.

Deathridge, John, and Carl Dahlhaus. *The New Grove Wagner.* London: Macmillan, 1984.

Deathridge, John, Martin Geck, Egon Voss, and Isolde Vetter. *Wagner Werk-Verzeichnis.* Mainz: Schott, 1986.

De Sanctis, Francesco. *Epistolario (1856–1858).* Edited by Giovanni Ferretti and Muzio Mazzocchi Alemanni. Turin: Einaudi, 1965.

———. *Lettere dall'esilio (1853–1860).* Edited by Benedetto Croce. Bari: Gius. Laterza, 1938.

———. *Scelta di scritti critici e ricordi.* Edited by Gianfranco Contini. Turin: Unione Tipograficao, 1969.

———. *Storia della letteratura italiana.* Milan: TEA, 1989.

Döge, Klaus, Christa Jost, and Peter Jost. *"Schlagen Sie die Kraft der Reflexion nicht zu gering an."* Mainz: Schott, 2002.

Drüner, Ulrich. *Schöpfer und Zerstörer: Richard Wagner als Künstler.* Cologne: Böhlau, 2003.

Eösze, László. "Neue Aspekte eines Künstlerbundes." In *Studia Musicologica Academiae Scientiarum Hungaricae* 28 (1986): 195–200.

Erismann, Adolf. *Über den gegenwärtigen Stand der Hydrotherapie: Ein Beitrag zur wissenschaftlichen Begründung des Priessnitz'schen Heilverfahrens; Nebst einem Anhange: Die Ergebnisse des hydrotherapeutischen Heilverfahrens in der Wasserheilanstalt Brestenberg am Hallwylersee.* Baden: J. Zehnder, 1846.

Erismann, Hans. " 'Albert R. Fäsy, Enge': Ein unbekannter Zürcher Komponist des 19. Jahrhunderts." In *Neue Zürcher Zeitung*, 20/21 March 1976.

———. *Das fing ja gut an . . . Geschichten und Geschichte des Opernhauses Zürich.* Zurich: Verlag Neue Zürcher Zeitung, 1984.

———. *Johannes Brahms und Zürich: Ein Beitrag zur Kulturgeschichte von Zürich.* Zurich: Fretz, 1974.

———. *Richard Wagner in Zurich.* Verlag Neue Zürcher Zeitung, 1987.

Ermatinger, Emil. *Gottfried Kellers Briefe und Tagebücher.* Stuttgart and Berlin: Cotta, 1916.

Eschmann, Johann Carl. *Ein Hundert Aphorismen: Erfahrungen, Ergänzungen, Berichtigungen, Anregungen, als Resultat einer 30jährigen Clavierlehrerpraxis.* Berlin and Leipzig: Luckhardt, 1878; Second ed., edited by Ernst Radecke: Berlin: Raabe & Plothow, 1899.

Eschmann-Dumur, Carl. *Guide du jeune pianiste: Classification méthodique et graduée d'oeuvres diverses pour piano.* Lausanne: E.-R. Spiess, 1884.

Ettmüller, Ludwig. *Herbstabende und Winternächte: Gespräche über Deutsche Dichtungen und Dichter*. Stuttgart: Cotta, 1865–67.

———. *Sigufrid: Schauspiel in fünf Handlungen*. Zurich: Bürkli, 1870.

———. *Der Singerkriec uf Wartburc*. Ilmenau, Germany: Voigt, 1830.

Fehr, Max. *Richard Wagners Schweizer Zeit*. Vol. 1. Aarau and Leipzig: Sauerländer, 1934; vol. 2. Aarau and Frankfurt am Main: Sauerländer, 1953.

Friedrich, Sven. *Richard Wagner: Deutung und Wirkung*. Würzburg: Königshausen & Neumann, 2004.

Fries, Willy. *Ein Zürcher Musiker unter Richard Wagner*. Typescript.

Fröhlich, Martin. *Le Palais Fédéral à Berne*. Basel: Société d'Histoire de l'Art en Suisse, 1979.

Gisbert, Paul (pseudonym of Paul Pniower). "Der Ring, der nie gelungen." In Borchmeyer and Kohler, *Wagner-Parodien*, 87–139. Frankfurt am Main: Insel, 1983.

Gottwald, Clytus. "'Herr Seifriz hält mit dem Jahrhundert Schritt': Max Seifriz (1827–1885) — Ein Dirigent der 'Neudeutschen Schule.'" In: *Musik in Baden-Württemberg, Jahrbuch 2003*, 211–28. Stuttgart, Weimar: Metzler-Verlag, 2003.

Gregor-Dellin, Martin. *Richard Wagner: Sein Leben. Sein Werk. Sein Jahrhundert*. Munich and Zurich: Piper, 1980.

Grey, Thomas S. "Wagner, the Overture, and the Aesthetics of Musical Form." In *19th-Century Music* 12, no. 1 (Summer 1988): 3–22.

———. *Wagner's Musical Prose: Texts and Contexts*. Cambridge and New York: Cambridge UP, 1995.

———, ed. *Richard Wagner: Der fliegende Hollaňder*. Cambridge and New York: Cambridge UP, 2000.

Gysi, Fritz. *Wagner und die Schweiz*. Frauenfeld and Leipzig: Huber, 1929.

Hauer, Stanley R. "Wagner and the 'Völospá.'" In *19th-Century Music* 15, no. 1 (Summer 1991): 52–63.

Hegar, Friedrich. "Brief an den Verwaltungsrat und an die Direktion des Konservatoriums für Musik in Zürich." In *Festschrift zum fünfzigjährigen Jubiläum des Konservatoriums für Musik in Zürich, 1876–1926*, ed. Hans Jelmoli. Zurich: Orell Füssli, 1926.

Heinel, Norbert. *Richard Wagner als Dirigent*. Vienna: Praesens Verlag, 2006.

Heintz, Albert. "Richard Wagner in Zürich." In *Allgemeine Musikzeitung* 23, no. 7 (1896): 91–94.

Hofmann, Kurt, and Renate Hofmann. "Johannes Brahms als 'Autographensammler.'" In *Bunte Blätter: Klaus Mecklenburg zum 23. February 2000*, edited by Rudolf Elvers and Alain Moirandat, 99–123. Basel: Moirandat, 2000.

———. "Zu den Beziehungen zwischen Johannes Brahms und Mathilde Wesendonck." In Langer and Walton, *Minne, Muse und Mäzen: Otto und Mathilde Wesendonck und ihr Zürcher Künstlerzirkel*, 130–40.

Hofmann, Renate. *Clara Schumanns Briefe an Theodor Kirchner*. Tutzing, Germany: Schneider, 1996.

Holden, Raymond. *The Virtuoso Conductors: The Central European Tradition from Wagner to Karajan*. New Haven and London: Yale UP, 2005.

Hornstein, Robert von. *Memoiren*. Edited by Ferdinand von Hornstein. Munich: Süddeutsche Monatshefte, 1908.

Huber, Roger. *Im Reich der Töne erblüht das Schöne: Geschichte/Chronik der Stadtmusik Zürich von 1846 bis 1996; Jubiläumsbuch "150 Jahre Stadtmusik Zürich."* Zurich: Stadtmusik Zürich, 1996.

Hunziker, Rudolf, ed. *Der junge Hans Georg Nägeli: Achtzehn Briefe aus den Jahren 1790–1808*. Zurich: Hug, 1937.

———. "Theodor Kirchner in Winterthur." In *Schweizerische Musikzeitung* 74, no. 7 (1 April 1935): 229–42.

Hunziker, Rudolf, and Paul Schaffner. *August Corrodi als Dichter und Maler*. Winterthur: Literarische Vereinigung, 1930.

Jelmoli, Hans. *Festschrift zum fünfzigjährigen Jubiläum des Konservatoriums für Musik in Zürich, 1876–1926*. Zurich: Orell Füssli, 1926.

Jenny, Markus. *Zwinglis Stellung zur Musik im Gottesdienst*. Zurich: Zwingli Verlag, 1966.

Joelson-Strohbach, Harry. "Theodor Kirchner bei Mathilde Wesendonck." In Langer and Walton, *Minne, Muse und Mäzen: Otto und Mathilde Wesendonck und ihr Zürcher Künstlerzirkel*, 143–58.

Jung, Ute. *Die Rezeption der Kunst Richard Wagners in Italien*. Regensburg: Gustav Bosse, 1974.

Keller, Walter. "Richard Wagners Freundschaften aus der Revolutionszeit." In *Nachrichtenblatt, 1981–83*, 299–306. Graz: Österreichische Richard-Wagner-Gesellschaft, 1983.

Kietz, Gustav Adolph. *Richard Wagner in den Jahren 1842–1849 und 1873–1875*. Edited by Marie Kietz. Dresden: Carl Reissner, 1905.

———. "Das 'Rigigespenst.'" In *Richard Wagner-Jahrbuch*, vol. 2, edited by Ludwig Frankenstein. 431–32. Berlin: Hermann Paetel, 1907.

Kirchmeyer, Helmut. *Situationsgeschichte der Musikkritik und des musikalischen Pressewesens in Deutschland, dargestellt vom Ausgange des 18. bis zum Beginn des 20. Jahrhunderts*. Part 4, vol. 2: "Das zeitgenössische Wagnerbild," in seven volumes. Regensburg: Gustav Bosse, 1967–85.

Köhler, Joachim. *Der letzte der Titanen: Richard Wagners Leben und Werk*. Munich: Claassen, 2001.

Kramer, Bernd. *"Lasst uns die Schwerter ziehen, damit die Kette bricht . . ." Michael Bakunin, Richard Wagner und andere während der Dresdner Mai-Revolution 1849*. Berlin: Karin Kramer Verlag, 1999.

Krueger, Ingeborg. ". . . fast nur Gutes und einiges ganz Treffliche . . . Zu Otto Wesendoncks Gemäldesammlung." In Langer and Walton, *Minne,*

Muse und Mäzen: Otto und Mathilde Wesendonck und ihr Zürcher Künstlerzirkel, 100–113.

La Mara (Ida Marie Lipsius), ed. *Franz Liszts Briefe*, vol. 2: *Von Rom bis an's Ende*. Leipzig: Breitkopf & Härtel, 1893.

———. *Franz Liszts Briefe*, vol. 3. *Franz Liszts Briefe an eine Freundin*. Leipzig: Breitkopf & Härtel, 1894.

———. *Franz Liszts Briefe*, vol. 4. *Franz Liszt's Briefe an die Fürstin Carolyne Sayn-Wittgenstein*. Leipzig: Breitkopf & Härtel, 1899.

Labhart, Walter, ed. *"Vom Alphornruf zum Synthesizerklang": Schweizer Musik aus 150 Jahren*. Exhibition catalogue. Lucerne: Internationale Musikfestwochen, 1991.

Langer, Axel, and Chris Walton, eds. *Minne, Muse und Mäzen: Otto und Mathilde Wesendonck und ihr Zürcher Künstlerzirkel*. Zurich: Museum Rietberg, 2002.

Largiadèr, Anton. *Geschichte von Stadt und Landschaft Zürich*. Vol. 2. Erlenbach: Eugen Rentsch, 1945.

Leemann-van Elck, Paul. *Druck, Verlag, Buchhandel im Kanton Zürich von den Anfängen bis um 1850*. Zurich: Leemann, 1950.

Leverett, Adelyn Peck. "Liszt, Wagner and Heinrich Dorn's 'Die Nibelungen.'" In *Cambridge Opera Journal* 2, no. 2 (July 1990): 121–44.

London, S. J. "Anton Pusinelli, M.D. (1815–1878): Janissary to a Genius." In *New York State Journal of Medicine* 69, no. 12 (June 1969): 1451–61.

Lütteken, Laurenz. "Wagner dirigiert Mozart." In *Musikalische Quellen — Quellen zur Musikgeschichte: Festschrift für Martin Staehelin zum 65. Geburtstag*, edited by Ulrich Konrad, Jürgen Heidrich, and Hans Joachim Marx, 425–37. Göttingen: Vandenhoeck & Ruprecht, 2002.

Marni, A. "Francesco De Sanctis and Goethe." In *The German Quarterly* 22, no. 4 (Nov. 1949): 215–22.

McGlathery, James M. *Wagner's Operas and Desire*. New York: Peter Lang, 1998.

Meienberg, Niklaus. *Die Welt als Wille und Wahn*. Zurich: Limmat Verlag, 1988.

Mertens, Volker. "Wagner's Middle Ages." In *Wagner Handbook*, ed. Ulrich Müller and Peter Wapnewski, 233–68. Cambridge, MA.: Harvard UP, 1992.

Millington, Barry. *Wagner*. London: Dent, 1984.

Moleschott, Jacob. *Für meine Freunde: Lebens-Erinnerungen*. Giessen: Emil Roth, 1894.

Müller, Ulrich, and Peter Wapnewski, eds. *Wagner Handbook*. Cambridge, MA: Harvard UP, 1992.

Mungen, Anno. "Entering the Musical Picture: Richard Wagner and Nineteenth-Century Multimedia Entertainments." In *Music in Art* 26, nos. 1–2 (2001): 123–29.

Münster, Robert. "Eine *Serenade* von Richard Wagner." In: *Studien zur Musikgeschichte: Eine Festschrift für Ludwig Finscher*, edited by Annegrit Laubenthal, 614–21. Wiesbaden: Bärenreiter, 1995.

Muscetta, Carlo. *Francesco De Sanctis.* Rome: Laterza, 1975.

Nattiez, Jean-Jacques. *Wagner Androgyne.* Translated by Stewart Spencer. Princeton: Princeton UP, 1993.

Neubauer, Franz Christoph. *Fernando und Yariko.* Zurich: Orell, Gessner & Füssli, 1786.

Newman, Ernest. *The Life of Richard Wagner.* Cambridge: Cambridge UP, 1976.

Nietzsche, Friedrich. "Richard Wagner in Bayreuth." In *Unzeitgemässe Betrachtungen*, edited by Peter Pütz, 225–89. Munich: Goldmann, 1992.

Paravicini, E. *Die Wasserheil-Anstalt Albisbrunn.* Albisbrunn: Paravicini, 1886.

Pechotsch-Feichtinger, Inge. "Briefe von Ödön von Mihalovich an Mathilde Wesendonck." In *Studia Musicologica Academiae Scientiarum Hungaricae* 40, no. 1 (1999): 249–301.

Pfenninger, Friedemann Arthur. *Zürich und sein Theater im Biedermeier.* Zurich: Hug, 1980.

Praeger, Ferdinand. *Wagner as I Knew Him.* New York: Longmans, Green, 1892.

Puffett, Derrick. " 'Lass er die Musi, wo sie ist': Pitch Specificity in Strauss" and "A Notational Peculiarity in Webern." Both in *Derrick Puffett on Music*, ed. Kathryn Bailey Puffett. Aldershot, UK: Ashgate, 2001. 661–86 and 488–97.

Rank, Otto. *Das Inzest-Motiv in Dichtung und Sage.* Leipzig: Deuticke, 1912.

Rapone, Anita. *The Guardian Life Insurance Company, 1860–1920: A History of a German-American Enterprise.* New York and London: New York UP, 1987.

Rieger, Eva. *Minna und Richard Wagner: Stationen einer Liebe.* Düsseldorf and Zurich: Artemis & Winkler, 2003.

Rüegg, Reinhold. *Die ersten 50 Jahre des Zürcher Stadttheater, 1834–1884.* Zurich: Verlag der Züricher Post, 1925.

Schad, Martha. *"Meine erste und einzige Liebe": Richard Wagner und Mathilde Wesendonck.* Munich: Langen Müller, 2002.

Scheck, Raffael. "Swiss Funding for the Early Nazi Movement: Motivation, Context, and Continuities." In *The Journal of Modern History* 71, no. 4 (December 1999): 793–813.

Schneider, Peter Otto, ed. *Theodor Kirchner: Briefe aus den Jahren 1860–1868.* Zurich: Hug, 1949.

Schnyder von Wartensee, Xaver. *Lebenserinnerungen.* Zurich: Hug, 1887.

Schollenberger, Hermann. *Geschichte des Sängervereins Harmonie Zürich, 1841–1921: Jubiläumsgabe zur Feier des achtzigjährigen Bestandes 12. February 1921.* Zurich: Harmonie, 1921.

Schumann, Robert. *Gesammelte Schriften über Musik und Musiker.* Vol. 3. Edited by Heinrich Simon. Leipzig: Reclam, 1888.

Schurz, Carl. *Worte gesprochen am Sarge von Frau Wilhelmine Wesendonck geboren zu Crefeld am 10ten April 1820, gestorben zu Ems am 24sten August 1889 und auf Greenwood Cemetry zur Ruhe bestattet am 16ten September 1889.* New York: n.p., 1889.

Schwetschke, Gustav. *Jubiläums-Ausgabe der Novae epistolae obscurorum virorum: Zum ersten Male mit Erläuterungen versehen; Erinnerungen aus den Frankfurter Parlamentstagen.* Halle: G. Schwetschke'scher Verlag, 1874.

Scruton, Roger. *Death-Devoted Heart: Sex and the Sacred in Wagner's "Tristan and Isolde."* Oxford: Oxford UP, 2004.

Sietz, Reinhold. *Theodor Kirchner: Ein Klaviermeister der deutschen Romantik.* Regensburg: Gustav Bosse, 1971.

Spencer, Stewart. Review of *Wagner: Race and Revolution*, by Paul Lawrence Rose. In *Wagner* 16, no. 1 (January 1995): 46–48.

Spohr, Louis. *Selbstbiographie.* Basel: Bärenreiter, 1954.

Staub, Urs. Untitled presentation given in the Bundeshaus on the building's 100th anniversary, at http://www.parlament.ch/ab/frameset/f/v/4612/56958/f_v_4612_56958_56959.htm, accessed September 2006.

Steiner, Adolf. *Richard Wagner in Zürich.* Three vols. Zurich: Orell Füssli, 1901–3.

Sternberg, Rolf. "Fantasy, Geography, Wagner, and Opera." In *Geographical Review* 88, no. 3 (July 1998): 327–48.

Strauss, Richard. *Betrachtungen und Erinnerungen.* Edited by Willi Schuh. Munich/Mainz: Piper/Schott, 1981.

Strobel, Otto. *Richard Wagner: Leben und Schaffen; Eine Zeittafel.* Bayreuth: Verlag der Festspielleitung, 1952.

Thiery, Joachim, and Dietrich Seidel. " 'I Feel Only Discontent': Wagner and His Doctors." In: *Wagner* 16, no. 1 (January 1995): 3–22.

Thomann, Robert. *Der Eidgenössische Sängerverein, 1842–1942.* Zurich: Orell Füssli, 1942.

Treadwell, James. *Interpreting Wagner.* New Haven and London: Yale UP, 2003.

Vazsonyi, Nicholas. *Wagner's "Meistersinger": Performance, History, Representation.* Rochester, NY: U of Rochester P, 2003.

Vetter, Isolde. "Wagner in the History of Psychology." In Müller and Wapnewski, *Wagner Handbook*, 118–55. Cambridge, MA. and London: Harvard UP, 1992.

Vogt, Matthias Theodor. "Die Geburt des Festspielgedankens aus dem Geist der Bäderkur." In *Welttheater, Mysterienspiel, rituelles Theater "Vom Himmel durch die Welt zur Hölle,"* edited by Peter Csobádi, Gernot Gruber, Jürgen Kühnel, Ulrich Müller, Oswald Panagl, and Franz V. Spechtler, 343–64. Anif/Salzburg: Verlag Ursula Müller-Speiser, 1992.

Voss, Egon. " '*ein göttliches, unvergleichliches Werk'* — '*leider alles unkonzentriert'*: Richard Wagner und *Don Giovanni.*" In *Festschrift Christoph-Hellmut Mahling zum 65. Geburtstag*, edited by Axel Beer, Kristina Pfarr, and Wolfgang Ruf, 1463–73. Tutzing, Germany: Schneider, 1997.

———. "Die 'schwarze und die weiße Flagge': Zur Entstehung von Wagners 'Tristan.' " In *Archiv für Musikwissenschaft* 54, no. 3 (1997): 210–27.

———. "Der Vergessenheit anheimgefallen: Der Musikdirektor Carl Ludwig Eberle." In *Im Dienst der Quellen zur Musik: Festschrift Gertraut Haberkamp zum 65. Geburtstag*, edited by Paul Mai, 575–83. Tutzing, Germany: Schneider, 2002.

———. *Wagner und kein Ende*. Mainz and Zurich: Atlantis Musikbuch-Verlag, 1996.

———. "Die Wesendoncks und Richard Wagner." In Langer and Walton, *Minne, Muse und Mäzen: Otto und Mathilde Wesendonck und ihr Zürcher Künstlerzirkel*, 117–29.

Walton, Chris. "Flickarbeit oder Bearbeitung?" In *Neue Zürcher Zeitung*, 14/15 December 1996.

———. "Furtwängler the Apolitical?" In *The Musical Times* 146, no. 1889 (Winter 2004): 5–25.

———. *Heinrich Schulz-Beuthen (1838–1915): Eine biographische Skizze*. Zurich: Hug, 2003.

———. "Im Klang der Zeit: Ausgrabung einer Gluck-Bearbeitung Richard Wagners." In *Neue Zürcher Zeitung*, 25 March 1998.

———. "*Iphigenia* Lost and Found: A Newly-Discovered Gluck arrangement by Richard Wagner." In *Fontes artis musicae* 45, nos. 3–4 (1998): 227–36.

———. "Lost Without Trace: Hunting for Heinrich Schulz-Beuthen." In *The Musical Times* 147, no. 1895 (Summer 2006): 25–38.

———. "*Parsifal* in Zurich." In: *Wagner Society of Scotland: Journal* 2 (2005): 7–16.

———. "Pocahontas in the Alps: Masonic Traces in the Stage Works of Franz Christoph Neubauer." In *The Musical Times* 146, no. 1892 (Autumn 2005): 43–56.

———. "Richard Wagner als Dirigent in Zürich." In *Tribschener Blätter* 55/56 (1998): 2–45.

———. "Richard Wagner und seine 'schöne Märchen-Frau.' " In *Neue Zürcher Zeitung*, 29/30 May 1999.

———. *Richard Wagners Zürcher Jahre, 1849–1858: Ein biographischer Index*. Zurich: Hug, 2000.

———. "Die 'Synopsis isagoges musicae' von Johannes Fries 1552." In *Zentralbibliothek Zürich: Alte und Neue Schätze*, edited by Alfred Cattani, Michael Kotrba, and Agnes Rutz, 66–69. Zurich: Verlag Neue Zürcher Zeitung, 1993.

Walton, Chris. "Three Men for All Seasons: Musico-Horticultural Flights in Enlightenment Zurich." In *Bunte Blätter: Klaus Mecklenburg zum 23. Februar 2000*, edited by Rudolf Elvers and Alain Moirandat, 315–39. Basel: Moirandat Company AG, 2000.

———. " '. . .Unsre gute jungfer Fanny Hühnerwadel [*sic*] . . .' — Eine Schweizer Komponistin in Wagners Zürcher Entourage." In *Bulletin der Peter-Mieg-Stiftung*. 12 (1998): 21–26.

———. "Von Kunst und Staat: Wagners *Siegfried-Idyll*." In *Neue Zürcher Zeitung*, 22/23 April 1995.

———. "Wagner-Quellen in der Zentralbiblithek Zürich: Verleger, Kopisten, Dirigate." In Döge, Jost, and Jost, *"Schlagen Sie die Kraft der Reflexion nicht zu gering an,"* 92–113.

———. "Wagner's Peculiar Oboist: Philipp Joseph Fries." In *Fontes artis musicae* 49, no. 4 (2002): 271–84.

———. "The Zurich Music Publisher P. J. Fries: List of Publications, 1851–ca. 1872." In *Fontes artis musicae* 49, no. 4 (2002): 285–95.

Weber, Heinrich. *Vierundsiebzigstes Neujahrsblatt der Allgemeinen Musikgesellschaft in Zürich*. Zurich: Orell Füssli, 1886.

———. *Zürichs Musikleben von 1812–1850*. Vol. 1. Zurich: Allgemeine Musikgesellschaft, 1874.

Wesendonck, Hugo. *Erinnerungen aus dem Jahre 1848*. New York: n.p., 1898.

Westernhagen, Curt von. *Richard Wagners Dresdener Bibliothek, 1842–1849*. Wiesbaden: Brockhaus, 1966.

Widmer, C. (first name unknown). *Wilhelm Baumgartner: Ein Lebensbild*. Zurich: David Bürkli, 1868.

Wiesend, Reinhard. "Die Entstehung des 'Rheingold'-Vorspiels und ihr Mythos." In *Archiv für Musikwissenschaft* 49, no. 2 (1992): 122–45.

Wille, Eliza. *Erinnerungen an Richard Wagner: Mit 15 Briefen Richard Wagners*. Zurich: Atlantis Musikbuch-Verlag, 1982.

Wille, Jürg. "Das 'Asyl' Richard Wagners (Frühling 1857–Sommer 1858) in der heutigen Villa Schönberg." In Zimmermann, *Richard Wagner in Zürich: Eine Chronik*.

———. "Rieter im Rietberg." In Langer and Walton, *Minne, Muse und Mäzen: Otto und Mathilde Wesendonck und ihr Zürcher Künstlerzirkel*, 168–73.

Winkler, Jürg. *"Ich möchte dir meine Heimat einmal zeigen": Biographisches zu Johanna Spyri, Autorin des "Heidi" und ihren Hirzler Vorfahren*. Hirzel, Switzerland: Jürg Winkler, 1982.

Wittgenstein, Ludwig. *Lectures and Conversations on Aesthetics, Psychology and Religious Belief*. Edited by Cyril Barrett. Oxford: Blackwell, 1978.

Zehle, Sibylle. *Minna Wagner: Eine Spurensuche*. Hamburg: Hoffmann & Campe, 2004.

Zimmermann, Werner G. *Brahms in der Schweiz: Eine Dokumentation.* Zurich: Atlantis Musikbuch-Verlag, 1983.

———, ed. *Richard Wagner in Zürich: Eine Chronik.* Second, expanded edition. Zurich: Präsidialabteilung, 1987.

———. *Richard Wagner in Zürich: Materialien zu Aufenthalt und Wirken.* Vol. 1, Zurich: Hug, 1986; vol. 2, Zurich: Hug, 1988.

Zimmermann, Werner G. et al., eds. *Alfred Escher: Ausstellung in der Galerie "le point" am Hauptsitz der Schweizerischen Kreditanstalt.* Zurich: Schweizerische Kreditanstalt, 1994.

Zosel, Alois. *Heinrich Schulz-Beuthen, 1838–1915: Leben und Werke; Ein Beitrag zur Geschichte der neueren Programmusik.* Würzburg-Aumühle: Triltsch, 1931.

Index